Lieder in America

MUSIC IN AMERICAN LIFE

*A list of books in the series appears
at the end of this book.*

Lieder in America

On Stages and In Parlors

HEATHER PLATT

UNIVERSITY OF ILLINOIS PRESS
Urbana, Chicago, and Springfield

© 2023 by the Board of Trustees
of the University of Illinois
All rights reserved
1 2 3 4 5 C P 5 4 3 2 1
♾ This book is printed on acid-free paper.

Funding provided by the Aspire Program's Published
Scholarship Support at Ball State University and the John
Daverio Fund and by the General Fund of the American
Musicological Society, supported in part by the National
Endowment for the Humanities and the Andrew W.
Mellon Foundation.

Library of Congress Cataloging-in-Publication Data
Names: Platt, Heather Anne, author.
Title: Lieder in America : on stages and in parlors /
    Heather Platt.
Description: Urbana : University of Illinois Press,
    2023. | Series: Music in American life | Includes
    bibliographical references and index.
Identifiers: LCCN 2023008541 (print) | LCCN
    2023008542 (ebook) | ISBN 9780252045486
    (cloth) | ISBN 9780252087592 (paperback) | ISBN
    9780252055102 (ebook)
Subjects: LCSH: Songs—United States—History and
    criticism. | Songs, German—United States—History
    and criticism. | Music—United States—German
    influences. | Concerts—United States—History.
Classification: LCC ML2811 .P53 2023 (print) | LCC
    ML2811 (ebook) | DDC 782.421680973—dc23/
    eng/20230307
LC record available at https://lccn.loc.gov/2023008541
LC ebook record available at https://lccn.loc.gov/2023008542

Contents

Acknowledgments   vii

Notes Regarding Titles of Compositions and Sources   xi

Introduction   1

1 Introducing a "Higher Class" of Song to American Audiences   23

2 Song Recitals and Song Recital Series   48

3 The Henschels' Polyglot "Vocal Recitals"   72

4 Max Heinrich's "Classical Song Recitals"   95

5 Max Heinrich's Expanding Stylistic and Geographic Vistas   116

6 Villa Whitney White and Women's Music Clubs   142

7 David Bispham and the Heyday of Song Recitals   167

Epilogue: The End of an Era   197

Appendix: Milestones in the Development of Song Recitals   213

Notes   217

Bibliography   275

Index   293

Acknowledgments

After years of examining the rich, structural intricacies and reception history of Brahms's lieder, I began my exploration of performances of lieder in America as a result of two chance invitations. Jim Sobaskie invited me to review the digital platform known as VIFA (now known as Musiconn, https://www.musiconn.de/aus-vifamusik-wird-musiconn) for *Nineteenth Century Music Review* (NCMR). I quickly became hooked on digitized sources and search engines that enabled me to immediately access hundreds of resources on numerous subjects. I am extremely grateful to Jim and to Bennett Zon (the general editor of NCMR) for this opportunity because it led to an invitation to become the digital reviews editor for NCMR. While commissioning a review of the services housing digitized nineteenth-century US newspapers, I joined the growing number of scholars who are captivated by the wealth of material chronicling American musical life that the search engines of these services reveal. On a whim, I searched for Brahms and Magelone (in reference to the composer's op. 33 lieder cycle, the *Magelone Romances*). I was surprised to locate records of complete performances of this cycle in the United States during the 1890s. Brahms had not encouraged such complete performances, and even in the 1890s they were still uncommon in Europe. Fortuitously, around the same time Natasha Loges and Laura Tunbridge were hosting a conference at the Royal College of Music, and they graciously accepted my proposal concerning US performances of lieder cycles in the nineteenth century.

Just as I had been amazed by the results of my first searches, so, too, the conference attendees were amazed that Americans were singing complete cycles by Schubert and Schumann, let alone Brahms's cycles. *Lieder in America* expands on this original study and focuses on the singers and advocates of lieder who established song recitals, which became one of the most important avenues in the US dissemination of lieder. In researching the questions Natasha and Laura and their conference attendees posed, I came to realize that many American musicians and historians are unaware of the development and significance of nineteenth-century song recitals and the frequency with which lieder were performed in public during the 1890s and early 1900s. I am most grateful to Natasha and Laura for their numerous suggestions, penetrating questions, and patience as they guided my chapter in *German Song Onstage* through the publication process. Moreover, in the following years Natasha offered invaluable assistance in locating sources in Europe, and she introduced me to other European scholars who were also exploring performances of lieder. Her own publications on lieder have influenced every chapter of this book.

As an Australian American who studied lieder, I never expected to research American musical culture. I am extremely grateful to all the Americanists who encouraged my work and introduced me to nineteenth-century American musical life and the associated disciplinary practices and important sources. I am particularly grateful for the generous support and advice Douglas Bomberger gave me as I began to dive deeper into this project and for the encouragement and highly perceptive questions and suggestions of my Ball State University colleague Linda Pohly. Over the years, many other scholars including Heike Bungert, Therese Ellsworth, John Graziano, Marian Wilson Kimber, Katherine Preston, and Douglas Shadle provided advice and shared sources. Like many mid-career scholars, I gradually learned of digital aggregators and services, as well as methodologies for manipulating and compiling vast numbers of digitized sources. During this process I greatly benefited from opportunities provided by what was then Ball State University's Digital Scholarship Lab and from the advice of its leaders, James Connolly and Doug Seefeldt.

My work, like that of all lieder scholars of the past few decades, has been immensely influenced by Susan Youens, and numerous other lieder scholars have also been of great assistance and inspiration to this book. They include Benjamin Binder, Katy Hamilton, Jennifer Ronyak, and Chanda VanderHart.

Although I acquired most of the sources for this study through digitized services, I was able to locate archival materials with the assistance of numerous librarians and archivists. Rebecca Littman, of the New York Public Library for the Performing Arts, was extraordinarily helpful in assisting me in locating material on Max Heinrich and David Bispham during the COVID months of 2020. Others gave me invaluable advice and assistance during the earlier years of my research, including Dr. Otto Biba, who served as the director of the Archiv, Bibliothek, und Sammlungen der Gesellschaft der Musikfreunde in Vienna; Bridget Carr, Archives and Digital Collections, Boston Symphony Orchestra; Andrea Cawelti, Houghton Library, Harvard University; David Coppen, special collections librarian and archivist, Sibley Music Library, Eastman School of

Music; Katy Darr, Newberry Library; Rebecca Jewett, Special Collections Area, Music and Dance Library, Ohio State University; Ellen Keith, Chicago History Museum Research Center; and Maryalice Perrin-Mohr, Blumenthal Family Library, New England Conservatory of Music. Staff at many other institutions have assisted me in navigating their collections or emailing me copies of programs, including the staff at the Boston Public Library; the British Library; Cambridge University Library; the Historical Society of Washington, DC; Indiana University at Bloomington; the Oregon Historical Society; Smith College; and the Wienbibliothek im Rathus (Vienna). The librarians at Ball State University assisted me in numerous ways, and I'm particularly grateful to Elaine Nelson and the amazing, dedicated staff in the Interlibrary Loan department, and to Jan Vance, who often came to my rescue when I was using microfilm. Michael Twigg assisted me in gaining access to numerous digital services, Angela Gibson produced maps charting the tours of Villa Whitney White for some of my conference presentations, and Amy Edmonds was always available to help me track down important leads.

Much of the property of the singers whose careers this book charts has been dispersed or lost, and surviving descendants are few. However, I was able to contact two relatives of Villa Whitney White: John White and Nancy Dalrymple. I'm deeply thankful for the insights into their extended family that they shared with me and for Nancy's own research at the Mary Baker Eddy Library of the Church of Christian Science in Boston and at New England colleges.

Several people gave invaluable assistance with editing and proofreading the manuscript for this book. Faedra Weiss's suggestions and corrections, her vast knowledge of German culture and music, and love of vocal music immeasurably enriched my work. Valerie Weingart (who independently researched Marguerite Hall, one of the singers this book touches on) and Ashley Buegner gave me important advice on some of the chapters, and Jane Zanichkowsky, my copyeditor at the University of Illinois Press, further honed my writing. Across the years, a variety of students also assisted me. Andrew Van Dyke toiled for countless hours compiling information from thousands of newspaper notices into spreadsheets. Hayden Giesseman, Rachel Jordan, and Terrilyn Shepherd all proofread various versions of some of the chapters, and Luke Vasilarakos created the music examples.

I am indebted to Murray Steib, the coordinator for Ball State University's Music History Area, for assigning students to work with me and supporting my research in countless other ways. Seth Beckman, the dean of the College of Fine Arts at Ball State University, and Ryan Hourigan, the former director of the School of Music, also supported my work, principally through invaluable course releases. I was also supported by a 2017 Ball State University Create Award and a 2022 award from the university's Published Scholarship Support Aspire Program. The publication of this book was also assisted by the John Daverio Fund and by the General Fund of the American Musicological Society, supported in part by the National Endowment for the Humanities and the Andrew W. Mellon Foundation.

Laurie Matheson of the University of Illinois Press had numerous probing questions that significantly strengthened the book. My work also benefited from the comments of the anonymous reviewers of the manuscript of this book and of my related articles for *American Music* and *German Song Onstage*.

Throughout the years my friends and family supported and sustained me, reminded me to laugh, and heroically listened to more details about lieder and singers than they ever wanted to know. I'm grateful for the support and encouragement of Elizabeth Crawford, Valerie Woodring Goertzen, Ben Korstvedt, Joel Lester, Roger McConnell, Peter H. Smith, Gloria Storey, Larry Todd, and Channan Willner. Above all, this book never would have come into existence without the love, patience, and humor of my husband Mark H. Kaplan.

Chapters 1 through 4 expand on material first presented in "'Something New in the Musical Line': The Emergence of the Song Recital During the 1870s and '80s," *American Music* 38, no. 1 (2020): 454–84. This article also included figures 2.1, 2.2a and b, 4.1, and 4.2. Similarly, some of the information on song cycles in Chapters 5 through 7 appeared in "'For Any Ordinary Performer It Would Be Absurd, Ridiculous or Offensive': Performing Lieder Cycles on the American Stage," in *German Song Onstage: Lieder Performance in the Nineteenth and Early Twentieth Centuries*, ed. Natasha Loges and Laura Tunbridge, 111–31 (Bloomington, IN: Indiana University Press, 2020).

Notes Regarding Titles of Compositions and Sources

The first time a lied or lieder cycle is referenced it is accompanied by its opus or catalog number (if there is one). The index lists some lieder referenced in the book, and it also provides these identifying numbers for them. American publications of the nineteenth century referred to lieder by their German and English titles. The original German titles are frequently used in this book, but English titles are used for the songs that were often performed in English and in cases where a publication under discussion used them.

Concert and recital programs printed in nineteenth-century newspapers and journals, as well as those given to audience members, did not follow a consistent format. The first names of composers were often omitted. Opus numbers, dates of composition, and birth and death dates of composers were usually omitted. Lieder were identified by English or German titles, not both. A single program might use English for a few lieder and German for others; this usually reflected the languages employed by the singer. The programs transcribed throughout this book provide the information as given in the sources; only spelling mistakes have been corrected. Occasionally a piece of information such as a title or the name of an encore has been added on the basis of information in contemporary newspapers. These additions are indicated by square brackets.

The vast majority of newspaper and journal articles cited in this study are not signed. In cases where the identity of the music critic is known, his name has been added to the citations but placed in square brackets. The bibliography only includes the signed publications.

Lieder in America

Introduction

"I introduced German lieder in America at a time when the singing of a German song was as likely to bring stale vegetables as it was to evoke applause!"[1] So claimed Max Heinrich (1853–1916), one of the most admired recitalists of the 1880s and 1890s. Although Heinrich was prone to hyperbole and self-promotion, and although singers had begun to tentatively introduce lieder to US audiences during the 1850s, his statement reflects the state of lieder in US concert life through the mid-1880s. In contrast, by 1900, observers reported that stale vegetables had given way to bouquets: "The day of appreciation of the German lied is at its noon; even the most ambitious singers are giving song-recitals rather than operatic concerts, and thither flock both the instructed and the uninstructed lovers of music."[2] *Lieder in America* explores how the situation in 1900 came about by examining the ways in which advocates of German instrumental music and cultural uplift, women's music clubs, and domestic music makers supported the singers who established the lied as a concert repertoire and at the same time developed song recitals dedicated to art songs.

The history of the establishment of the lied on US stages is documented by the concerts and recitals of lauded exponents of the genre, notably August Kreissmann (1823–1879), George Werrenrath (1838–1898), George Henschel (1850–1934)[3] and his American wife Lillian (1860–1901), Max Heinrich, Villa Whitney White (1858–1933), and David Bispham (1857–1921). These singers contributed to the canonization of lieder by Beethoven, Brahms, Robert Franz, Schubert, and Schumann,[4] and they introduced Americans to countless other European song composers including Dvořák, Grieg, and Loewe. In varying degrees, their careers and the US adoption of the lied were influenced by members of the network of critics and performers, including John Sullivan Dwight (1813–1893) and Theodore Thomas (1835–1905), who were endeavoring to improve US concert life by promoting performances of classical, predominantly German, instrumental music. Women also played a role in the dissemination of the lied. Women gave some of the early performances of lieder in concert settings, contributed to the earliest song recitals, fostered the proliferation of song recitals, and purchased scores of their favorite lieder. While some of the singers and pianists who initially advocated for the lied were German immigrants, they joined American-born musicians in addressing heterogeneous audiences. To this end lieder were given in both German and English, press reports used the word "songs" rather than "lieder," and numerous singers and critics aided in the dissemination of English-language scores of lieder.

From sporadic performances during the multi-genre vocal and instrumental concerts that were in vogue during the first half of the nineteenth century, lieder gradually emerged as a major component of the professional song recitals that flourished at the turn of the century. A wide variety of European and American songs could be heard in many venues, but the term "song recital" designated the performance of solo songs viewed as "high art." Unlike *concerts* comprised of popular ballads and arias from well-known nineteenth-century Italian operas, and recitals including recitations, *song recitals* emphasized art songs, and especially lieder. While some recitals were comprised entirely of lieder, many audiences and critics preferred lieder to be combined with other genres, including a few arias from Baroque and Classical Italian, French, German, or English operas and oratorios. Some programs followed lieder with a few lighter songs, folksongs (usually from the British Isles), or newly composed songs written in folk style. At the turn of the century, singers responded to the growing influence of the conjoined forces of antagonism to German culture and pride in the American nation and its music by programming lieder with recently composed American art songs and French *mélodies*.

Whereas modern recitalists often create programs with a unifying theme, nineteenth-century recitals were characterized by variety. Programs comprised lieder by multiple composers and ones in different styles and moods, and many included contrasting genres in various languages. But no matter the genre or language, audiences appreciated beautiful melodies, love songs, and dramatic ballads. And they responded to singers they could relate to, and who passionately conveyed the emotions and narratives of the songs.

The Lied and the Transatlantic Transfer of "High Art"

Efforts to establish the lied as a concert genre during the 1850s and 1860s were guided by both Americans and German immigrant musicians who arrived in the United States following the failed 1848 revolutions in Europe. Recent scholars have studied the process through which German compositions came to dominate the canon of works performed in US concert halls and opera houses, and the transatlantic transfer of German culture in general, but to date there has not been an investigation of performances of lieder. In fact, although the genre is central to German Romanticism, it is scarcely acknowledged. Nancy Reich's study of US performances of Schumann's music is one of the few to briefly consider lieder.[5] There are also gaps, however, in the examination of the transfer of other genres. Nancy Newman, for instance, concludes that "surprisingly little is known about the numerous individuals who immigrated to the United States at mid-century and affected our musical life so profoundly. The precise mechanism by which the 'classical,' predominantly German, repertory of instrumental works found its way into American concert halls is just beginning to be explored."[6] Newman's remarks apply even more strongly to lieder. By "mechanism" she means such issues as the relationships between students and teachers and the transmission of scores from Europe. In the process of excavating performances of lieder and constructing a history of song recitals, the present study contributes to the investigation of this mechanism in that it reveals that the early advocates of the lied were central members of the extensive network of music lovers—including singers, instrumentalists, and critics—who fostered the dissemination of other German genres.

Initially, advocates of German music such as Thomas, Leopold Damrosch (1832–1885), Otto Dresel (1826–1890), and Carl Wolfsohn (1834–1907) advanced the cause of lieder by inviting singers to perform during orchestral and chamber concerts. Others, including Dwight and W(illiam) S(mythe) B(abcock) Mathews (1837–1912), promoted performances and scores of lieder through reviews and articles in journals, taught and collaborated with singers, and influenced the publication of lieder in English-language sheet music.[7] Whereas scholars have long since established Dwight's role in the dissemination of German instrumental music, they have overlooked his advocacy of the lied, perhaps because they were influenced by his well-known preference for music without text. Nevertheless, he valued the lieder of Schubert, Schumann, and Franz, along with sonatas, symphonies, and Bach's chorales, because the music spoke to and enriched the soul.[8] In this sense, he joined numerous writers in Europe and the United States in viewing German music as universal.

The transatlantic transfer of lieder was predicated on the view that these songs, like German symphonies and chamber music, were edifying high art. Critics, including Dwight, praised the main exponents of the lied for performing a "high" class of song. Paralleling developments in Europe, the classification of some genres as superior to others contributed to the development of the musical canon. Throughout the century the canon expanded, encompassing works by Mozart and Beethoven and more recent composers including Schubert,

Introduction   3

Schumann, Wagner, and Brahms. Lieder by these composers were gradually introduced to US music lovers, and by the start of the 1890s the genre had found a place in the canon of US concert repertoire. Dwight and his colleagues heavily influenced the formation of this canon. He believed music was a "civilizing agency," and, with his like-minded colleagues, he viewed the promotion of German music as a way to educate and elevate musical taste and society in general.[9] The belief in music's enriching and moral qualities continued to influence the dissemination of lieder through the closing years of the long nineteenth century. It was endorsed by advocates of the lied including women's music clubs, singers such as David Bispham, and music critics such as Henry Krehbiel (1873–1923).[10]

In recent decades, the types of elitist attitudes that created the cultural hierarchy that canonized classical music have been exposed as flawed and as failing to recognize the richness of indigenous and vernacular musics and the importance of their cultural and societal roles. Nevertheless, the fact remains that lieder were first established as a concert genre in the United States because critics and performers valued these songs as high art, and their opinions were repeated and therefore endorsed by media outlets throughout the country. Although the separation of "cultivated" and "vernacular" or "elite" and "popular" music tentatively began during the first half of the nineteenth century,[11] the propagation of repertoire believed to be high took on added significance during the second half of the century, when "American elites purposefully adopted trends of European high culture in search of taste, class, refinement, and philanthropy."[12] In an era when self-improvement was promoted as a means to a better life and when attendance at classical concerts and a piano prominently positioned in a family's parlor symbolized social standing and taste, the marketing of lieder as high art became an important selling point. Ultimately the lied attracted far more music lovers than it does in current times. Nevertheless, despite adhering to notions of progress and uplift and facilitating the publication of singable English-language scores, champions of the lied made limited attempts to reach all Americans. Advocates rarely explained the nature of the genre or the cultural significance or meaning of the songs' texts to the uninitiated, and throughout much of the century tickets for performances of lieder were not as cheap as those for entertainments marketed to the masses. Performers, however, occasionally presented recitals at "popular" prices. These tickets were priced as low as twenty-five cents, whereas the lowest price for tickets to recitals given by eminent singers was usually at least one dollar, around the same price as good seats at an opera or orchestral concert. According to newspaper reports, early lieder performances were attended by exclusive audiences of educated musicians and socialites, and the venues for these performances often seated fewer than one thousand. In contrast, from the late 1890s to at least 1917 the lied's market share increased, advertisements targeted a broader audience, and lieder were performed in more varied venues. In our own time lieder are attracting smaller and smaller audiences, in part because performers, teachers, and commentators have failed to convince the general public of the genre's relevancy. In effect, the genre has not been able to throw off the branding and elitist implications of "high art" that initially ensured its successful dissemination in the United States.

Navigating High and Low Styles

While nineteenth-century critics and performers classified lieder by such composers as Beethoven, Schubert, and Schumann as high art, the types of songs that were viewed as representing lower or popular art were not so clearly identified. Some critics preferred lieder to English and German songs with folklike melodies and simple piano accompaniments. For instance, a reviewer in *Dwight's Journal of Music* (likely Dwight himself) reported that the first six series of scores published under the title *Gems of German Song* had whetted the appetite of music lovers "who had only known English songs and ballads, sentimental love-strains with the most meager common chord accompaniments."[13] Although he praised the publication of lieder by Schubert, he was disappointed that many of the sixty songs in this series were not of the same artistic level.

The German songs that this critic—like those in Europe—believed were of a lower standard than those by Beethoven and Schubert were composed by Franz Abt (1819–1885), Friedrich Wilhelm Kücken (1810–1882), and Friedrich Silcher (1789–1860), among others. These works had lyrical melodic lines and simple accompaniments that supported the melody and could be easily learned by amateurs. They usually did not explore the type of subtle relationships between the text and music that are noteworthy of lieder by Schubert and Schumann. Nevertheless, as in Europe, these works were widely performed in concert settings—even by opera stars—as well as by amateurs at home. Scores subjected to various contrafactum processes were distributed by numerous US publishers, who in some cases did not clearly indicate that the songs were originally written in German. Critics complained of the poor translations and derided the songs as "sweet things,"[14] but nevertheless they were thoroughly assimilated into American musical life.[15] Charles Hamm was able to conclude that German song "enjoyed some vogue in America at mid-century" because of the wide dissemination of these works, which, he observed, were published in much greater numbers than were German art songs by the likes of Schumann.[16]

Richard Middleton and Peter Manuel define popular music as "types of music that are considered to be of lower value and complexity than art music" and that are "readily accessible" to "musically uneducated listeners."[17] Abt's and Kücken's songs meet these criteria, and the dissemination of their scores likewise demonstrates Derek Scott's and Hamm's conclusion that sheet music sales influenced

Introduction 5

the creation of popular music.[18] Songs identified as folk music, however, are somewhat more difficult to classify, as Scott has noted. Some of the singers and writers to be discussed in the following chapters greatly valued European folksongs and believed that sacred and secular art music derived from them. Nevertheless, folksongs meet Middleton and Manuel's definition of popular music, and arrangements of folksongs were widely disseminated through scores and performances by professionals and amateurs. In contrast, Scott maintains that by the end of the century the English viewed folksong as a type of national music distinct from commercial popular music. While this is also evident in the United States, many recitalists (even those who acknowledged the artistry of these works) tended to program folksongs or works composed in folk style as popular, light audience pleasers that provided a contrast to complex lieder.

Although there were numerous songs that critics and performers consistently classified as either high or low art, there were others that occupied a hybrid region in that they attained commercial success while being recognized as high art. As with many Italian operas that likewise were simultaneously popular and high art,[19] these lieder were usually sung in English. American audiences favored these works over all other lieder. Throughout the century, professional singers repeatedly programmed them, they were included on recitals marketed as popular and on "request" programs, and English-language scores of many of these works were released by multiple US publishers. Typically, these lieder had attractive melodies. Many had texts about love, but others were dramatic and had a narrative set to contrasting sections of music, or, in many fewer cases, they invoked religious beliefs. Some conveyed themes such as courtship or childhood that were frequently associated with the woman's sphere. All of these songs had texts that Americans could relate to even if they did not understand the nuances of the original German poems. Schubert's "Ständchen" ("Serenade," D. 957) and Mendelssohn's "Auf Flügeln des Gesanges" ("On Wings of Song," op. 34, no. 2) fall into this category. They were among the first lieder to be performed on US stages during the 1850s, in large part because they had already achieved some degree of renown through the dissemination of English-language sheet music produced for home music making. "Serenade" was so popular that between 1850 and 1880 there were no fewer than fifteen adaptations of it in circulation, and it was recognized as one of the "top selling foreign songs" in 1870.[20] The song's success can in part be attributed to its similarities to popular parlor songs, including a chordal accompaniment that could be played by amateurs.[21] Although "Serenade" and "Auf Flügeln des Gesanges" continued to be popular into the twentieth century, they did not dominate concert repertoire in the same way they did at mid-century, likely because so many other German and American songs were being disseminated and programmed.

There were other well-known lieder, however, that retained their popularity. These included Schubert's "Erlkönig" (D. 328) and Schumann's "Die beiden Grenadiere" (op. 49, no. 1). Dramatic ballads such as these two were particularly well suited to the concert hall, but part of the appeal of "Die beiden Grenadiere" was its quotation of the extremely popular "La Marseillaise." Written during the French Revolution, "La Marseillaise" immediately became known in America, where during the 1790s it became "a symbol of opposition to both England and Federalism, and in support of republican government."[22] During the nineteenth century it was often played alongside patriotic American songs such as "Yankee Doodle" during band concerts and other popular fora. English-language sheet music of "Die beiden Grenadiere" was released in the United States during the 1840s, shortly after the composition of the song.[23] This was highly unusual because at the time few scores of Schumann's lieder were being released by American publishers. As song recitals proliferated, this work became part of the standard repertoire for baritones, whose performances were frequently greeted with calls for an encore. That Bispham and other Americans continued to sing "The Two Grenadiers" during World War I suggests that singers and audiences were not cognizant of the type of German nationalist overtones that Susan Youens has located in this work.[24] More broadly, the reception of this lied demonstrates the flexibility of the genre: It was able to be "at the same time or in alternation, both elitist and popular,"[25] and it was able to withstand transmission to other cultures. Such flexibility was not confined to the US marketplace, but, rather, was an important element of the lied that had already emerged in early nineteenth-century Europe.

Numerous investigators of the transatlantic transfer of classical music have followed cultural historians Paul DiMaggio and Lawrence Levine in concluding that by the closing decades of the nineteenth century concert programs eliminated "lowbrow" repertoire while concentrating on "highbrow" works. And Levine has compared this change to similar changes in other aspects of culture, including the theater.[26] However, although nineteenth-century critics often praised singers for programming "high class" lieder, song recitals at the end of the century frequently included a few lighter numbers. This contrasts with the type of increasing homogeneity that has been observed in the development of orchestral concerts.[27] In addition to a few folksongs from the British Isles, at that time the more accessible numbers often included new American songs such as those by Ethelbert Nevin (1862–1901) that straddled the divide between art songs and popular songs.[28] Few commentators protested such combinations of complex lieder and lighter works, or that of German lieder and songs by American composers, in large part because, like audiences, they valued variety.

Introduction 7

Women Patrons and Music Makers

Dwight's journal promoted performances of lieder by men and women, and, in the closing decades of the long nineteenth century, women played an increasingly important role in the US dissemination of the genre and in various ways reinforced its status as high art. According to Beatrix Borchard, the gender of audiences for lieder in Europe has not been established, but she assumes they were largely comprised of middle-class women because the lied was "connotated as female" and "it was predominantly women who received singing lessons, acquired scores, and sang lieder in the domestic sphere."[29] This situation was replicated in the United States, where, Walter Damrosch recalled, music was initially the domain of women and was considered effeminate.[30] Women were responsible for running the house and raising the children, and these duties extended to cultural matters such as music making. Middle- and upper-class women played decisive roles not only in fostering music at home but also in serving as teachers and attending concerts given by professional musicians.[31] Society women also hosted performances by professional musicians in their homes. All these activities included lieder.

Throughout the nineteenth century the growing middle class in the United States embraced music for pleasure but, as in Europe, it also tapped into the social prestige associated with classical music. During the second half of the century piano builders produced affordable, reliable instruments for amateurs, and, aided by the flourishing economy as well as by the interest in touring virtuosi, sales of pianos dramatically increased. According to Richard Crawford, "It has been estimated that one out of 4,800 Americans bought a new piano in 1829; in 1910, a year in which 350,000 pianos were made [in the United States,] one out of 252 bought one."[32] In middle-class families throughout the country the piano was the centerpiece of the parlor, signifying its importance to family life but also the family's prosperity, "social respectability and female accomplishment."[33] Etiquette books frequently extolled piano playing and singing as enhancing morals, and authors reinforced the belief that these skills were a sign of a cultured woman.[34] In both Europe and the United States, piano ownership contributed to the increasing rates of music education and the production of sheet music. Publishers catered to consumers who were particularly interested in songs (as opposed to technically demanding piano sonatas). By the middle of the century the sheet music trade was producing more than five thousand titles per year.[35] Lieder, usually with singable English translations, were part of this expansion. The list of German songs published in the Board of Music Trade's 1870 *Complete Catalog of Sheet Music and Musical Works* comprised ten pages, including 235 works by Beethoven, Franz, Mendelssohn, Schubert, and Schumann. (In contrast, songs composed in English were far more numerous, and the list of Italian songs filled thirteen pages.)[36] Throughout the century, the firm of Oliver Ditson led the way in publishing lieder, and, like European publishers, this company worked with well-known singers to market its scores.[37]

During the 1890s the integration of song recitals into musical life across the country was facilitated by the rapid growth in the number of women's music clubs. By 1919, there were more than six hundred active women's clubs with an estimated two hundred thousand members.[38] Many of these clubs strove to elevate their city's culture by instituting a visiting artist series that presented performers and lecturers of national renown, including those who specialized in lieder. While the roles music clubs played in the formation of institutions such as the Cincinnati Symphony and in supporting touring instrumentalists has already been acknowledged, their contribution to the dissemination of lieder and the promotion of the most acclaimed lieder recitalists has not. Yet these clubs did more to promote lieder to heterogeneous communities throughout the United States than did *Männerchöre* or any other German organization. Whereas recitals given by amateurs in the homes of club members were often open only to fellow members, those given by professional singers were marketed to the public. All the major lied recitalists performed before clubs, including those in small, remote locations.

In Europe the lied was already associated with the feminine, domestic sphere in the early nineteenth century, and David Gramit has argued that this was such a strong negative association that at first the genre was not taken as seriously as other high art.[39] Marcia Citron and others have similarly shown that small-scale genres were often associated with the woman's domain. Citron's argument regarding the status of compositional genres can be applied not only to the works themselves but also to concerts that emphasized specific genres (for instance, recitals devoted to lieder as opposed to symphony concerts). According to Citron, genre is a "convention whose internal divisions are based on criteria that reflect social values, such as a preference for largeness and for non-functionality that implies transcendence. The criteria establish hierarchies that are linked with gender: maleness with the large, the non-functional, and the intellectual, which are valued; femaleness with the small and the functional (and the private), which are devalued."[40] In the nineteenth century the press occasionally derided the female-dominated audiences of song recitals, and in more recent times the failure of scholars to acknowledge the success of such recitals is in part driven by this type of privileging of large (male) genres.

Many of the chapters in *Lieder in America* document performances of lieder that the main exponents of the genre gave to women's clubs, with Chapter 6 specifically debunking the satires of recitals held by clubs. In addition, each chapter documents the contributions of numerous women singers in establishing song recitals and disseminating the lied; they include Fanny Raymond

Introduction   9

Ritter (ca. 1840–1890), Grace Hiltz (ca. 1855–1930), Ernestine Schumann-Heink (1861–1936), and Villa Whitney White. In the closing decades of the long century, women's clubs extended their advocacy of classical music to embrace songs by American composers. As a result, their members performed songs by numerous American women, and artists such as Schumann-Heink programmed these works in recitals and recorded them.

American Art Song and the Lied

Despite the influence and success of the network of musicians promoting German instrumental and vocal repertoire, their efforts met with increasing opposition. As early as the 1880s, a few critics who praised the performances of lieder by artists such as Henschel and Heinrich also occasionally voiced reservations about performing too many German songs. Such complaints reflected the preference for recitals to encompass a variety of styles and genres and reservations about repertoire sung in the German language, as opposed to English. During the 1890s critics, composers, and performers began to give increasing attention to compositions by Americans, a development that Douglas Shadle, among others, has tied to wider sociopolitical developments and nation building not only in the United States but also in Europe.[41] Campaigns to promote the composition and performance of American instrumental music were mirrored by recital programs encompassing an increasing number of songs by Americans and by related articles and reviews in newspapers and music journals. Initially recitalists tended to favor songs by the composers of the Second New England School who pioneered the American art song, principally Arthur Foote (1853–1937), George Chadwick (1854–1931), Edward MacDowell (1861–1908), and Amy Beach (1867–1944). But by the second decade of the twentieth century, singers such as Bispham programmed lieder with works by a much greater array of American men and women, including arrangements of African American and Native American songs.

Since Americans preferred programs presenting a variety of songs and because many were not aware of the nationalistic connotations of lieder (in part because these works were often sung in English), programs combining lieder with American songs were not viewed as problematic, and any possible ideological conflicts in such combinations were not publicly discussed by critics or performers. Ultimately the American assimilation of the lied was so successful that even after the outbreak of war in Europe, American recitalists programmed lieder alongside patriotic American numbers, and while many performers gave lieder in English, some continued to sing in German. A few even continued to program lieder after America entered the war in 1917.

How Were Lieder Understood by Americans?

Although German immigrants sang lieder in their homes and during meetings of their social groups, their organizations did not guide the American dissemination of lieder. Rather this was left to individual singers and the network of American and German musicians surrounding Dwight who were fostering classical instrumental music. These early advocates promoted lieder to the general concertgoing community, many of whose members were Anglophones, and not just to the German population. Although some of the singers highlighted in this book occasionally performed before German clubs, most of their performances were in venues catering to music lovers generally. Furthermore, it will become clear that some cities with significant German populations, including Cincinnati, were not among the main trendsetters in the development of the song recital, while in others, including New York, early recitals were not always well attended. Some of the song recitals that will be referenced were advertised in German newspapers, but such notices were not more informative than those in the Anglophone press. Moreover, despite the prominence of the German immigrant community in New York, the *New York Times* advertised far more song recitals and performances of lieder than did the *New Yorker Staats-Zeitung*, a German paper that carried numerous notices about concerts and operas. The numerous English-language scores, performances in English, and advertisements and reviews using English translations of the titles of lieder all demonstrate the ways lieder were being disseminated to Anglophone audiences.

Beyond accepting the media's descriptions of lieder as high art, Anglophone Americans perceived this genre and the meaning of individual songs in contrasting ways, as did Germans. As late as 1884, the Chicago critic and pedagogue Frederick Grant Gleason (1848–1903) asserted that "a German song to an American audience is nothing else than a vocal solo,"[42] and despite the increasing number of singers taking up the lied, this situation remained largely unchanged through the rest of the century. Although Gleason argued that providing translations of the texts was not enough to inform listeners, his publications, most of which were newspaper columns, do not explore the multiple levels of meaning in a lied. In Europe the lied carried nationalistic connotations that encompassed their introverted contemplations of human nature and implications of intimacy. Much of this was lost when the lied was transferred to the United States, but even in Europe there were varying levels of appreciation of the genre.

In Europe the lied was viewed as quintessentially German. In a review of the score of Schubert's *Winterreise* (D. 911) in the 1828 *Theaterzeitung* a Viennese critic championed the national significance of the work and the composer: "Herein lies the nature of German Romantic being and art, and in this sense

Introduction   11

Schubert is a German composer through and through, who does honor to our fatherland and our time. It is this spirit that is breathed by the present songs."[43] Similarly, Eduard Hanslick (1825–1904), an influential Viennese music critic (and close friend of Brahms and numerous lieder singers), frequently invoked the German spirit of lieder, including during discussions of such renowned exponents of the lied as Julius Stockhausen (1826–1906).[44] Throughout the century, German writers explored the important place of *Innigkeit* (inwardness) in German culture and, in particular, as embodied by the lied.[45] In contrast, American commentaries on the lied rarely invoked this concept—let alone its cultural connotations. While German performers and audiences in the United States might well have appreciated the cultural significance of the lied, many Anglophones had a limited appreciation of the strength of this relationship because performers and critics made only limited attempts to educate them.

In Germany and Austria, the lied's national significance was reinforced when singers programmed lieder with German folksongs, the importance of which was instilled in Germans of all classes. In addition to school curricula, this was achieved through published scores marketed to amateurs, educational concerts that modeled bourgeois ideology,[46] and lieder by the likes of Brahms that were written in the style of folksongs. While some singers in the United States explicitly connected German folksongs to art songs, others did not, and in some cases German folksongs or folk-inspired songs were grouped with folksongs from other countries and were used to lighten programs rather that to reinforce German identity.

Beyond issues concerning the status of the genre, assessing the extent to which European and Anglophone audiences understood the subtleties of either the texts or the ways the music interpreted the texts is difficult because reviews of lieder performances rarely referenced anything more than obvious audience responses such as calls for encores. It is an oft-repeated truism that Anglophones cannot hear lieder in the same ways as native German speakers. Although highly educated Americans might well have recognized all the tropes of German Romanticism in Schubert's "Der Wanderer" (D. 489), which was highly popular in both Europe and the United States, numerous others who attended song recitals or purchased sheet music likely did not. Moreover, it is unlikely that many appreciated the difference in the poetic styles of, for instance, Heine and Goethe.[47] But even in German-speaking countries lieder were heard by diverse audiences. Gramit contrasts the elite educated Germans who had the wherewithal to study German Romantic poets to the many other readers "whose literary tastes were perceived to be less refined."[48] Similarly, Susan Youens argues that as early as the 1820s, European audiences were not monolithic, and composers, singers, and critics discriminated between songs exploring deep levels of subjectivity through highly nuanced compositional techniques and simpler ones addressed to a public who "merely wanted their ears tickled."[49] The same applies to singers and audiences in the United States.

The following chapters reveal that audiences in different parts of the United States had contrasting opportunities to hear lieder and that even during the peak of song recitals in the early 1900s singers gave different types of programs to audiences in major cultural hubs than to those in smaller locales in the middle of the country and on the West Coast. This type of differentiation of audiences is, of course, still evident today, and is the case in Europe as well as the United States.[50] Even in a city like New York, nineteenth-century recitalists attuned to audience preferences offered a range of programs, with those for request or "popular" recitals, or for performances at other types of popular concerts, being confined to English versions of well-known lieder that were circulating in sheet music. Whereas modern scholars of the lied and recent performers are enthralled by the introspective aspects of the genre, the most popular lieder in nineteenth-century America were lyrical, often upbeat numbers about love or spring and dramatic narratives comprising contrasting sections. These preferences align with the types of piano music that, Crawford concluded, appealed to women because they touched "the player's or listener's imagination or emotions."[51] Lieder characterized by searing explorations of the human condition, such as some of those in *Winterreise*, posed more challenges. In some cases, the music did not have an immediate appeal, and an appreciation of the depth of the songs' beauty required detailed study of the music and the words, as well as multiple hearings.

The extent to which concertgoers—in Europe or the United States—studied the structure of the songs at home, as opposed to being concerned with the technical aspects of learning how to perform them, is not known. Laura Tunbridge recently cautioned against imposing modern scholars' understanding of the lied as a fusion of text and music and its possible role in *Bildung* by recalling the ways performances of Wilhelm Müller and Ludwig Berger's *Die schöne Müllerin*, op. 11 (1818) served primarily as "entertainment" for the amateur music makers at an early nineteenth-century house party in Berlin.[52] Some of the works of art that portray early Schubertiades likewise convey a playful environment, rather than introverted study. Descriptions of August Kreissmann's performances at private concerts and informal meetings of his Boston *Männerchor*, the Orpheus Club, similarly project a relaxed, convivial environment. And while these events might have provided German immigrants with a sense of comradery and nostalgia for their homeland, the few sources describing them do not indicate a deeper level of interaction with the songs. Regardless of the extent to which audience members had studied a song, reviews of American performances indicate that audiences at least perceived the main topics of many lieder and valued the ways in which the singers (and, by implication, the music) brought the narrative

Introduction   13

personae to life. In Europe and the United States audiences greatly appreciated singers who dramatized each song and in this way made the overall meaning or narrative clear and convincing.

Although European composers and publishers of the early nineteenth century marketed lieder for domestic consumption, from as early as the 1830s lieder were increasingly performed in public spaces, and by the turn of the century, despite some conservative German critics' protests, the genre was viewed as a concert genre. Complex new works by the likes of Brahms and Wolf were written for highly trained professional singers, rather than for amateurs. In both Europe and the United States lieder were performed in concert halls accommodating more than a thousand people, but more often they were performed in smaller venues with capacities of between two hundred and six hundred. In Europe, the perception of the genre's intimacy and immediacy, and the expectation of the performance of authentic emotions, were initially viewed as conflicting with performances in public concert halls. However, Vienna's six-hundred-seat Bösendorfer Hall, which opened in 1872, mediated the salon–concert hall dichotomy because, unlike an opera house, it was designed to promote a rapport between the singer and the audience.[53] While German aestheticians and historians have theorized the shift from the salon to the concert hall, which involved a departure from the sociability initially associated with lieder, US nineteenth-century lied scholars and music critics did not broach these broader topics. Yet from the late 1880s onwards some indicated that they were aware of the genre's connotations of intimacy in that they lauded performers who created a direct, meaningful rapport with their audiences. In contrast, the few times the size of the venue was criticized, it was in relation to a singer's lack of vocal power, rather than in relation to the inherent characteristics of the genre.

The success of the lied relied on its flexibility. The genre embraced aspects of both high and popular art, it was performed in intimate and public venues, and in varying ways was embraced by both Europeans and Americans. Its changing cultural connotations are a reminder that the meanings of the genre and of individual songs are contingent on numerous factors and are not inscribed solely by the composer.

Sources

The nationwide success and profitability achieved by recitals featuring lieder at the end of the long nineteenth century have never been replicated by recitals in modern times. By the late twentieth century not only were the number of recitals declining, but also any trace of the previous popularity of this genre seems to have disappeared from the collective cultural memory, replaced by claims of the death of the song recital.[54] This cultural amnesia, the current lowly status of song recitals, scholarly preferences for large genres, and possibly remnants of the association of lieder and song recitals with the woman's sphere, have likely deterred scholars from researching this mode of entertainment. Moreover, studying American performances of lieder prior to the age of the digital humanities was difficult in large part because primary sources such as program leaflets and booklets were not systematically preserved. As a result, there are insufficient archived documents to establish the initial development of song recitals or the gradual acceptance of the lied as a concert genre. Furthermore, the programs that have survived are not easily accessible because library catalogs often do not fully describe such ephemera. Institutions such as the Boston Public Library, the New York Public Library, and Chicago's Newberry Library hold a significant number of programs for recitals and concerts featuring lieder from the 1890s, but their holdings of artifacts from earlier concerts are significantly smaller. Successful choral organizations such as New York's Liederkranz and Arion Society did not archive their concert programs. Moreover, some of the printed programs that have survived do not provide detailed information about the lieder that were performed. For instance, the few extant early programs of the Philadelphia Männerchor, which are held by the Historical Society of Philadelphia, sometimes just state that a solo lied was to be presented, without giving its name or that of the composer. The practices of the *Männerchöre* are mirrored by those of women's clubs. At first many of the early clubs did not print programs, and when they did, many did not archive them. This situation resembles that in Europe, and on both continents the surviving programs often do not include the texts of songs or the names of accompanists.[55]

Music journals proffer more information about concerts including lieder than do archival sources, but most of these publications did not devote the same level of coverage to performances of songs as they did to operas and instrumental music. *Dwight's Journal of Music* is exceptional because it provided programs and reviews of numerous lieder performances in Boston and a small sample of those from other cities. Though this journal is an excellent source of information, it ran from 1852 to 1881, ceasing publication right at the time when song recitals featuring lieder began to gain currency. Briefer reports in the *Musical Courier*, which was first published in 1880, enable historians to track the subsequent growth in song recitals. Nevertheless, while this journal covered many of the major singers and printed representative programs from across the country, by its very nature as a trade journal it has significant gaps in coverage, and its reports include few sustained discussions of songs or their composers. Numerous other journals, as well as early histories of musical life in America, occasionally mention song composers or performers. Such publications do not, however, provide enough information to construct a history of song recitals or of lieder performances.

Introduction   15

In contrast, English- and German-language newspapers from around the country frequently reference recitals and performances of lieder. This study draws on about ten thousand articles, promotional pieces, and advertisements, most of which were published in newspapers that were accessed in digitized formats and on microfilm.[56] Many of the individual notices by themselves contain little information, often no more than the name of the singer, a listing of some of the composers whose works were sung, and the date and location of the concert. But when they are assembled with thousands of others, one can track the acceptance of the lied, the development of song recitals, and the careers of singers who have not been discussed in recent histories of American music. These sources also demonstrate trends in programming: They identify songs and composers that were performed more frequently than others, document when later lied composers such as Richard Strauss and Wolf began to be included in recitals, and reveal when American and French art songs began to be programmed with lieder. Moreover, digitized sources reveal the emergence of the US song recital during the 1870s, whereas previously the recital was thought to have begun with Henschel's first visit to the country in 1880–1881.[57]

Nevertheless, newspaper notices prompt as many questions as they answer, if not more. In general, fewer papers from the early and middle decades of the century have survived. Other limitations are posed by the mechanism of digital searches. The quality of optical character recognition impacts retrievability, as do alternative titles and spellings (which are particularly problematic when dealing with titles of compositions such as lieder in English-language papers). To address these concerns, this study is based on numerous digital archives whose content overlaps. Advertisements and reviews of performances often gave the titles of lieder in German or English, usually without opus numbers and without clearly indicating the language used by the performer.[58] Often a single notice would supply titles for some songs in German and others in English, but only a few reviews confirm the language or languages that the singer employed.[59] Some composers used identical or similar titles for multiple lieder, as is the case of the spring songs of Mendelssohn and Franz. Ascertaining which of these songs an advertisement or review is referencing can be impossible, but on rare occasions the identity of such a song becomes clear after an examination of multiple sources for a performance.

The concluding decades of the nineteenth century witnessed significant developments in music criticism. Erudite critics such as Louis C. Elson (1848–1920), Philip Hale (1854–1934), and Henry Krehbiel rose to the fore for their newspaper commentaries, and these men, as well as others such as W. S. B. Mathews, also contributed to music journals. In addition to their reviews of symphonic music and operas, they offered perceptive coverage of lieder and advocated

16   Introduction

for art songs by authoring lectures and publications on various aspects of the history of song, as well as editing anthologies of lieder and French art songs. Nevertheless, press reports of lieder performances in major cities and smaller locales, and in American and German-language newspapers, were usually quite terse (as was the case in Europe). Longer reports, including a few in the *New Yorker Staats-Zeitung*, occasionally referenced a singer's execution of a phrase or two in a given song, but assessments of the compositions were rarely provided. Although names of composers were often listed, poets and translators were rarely acknowledged.[60]

Discussions about song recitals in newspapers and journals in the United States and Europe rarely provided demographic information about audiences, and while the general profile of those attending private performances hosted by clubs or socialites can sometimes be deduced, documents about audiences at most of the performances discussed in this book have not come to light. Whereas the advertising, sizes of concert venues, and ticket prices point to recitals being marketed to the educated upper classes, there are no records or indications concerning the percentage of German immigrants attending concerts, nor are there accurate indications of the number of women in audiences. Recitals were not scheduled at a set time; they could be held on any day of the week (though usually not Sunday), and the most popular artists offered both daytime (morning or afternoon) and evening recitals. Scholars investigating instrumental concerts have assumed that audiences for daytime events were dominated by women of the middle and upper classes, and this was likely the case with song recitals as well.

Sources describing performances of lieder in private homes are even more limited than those documenting public concerts and recitals. The social columns in newspapers that sometimes reference recitals in homes provide very limited information. A few indicate the number of people who were invited (which could encompass a few hundred) and the names of the performers, but the compositions that were performed are rarely named. Although a few notices indicate refreshments would be served, many provide no such details about the atmosphere; it was assumed that if you had the wherewithal to attend you already knew the relevant social conventions. Lieder were also sung in less formal circumstances, such as friends and family gathering around the piano at home. The diary of William Steinway is one of the rare surviving documents describing such domestic music making, and it is also exceptional because it names some of the lieder he sang.[61] European sources concerning domestic music making are similarly limited.[62] Furthermore, while the US production of English-language sheet music reflects consumer interest in lieder, records of sales and print runs have not survived, nor are there records of US sales of scores

Introduction 17

printed in Europe.[63] Whereas recent studies have highlighted the significance of binders' volumes, that is, collections of sheet music that were often compiled by women, the practice of creating such volumes peaked in the middle of the century, when lieder were being introduced to the United States, and as a result the binders that have been studied include few lieder.[64] Moreover, most of these lieder are the same few works by Schubert and Schumann that were being sung in mid-century mixed-genre concerts, as well as lighter numbers by composers such as Abt and Kücken.

It might be surmised that singers in the United States were directly modeling their recital programs and lieder performances on those in Europe, but the available evidence suggests that this was not entirely the case. American performers were influenced by their social, political, and musical milieus and in some cases anticipated trends in Europe. The extent to which their programming practices developed independently, however, will only be accurately gauged after more thorough studies of the situation on the Continent have been undertaken. Although there have been studies of the careers and repertoire of such leading singers as Stockhausen, Amalie Joachim (1839–1899), Gustav Walter (1834–1910), and Pauline Viardot-Garcia (1821–1910), as well as of the UK performances of George Henschel, the accomplishments of other lieder performers have not been investigated, and any such study will likely be hampered by the limitations of the sources.[65] Ironically, most of the brief notices of concerts that included lieder in German newspapers and music journals such as the *Allgemeine musikalische Zeitung* do not offer as many itemized programs as do US newspapers. Other studies of European concert life, including those by William Weber and Edward Kravitt, acknowledge the significance of Stockhausen's concerts and Walter's Viennese *Liederabende* of the 1870s and 1880s in establishing lieder recitals in Europe, but they do not systematically trace the activities of these singers' contemporaries. Similarly, McVeigh and Weber's survey of performances of lieder in England touches on the 1870s and 1880s but emphasizes the sharp increase in the number of performances at the turn of the century.[66]

In addition to studies concerning specific European singers, three recent volumes have explored the performance of lieder, a new trend in lieder scholarship that contrasts with the traditional emphasis on hermeneutic readings of individual songs and their texts. Jennifer Ronyak takes a speculative approach in teasing out the paradoxes of performing a genre that was known for its interiority in various types of public places from the salon to the concert hall. She concentrates on Germany in the first quarter of the nineteenth century, and, with the exception of Beethoven's "Adelaide" (op. 46), on works such as songs by Carl Friedrich Zelter (1758–1832) that were not taken up by many professional singers in America. Laura Tunbridge, by contrast, explores lieder performances in concerts and recordings in New York and London between the two world wars. The singers she discusses, however, were building on the accomplishments of those described in the present study. *German Song Onstage* presents a series of case studies by various authors exploring performances of lieder from the mid-nineteenth century to the early twentieth century in the United Kingdom, Russia, Germany, and the United States, many of which offer informative points of comparison with the performances of lieder discussed in the following chapters.[67]

Overview

The chapters in *Lieder in America* cover two sequential periods. With an overall trajectory from the early nineteenth century to the late 1870s, Chapters 1 and 2 document the environment that fostered the emergence of "song recitals." Spanning the 1880s to 1917, Chapters 3 to 7 deal with the period when song recitals proliferated and singers, rather than instrumentalists, drove the campaign to introduce a greater number of Americans to lieder. Since the chapters focus on individual performers whose careers overlapped, a chronological snapshot of the performances that represent milestones in the development of song recitals is presented in the appendix. Each chapter ties prominent singers to the network promoting German instrumental music as a means of enriching US concert life. This network's influence continued to reverberate at the end of the century, when women's clubs promoted cultural uplift, but increasingly singers balanced their commitment to lieder with the necessity of responding to rising American nationalism and to a flood of new American songs.

Chapter 1, "Introducing a 'Higher Class' of Song to American Audiences," highlights the advocacy of the lied by German immigrants and American musicians and critics in Boston, including Kreissmann, Dresel, and Dwight. In addition to addressing the beauty of individual songs, they established the view that lieder, like German instrumental music, were "high art." They contributed and influenced performances of lieder during Boston chamber concerts and the publication of English-language sheet music, which began the process of canonizing the lieder of Beethoven, Schubert, Schumann, and Franz.

Chapter 2, "Song Recitals and Song Recital Series," is devoted to musicians including Fanny Raymond Ritter, W. S. B. Mathews, and George Werrenrath who championed German repertoire and contributed to the development of the "song recital." Some of the earliest song recitals were at normal schools for music teachers, where they were given by women singers (often with men at the piano) and women populated the audiences. These events contributed to the association of recitals with the woman's sphere, an association that was perpetuated throughout the rest of the century. Nevertheless, men often led the way, and in 1879 in Chicago, Werrenrath and Wolfsohn presented a series of

Introduction   19

four song recitals that encompassed more than fifty lieder. This series predated Walter's series of *Liederabende* in Vienna, and it influenced subsequent song recitalists in the United States including Henschel and Heinrich.

Chapters 3, "The Henschels' Polyglot 'Vocal Recitals,'" and 4, "Max Heinrich's 'Classical Song Recitals,'" explore the performances of George and Lillian Henschel and the early career of Max Heinrich, respectively. During the 1880s, these performers solidified the song recital as a significant concert genre. The Henschels' programs emphasized lieder while also embracing a variety of genres, periods, and languages. Some included George's own parlor songs, which were published as sheet music by US companies and marketed to women. When the couple returned to England in 1884 Heinrich became the foremost promoter of lieder in the United States. Like Henschel, he accompanied himself, he was often joined by a woman singer, and he did not program instrumental solos. Unlike recitals by Henschel and European singers of the 1880s, Heinrich's were devoted to lieder.

Chapter 5, "Max Heinrich's Expanding Geographic and Stylistic Vistas," explores Heinrich at the zenith of his fame, when he was repeatedly extolled for his profound understanding and interpretation of lieder. During the second half of his career, he resided in Boston (1891–1899), Chicago (1899–1904, 1906–1909), La Jolla (1904–1906), and New York (1909–1916), but throughout these years he undertook extensive tours. Unlike the Henschels, Heinrich responded to changes in both musical and societal landscapes. In response to programs by contemporaries and audiences who preferred variety, his wife, whom the press always referred to as Mrs. Heinrich (ca. 1853–1900), and eldest daughter Julia (1877–1917) sometimes sang French songs, including ones by Cécile Chaminade (1857–1944). He acknowledged the rise of anti-German sentiment by frequently singing lieder in English translation and programming songs written in English by composers such as Alexander Campbell MacKenzie (1847–1935), Foote, and Chadwick. Like his colleagues, he also began programming a few lighter popular numbers. Such repertoire was particularly important in addressing new audiences in venues beyond the major cosmopolitan areas, including those supported by the increasing number of women's clubs. He remained committed to the lied, however, and in the last years of his life created English-language editions of more than two hundred lieder.

Chapter 6, "Villa Whitney White and Women's Music Clubs," chronicles White's rapid rise to national prominence in 1895 after a series of lecture-recitals on the history of German song before Chicago's Amateur Musical Club. Although she was primarily known for performances of lieder, in 1898 she gave one of the earliest recitals to embrace diverse American folksongs, including ones by African and Indigenous Americans. Countering satirical portrayals of women's clubs in contemporary press reports, this chapter highlights the challenging works that clubs explored. It also demonstrates the development of the clubs' role in facilitating national tours of major recitalists, on which subsequent singers capitalized.

At the peak of the song recital's popularity, 1897–1916, newspapers attracted the attention of women by publishing stories about the private lives of their favorite singers, and singers developed personal brands to ensure success. Chapter 7, "David Bispham and the Heyday of Song Recitals," focuses on the ways Bispham shaped and marketed his recitals to distinguish himself in what was now a crowded market of lieder recitalists. During the early decades of the twentieth century opera stars such as Bispham, Nordica (Lillian Norton; 1857–1914), and Schumann-Heink presented recitals throughout the country, including states where previous recitalists had not performed. Some contributed to the commodification of the lied by marketing scores for home music makers and making gramophone recordings. Bispham's English-language recitals, featuring lieder sung in translation and songs by Americans, were well calibrated to the increasingly strong reactions against repertoire sung in German, the growing American nationalism of the prewar years, and the burgeoning production of songs by American men and women.

Throughout the nineteenth century, performances and English-language sheet music produced by US publishers contributed to the formation of the lied canon. The epilogue summarizes the ways in which published anthologies of lieder scores supported this canon before briefly considering the fate of the lied and the recital during and after World War I. The conditions that enabled lieder to flourish during the nineteenth century no longer applied in the twentieth, and this led to the continual decline in popularity of the song recital, and thereby also of the lied.

* * *

Whereas the careers of opera stars have been widely documented—and there is a growing body of research on African American singers who performed classical, predominantly operatic repertoire[68]—the accomplishments of singers who advocated for lieder and established song recitals have not. But during their lives, their performances were widely advertised and reviewed, and the celebrity status achieved by Henschel, Heinrich, and Bispham led to biographical news being reproduced in newspapers throughout the country—including places where they did not perform. These singers were also acknowledged in contemporary volumes chronicling the musical life of America and, in addition to their public performances, they were sought out for entertainments in private homes. Like the advocates for German instrumental music and operas and many leaders of women's clubs, they viewed themselves as missionaries, with goals of educating and uplifting their audiences. This study highlights their significance to nineteenth-century Americans and demonstrates that, in contrast to today, song recitals and lieder had a vital place in US musical life.

Introduction   21

1

Introducing a "Higher Class" of Song to American Audiences

A memorial for August Kreissmann, the most admired performer of the lied in the United States during the 1850s and 1860s, reads:

> From him the Boston public first heard the incomparable beauty of Schubert, Franz, and Schumann . . . and the immortal strains of the "Adelaide" of Beethoven. . . . People who had starved upon the inanities of modern psalmody, who were tired of the forced brilliancy of Italian opera, and were disgusted with the commonplaces of British composers, found in the overflowing fountain of German song the sources of the keenest and most lasting pleasure.[1]

Over and above memorializing an esteemed colleague, this statement paints a vivid picture of the concert scene in Boston before Kreissmann rose to prominence. Although somewhat hyperbolic in that some musicians likely had heard "Adelaide" and a few songs by Schubert before Kreissmann's performances, its insinuation of the general neglect of lieder could be applied to the state of concertgiving in the rest of the country as late as the early 1870s. The writer, F. H. Underwood (a member of the *Männerchor* that Kreissmann had conducted) cherished lieder because they embodied a "composite idea" in which the "words and music, thought and form, melody and accompaniment" worked together as one. With these words he distinguished lieder from lighter English songs. More broadly, his statement also reflected the change in aesthetics that was already well under way, during which German opera supplanted Italian opera in critical esteem, and complexities of such stylistic elements as harmony were valued more highly than an immediately pleasing, lyrical melody.[2] Underwood's position paralleled the enthusiasm for German music that was expressed in many other articles in *Dwight's Journal of Music* and also the journal's endorsement of the lied as high art. Although later singers were somewhat more inclusive in their programming than Kreissmann, the early advocates of the lied shared these opinions.

Lieder were rarely performed in US concerts before the 1850s, as noted by an unnamed German visitor to New York in 1849 who complained of the backward state of song and of the preponderance of Italian arias.[3] The few lieder that were performed on US stages were normally placed in concerts presenting a variety of larger, more familiar genres, as was the tradition in Europe. These types of concerts usually programmed lieder that were already available in English-language scores marketed for domestic music making by amateurs. In contrast, from the 1850s through the 1870s Boston witnessed numerous chamber concerts that programmed more lieder than did other types of concerts, and the singers introduced works that were not already circulating as parlor songs. Whereas singers in other locales typically sang lieder in English, these performers used both German and English.

The performers in Boston, including Kreissmann, his fellow tenor George L. Osgood (1844–1922), and the pianist Otto Dresel were associated with the network of musicians and writers including John Sullivan Dwight, Theodore Thomas, and Carl Wolfsohn who strongly believed in music's power to uplift the country's culture, and toward this end they promoted music by German composers.[4] The performances supported by these men and other like-minded music lovers began the process through which lieder were canonized in the United States. English-language sheet music, which Dwight and his colleagues assisted in creating and promoting, also contributed to this process. While musicians in Boston initiated trends in lieder consumption that would be followed elsewhere, they also created a few anomalies. In particular, because of the efforts of Dwight and Dresel, songs by Franz were often given far greater attention than those by other composers, and this might have limited the number of performances of lieder by Schubert and Schumann. Moreover, despite the enthusiasm that Boston musicians displayed for the lied, it is likely that some audience members and amateur musicians were not as well versed in the subtleties of the lied as were Dwight and his colleagues.

Mixed-Genre Concerts

During the first half of the nineteenth century the United States witnessed numerous vocal music concerts, but very few included lieder. Events under such titles as Grand Concert, Concert of Vocal Music, Grand Operatic and Ballad Concert, and Benefit Concert typically comprised a miscellany of operatic excerpts, popular numbers such as folksongs from the British Isles, and instrumental works.[5] While some of these concerts, such as those given by Teresa Parodi (1827–after 1878), Amelia Patti (1831–1915), and Elizabeth Taylor

Greenfield (1819–1876), were dominated by solo songs performed by one or two singers, many others were given by groups of soloists who also performed a few ensemble pieces, and many also included instrumental numbers. Rarely were more than one or two lieder sung when they were programmed at all. This was even the case in US concerts given by Jenny Lind (1820–1887), Henriette Sontag (1806–1854), and Stigelli (Georg Stiegel[e] or Giorgio Stigelli, ca. 1819–1868), who had burnished reputations in Europe for excellent performances of lieder. Although Lind's lieder interpretations were admired by highly selective musicians such as Schumann, only a small number of her US concerts included this genre. For instance, during an 1851 concert in New York she sang only one art song, Schumann's "To the Sunshine" ("An den Sonnenschein," op. 36, no. 4). Rather than introducing US audiences to more of Schumann's songs, she favored the crowd-pleasing, highly ornamented "The Bird Song," which Wilhelm Taubert (1811–1891) had written for her. As a result of such programming, one commentator begged Lind to perform "a higher style of music," including the "best of Schubert's songs," rather than "light roulades" and virtuosic pieces that pleased the "masses."[6]

Other types of mixed-genre concerts featuring choral and instrumental music likewise only sporadically presented lieder. Although some German immigrants performed lieder at home,[7] *Männerchöre* and *Turnverein* concerts did not present solo lieder on a regular basis; instead they focused on community-building choral works by German composers and popular excerpts from Italian operas by Donizetti and Bellini.[8] While orchestral concerts, including those conducted by Thomas as well as ones given by explicitly German ensembles such as Philadelphia's Germania Orchestra, occasionally programmed solo lieder with piano accompaniment, they, too, rarely included more than two or three.

Reviews of such mixed-genre concerts usually did not highlight lieder, but in reviewing a concert by New York's Liederkranz (a prominent German choral organization) one critic urged soloists to perform lieder rather than "hackneyed Italian arias, ground to death by every hand-organ in the city."[9] Others who championed the lied over Italian arias often exhibited similar elitist and biased complaints. But this was not unique to the United States; in Austria as late as 1858 Schubert's friend Josef von Spaun (1788–1865) complained that admirers of *Rigoletto* outnumbered those of Schubert's lieder.[10]

When concerts did include lieder, singers usually repeated the same few familiar works. Before the 1870s, concerts presenting a miscellany of vocal works or vocal and instrumental works usually confined their selections to lieder such as Schubert's "Der Wanderer" and "Serenade" and Mendelssohn's "On Wings of Song." It is highly likely that these songs, which were also popular in Europe, were selected in part because some audience members had come to know them through hearing or playing English versions at home.[11] An increasing number

Introducing a "Higher Class" of Song to American Audiences   25

of lieder were being distributed in English-language sheet music issued by US publishers, and bilingual scores were published in music journals. These scores and the performances of lieder in mixed-genre concerts seem to have raised enough interest in Schubert that occasionally music journals of the 1850s and 1860s referenced the poets he set, but some of these, including ones concerning Mayrhofer, focused on biographical information rather than literary style or cultural context.[12]

Nevertheless, at mid-century the lied was not the most popular genre. The few lieder scores in magazines were often outnumbered by part songs and piano pieces such as selections from Mendelssohn's *Songs Without Words*.[13] Advertisements for Benjamin Hitchcock's 1869 series "half dime music" listed 150 songs, but only one was a lied, "Praise of Tears," an Englished version of Schubert's "Lob der Tränen" (D. 711). This song was issued by other US publishers and was among those performed in concerts of the time.[14] Similarly, while English versions of songs by Schubert and Mendelssohn appear in the women's binder volumes currently housed at the Library of Congress, they are significantly outweighed by lighter English and American songs and operatic excerpts.[15]

A few lieder scores were produced as part of the merchandizing of Lind's tour, but they were far less significant than the clothing, household decorations, and paper dolls of Italian opera characters. Nevertheless, they demonstrate the lied's association with women. Schumann's "Canzonet: The Little Golden Ring," an Englished version of "Du Ring an meinem Finger" (op. 42, no. 4) was a perfect fit with the other merchandise because it was excerpted from the cycle *Frauenliebe und -leben*, whose texts by Adelbert von Chamisso modeled the mores and behavior that society expected of young women of the period.[16] In some respects Lind herself modeled this behavior, and the press repeatedly extolled her virtues and selflessness. Two other lieder that were released as part of the marketing of her tour were love songs from *Dichterliebe*, "The Rose and the Lily" and "I Can but Weep" (op. 48, nos. 3 and 4). These two scores were accompanied by a photograph of Lind, and their covers were decorated with delicate, feminine flowers, and music-making angels and cherubs (figure 1.1). These types of drawings were characteristic of sheet music marketed to women, and they reinforced the association of women with beauty and nature, as well as their aspirations for gentility.[17] Schumann's short, lyrical songs, whose general sentiments (if not the subtleties of the Heine texts) could be easily grasped, were precisely the types of lieder that were favored by American audiences. But scores like these did little to educate the consumer. Although Schumann is identified on the first page of the music, his name is not included on the list of songs on the cover, nor is the name of the poet, and there is no reference to the fact that these songs belonged to a cycle.

26   CHAPTER 1

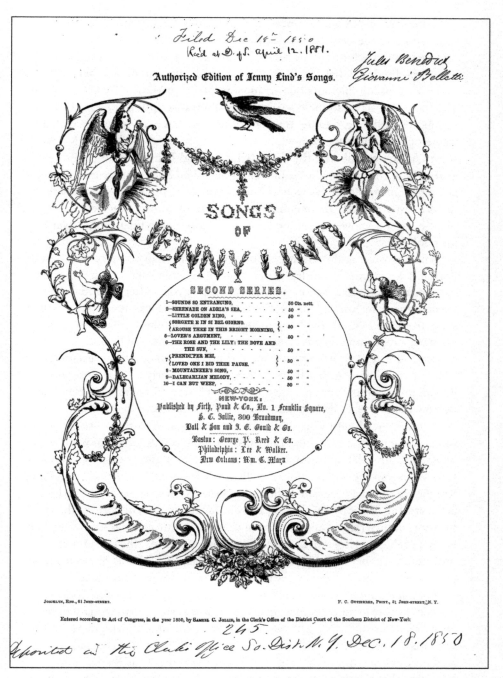

FIG. 1.1. Cover used for sheet music of some of the songs Jenny Lind performed in the United States, including Schumann's "I Can but Weep" (New York: Firth, Pond, 1850). Library of Congress, Music Division.

Scores and mixed-genre concerts also disseminated instrumental transcriptions and arrangements of well-known lieder. Thomas created an orchestral arrangement of Schubert's "Serenade," in addition to which a trombonist in his orchestra, Frederick Letsch (1829–1919), played a version of Schubert's "Wanderer" and Joseph Eller an oboe arrangement of "Ave Maria" (D. 839). A few of Thomas's concerts also included Liszt's piano transcriptions of songs such as Schubert's "Erlkönig."[18] Other transcriptions and arrangements were created by numerous American instrumentalists, including members of Boston's Mendelssohn Quintette Club and the pianists Dresel and Ernst Perabo (1845–1920). Throughout the century in Europe and the United States, many instrumental arrangements of lieder (as well as popular operatic numbers) were made for the domestic market. These enhanced the dissemination of the genre (even if players had no knowledge of the texts) while also being financially rewarding for publishers.[19]

Whereas vocal and orchestral concerts given in many diverse cities, from Portland, Maine, to New Orleans, occasionally included one or two lieder, Boston concerts were much more supportive of the genre. After an initial controversial concert by Joseph Philip Knight (1812–1887) that was devoted to German song, from the 1850s through the 1870s chamber and piano concerts in Boston regularly programmed an increasing number and variety of lieder.

Ironically, it was an Englishman, and not a German, who presented one of the first public concerts highlighting lieder. As early as 1839, Joseph Phillip Knight, a composer and singer, presented "Grand Concerts" in New York, Boston, Baltimore, Philadelphia, Schenectady, and Albany. In many cases songs were interspersed with a small number of instrumental works, usually piano solos. These programs favored English-language ballads (some of which were by Knight himself) and popular operatic arias by Italian composers and by Carl Maria von Weber. In contrast, at Boston's Tremont Temple in March 1840, Knight presented a program dedicated to works viewed as representing higher art, featuring lieder by Beethoven, Haydn, Mozart, and Schubert. At the time, this type of program would have been unusual in Europe, and its novelty was likely a problem in Boston. Dwight praised the concert as "the first and the only promiscuous concert in this place, composed entirely of classic pieces from the great masters," but he observed that the event was not well attended.[20]

Although another reviewer similarly asserted that this "classical concert . . . opened the way to the enjoyment of a higher class of songs than we have hitherto been used to hear,"[21] aspects of the concert were problematic. Knight performed versions of Beethoven's "Adelaide" and Schubert's "Erlkönig" that had been created for domestic music making. The English version of "Adelaide" (known as "Rosalie") that Knight sang was created by Charles Edward Horn (1786–1849) in 1828. In addition to tampering with the text, Horn altered the voice and piano

28   CHAPTER 1

parts, a liberty that was criticized by a number of writers but one that mirrored Englished versions of popular operas.[22] In 1835, when Schubert's instrumental works had yet to be introduced to American audiences, Horn created a similarly free arrangement of "Erlkönig," which was published under the title "The Elf King."[23] Knight likely sang this version in his 1840 concert. One reviewer, presumably the editor of the *Musical Magazine*, H. Theodore Hach, harshly critiqued the English-language version of "Adelaide" that Knight sang, and he complained that Knight gave an "energetic" performance without the delicacy the music and text required. In the same vein, he asserted that Knight did not sufficiently differentiate the three characters in "The Elf King."[24] Not only was Knight's program unusual, but also the specificity of this critique was rarely matched by contemporary reviewers of other performances of lieder. Moreover, later reviews of lieder performances in *Dwight's Journal* likewise only occasionally acknowledged specific relationships between the text and music of a lied or how such elements were interpreted by a performer. Despite the praise for the concept of a concert devoted to German classical song, Knight's program remained an anomaly, even as Boston chamber musicians began to show more interest in the lied in the following decades.

Chamber Music Concerts

From the 1850s through the early 1870s, Boston was the American epicenter of the lied. This city witnessed more lieder performances during public concerts than any other US city, and there was a greater variety of lieder being performed, with many being sung in German. That Boston, and not New York, became the hub for lieder is particularly ironic because the former had a smaller German immigrant community than did the larger metropolis. Nevertheless, many of the most influential members of the Boston music community, including the music teachers, were German, or, like Dwight, they favored German repertoire.[25] German immigrant musicians participated in orchestras that played classical repertoire, including the Germania Musical Society, based in Boston from 1851 to 1854, and the Harvard Musical Association. Many of these instrumentalists, including Carl Bergmann (1821–1876), also contributed to the rapid expansion of chamber music concerts, a type of concert that was not as successful in New York and one that accommodated performances of lieder.[26] In his examination of orchestral concerts, Paul DiMaggio argued that the "cultural capitalists" in Boston facilitated the sacralization of high art, which gained momentum after Henry Lee Higginson's (1834–1919) founding of the Boston Symphony Orchestra in 1881.[27] But the earlier chamber concerts by Bergmann and his colleagues were already establishing exclusive audiences for performances of works considered to be high art. In Europe, chamber music concerts distinguished themselves

Introducing a "Higher Class" of Song to American Audiences   29

from orchestral and vocal miscellany concerts in that they were associated with classical repertoire, and it was in these venues that Schubert's lieder were "first treated in canonic terms."[28] This was the case in the United States as well.

At mid-century Boston was creating a welcoming environment for chamber and piano concerts, which, as in Europe, were often referred to as soirées. Although these concerts programmed more lieder than did orchestral concerts, many of them reached smaller audiences. They were presented in public venues with less than half the seating capacity of the halls Thomas used for his orchestral concerts; many, including the rooms of the Chickering piano company, accommodated fewer than six hundred people.[29] Similarly, in Europe chamber concerts were attended by far fewer people than they might be today,[30] and even highly esteemed lieder singers such as Julius Stockhausen usually performed in such small halls. Unlike Thomas's garden concerts, these types of chamber concerts were marketed to the musical intelligentsia of the middle and upper classes, and reviews sometimes recorded the attendance of the elite social set or educated musicians. While the development of concerts featuring demanding repertoire was influenced by the influx of German immigrants and, in particular, by programs of the Germania Musical Society, other factors also contributed to an environment that could support chamber musicians and lieder singers. These included the success of the Handel and Haydn Society, the rising number of people receiving music education (which was greatly influenced by Lowell Mason [1792–1872]), and the community's commitment to self-improvement and cultural uplift. Similar factors also contributed to changes in concert life in Europe and to the development of chamber concerts in Victorian England in particular.[31]

Germans dominated Boston's musical circles, and therefore it is highly likely that the audiences for chamber concerts were in part populated by Germans and by Americans who were their students or part of their professional networks. Nevertheless, performances of lieder were promoted to the Anglophone community, and some of the lieder were sung in English. Katherine Preston has argued that during the 1870s and 1880s middle-class audiences were attracted to operas sung in translation while foreign-language performances were considered the bastion of the wealthy.[32] In contrast, because performers realized that an appreciation of the text was key to understanding the songs, lieder sung in English were performed for audiences comprised of both classes.

The Mendelssohn Quintette Club, the pianists Dresel, Hugo Leonhard (d. 1880), and Perabo, and the violinist Julius Eichberg (1824–1893) numbered among the musicians who introduced Boston audiences to classical, predominantly German repertoire. In addition to chamber and piano works, their concerts sometimes included lieder. Through performances in these types of concerts, August Kreissmann quickly became the most admired exponent of the genre, though other singers such as Caroline Lehmann (an opera singer from

30 CHAPTER 1

Europe and the sister of a member of the Mendelssohn Quintette Club) were also favored. The *Boston Transcript* was among the outlets to praise the efforts of the Quintette Club and its high level of programming. This review, like some of the elitist responses to performances of lieder in New York, commented on the pleasure of hearing the songs of Mozart, Beethoven, and Haydn "instead of the paltry trash with which, not long ago, we were regaled when we were rash enough to ask for a song."[33]

Chamber concerts in New York and Philadelphia that had goals and repertoire similar to those in Boston likewise sometimes included lieder. Beginning in the 1850s Theodore Eisfeld (1816–1882) presented chamber music concerts in New York, as did Bergmann, the pianist William Mason (1829–1908), and Thomas. Thomas also collaborated with the pianist Carl Wolfsohn in chamber concerts in Philadelphia.[34] One critic indicated that Bergmann and Mason intended to present songs of Schubert, Schumann, and Franz, and in doing so, their concert series would demonstrate the developments in both chamber music and song.[35] But few New York concerts, including theirs, highlighted lieder in the same manner as did those in Boston. Although the 1856 Mason-Thomas series included a performance of Franz's "Ave Maria" (op. 17, no. 1), lieder were not a standard feature of their programs and, compared to the instrumental offerings (which included the 1855 American premiere of Brahms's op. 8 Piano Trio), the lieder that were sung were often somewhat conventional choices and resembled the repertoire in orchestral concerts. For example, at a March 1860 Mason-Thomas concert Stigelli sang his own "Die Thräne" and Schubert's "Trockne Blumen" (D. 795, no. 18).[36] Similarly, lieder were usually not highlighted in Philadelphia's chamber concerts, though on one occasion the admired German opera singer Bertha Johannsen (1820–1893) was praised for her performance of lieder by Schubert, Schumann, and Mendelssohn.[37]

Although reviews in New York and Philadelphia papers demonstrate that some critics were quite knowledgeable about the lied,[38] neither city had a writer who supported the genre in the same way Dwight did in Boston. The journal he founded avidly covered chamber music concerts, in large part because the classical repertoire and high-quality performances aligned with his aspirations to enrich US concert life and his ethos of cultural uplift. Furthermore, Dwight joined chamber musicians in promoting lieder, especially those by Dresel's idol, Robert Franz.

Dwight and Dresel's Promotion of Lieder by Robert Franz

Dwight's Journal of Music published numerous items about lieder, including reviews and advertisements of concerts as well as short articles about composers. The first volume of the journal published an introductory overview of

Schubert's music. The author, Mr. H. Perabeau, a local pianist, observed that "Die Waldesnacht" (a.k.a. "Im Walde," D. 708) is "undoubtedly the greatest of all his songs. The figures in the accompaniment carry you on like the storm-wind through the old pine-woods, which fall cracking before this mighty element."[39] Despite this enthusiastic endorsement, "Die Waldesnacht" was not frequently sung on Boston stages of the time. Furthermore, the reference to the piano's graphic representation of specific images in the text was atypical of contemporary notices in this and other music journals. In general, the few articles in *Dwight's* that went further than merely naming lieder, such as a translation of Theodore Hagen's brief essay on Schubert, often limited themselves to evocative references to the overall emotional tone of a work and to occasionally naming the poets whose works the composers set.[40] The same applies to reviews and advertisements of lieder performances, with the reviews often only providing an overall, usually positive, assessment of the performance. This lack of technical detail, however, should not be taken to imply that the writers had only a superficial appreciation of the genre; indeed, Dwight had an in-depth understanding of its literary aspects.

During his student years at Harvard, Dwight published a book of translations of poems by Goethe and Schiller. His translations of other lieder texts appeared in his journal and in scores published by Ditson (the same company that published his journal), but the preface to his book gives the clearest indication of his engagement with the types of poems that German composers set to music. Dwight believed that German Romantic poetry transcended national boundaries and modeled values of beauty, edification, and spirituality that he held dear. To him the poetry spoke to all men: "It explores that great common field, and tells us, with the glow of ever-fresh discovery, how boundless are its riches; how life, and thought, and poetry, and beauty, are the inheritance of Man, and not of any class, or age, or nation; and how each, however humble, by fidelity to himself, shall find the natural current of his own being leading back into the very bosom of that ocean."[41] Dwight heard these same universal spiritual qualities in German Romantic instrumental music, and although he valued "pure" instrumental music more highly than program music or vocal music, he understood that lieder shared this ethos. Yet his knowledge of the literary tradition of lieder rarely surfaces in his journal. In general, it seems that like other Boston musicians he was more focused on fostering performances of lieder than on providing concertgoers with an understanding of the imagery in their texts or their place in German culture. He likely assumed that the readers of his journal and the musically educated people who attended concerts where lieder were performed had some familiarity with the German literary traditions of the genre. The same could be said of the Bostonians who performed lieder, including Dresel. But such elitist attitudes ultimately meant that some audiences and consumers of lieder appreciated the sound of the music but did not comprehend the complex and subtle meaning of the words.

By organizing chamber music concerts and collaborating with singers, Dresel significantly shaped performances of lieder in Boston. During the early 1840s, as a student in Europe, he met numerous eminent composers including Liszt, Mendelssohn, and Schumann. More significant, he commenced an enduring friendship with Franz. In the aftermath of the 1848 revolutions, Dresel immigrated to the United States. He arrived in New York in December 1848 and began collaborating with other German musicians, including Eisfeld. In October 1852, after a sojourn in Europe, he established himself in Boston, where Dwight introduced him to local musicians. By the end of the year, he was organizing chamber concerts and collaborating with members of the Germania Musical Society.[42]

Dwight lauded the ambitious, serious programs that Dresel presented in his chamber concerts. These events introduced audiences to chamber works, piano solos, and lieder by such composers as Chopin, Franz, Schubert, and Schumann.[43] In addition to numerous complex instrumental works, they presented lieder, sung in German, that were not already circulating in English editions. This represents a distinct departure from the type of programming that was typical of mixed-genre concerts headlined by opera stars who often sang in English. Dresel composed lieder, but he did not program them very frequently, even though he typically placed lieder on both halves of his programs (as was the practice in European concerts). While Bergman, drawing on his experiences with the marketing of the matinees given by the Germania Musical Society, scheduled his New York chamber concerts with Mason and Thomas during the day so that women could attend,[44] Dresel often gave concerts in the evening, and reports do not indicate whether women made up a significant proportion of the audiences. The press, however, did allude to the upper-class and educated people in attendance.

Dwight observed the exclusivity of Dresel's events. Reviewing the first soirée of the 1851–1852 season he wrote: "This was none of your grand and showy concerts. It was more like a gathering of the true disciples. . . . There were perhaps one hundred and fifty present, and there was room for as many more. The programme was the choicest we have ever heard" (see figure 1.2).[45] In short, Dresel's concerts exemplified Dwight's vision of high-quality programming and a reverent audience, and as such they might be interpreted as contributing to the sacralization of the concert hall as theorized by Lawrence Levine.[46] Moreover, Dwight's attitude that lieder were among the works appropriate for the educated elite mirrors attitudes in Europe, and in particular, those of Schubert and his colleagues.[47]

Dresel introduced numerous singers including Kreissmann and Lehmann, as well as, in the 1870s, Clara Doria (1844–1931) and Osgood, to Franz's lieder.

Introducing a "Higher Class" of Song to American Audiences   33

Part I

1. First Allegro from a Sonata for Piano four hands   Moscheles
   Alfred Jaëll and Otto Dresel

2. Andante and Intermezzo from a Quartet for Piano,
   Violin, Viola, and 'Cello   Otto Dresel
   Otto Dresel, Mr. Schultze, Mr. Meissel, Carl Bergmann

3. German Songs:—
   a. Er ist gekommen in Sturm und in Regen,
      and Weil' auf mir du dunkles Auge   Rob't Franz
   b. Du meine Seele, du mein Herz   Rob't Schumann
      Miss Caroline Lehmann

4. Sonata for Piano Solo, E flat, op. 20   Beethoven
   a. Allegro– b. Scherzo– c. Minuetto– d. Finale
      Otto Dresel

Part II

5. First Trio for Piano, Violin, and 'Cello   Mendelssohn
   a. Allegro agitato– b. Andante tranquillo–
   c. Scherzo– d. Finale
      Otto Dresel, Mr. Schultze, and Carl Bergmann

6. German Songs:–
   a. Mother, Oh Sing Me to Rest, as in My Bright   Robert Franz
   b. Trockne Blumen   Franz Schubert
      Miss Caroline Lehmann

7. Piano Solos:– a. Notturno and Mazourka,   Chopin
   b. Spring Song   Mendelssohn
      Otto Dresel

FIG. 1.2. Advertisement for Otto Dresel's first monthly musical soirée, Wednesday, December 22, 1852, 7:30 p.m., at Johnson's Music Hall. As reported in "The Concerts," *Dwight's Journal of Music* 2, no. 11 (December 18, 1852): 87.

As a result of his enthusiasm for this composer, in some years more of Franz's songs were performed than those of Schubert or Schumann. A survey of selected concerts demonstrating "taste and culture" in Boston's 1866–1867 season reported that sixteen songs by Franz were performed, eleven by Schubert, and only six by Schumann.[48] This bias toward Franz was evident in no other US city.

Dwight lavishly praised Dresel's accompanying of lieder, and he fully supported Dresel's project to promote those by Franz. In one review of a concert that included six lieder by Franz, Dwight described Dresel's accompaniments as "marvelously beautiful and full of meaning, . . . Mr. Dresel shows how intimately he has made Franz songs his own."[49] Some of Dwight's observations, however, praise Franz at the expense of Schubert or Schumann. This was the case in a review of Dresel's January 1853 concert in which Dwight rhapsodized: "That 'Ave Maria' by Robert Franz is the most precious acquisition made to the Song-Album of our memory for a long time. It is a real Ave Maria—not a strain of romance, with common *arpeggio* accompaniment, like Schubert's but a deep, religious composition, reminding one of the old Italian masters, and yet original. The impression of it lived through the whole, and it was re-demanded at the end."[50] In this case, the conservative Dwight preferred the hymn-like melody and texture of Franz's lied, but he was likely also reacting against the popularity of Schubert's setting and its use of a type of accompaniment found in numerous popular arias that he disdained. Yet the specificity of this remark is highly unusual. Indeed, because of the brevity of most of Dwight's observations, it is impossible to judge the extent to which his preference for Franz was colored by the influence of Dresel, his own aesthetics, his personal affinity for the unassuming Franz, or his initial lack of sympathy for modern composers such as Schumann and Brahms. However, in light of recent critiques of Dwight's judgment of other types of compositions and the way his preconceptions of the universal nature of German music influenced his assessments, it is highly likely that his endorsement of Franz's lieder was not solely based on structural or stylistic elements of the music.[51]

Dwight's Journal published numerous articles about composers, including lieder composers such as Mendelssohn and Schubert, but it devoted far more space to Franz. Aside from reviewing and advertising performances of Franz's songs, the journal published English translations of German essays about the composer. In varying ways, the essays by Schumann and Liszt, both of which lieder scholars have often cited, along with ones by August Ambros (1816–1876), a distinguished historian and critic, and August Saran (1836–1922), a student of Franz, placed Franz's songs in the context of the history of the lied and in relation to German folksong. In so doing they gave greater insight into the genre of the lied and its relation to German culture than did many other articles in *Dwight's*. In addition, the journal endorsed two American benefits to aid the composer, as well as the 1873 benefit in Leipzig organized by Liszt.[52] Dwight's advocacy of Franz led him to create English translations of the texts of some of the composer's songs, some of which appeared in Ditson's 1865 series of twenty-five Franz songs. Occasionally a review would specifically reference the Ditson score of a song that was performed, making this commodification of lieder clear.[53]

Although notices in *Dwight's* do not proffer firm evidence that Boston audiences favored Franz to the same degree as did Dresel and Dwight, the number of published scores indicate that there certainly was interest in this composer. Ditson published anthologies of songs based on successful sales of sheet music.[54] The company's 1866 anthology of one hundred German songs included only one song by Schumann—"Dedication" ("Widmung," op. 25, no. 1)—but nine by Franz.[55] In addition to Ditson, which released another series of twenty-one Franz songs in 1868, at least three other Boston companies—G. P. Reed, Nathan Richards, and Henry Tolman—published bilingual versions of this composer's songs. The availability of these scores resulted in performers, including those in Boston, giving some of the songs in English.

Beginning in the mid-1850s Dresel published his piano arrangements of twelve of Franz's songs.[56] In creating this project, he was inspired by Liszt's 1848 transcriptions of a contrasting selection of twelve songs by Franz, some of which were performed by other Boston pianists. Scores of Dresel's arrangements appeared under a variety of imprints, including S. Brainard's Sons in Cleveland and Root & Cady in Chicago. In this way, Dresel's advocacy for Franz extended beyond Boston. Dresel selected songs from Franz's opp. 1 to 21, including "Mutter, O sing' mich zu Ruh'" (op. 10, no. 3). A lament of a dying child, this song was performed by Kreissmann and other singers throughout the century and was published in multiple English-language scores. Some of these scores were designed to appeal to women. For instance, this song was part of a series titled *Flower of Germany* that also included other songs viewed as appropriate to the feminine sphere, such as lullabies and Schumann's much-loved and frequently programmed rapturous love song "Widmung."[57]

The commodification of lieder such that the songs and arrangements were performed in public concerts and distributed as sheet music also involved lieder by other composers, including Schubert. The Germania Musical Society had earlier realized that sheet music sold to women, so they could perform the pieces they heard in concerts at home, was an important marketing tool. Dwight and Dresel likely also realized the importance of arrangements and sheet music, but it is not clear whether they were fully aware of the power of women consumers. Yet a few of Franz's songs, including his "Ave Maria," were among the small number of lieder scores that mid-century women assembled into binders' volumes.[58] Although later singers contributed to the publication and marketing of lieder scores, only a few early singers were involved in the production of English-language sheet music.[59] Whereas Kreissmann and Osgood published scores of their own English-language songs, it seems they did not participate in the production or marketing of scores of lieder by other composers.

August Kreissmann

Born in Germany, Kreissmann studied at the Leipzig Conservatory in 1844 and then for two years in Milan. He arrived in New York in 1848 and for a time

36   CHAPTER 1

worked with Lowell Mason. Establishing himself in Boston during the 1850s, he was primarily a church musician and teacher, in addition to which he sang lieder in numerous concert settings.[60] He concertized with Boston's leading musicians, including the Mendelssohn Quintette Club, Dresel, Perabo, Alfred Jaëll (1832–1882), and two fellow graduates of the Leipzig Conservatory, Eichberg and Leonhard. Whereas singers were usually billed as supporting artists in chamber concerts, Kreissmann was sometimes accorded equal billing with the instrumentalists, including in the concerts that he organized with Eichberg and Leonhard. Although there are occasional vague hints of technical deficiencies in his voice, his performances of lieder were frequently lauded, and *Dwight's* repeatedly credited him with introducing Boston audiences to the songs of Beethoven, Franz, Schubert, and Schumann. At the high point of his career, during the 1860s, at least one journal in Germany also acknowledged his contributions to familiarizing Bostonians with the lied.[61] Most of Kreissmann's performances took place during chamber or piano concerts, but he also performed during private concerts and rehearsals of the Orpheus Society, a *Männerchor* that he founded in 1854.[62]

Under Dresel's influence Kreissmann programed more songs by Franz than any other composer, but his performances of Schumann's lieder were also significant. Whereas he had around forty lieder by Franz in his repertoire, he sang less than half that number by Schumann. Still, he performed more songs by Schumann than ones by Schubert, and he was credited with introducing Boston audiences to Schumann's *Dichterliebe*.[63] He sang excerpts from this cycle on numerous occasions, but the largest number of songs he gave in a single performance was eight, and his selections always came from the first eight songs of the sixteen-song cycle.

In contrast, in Europe during the 1860s Stockhausen gave performances of the entire *Dichterliebe*, sometimes with Clara Schumann at the piano. Kreissmann initially left Europe around the time Stockhausen was beginning to develop his reputation as an interpreter of the lied. It is not known whether he heard Stockhausen sing during his trips to Europe, but it is likely that he at least learned about Stockhausen from his European colleagues or from reports in music journals. On occasion, Americans favorably compared him to Stockhausen.[64] The comparison is apt because even though Kreissmann did not have Stockhausen's technique, his status as an advocate of the lied in the United States, and in particular his performances of songs from *Dichterliebe*, could be justly compared to Stockhausen's advocacy for the genre and for Schumann in Europe.

Schumann's works were not immediately taken up by Americans. A notice in an 1852 issue of the *New York Tribune* asserted incorrectly that Schumann was "a scholar" and "an imitator of Mendelssohn."[65] The reception of this composer's lieder in concerts in Boston was to some degree impacted by the preference for Franz. Dwight acknowledged the beauty of Schumann's lieder, and his transla-

Introducing a "Higher Class" of Song to American Audiences 37

tions of the texts of five songs from *Dichterliebe*, which were published in his journal and in one of Ditson's collections of Schumann's songs, indicate his interest in promoting these works.[66] Nevertheless, Dwight's bias toward Franz's works crept into reviews. A report of an 1861 chamber concert offers a telling comparison between the Schumann and Franz selections: "We all love to hear [Kreissmann's] fine voice, and we all recognize the intellectual power and discrimination which his singing shows. He favored us with an unusual number of pieces, embracing many well-contrasted styles. Schumann's *Dichterliebe* displays a vigorous dramatic conception, and is filled with an intensity of passion; but the songs of Franz are more enjoyable, certainly more pleasing to the general public."[67] Whether "the general public" preferred Franz's songs cannot be verified; however, there were other American critics who had reservations about Schumann's lieder, in large part because his vocal lines were viewed as unsuited to the voice. Louis Elson, a student of both Dresel and Kreissmann, was among those to discuss this reservation, though he nevertheless acknowledged the beauty of these works and the richness of their piano parts.[68]

Throughout his career Kreissmann gave multiple performances of Beethoven's "Adelaide" and *An die ferne Geliebte* (op. 98), a cycle of six lieder. The review of Kreissmann and Dresel's 1859 performance of *An die ferne Geliebte* in *Dwight's Journal* claimed it was probably the first time the cycle had been performed in Boston, though there is evidence it had been performed earlier in at least one private home.[69] The occasions during which Kreissmann gave this cycle are significant because these concerts embraced as many as ten lieder, a number that, as Dwight acknowledged, was quite high.[70] The programming of these concerts, however, was analogous to that of the European chamber and piano concerts in which Stockhausen presented Beethoven's cycle.

Although Franz, Schumann, and Beethoven were the mainstays of Kreissmann's repertoire, he also performed at least one ballad by Loewe. During an 1870 soirée with Perabo at the piano he performed Loewe's "Hochzeitslied" (op. 20, no. 1).[71] Whereas Dresel inspired Kreissmann's interest in Franz, it is possible that it was Perabo who prompted this performance. Loewe's works were given by other singers during two of Perabo's 1869 concerts, and Perabo also transcribed some of this composer's other songs.[72] Previously *Dwight's Journal* had occasionally noted European performances of Loewe's works, and in 1861 Dwight himself published an adaptation and translation of "Der Wirthin Töchterlein" (op. 1, no. 2) for the *Gems of German Song* series.[73]

In addition to his concerts in Boston, Kreissmann collaborated in a few concerts in other cities. During an 1863 Mason-Thomas chamber concert he sang the first eight songs from *Dichterliebe* and three songs by Franz (figure 1.3). A concert featuring so many lieder was unusual in New York and was not typical of the Mason-Thomas concerts. The *New York Post* observed that Kreissmann

Concerto in C major for two pianos, with two violins, viol and cello [BWV 1061]	Bach
Dichterliebe, opus 48, nos. 1–8 August Kreissmann and Henry C. Timm	Schumann
Adagio e Variazioni [String Quartet, op. 76, no. 2, second movement]	Haydn

Songs: Erinnerung op. 5, no. 10
    Im wunderschönen Monat Mai, op. 25, no. 5
    Willkommen mein Wald, op. 21, no. 1
	Franz

Quartet in C-sharp minor	Beethoven

FIG. 1.3. Mason-Thomas chamber music concert in Dodworth Hall, New York, NY, Tuesday, April 21, 1863, 8 p.m. Theodore Thomas Programs, Box 226, Concerts, Newberry Library, Chicago.

"was repeatedly encored" and that his "tenor is of a beautifully delicate quality, while his manner is vigorous and his style of delivery dramatic."[74] This concert's complex instrumental repertoire also demonstrates Thomas's efforts to elevate programming in US concerts, a commitment he shared with Dwight and Dresel.[75]

In 1865 Kreissmann returned to New York to participate in another Mason-Thomas concert. With Mason at the piano, he performed Schumann's "Waldesgespräch" (op. 39, no. 3), "Mondnacht" (op. 39, no. 5), and "Frühlingsnacht" (op. 39, no. 12) along with Franz's "Frühlingsgedränge" (op. 7, no. 5), "Für Musik" (op. 10, no. 1), and "Gewitternacht" (op. 8, no. 6). As with his previous appearance in this city, these were songs he had repeatedly given in Boston, but they were performed less frequently, if at all, on New York stages during this decade. The *New York Times* report of this concert is unusual in that the discussion concentrates almost exclusively on the songs rather than the instrumental works. It also provides a critique of Franz's songs that is in striking contrast to the adulation Boston writers accorded Franz:

> An unusual but acceptable vocal innovation was made by Mr. August Kreismann [*sic*], a capital concert singer, who sang half a dozen German songs with rare intelligence and nicety of feeling. Three were by Schumann and three by Franz—the last a composer who is steadily making his way in classic esteem. Franz's treatment of a film of melody, of an atomic idea, is generally good and frequently singularly delicate and fresh. It is not difficult, however, to detect a very strong tendency toward Schubert. Without the pleasant plashing of the piano, it would be difficult to attach either meaning or importance to the very turgid sentences which are here supposed to pass muster as songs. They are in fact mere suggestions for the spirited repartée of the piano; occa-

sions for skillful embroidery; opportunities for answering neat little musical questions, and doing it rather learnedly. Such works lack strength, but they are polished, and in a certain way, perfect, especially when interpreted by an intelligent singer like Mr. Kreissmann, and an admirable accompanyist [sic] like Mr. William Mason.[76]

Perhaps what are regarded here as weaknesses—that is, the fragmentary aspect of Franz's lieder and the learned aspects of the accompaniment—are some of the elements that appealed to Dwight. A review of Kreissmann's 1863 New York performance is somewhat similar in that while the critic admired Franz's melancholy and reflections of the past, he concluded, "Franz is a great *talent*; perfected, and in a certain measure, *made*; Schumann is a *genius*; god anointed."[77] (This reviewer also called for more concerts to include lieder.)

In 1864 Kreissmann visited Philadelphia, where he performed in one of Wolfsohn and Thomas's chamber concerts and in several other public and private events. As usual, he gave selections from *Dichterliebe*, as well as lieder by Schubert and Franz. A glowing review of the chamber concert praised his interpretations of both impassioned and tender moments and implied that such performances were not the norm in Philadelphia: "To some it must have come as a new revelation of the beauty and the depth of German poesy."[78]

From the mid-1860s Kreissmann suffered various bouts of ill health. In 1866, after a period of recuperation in Germany, he was well enough to teach at Eichberg's recently opened Boston Conservatory, but subsequently his health declined, and he returned to Germany in 1873, where he died in 1879. Charles H. Brittan (ca. 1845–1903), one of his former students, published a moving memorial that spoke of his interpretative skills: his keen analysis and the way in which he penetrated to the emotional core of lieder. In particular, Brittan recalled the intensity of Kreissmann's rendering of Schubert's "Aufenthalt" (D. 957, no. 5).[79] This type of observation clearly demonstrates the emotional depth of Kreissmann's performances. In contrast, it is not clear whether the singer communicated the nature of the lied as a genre or the complexities and cultural associations of its German texts to Anglophone concertgoers who had not studied German culture.

Kreissmann, Dresel, and Dwight influenced numerous Boston musicians, some of whom had a larger audience than they did. Their enthusiasm for Franz was echoed by later Boston critics, including Elson and Brittan, both of whom studied with Dresel and Kreissmann, as well as William Apthorp (1848–1913). Whereas Elson was based in Boston, Brittan trained in Boston before working in Chicago. Elson became an authority on the lied, and during the 1880s toured the United States giving lectures on this genre. He dedicated his monograph *The History of German Song* to Franz and discussed his time with Franz during his recollections of his European travels.[80] That Boston performers' infatuation

40   CHAPTER 1

with Franz was somewhat short-lived and that other composers attracted the attention of later singers is hinted at in Elson's reviews of lieder performances during the 1880s and 1890s, which often called for increased performances of lieder by his favored composer. Brittan was not as prominent as Elson, yet his colleague W. S. B. Mathews credited him as "the first singer to introduce the songs of Robert Franz, Schubert, and Schumann to the general public in Chicago."[81] Brittan replaced Mathews as the Chicago reporter for *Dwight's Journal of Music*, and although he occasionally performed lieder in public settings, he was primarily known as a pedagogue, a role that also enabled him to foster American performances of lieder. Apthorp, who was another member of the Boston musical establishment, likewise championed Franz in various publications, including an English-language anthology of the composer's lieder.[82] Mathews was also interested in Franz, and his journal published a discussion of the composer's style that noted that the impoverished Franz was most grateful for the revenues he earned from the sale of scores in the United States.[83] While Dresel's and Kreissmann's influence was absorbed by later generations through the writings of these critics, at a more immediate level, they also influenced the singers who came to the fore in Boston during the 1870s, including Osgood.

George L. Osgood

After Kreissmann returned to Europe, Osgood established himself as a champion of the lied in Boston. Whereas many of the performers who presented lieder in concert settings before the late 1870s were immigrants, Osgood was a Bostonian whose family traced its origins to the Puritans.[84] Initially, he trained in Boston, where he interacted with many of the German immigrants who had been promoting lieder, including Dresel. He then studied in Germany, where he established a friendship with Franz. From 1867 through 1871 he studied voice in Milan with the renowned instructor Francesco Lamperti (1813–1892), who trained numerous other Americans. While Osgood was still in Europe, Thomas hired him to sing lieder during his orchestra's 1872–1873 US tour. These concerts were heavily marketed, with numerous publications reprinting Osgood's biography and inflated claims of his successes in Europe, for example, "The Germans pronounce him to be the most perfect interpreter living of Schubert's, Schumann's, and Robert Franz's songs."[85] Perhaps this hype served to balance the still-lowly status of the lied, as at the start of the 1870s many American concertgoers still considered lieder to be a new, challenging genre. Even a reviewer in *Dwight's* referred to Osgood's repertoire as a "peculiar class of songs."[86]

The Thomas Orchestra's tour took Osgood to more than twenty cities, from Buffalo, New York, to Madison, Wisconsin. In many of the larger cities the orchestra gave multiple concerts, with Osgood performing different selections

Introducing a "Higher Class" of Song to American Audiences   41

Overture to "King Lear"	Berlioz
Piano Concerto no. 4, first movement	Beethoven
Anna Mehlig, soloist	
The Erl-King	Schubert
Osgood	
Hunnenschlacht	Liszt
Violin Concerto, op. 26	Bruch
Ballet from *Faust*	Gounod
Five Songs, op. 90 (Lenau)	Schumann
Lied eines Schmiedes	
Meine Rose	
Kommen und Scheiden	
Die Sennin	
Der Schwere Abend	
Osgood	
Overture to *Tannhäuser*	Wagner

FIG. 1.4. Program for a Theodore Thomas concert with Osgood. Boston Music Hall, Tuesday, December 3, 1872, 8 p.m. Program held at the Blumenthal Family Library, New England Conservatory of Music, Boston.

of lieder in each one. The number of lieder that he sang in each concert ranged from as few as one to as many as six. The larger groups of songs, as for instance in the program shown in figure 1.4, were atypical for orchestral concerts, but these particular songs by Schumann are quite short. Osgood sang some of the lieder in German and others in English, sometimes using his own translations.[87] The programs distributed to the audiences provided English translations of the lieder, and some also gave a few other details. The one for a concert in Rochester, New York, printed a translation of the text of Schubert's "Erlkönig" with the name of each character (father, son, and Erlking) next to the corresponding lines of poetry. There were also two sentences briefly identifying the Erlking as a goblin or King of Death.[88] These types of annotations were highly unusual for the time, and even at the end of the century, when program notes were published with greater frequency, explanatory remarks about lieder were usually not provided.

In all, Osgood's repertoire for the tour encompassed about thirty lieder, including many by Schumann and Franz that had not been performed in concerts beyond the Boston area, as well as a few arias by eighteenth-century composers and English-language songs that he had composed. Mathews and the *Chicago Tribune* reacted in the same way as many other critics by acknowledging Osgood for introducing "songs of a higher order than we usually get in a concert room."[89]

In Cincinnati, Osgood's performance prompted diverse responses. One of the more positive notices took a broad view and lauded America's growing appreciation of Schubert's lieder. Although Osgood gave songs such as "Erlkönig" that had received numerous performances elsewhere and had been circulating in sheet music for decades, the *Cincinnati Daily Gazette* described the lieder he performed as unfamiliar and bewildering to the audience. This claim is particularly surprising because Cincinnati had a large German population, and it suggests that local German communities were not strongly promoting lieder to Anglophone concertgoers. More broadly, the paper acknowledged Osgood and Thomas's altruistic efforts to raise the level of concert programs.[90]

Osgood's voice and technique had a mixed reception, with most critics lauding his interpretations but a few observing that his voice was not suited to large halls. Although Thomas hired Doria, who also had a somewhat small voice, for some of the concerts on his next tour, during the following years he favored arrangements of lieder with orchestral accompaniments and singers with more powerful voices, most notably Franz Remmertz (1834–1903) and Emma Juch (1863–1939).[91] His concerts often reprised the same few lieder, including Schubert's "Serenade" and "Doppelgänger" (D. 957, no. 13), and therefore they did not significantly broaden the US appreciation of the genre. After the 1872–1873 tour, Osgood was based in New England, where he was uniformly praised for the expressiveness of his singing and for his leadership of the Boylston Club, a choral society of more than two hundred voices.[92]

Like Kreissmann, Osgood was both a sought-after teacher and a composer. His 1874 *Guide in the Art of Singing*, which consists mainly of untexted technical exercises, attained enough success that it was released in at least eight editions. The section on declamation proffers a cursory observation on the importance of lieder texts and a bilingual score of Franz's "Mailied" (op. 33, no. 3). There is no explanation of this song's words, however, nor any other guidance about performing it. Moreover, the rest of the book has little to say about lieder.

Osgood's compositions included more than fifty songs and anthems. The high point of his career as a composer came in October 1877, when the *Atlantic Monthly* published the score of his song "Dear Love, Let This My Song Fly to You." This was part of the magazine's much-advertised project in which four respected composers, including John Knowles Paine (1839–1906), each set a text by one of the magazine's contributing poets. Osgood set a poem by G. P. Lathrop (1851–1898), an associate editor of the journal and a son in-law of Nathaniel Hawthorne.[93] Although Osgood's compositions were sufficiently admired that they were performed in other parts of the country, Elson's assertion that "Osgood is one of the finest melodists that America has ever possessed"[94] was overly generous, and by the end of the century most of his songs had been forgotten.

Introducing a "Higher Class" of Song to American Audiences   43

During the 1870s Boston was home to numerous highly praised lieder singers, and as a result the city witnessed an increasing number of concerts with lieder. Facing pages of an April 1874 issue of *Dwight's* included reports of five recent concerts presenting lieder performed by admired singers such as Osgood, Clara Doria, Nelson Varley (1844–1883), and Charles R. Hayden (ca. 1846–1886).[95] Doria, who had sung on European stages before coming to the United States, praised Boston as a "hotbed of literature, art and science" and recalled that when she first visited the city in 1873 she was told that songs by Schubert, Schumann, and Franz were "greatly in vogue in amateur circles." Like others, she recognized the city as culturally superior to New York.[96] While Osgood and his colleagues continued to perform works by composers who had been introduced to Boston audiences as early as the 1850s, they no longer relied on well-known numbers such as Schubert's "Der Wanderer" in the same way as did earlier singers. Their expansion of the lied repertoire was facilitated by audiences' growing acceptance of the lied as a concert genre and the availability of an increasing number of English-language editions of lieder. In addition to programming works by well-known composers such as Schubert and Franz that had not previously been performed during concerts, singers introduced lieder by other composers, including Grieg, and they gave other types of songs by composers such as Gounod who today are better known for compositions in larger genres.[97]

Osgood's career as a solo singer peaked during the second half of the 1870s. Some of his most significant performances of lieder occurred in March 1874, when he collaborated with Leonhard, one of Kreissmann's former pianists, in a series of four concerts at Mechanics Hall in Worcester, Massachusetts. Although they were held on Wednesday afternoons, they were widely advertised in the Boston press, they attracted large audiences, and music journals and newspapers reviewed each concert. In some ways, these programs were like those given in Europe from the 1850s onwards by Stockhausen and pianists including Clara Schumann, Theodor Kirchner (1823–1903), and Brahms, and those in Vienna by Gustav Walter and the pianist Anton Door (1833–1919). The number of songs that these European singers performed in each concert varied, with eleven being on the higher end of the spectrum.[98] Similarly, during his concerts in Worcester, Osgood performed between six and twelve songs, most of which were lieder. Leonhard's contributions to these programs, which were accorded somewhat more discussion by the critic for *Dwight's*, were likewise similar to Door's repertoire in Walter's concerts. In each concert, he performed at least one substantial piano sonata (by Beethoven or another nineteenth-century composer) in addition to four or five shorter works by Chopin or Schumann.

Dwight's described some of the songs that Osgood performed during this Worcester series as little known, but at least some concertgoers likely had played

44   CHAPTER 1

or heard the ones circulating in sheet music. During the second concert Osgood sang nine songs, including two by Haydn, a repertoire that was less frequently performed in public in the 1870s than in the preceding decades. The gradual pace at which educated musicians came to appreciate Schubert's lieder is demonstrated by a comment in *Dwight's Journal* that the four Schubert songs that Osgood performed were unfamiliar. These included "The Trout" (D. 550), which the journal indicated was best known through Liszt's piano transcription. Similarly, Beethoven's "Kennst du das Land?" (op. 75, no. 1), also on Osgood's program, was said to be rarely performed in concerts. This song elicited an unusually precise observation in *Dwight's*, with the critic praising the sensitive setting of the text, and particularly the "natural excitement" at "Dahin! Dahin!" (There! O There!).[99] The full meaning of this type of remark could only be appreciated by a reader with some familiarity with the song and the German poem it set. In contrast, a review in the *Boston Daily Advertiser* informed a wider public that the meaning of a lied relies on the text rather than merely on the melody—a characteristic of the genre that newspapers rarely mentioned.[100]

Osgood also performed well-known audience pleasers including Schumann's "Der Nussbaum" (op. 25, no. 3) and a selection from *Dichterliebe*, as well as songs by Mendelssohn. Other singers tended to confine themselves to Mendelssohn's most popular songs, "Auf Flügeln des Gesanges" and "Spring Song" (op. 8, no. 6), but perhaps to please the women in the audience, Osgood gave many others, some of which, including "An die Entfernte" (op. 71, no. 3), were available in sheet music. Numerous songs by this composer were circulating in English versions. Boosey (in New York), for example, issued a collection of twenty songs by Mendelssohn as part of its Musical Cabinet, a series of "standard and popular vocal and pianoforte music." The cover of this volume featured stereotypical drawings of idealized young women socializing and making music in garden settings, images that were characteristic of sheet music and other types of publications that likewise conveyed idealized notions of genteel feminine sensibility.[101]

During evening concerts in 1876 and 1879, Osgood gave Schumann's *Frauen-liebe und -leben* in its entirety. In the first he was accompanied by Perabo and during the second by Benjamin J. (B. J.) Lang (1837–1909). The 1876 performance was said to be the first time the entire cycle had been given in the country. Although the performance was significant enough to be reported as far afield as Milwaukee, it is possible that amateurs at home had already given the cycle, because Schirmer had published an English-language score in 1871.[102] Today the cycle is usually performed by women, but Stockhausen, a baritone, gave the first complete performance in Europe, during which he was accompanied by the composer's widow, Clara. In general, nineteenth-century performers did not link the narrative persona of a song and the gender of the performer as consis-

Introducing a "Higher Class" of Song to American Audiences   45

tently as did musicians in the following centuries.[103] Nevertheless, throughout the nineteenth century, the songs in this cycle were more frequently performed by women than by men, and versions in English-language sheet music issued by a variety of US companies were marketed to women.

Both of Osgood's concerts presented a miscellany of other genres, including choruses and instrumental works.[104] During the 1879 event he performed a total of sixteen lieder. In addition to the eight songs of *Frauenliebe* he sang six lieder by Franz and two by Anton Rubinstein (1829–1894). Although Rubinstein had not promoted his lieder during his much-publicized US piano concerts in 1872–1873, numerous artists subsequently programmed them, with "Der Asra" (op. 32, no. 6, ca. 1856)—one of the pieces that Osgood sang—becoming a particular favorite. This song was also well known in Europe, and part of its appeal was likely the exoticism of Heine's poem, which tells of a slave boy from Yemen. Osgood sang more songs in this concert than many later European singers gave in their *Liederabende* or in their US recitals. Ironically, while his career as a singer was winding down at the end of the 1870s, the song recital was just beginning to emerge.

*   *   *

The concerts during which Kreissmann and Osgood performed multiple lieder paved the way for the development of song recitals in which lieder dominated. These singers and their contemporaries also began the process by which the lieder of Beethoven, Franz, Schubert, and Schumann became part of the canonic US concert repertoire. Yet their achievements would not have been possible without the support of a network of musicians who were not singers. Dresel in Boston, and Thomas and Wolfsohn in New York and Philadelphia, folded lieder into their project to promote programs of serious classical repertoire. Critics in New York and Boston lauded singers for performing lieder, which they considered to be high art, and they entreated them to perform such works more frequently. Whereas initially singers in mixed-genre concerts programmed lieder that had already been published in English-language scores, Dwight and his colleagues contributed to the publication and dissemination of some of the lieder that were first heard in chamber concerts in Boston. That Dwight's journal was published by Ditson, one of the country's leading music publishers, likely facilitated this process.

There is little doubt that Kreissmann explored the intricacies of the lied, including the significance of the texts, with his students, and Dwight and others should be lauded for publishing reliable English translations of lieder texts that could be sung. But the cursory descriptions of lieder in journals and the scanty program notes, along with the practice of creating instrumental arrange-

46   CHAPTER 1

ments, suggests that at this time advocates of the lied seem to have been more interested in introducing the *sound* of lieder to audiences than in providing a holistic understanding of the genre to people who were not part of their musically educated circles. In contrast, later musicians, including Mathews and Elson as well as members of women's music clubs, published commentaries and gave lectures to broader audiences and music makers that aimed to bridge this gap.

2

Song Recitals and
Song Recital Series

Song recitals, including those highlighting lieder, began to emerge in the middle of the 1870s. These recitals owed their origins to the earlier piano recitals and chamber concerts that presented lieder, as well as to recitals like Fanny Raymond Ritter's 1869 series "Historical Recitals of Vocal and Piano-Forte Music." Song recitals comprising art songs (rather than popular operatic arias) seem to have first gained currency in the mid-1870s during summertime normal schools for music teachers, many of whom were women.[1] Recitals at normal schools in New York State and in Illinois paved the way for George Werrenrath and Carl Wolfsohn's 1879 series of four song recitals in Chicago, which encompassed more than fifty lieder. From this point onwards, the number of public song recitals dramatically increased, with Grace Hiltz's recitals in the Midwest and Werrenrath's series of recitals in Brooklyn being particularly noteworthy. It is highly likely that performers in the United States were familiar with some of the European concerts that included lieder, but Werrenrath and Wolfsohn's programs departed from European models in significant ways. More broadly, a comparison between US and European lieder performances reveals that US song recitals developed in a somewhat different way than *Liederabende*. As with the musicians who promoted lieder in the 1860s, many of those who led the way in establishing song recitals as a US concert genre were part of the extended network of musicians promoting performances of German classical instrumental music, and they had contact with either Dwight or Thomas.

The Development of European Lieder Recitals

In Europe, one of the earliest public concerts devoted to lieder took place in Vienna in 1846. Johann Baptist Pischek (1814–1873) gave a concert at the

Musikverein Hall that closely resembles what is now called a lieder recital. Though comprised entirely of lieder, it was titled "Farewell-Concert" (*Abschieds-Concert*). The *Wiener Zeitung* pointed out that it was quite unusual for a concert to be devoted to one artist and compared this event to Liszt's piano recitals. Another reviewer labeled the event as a "Lieder Concert," a designation that was not in widespread use during the 1840s; even in the 1850s it was employed only in the occasional review or advertisement. Reviews indicate that Pischek, an admired operatic baritone whose lieder singing earned Berlioz's praise, had planned to perform twelve lieder, many of which he had previously sung in Vienna.[2] In response to the audience's applause and calls for encores, however, he sang twenty or twenty-one. In addition to Schubert's "Im Walde" (a.k.a. "Waldesnacht"), Pischek presented lighter popular songs by composers such as Heinrich Esser (1818–1872), Gustav Hölzel (1813–1883), Peter Josef Lindpaintner (1791–1856), Heinrich Proch (1809–1878), and Josef Staudigl (1807–1861).[3] But ironically, it seems likely that J. P. Knight's Boston concert in 1840, which was described in Chapter 1, encompassed a greater number of art songs by the likes of Schubert and Beethoven than this 1846 concert in Vienna.

While neither Pischek's nor Knight's event initiated an immediate trend, the 1850s witnessed a slight increase in the number of performances devoted to lieder. In 1853 Stigelli presented a "Lieder Concert" in Vienna. While a review noted he performed two lieder by Schumann, it did not describe the rest of the program.[4] During the same decade, Stockhausen also occasionally gave concerts emphasizing lieder, but his all-lieder concerts were limited to performances of Schubert's *Die schöne Müllerin* (D. 795) or *Winterreise*.[5] Each of these two cycles is long enough to fill a short recital. Nevertheless, Stockhausen's performances were not titled Lieder Concert or *Liederabend*. Similarly, Karl Wallenreiter (d. 1874), a former pupil of Pauline Viardot-Garcia, did not consistently use these titles when he presented solo programs devoted to the lieder cycles by Schubert and Schumann.[6] Although these performances of song cycles lacked a uniform nomenclature, they are nevertheless more closely related to later lieder recitals or *Liederabende* than to the miscellany programs in which lieder were usually given. Stockhausen's and Wallenreiter's performances of complete cycles anticipated Gustav Walter's and Adolf Wallnöfer's (1854–1946) "concerts" in the 1870s, in which the lieder held a more significant place than the instrumental works. The term *Liederabend* seems to have become the accepted designation for such events following Walter's 1876 Schubert-*Abend* in Vienna. This performance was so successful that Walter gave a Schubert-*Abend* in each of the following years. Eventually his concert manager, Albert Gutmann (1852–1915), encouraged him to present a series of *Liederabende*, the first of which comprised three programs and took place in 1881. Walter's performances attracted so much attention they were referenced in *Harper's* in the United States.[7] Subsequently

Song Recitals and Song Recital Series   49

Gutmann engaged other professional singers to present similar series.[8] Although Lilli Lehmann (1848–1929) was one of these singers, she did not use the term *Liederabend* until 1885.[9]

Whereas performances of complete lieder cycles predated the establishment of *Liederabende* in Europe, in the United States song recitals developed before the cycles of Schubert and Schumann were performed in public in their entirety. Indeed, although some of Stockhausen's and Wallenreiter's performances of cycles were likely known to US musicians, they had no direct impact on American concert life in the 1860s. Evidence in newspapers and music journals suggests that, with the exception of *An die ferne Geliebte*, complete lieder cycles were rarely performed on US stages before the late 1880s, almost a decade after the initial "song recitals" held during summertime normal schools. Song recital programs dominated by lieder, like Werrenrath's, also seem to have predated similar ones in Europe.

Fanny Raymond Ritter

Unlike many contemporary lieder singers in the United States, Fanny Raymond Ritter was not a German immigrant; rather, her family came from the United Kingdom. From at least 1844 her father, Richard Malone Raymond (known as Malone; 1832–1916) and her mother (whom the press identifies only as Mrs. Raymond) made numerous appearances in England presenting an "Entertainment" often titled "An Hour in Ireland." Performances included humorous anecdotes told in a "rich, racy brogue" along with Irish songs.[10] In early 1848 the couple migrated to the United States, where they gave similar programs, some of which included performances by their three daughters, Fanny, Emily, and Louisa. The family appeared in numerous cities including New York, Boston, Worcester (Massachusetts), Hartford (Connecticut), and New Orleans.[11]

In the 1850s Fanny Raymond emerged as a performer of classical songs, a repertoire distinctly different from her family's. It is not clear when she started performing these works, but reports dating from the 1850s (when her family was living in Ohio) indicate that she was moving in circles of classically trained musicians. In Ohio, Fanny met Frédéric Louis Ritter (ca. 1834–1891), and he became her principal mentor. Migrating from Strasbourg in 1856 at the age of twenty-two, Ritter first settled in Cincinnati, where he founded and directed the Cecilia Society. Raymond often appeared as a soloist during this chorus's concerts, for instance, singing "Erlkönig" during an 1858 performance. Some of the chorus's concerts were favorably reviewed in *Dwight's Journal of Music*, and through this journal, Ritter and Raymond likely came in contact with, or at least became familiar with, the network of East Coast musicians who were also promoting performances of classical music.

50   CHAPTER 2

Raymond and Ritter settled in New York during the early 1860s and began collaborating with musicians who were campaigning for performances of German repertoire. In 1862 Ritter became the director of the Harmonic Society and in 1864 the conductor of the Arion Society; in 1867 he was named professor of music at Vassar College in Poughkeepsie, New York. From 1864, Raymond sang lieder and arias in some of Thomas's orchestral and chamber concerts, and on one occasion in 1866, Thomas played the violin in a recital that Fanny herself headlined. Having married Ritter in 1865, she now used her married name, Fanny Raymond Ritter.[12]

At a time when songs by Schumann, Loewe, and Liszt were rarely heard on New York stages, Raymond Ritter performed Schumann's "Ich wandelte unter den Bäumen," "Schöne Wiege meiner Leiden," and "Die Lotosblume" (op. 24, nos. 3 and 5 and op. 25, no. 7); Loewe's "Die Überfahrt" (op. 94, no. 1); and Liszt's "Der du von dem Himmel bist" (S. 279).[13] She also sang some of the Irish melodies Beethoven arranged for voice and piano trio (WoO 152 and 153). Although rarely programmed in the twenty-first century, these works were occasionally performed in mid-nineteenth century chamber concerts. Raymond Ritter also presented "Lascia ch'io pianga mia cruda sorte" from Handel's *Rinaldo* (1711) and "O del mio dolce ardor" from Gluck's *Paride ed Elena* (1770). Although Kreissmann usually did not sing this type of early repertoire, later recitalists frequently programed eighteenth-century arias with lieder, and arias from Handel's oratorios were quite common in concerts in both Europe and the United States.[14]

In 1869 Raymond Ritter traced the history of song and keyboard literature in a series titled "Historical Recitals of Vocal and Piano-Forte Music by Mrs. Fanny Raymond Ritter and S. B. Mills." (While Sebastian Bach Mills [1838–1898] played the solo piano works, S[amuel] P. Warren (1841–1915) accompanied Raymond Ritter's songs.) In addition to Raymond Ritter's name being placed before Mills's, reviews gave her greater prominence. The nomenclature of this series was also significant. The events were labeled "recitals," as opposed to "concerts" or "soirées," with "vocal" placed before "pianoforte." One of the advertisements in *Watson's Art Journal* rammed the latter point home by printing the word "vocal" in a font that was three times the size of that for "pianoforte."[15] As media reports indicated, Frédéric Ritter influenced the series, and he stated that the scores for the earlier works were drawn from his library.[16] Ritter was an avid historian who subsequently published a number of books, at least one of which touched on lieder.[17]

Raymond Ritter's New York recitals were well attended, with reviews indicating that the receptive audiences filled Steinway's four-hundred-seat hall. They were held during the day on Saturdays, reportedly so that out-of-towners could attend. *Watson's* praised Raymond Ritter's warmth, enthusiasm, and ability to convey the sentiments of the songs but expressed regret that she did not modu-

Song Recitals and Song Recital Series   51

late her voice to suit the hall. The critic hoped that in the following year there would be a longer series and anticipated that subscriptions could be obtained for six programs. Although this larger project did not materialize, Raymond Ritter, accompanied by her husband, presented another pair of historical recitals at Vassar College in 1869. These drew on repertoire from their New York programs.[18]

Raymond Ritter's series was unusual for the United States, though readers of *Dwight's* were already familiar with the concept of historical programs. Frédéric Ritter owned copies of this journal, and it is therefore likely that prior to formulating their own series, the couple had read at least some of the reports about historically themed concerts. This suggests that aside from Ritter's interest in history, *Dwight's* or earlier historical series could have influenced Raymond Ritter's series. As early as its third volume in July 1853, *Dwight's* carried reports of historical concerts in Europe, but most of them presented choral and instrumental music, rather than solo songs. An 1863 series in Bremen titled Historical Musical Evenings was exceptional in that it included a small number of lieder by Schubert, Schumann, and Mendelssohn in its survey of compositions from Bach to the mid-nineteenth century.[19]

On numerous occasions Dwight begged for performances of historical concerts in the United States, and his journal reported early efforts to create such programs. These included the series of four "classical chamber concerts" given by Frederick Nicholls Crouch (1808–1896) and Hermann Kotzschmar (1829–1908) in their respective Boston studios in 1853. Their small-scale concerts, each of which included ten numbers, covered eighteenth- and nineteenth-century repertoire. The only lieder included were Schubert's "Serenade" and "Ave Maria," along with Beethoven's "Knowest Thou the Land." As in the Ritters' later series, the songs outnumbered the instrumental works, which were restricted to piano solos and duets. Throughout the 1850s and 1860s Boston also hosted a few historically themed sacred music concerts. Although some of these encompassed chant, most emphasized choral music and therefore were not as similar to the Ritters' series as those that included solo songs.[20]

The Ritters' series was more ambitious than Crouch and Kotzschmar's and included older repertoire. Their first recital presented works from about 1200 to the eighteenth century, including "Sumer Is Icumen In" and songs by Purcell and Pergolesi. The second comprised twenty-six numbers spanning the period from Lully to Liszt, with an emphasis on eighteenth-century French and German songs. Both these programs presented a variety of keyboard works ranging from Byrd's "Carman's Whistle" to pieces by nineteenth-century composers, and both included folksongs. The third recital, titled "Modern German School," included eight lieder (see figure 2.1). According to Ritter's *Music in America*, Raymond Ritter was responsible for the program annotations and the versified

Air and Variations in G major	Beethoven. Born 1770, died 1827
Wonne der Wehmut	Beethoven
Sonata appassionata, opus 57	Beethoven
Ellen's Song (words from "Lady of the Lake")	Schubert. Born 1797, died 1828
Gretchen am Spinnrade (from Goethe's *Faust*)	
Des Abends, Traumes Wirren and Ende vom Lied. From the *Fantasie-Stücke*, op. 12	Schumann. Born 1810, died 1856
Reiselied	Mendelssohn. Born 1809, died 1847
The Warrior's Death. Song	F. L. Ritter
Moments Musicaux, op. 94, nos. 1 and 2	Schubert
Elsas Ermahnung an Ortrud from *Lohengrin*	R. Wagner
Angiolin dal biondo crin	Liszt
Etude, C sharp minor, op. 25, no. 7	Chopin
Schoene Wiege meiner Leiden Song from op. 24	Schumann
Er ist gekommen	Franz
Hungarian Gypsy Melodies	Tausig

FIG. 2.1. Program of Fanny Raymond Ritter's "Modern German School" recital, April 17, 1869, at 2:30 p.m. in the small hall at Steinway and Co., New York. "New York," *Dwight's Journal of Music* 29, no. 3 (April 24, 1869): 23.

translation of many of the folksongs' texts. In performing these folksongs, she accompanied herself, playing piano parts of her own making.

The pedagogical dimension of the Ritters' recitals placed them ahead of developments in European programming. Although their programs did not follow an exact chronological order, the three recitals taken together moved from early to recent songs.[21] This organization was made explicit by the program notes, which were highly unusual for the time, and by the inclusion of some of the composers' birth and death dates, a feature that Frédéric Ritter specifically emphasized when writing about the series in *Music in America*. In contrast, according to Weber, this type of information was not given on European programs before the 1880s.[22]

The program annotations reprinted in *Dwight's* made the argument that the type of folksongs, national songs, and traditional airs that Raymond Ritter sang influenced art music from the middle ages to the nineteenth century.[23] Crouch had also programmed art songs with folksongs, and this was a well-known practice in Europe, where Herder's *Volksgeist* was a key element of German Romanticism. Singers trained under Manuel García (1805–1906), including Stockhausen and Lind, as well as Viardot-Garcia, admired this repertoire, and they sometimes paired folksongs with lieder in their concerts. In reviewing an 1874 performance by Stockhausen, Emil Krause (1840–1916), a critic in Hamburg, argued that placing folksongs, which he viewed as informal, on a program with art songs was not appropriate,[24] but most US writers did not discuss the merits of such pairings, and audiences on both continents appreciated programs providing variety rather than uniformity of genres. Whereas Raymond Ritter's programs presented national songs and airs from diverse European countries including Spain, other US singers confined their selections to German and British numbers and did not proffer greater variety until the end of the century.

Frédéric Ritter claimed that his wife's recital series became the model for subsequent recitalists. While one historical recital series in New Haven, Connecticut, closely followed their model,[25] other historical programs showed greater independence. Throughout 1876, for instance, B. D. (Benjamin Dwight) Allen (1831–1914), a well-known pedagogue, gave a series of ten illustrated "talks" in Worcester, the first of which encompassed repertoire from chant to the nineteenth century. As in Raymond Ritter's programs, he connected folksong to art music, performing three songs by Franz that were said to be influenced by folksong.[26] In 1875 Osgood joined Frédéric Boscovitz (1838–1903), a Hungarian pianist who had studied briefly with Chopin, in presenting a series of four historical concerts in Mechanics Hall in Worcester, each of which encompassed choruses, piano solos, and lieder. Although the Ritters might have influenced their series, Rubinstein's piano recitals and the illustrated lectures of John Knowles Paine (Osgood's former teacher at Harvard) were also cited as precedents.[27]

Following her series of historical recitals, Fanny Raymond Ritter retired as a performer and devoted herself to research and writing. Her original publications included *Woman as a Musician*, a fifteen-page booklet that traces women composers from the Middle Ages to the nineteenth century and argues for women to form organizations to cultivate music making in homes. This essay was widely disseminated and excerpted in *Dwight's*, to which Raymond Ritter was a regular contributor.[28] Other frequently cited publications included translations of an anthology of essays by Schumann titled *Music and Musicians: Essays and Criticisms* (1877) and *Letters on Music, to a Lady* (1870) by Louis Ehlert (1825–1884), a German critic and composer who aimed to introduce classical composers to a wide audience. Raymond Ritter's translation of Ehlert's essay

54   CHAPTER 2

"The German Lied: Schubert, Mendelssohn, Schumann, Franz, etc." was also reprinted in *Dwight's*. In this publication she did not insert her own voice, although she frequently expressed strong opinions when reviewing performances. Therefore, Ehlert's critique of the declamatory vocal lines in Schumann's lieder (a repertoire Raymond Ritter performed) went unchallenged.[29] Similarly, the reader is not informed whether Raymond Ritter agreed with Ehlert's preference for the intimate songs of Franz over the "intellectual" works of Schumann, an assessment that resonates with views expressed by other notices in *Dwight's*. The essay's slight praise of Brahms's songs and its mixed review of Rubinstein's *Persian Songs* (op. 34) had the potential to encourage readers to explore less-familiar works.

Whereas Dwight's journal and many of Raymond Ritter's publications were addressed to knowledgeable musicians, other outlets strove to promote a greater appreciation of the lied in the United States by providing less experienced musicians with the main composers' biographies and succinct overviews of the style of their songs. This was the case with an article on lieder composers by George T. Ferris (b. 1840) that was reprinted in *Whitney's Musical Guest*, a monthly magazine for home music makers that, typical of the era, included scores and stereotypical feminine artwork.[30] But these types of publications usually did not explore the cultural context of German lieder nor the imagery frequently encountered in lieder texts, and this situation persisted throughout the century.

The Emergence of "Song Recitals"

From the mid-1870s performers began giving song recitals featuring a more diverse selection of lieder than earlier multi-genre concerts. The designations of "song recital" and "vocal recital" rather than *Liederabend*, or lieder recital, were likely used to accommodate songs in a variety of genres and to attract the attention of Anglophone audiences who might have been uncomfortable with the German language.

In 1874 Clara Brinkerhoff (b. 1830) toured throughout the Midwest and New York giving performances titled "Unique Vocal Recitals" or "Classical Vocal Recitals." These performances encompassed a variety of genres, from arias to hymns in various languages, as well as her own songs and piano solos. Since she had previously performed lieder, including what was likely the first US performance of Brahms's "Liebestreu" (op. 3, no. 1), these vocal recitals probably included this genre.[31] In addition to singing, she introduced each song and explained its meaning, and on some occasions accompanied herself.

One advertisement implied that these recitals were originally viewed as "experiments," and in this way it drew attention to their innovative nature. The term "experiments" likely references the format of one singer presenting a program comprised almost exclusively of songs, as opposed to a miscellany of genres presented by an ensemble of performers or programs comprised of songs and recitations.[32] Although similarly formatted recitals began to proliferate, Brinkerhoff's term "vocal recital" was not widely adopted in the United States. In contrast, this title was used in England for performances of diverse repertoire, as well as for programs of classical songs.[33] At about the same time as Brinkerhoff's tours, summertime normal schools for music teachers in New York State and Illinois began to sponsor performances of art songs using the designation "song recital."[34]

Some of the earliest press reports that discuss "song recitals" featuring lieder are in reference to the normal school recitals of Mrs. J. Hull (b. ca. 1840) and W. S. B. Mathews, a pianist and pedagogue based in Chicago.[35] In 1875 Hull, one of the leading sopranos in Meadville, Pennsylvania, gave two song recitals at the normal school in Watertown, New York.[36] Before the first, the *Watertown Daily Times* complained that in numerous programs singers repeated the same well-known numbers, "hence it happens that the immense literature of German song lies entirely unknown to our musical amateurs generally." After Hull's performance, she was praised for offering a "copious selection of songs entirely new to our public, and all of them very beautiful." It was Mathews, however, who was said to be responsible for constructing the programs.[37] During the recitals, Mathews, who had praised Hull's singing during an 1873 normal school, briefly explained some of the pieces before they were performed.[38]

Despite the claim that the public was not familiar with the songs, much of the repertoire of these Watertown recitals had been repeatedly performed in other cities and at least one, Schumann's "Thou Ring upon My Finger," had been circulating in English-language sheet music since the 1850s. In her first recital, Hull presented three songs by Schubert and three by Schumann, as well as two arias from oratorios, a duet by Mozart, and Gounod's 1839 barcarolle "Tell me, Beautiful Maiden" ("Où voulez-vous aller"). During the 1876 normal school in Watertown, Hull presented two additional song recitals, both of which had programs similar to her previous performances. In addition, other women in Watertown and the surrounding towns also began giving song recitals.[39] Typically, these women, and those at normals, sang in English. Hull's recitals were held in a church during the afternoon, and because most music teachers were women, it can be assumed that the attendees at these events, like recitals at other normals, were mostly women.[40]

Normals and other schools in Illinois also began presenting song recitals. The 1876 normal at Wheaton, west of Chicago, included two recitals, one by Sarah Hershey (1837–1911), who had trained in Germany, and her star pupil Grace Hiltz, and the other by Mrs. E. A. Jewett (Jennie M. Jewett; 1848–1903), a well-known Chicago singer. Both programs were dominated by lieder, though both also included a few English songs.[41] Mathews fostered numerous song recitals at the Chicago-area institutions where he taught, including the Hershey School of Musical Art, which he co-founded with Sarah Hershey, and at the normal schools he conducted in Evanston and at Highland Hall, a female seminary in Highland Park, a few miles north of Evanston. At the 1880 Evanston normal, for instance, William Chamberlain (1847–1903), a professor of vocal culture at Oberlin College, presented three recitals, while a Miss Howe (of Cincinnati) gave four.[42]

Mathews also promoted lieder to Chicago and Evanston audiences through his illustrated lectures, which included performances by the likes of Hiltz and Jewett.[43] In some ways, these pedagogical projects could be considered analogous to educational experiences provided on the East Coast by the Ritters, B. D. Allen, and Osgood, all of which Mathews could have read about in *Dwight's*. As with the recitals in Watertown, many of these recitals and lectures took place in the afternoons and were held in small halls. Although they were advertised to the public, audiences were likely comprised of students and perhaps faculty, as well as women music lovers, but reviews usually did not record the demographics of the audiences.

Contemporary publications and later writers testify to the emergence of the song recital during the 1870s and early 1880s.[44] For instance, *Dwight's Journal of Music* began discussing song recitals in the mid-1870s. An advertisement for an 1881 song recital by local musicians in Wheeling, West Virginia, described these events as "something new in the musical line."[45] In 1882 Mrs. Henry Norton (Ida Fletcher Norton; ca. 1851–1931) began giving song recitals in San Francisco, some of which included lieder.[46] Two years later, newspapers reported that Henry B. Pasmore (1857–1944), who had just returned from studying at the Leipzig Conservatory, gave the first song recital by a man on the West Coast, but in so doing they also indicated a quickly growing perception that recitals were part of the woman's sphere.[47]

George Werrenrath's Chicago Song Recitals

In 1879 George Werrenrath and Carl Wolfsohn presented a series of four song recitals in Chicago. Although the two had not previously collaborated in recitals, this project was a logical development of their previous individual experiences, and especially of Wolfsohn's series of piano recitals. In 1865 and again in 1867–1868, he presented a ten-matinee series of piano recitals in Philadelphia comprising all of Beethoven's piano sonatas. He repeated this series in New York during the 1866–1867 season. Each program included a few vocal numbers, some of which were lieder. Ignaz Pollack, a former student of Stockhausen, sang at most of the recitals in the New York series and at least one in Philadelphia.[48]

Song Recitals and Song Recital Series   57

Wolfsohn built on this Beethoven series when he moved to Chicago. In contrast, Werrenrath had sung lieder in numerous concerts in Brooklyn, where he resided, and in Europe, but there is no evidence that he had previously presented a solo song recital.

Chicago witnessed an unprecedented burgeoning of cultural institutions during the era of rebuilding that followed the great fire of 1871. New organizations that immeasurably enriched the city's musical life included the choruses of the Apollo Musical Club (which started life as a *Männerchor* in 1873 and later became a mixed chorus) and the Beethoven Society, a mixed chorus of two hundred members, which Wolfsohn founded in 1873. The Beethoven Society performed numerous oratorios, often with high-profile solo artists from out of town. It also hosted Wolfsohn's chamber concerts and piano recitals. In 1874 he reprised his Beethoven piano sonata series; the recitals were held on Friday evenings in the rooms of the Beethoven Society. This time he programmed far more lieder and included *An die ferne Geliebte*.[49] Following the success of this series, he presented a new series of ten piano recitals dedicated to Schumann in 1875, and in 1876 a further ten dedicated to Chopin, both of which were held on Saturday afternoons. As with the Beethoven series, these series included a significant number of songs, and the singers were all locals who occasionally performed lieder in other venues.

During the Schumann series, Wolfsohn programed forty-four of the composer's lieder, "and of these many were first productions" in Chicago.[50] In one of the recitals Mrs. Clara D. Stacey, an admired Chicago singer, performed either fifteen or all sixteen songs of *Dichterliebe* in English. It was still unusual to perform the complete, or near-complete, cycle, and Stacey was praised for this ambitious undertaking.[51] Mathews lauded the series for attracting audiences of between five hundred and six hundred, but he criticized Wolfsohn's playing. (Numerous critics had similar reservations about Wolfsohn's technique.) Mathews believed Schumann was "in the apostolic succession, beyond question:—Bach, Beethoven, Schumann," and he bemoaned the fact that this composer's works were still not well known in Chicago.[52]

The tenth recital in Wolfsohn's 1876 Chopin series included art songs by the composer (which were sung in English), and each of the others incorporated a small selection of lieder by another nineteenth-century composer. They included Franz, Liszt, Mendelssohn, and Rubinstein, as well as composers who were never canonized: Esser, Adolf Jensen (1837–1879), Joachim Raff (1822–1882), and Ernst Friedrich Richter (1808–1879).[53] Many of the songs by these men were new to the audiences, but singers in other cities were also performing some of their works. Some of the repertoire, including songs by Liszt, Esser, and Jensen, posed significant difficulties for the singers and for Wolfsohn. In particular, James Gill, a Scotsman who had studied at the Leipzig Conservatory before joining the faculties at the Chicago Musical College and the Hershey School of Musical Arts, gave Esser's "Der Saengers Fluch" ("The Minstrel's Curse," op. 8), a dramatic ballad more than two hundred measures long.[54] The novelty of the lieder Wolfsohn presented notwithstanding, his Beethoven, Schumann, and Chopin series primarily focused on piano music. This was not the case, however, with his four-recital series with Werrenrath. These events were clearly labeled as song recitals, and lieder dominated the programs.

Prior to coming to the United States, Werrenrath, a Danish tenor, performed in Europe. After training in Hamburg he appeared in operas in Wiesbaden, Paris, and London. In the early 1870s he formed a friendship with Gounod and performed with him on tours of Belgium and England. Gounod also encouraged Werrenrath to study with Lamperti in Italy.[55] In 1876 General C. T. Christensen (a Danish American) hired Werrenrath for the choir at the Plymouth Church in Brooklyn after hearing him sing in a London concert that had also featured the popular American soprano Antoinette Sterling (1841–1904).[56] Founded in 1847, the Plymouth Church was led by the preacher Henry Ward Beecher (d. 1887), a leading abolitionist. In 1879, with Beecher officiating, Werrenrath married Aretta Camp, the daughter of Henry Camp, the church's choirmaster.[57]

As early as May 1877, the *Brooklyn Daily Eagle* described Werrenrath as a popular and successful performer.[58] In addition to his church duties, he performed in operas and presented excerpts from Wagner's operas in Thomas's New York and Philadelphia orchestral concerts. During the 1877 Wagner Festival he performed solo roles in the Brooklyn productions of *Lohengrin* and *Tannhäuser*. He appeared in *Der Freischütz*, *Tannhäuser*, and Meyerbeer's *Les Huguenots* in midwestern cities, including Chicago, as well as in Philadelphia. From the late 1870s through the 1880s, Werrenrath frequently performed lieder, songs by Gounod, and folksongs from a variety of European countries in Brooklyn.

In February 1879 Werrenrath fulfilled multiple engagements in Chicago before commencing his series of recitals with Wolfsohn. His main performance was the title role in the Beethoven Society's presentation of Bruch's *Odysseus*, which Wolfsohn conducted. The recitals comprised primarily nineteenth-century literature: lieder by Brahms, Franz, Jensen, Liszt, Rubinstein, Schubert, and Schumann, all sung in German, along with songs in English, French, and Italian. Unlike most previous and contemporary European and US recitals, songs dominated these programs, with Wolfsohn's piano solos being of secondary interest (despite their technical demands). The fact that this series took place in 1879 is significant because it predates Gustav Walter's first series of three *Liederabende* in Vienna in 1881. Although Kravitt and others accord these European performances significant attention, whether they were genuinely innovative is somewhat debatable. It is more likely that they (like Werrenrath's series) were a logical extension of contemporary concertgiving in which artists such as Walter

Song Recitals and Song Recital Series   59

and Door (in Europe) and Mathews (at normal schools in the United States) presented pairs of recitals.

According to an 1887 biography of Werrenrath, this was the first series of song recitals in the United States.[59] Although Raymond Ritter's 1869 recital series might be interpreted as a historical precedent, Werrenrath's series was far more ambitious, and it was also more ambitious than pairs of recitals in Europe. Therefore, a Chicago paper was more than justified in describing it as a "novelty."[60] Encompassing about twenty songs, as shown in figure 2.2, each of Werrenrath's programs was significantly longer than many of the contemporary song and piano concerts in Europe, including Walter's. Indeed, European music journals registered surprise when in February 1880 Amalie Joachim gave a concert in Bonn that consisted of twenty-one lieder.[61] Moreover, numerous *Liederabende* given in Vienna during the late 1880s and the early 1890s presented fewer songs.

Werrenrath's series encompassed both well-known songs and those that were new to his audiences. Some, including excerpts from *Dichterliebe* and *Die schöne Müllerin*, were already familiar to audiences in major US cities, and the song by Jensen and three of Rubinstein's had been performed during Wolfsohn's earlier Chopin series. Less frequently performed songs included "Träume" and "Schmerzen," two of Wagner's 1857 *Wesendonck Lieder* (WWV 91). Similarly, at a time when few of Brahms's songs were sung during US concerts, Werrenrath gave three: "Wiegenlied" (op. 49, no. 4), which was not as well known as it is today; "Sonntag" (47, no. 3); and "Ruhe, Süßliebchen" (op. 33, no. 9), all of which had been published in Europe during the 1860s. Subsequently, the songs by Wagner were taken up by numerous singers. "Ruhe, Süßliebchen" became the most frequently sung number from Brahms's *Magelone Romances* (op. 33), perhaps because its lyrical melody and the text, which is a lullaby sung by a man to his sweetheart, appealed to women.

Considering the number of lieder composers that Werrenrath included, it is somewhat surprising that there was nothing by Mendelssohn. By this time Mendelssohn was a well-known composer in America, and aside from the popularity of his oratorios, his piano works and songs were circulating in scores for domestic music makers.[62] Earlier performers on the East Coast frequently gave this composer's songs, as did the singers at the Hershey School and those contributing to Wolfsohn's recitals. In contrast, it seems that Werrenrath was not interested in them, and there are no reports that he performed them in his later recitals. Conversely, his inclusion of von Wolkenstein's (1376/77–1445) "Minnelied" ("Dein Mund geschwellt") is intriguing, in part because Walter did not include older numbers such as this one in his *Liederabende* until 1882,[63] though the song was performed in other European concerts before then.

60   CHAPTER 2

First Recital

Moments Musicaux	Schubert
Elegie [Impromptu op. 90, no. 3]	
7 songs from *Die schöne Müllerin*	
Novelette, F major	Schumann
Romanza, F sharp minor	
Dichterliebe, songs 1–4	
An den Sonnenschein	
Der Nussbaum	
Sonntags am Rhein	
Romanza	Rubinstein
Barcarolle (piano)	
Leise zieht durch mein Gemüt	
Der alte König	
Sehnsucht	
Frühlingslied	
Melodie in F major (piano)	Scharwenka
Loreley, op. 2 (piano)	Hans Seeling
There Is No Flock	Frederic Clay
Sands o' Dee	
Oft in the Stilly Night	Thomas Moore
from *Irish Melodies*	

Second Recital

Fantasia (piano)	Beethoven
An die ferne Geliebte	
Romanza, B flat minor	Henselt
Etude, F sharp major (piano)	
Ma belle amie est morte	Gounod
When in the Early Morn	
If Thou Art Sleeping, Maiden Awake	
Perche Piangi?	
Ho messo nuove corde al Mandolino	
Etude, *Waldesrauschen*	Liszt
Legende, Sermon to the Birds (piano)	
Lieder aus Schillers Wilhelm Tell:	
Der Hirt	
Der Alpenjäger	
Der Fischerknabe	
Idylle, B major	Jensen
Stille Liebe (piano)	
Lehn' deine Wang' an meine Wang'	
Minnelied	Wolkenstein
Am Rhein (op. 28, no. 4)	Goltermann

FIG. 2.2A. Werrenrath and Wolfsohn's first two song recitals, as reported in the *Inter Ocean* (Chicago), February 8, 1879, 6.

Third Recital

Work	Composer
Nocturne	Tchaikovsky
Humoresque (piano)	
Verfehlte Liebe, verfehltes Leben!	Franz
Die Letzte Rose	
Das macht das dunkelgrüne Laub	
Die blauen Frühlingsaugen	
Abends	
Widmung	
Variations on a Theme by R. Schumann	Brahms
Wiegenlied	
Sonntag	
Ruhe, Süßliebchen	
Elsa's Prayer from *Lohengrin* (piano)	Wagner
Schmerzen	
Träume	
Erzählung from *Lohengrin*	
Narrative, At the Spinning-wheel (piano)	Urich
The Angel and the Sunshine	
To a Faded Violet	
A Day Dream	
Meine Rose	

Fourth Recital

Work	Composer
Rondo, G minor	Beethoven
Wonne der Wehmut	
Adelaide	
Impromptu, B flat major	Schubert
Serenade	
Du bist die Ruh'	
Frühlingsglaube	
Am Meer	
Erlkönig	
Arabesque	Schumann
Lied ohne Ende (piano)	
Du bist wie eine Blume	
Mondnacht	
Widmung	
Dein Angesicht	
Frühlingsnacht	
Prelude and Fugue in E major	Rubinstein
Melodie	
Der alte König	
Du bist wie eine Blume	
Der Asra	
Waldeinsamkeit	
Es blinkt der Tau	
Consolation: Nocturne for piano	Wolfsohn
Ich hab' im Traum geweinet	
Die stille Wasserrose	

FIG. 2.2B. Werrenrath and Wolfsohn's third and fourth song recitals, as reported in the *Inter Ocean* (Chicago), February 8, 1879, 6.

The fourth program was the only one in which all the songs were lieder; the others included at least a few in contrasting languages and styles, as was typical of concerts given by lieder singers in Europe, including Stockhausen. The second recital included English, French, and Italian songs by Werrenrath's mentor and friend Gounod, all of which originated from the period when Gounod lived in England. Earlier US song recitals had also programmed some of Gounod's songs, but with the exception of "When in the Early Morn," which was published by Ditson in 1873, most of Werrenrath's selections do not appear to have been well known. Even in the 1880s, Gounod's "Ave Maria" and "Serenade" were more frequently performed than most of the numbers Werrenrath sang.[64]

While most of the songs in Werrenrath's Chicago series were art songs, there were also a few popular works, including Thomas Moore's "Oft in the Stilly Night" and Frederic Clay's "Sands o' Dee." Sheet music for Moore's (1779–1852) song had been circulating in America since the beginning of the century, and it was reported to be one of the top-selling foreign songs in the country in 1870.[65] Likewise, works by Frederic Clay (1838–1889) had been performed in parlors in the British Isles and the United States for some time. Werrenrath was not the only artist to program these songs in classical concerts; the previous year, "Sands o' Dee" was performed during a concert given by the Mendelssohn Quintette Club in Chicago.[66] Although earlier lieder singers such as Osgood were lauded because they forsook such popular songs, many later recitalists continued to combine this repertoire with lieder. This contradicts Levine's theory of the greater sacralization of concert life, and possibly does so in a matter that is clearer than recitals combining lieder and folksongs, which many artists considered as important predecessors of lieder.

Some of the other songs in the series were by less well-known composers. John Urich, for example, was an opera composer born in Trinidad. He worked mostly in London, where he studied with Gounod, before transferring to the United States around the time of World War I. In contrast, Georg Goltermann (1824–1898) was primarily known as a cellist in Germany. Although the songs by Gounod and Urich provided linguistic and stylistic contrasts to the German songs, these pieces, like Wolfsohn's lieder, were probably selected on the basis of the composers' relationships with Werrenrath. Nevertheless, this blending of different styles of song was not unique. George Henschel's later recitals were also characterized by similarly contrasting genres and styles, and throughout the late 1880s and 1890s critics frequently preferred this type of mixed program to ones comprised entirely of lieder sung in German.

Although Werrenrath and Wolfsohn's programs were not organized chrono-logically and were not specifically labeled as historical, their breadth of repertoire implies a historical dimension. While Wolfsohn's encyclopedic piano recitals likely informed the conception of the series, it is unclear whether other performers who had experimented with historically themed song programs influenced the two men. Both knew Frédéric Ritter. Wolfsohn was working in New York when the Ritters gave their series of recitals, and in December 1879 (the same year as the Chicago series) Werrenrath participated in a chamber concert at Vassar that Ritter organized. In addition to a selection of his usual lieder, he performed an unpublished song by his host.[67] Nevertheless, there is no documentation indicating that the Ritters' 1869 series influenced Werrenrath and Wolfsohn.

Despite the historical significance of this recital series and the involvement of such a well-known musician as Wolfsohn, the recitals had small audiences and attracted little critical attention. They were held on Thursday and Saturday evenings at the First Methodist Church auditorium, at the corner of Clark and Washington Streets, where some of the other concerts of the Beethoven Society were held. The seats for the entire cycle cost one dollar. This was the price for a seat at just one of Werrenrath's subsequent recitals, but it was comparable to prices for Hershey School recitals. Although local papers and the *American Art Journal* carried advertisements for the recitals, some of which printed the programs in full, the *Inter Ocean* was the only one to publish a review. It acknowledged the promise of the endeavor but also voiced disappointment at the poor attendance.[68] Given that Dwight's journal had displayed so much interest in lieder, it is surprising that this series rated only the briefest mention, and it occurred within a report from Chicago by Brittan. Only two months earlier Brittan, himself an advocate of the lied, had chronicled the vast improvement in the musical life of Chicago during the preceding decade.[69] Previously he had enjoyed the richness of Boston's musical life and therefore he would have realized the significance of the series, making the brevity of his report all the more surprising. This situation could, however, imply that there was some sort of professional jealousy or conflict with Wolfsohn or that the performances were less than satisfactory. Perhaps critics (and audiences) were hesitant to attend because Werrenrath had earlier given uneven performances in Chicago, which were attributed to his recent illness.[70]

Regardless of this lack of critical success, Werrenrath's recital series anticipated the growth in song recitals that took place throughout the 1880s, when both national- and regional-level artists quickly adopted this new medium. In 1880 Julius (Jules) Jordan (1850–1927), a student of Osgood, gave what appears to be the first US recital series devoted to Schubert's *Die schöne Müllerin*, *Winterreise*, and *Schwanengesang* (D. 957).[71] Whereas these recitals took place before small audiences in Providence and Newport, Rhode Island, Grace Hiltz presented recitals throughout the Midwest and New England. Just as Werrenrath was associated with instrumentalists championing German music, initially Hiltz collaborated with Mathews and the similarly Germanophile instructors at the Hershey School.

Grace Hiltz

Born in Portland, Maine, and raised in Providence, Rhode Island, Hiltz moved with her widowed mother to Chicago during the 1870s. There she began studying with Sarah Hershey, who had married her school's organist, Clarence Eddy (1851–1937). In 1887 *Brainard's* observed that "Under Mrs. Eddy's inspiration, . . . Miss Hiltz was among the first American vocalists to give song recitals sustaining a whole program—save one or two instrumental intervals."[72] Although this report references the influence of Sarah Eddy, it does not acknowledge that collaborating with Mathews in his normal school song recitals likely also influenced Hiltz's work. In 1879 she gave her first recitals at the Hershey School and at one of Mathew's normal schools in Evanston. This normal also featured a recital by the admired pianist Amy Fay (1844–1928), who had recently returned from Europe, where she had studied with Liszt.[73]

Hiltz's first two solo recitals were part of the Hershey School's 1879 series of eight recitals by its voice, piano, and organ students, which were held in the school's two-hundred-seat hall. During her first recital she sang three lieder by Mendelssohn, five from Schumann's *Dichterliebe*, nine by Franz, and five by Schubert (see figure 2.3).[74] She gave the same program, without instrumental solos, for her recital at the Evanston normal, where she was listed as one of the featured artists.[75] In contrast to this program, her second Hershey recital ranged from arias by Bach and Handel to five songs by Chicago composers, including Clarence Eddy and Gleason.

By comparing the Hershey School's song recital programs to student recitals at the New England Conservatory, it is possible to observe just how unusual they were for this period. The conservatory's student programs comprising vocal works and piano solos are not as substantial or as focused on lieder as many of the Hershey song recitals. The school's contrasting commitment to song recitals emphasizing lieder can be attributed to Mathews's interest in the genre and Hershey's training in Germany.[76] But some of the programs were also unusual compared to European recitals. Most of Hiltz's programs included between seventeen and twenty-three lieder, more than in Stockhausen's and Walter's recitals, and more than in most of the other recitals at the Hershey School. In other regards, some were like European programs in that they began with eighteenth-century numbers, including arias by Handel.

In 1880 Hiltz presented two recitals at the Hershey normal school, where she was a faculty member.[77] The first included Brahms's "Spanish Serenade" ("Spanisches Lied," op. 6, no. 1) and a complete performance of *Frauenliebe und -leben*, excerpts of which were frequently sung by other women at the Hershey School. Her second recital included a suite of six spring songs by Franz. These selections suggest that she might have been aware of Osgood's recent perfor-

Song Recitals and Song Recital Series   65

On the Wings of Music   Mendelssohn
Zuleika
Song of Spring, op. 71, no. 2

Five Songs from the "Poet's Love"   Schumann
    'Twas in the Lovely Month of May
    Where Fall My Bitter Tear Drops
    The Rose and the Lily
    When Gazing on Thy Beauteous Eyes
    A Young Man Loves a Maiden

Blondel's Song   Schumann

Organ: Christmas Pastorale   Merkel
                  Miss Carrie T. Kingman

Nine Songs   Franz
    Dance Song in May, op. 1, no 6
    In Vain, op. 10, no. 6
    Two Faded Roses, op. 13, no. 1
    May Song, op. 33, no. 2
    The Lotus Flower, op. 1, no. 3
    Rosemary, op. 13, no. 4
    Slumber Song, op. 1, no. 10
    O Tell Me Is My Wandering Love? op. 40, no. 1
    The Woods, op. 14, no. 3

Organ: Ave Maria   Arcadelt-Liszt
                  Miss Carrie T. Kingman

Five Songs   Schubert
    Barcarolle
    Thou Art the Rest
    Hark, Hark! the Lark
    Faith in Spring
    Whither?

FIG. 2.3. Program of Grace Hiltz's recital on Friday afternoon, May 9, 1879, at the Hershey School of Music Concert Hall. Program housed in Box 52 of the Frederick Grant Gleason Collection, Newberry Library, Chicago.

mances of these lieder in Boston, especially since other recitalists were not programming the Brahms song or the Franz suite.[78] Osgood's performances were chronicled in *Dwight's Journal of Music*, and it is possible that Hiltz had learned of them from associates such as Brittan and Matthews who contributed to this journal. Whereas Osgood sang in German, Hiltz sang in English, as was typical of singers at the Hershey School. In addition, unlike Osgood's programs and those in other cities, each of Hiltz's recitals included organ compositions played by Clarence Eddy.[79]

Having established herself as a professional singer in Chicago, Hiltz sought further instruction in New England and Europe. Beginning in the fall of 1880, she sang at the Union Congregationalist Church at Providence, where she earned a handsome salary of $1,000 per year. During this period, she studied with Boston singers renowned for lieder performances including Osgood, Henschel, Charles R. Adams (1834–1900), and Erminia Rudersdorff (1822–1882).[80] She also worked with Jules Jordan in Providence, where she sang in his Arion choir.[81] She performed solo songs she had given in Chicago in collaborative recitals and in her own recitals in Providence and Boston, as well as at the Oberlin Conservatory. After less than two years studying in Boston, Hiltz traveled to Europe, but once again this was only a short sojourn. In Paris, like many Americans, she studied with Viardot-Garcia and Anna Caroline de La Grange (1825–1905), as well as with Giovanni Sbriglia (1832–1916).[82] By the end of 1882, however, she was back in Chicago, where she re-established herself as a valued performer and teacher.

Hiltz was particularly admired in the Midwest, where she often gave song recitals and sang solos in concerts and oratorios, but she also made the occasional appearance in East Coast cities such as Boston. Her itinerary from the end of 1887 through the early months of 1888 gives an indication of her success. In addition to recitals in Chicago, Hiltz appeared in recitals and concerts in at least five cities in Minnesota, as well as in multiple cities in states such as Iowa, Michigan, Ohio, Pennsylvania, and Indiana.[83]

After the Hershey School closed in 1885, Hiltz organized and performed in concerts at Chicago's Haymarket Theater. Many of these, and those she organized subsequently, were collaborations with instrumentalists performing chamber music, and they included fewer songs than did her solo recitals in earlier years. On midwestern tours she often appeared during conferences organized by music educators and before women's music clubs. In 1892, for example, she collaborated with the Indiana pianist Josephine Large in a recital for the women's club Matinee Musicale at the First Baptist Church in Huntington, Indiana. Four hundred and twenty-five invitations were distributed for this event.[84] Throughout her career, her performances received positive reviews, and her programs usually pleased the critics. Unlike her early recitals, many of these programs included

Song Recitals and Song Recital Series   67

a few songs by English, French, and Italian composers, as well as lieder. Despite this variety, in most cases she sang all the works in English.[85] At a time when few major recitalists visited Texas, she gave recitals in Fort Worth in 1895,[86] and then, in search of a milder climate, briefly resided in that state. When she returned to Chicago her performance career had ended, though she continued to teach.

Werrenrath's Brooklyn Recitals

In contrast to Hiltz's appearances throughout the Midwest, most of Werrenrath's recitals took place in his hometown of Brooklyn. The few exceptions include the 1879 series in Chicago and, in 1881, recitals in Boston and Buffalo and at Wells College in Aurora, New York.[87] The recital at Wells College encompassed twenty songs, including ones by Grieg and one by the beloved music instructor at the college, Max Piutti (1852–1885). Subsequently, Werrenrath sang the songs in Piutti's lecture on Schubert for the Ladies' Afternoon Musicale, held in Buffalo.[88] After this, he seems not to have pursued recitals beyond Brooklyn, perhaps because his other performance obligations placed constraints on his time.[89] In Brooklyn he gave numerous recitals comprised of art songs and folksongs, most of which took place in the auditorium of the Long Island Historical Society.[90] He presented at least five series of song recitals, as well as numerous individual recitals. Most series consisted of three programs, though the first series was so successful that he added a request recital. Whereas his Chicago recitals were held in the evenings, the Brooklyn events were on Thursday or Friday afternoons. As with the Chicago series, they included a few piano solos.

The press's reaction to Werrenrath's first Brooklyn series in 1881 was consistently positive. In an announcement for this series, the *Musical Courier* claimed that Werrenrath was "too well known to need puffing."[91] The *New Yorker Staats-Zeitung* review of the first recital, which it labeled a "Lieder-Recitation," noted the difficult task of performing some fifteen lieder, implying that such recitals were a new concept.[92] According to the *American Art Journal*, the third attracted a larger audience than was typical of Brooklyn recitals; this was viewed as particularly surprising because seats were priced at one dollar. In general, Werrenrath impressed this journal, which praised his intelligence, "cultured expression," and programming of songs that were not frequently performed by others.[93]

The reviews in the *New Yorker Staats-Zeitung* and the *New York Times* referenced the number of women in Werrenrath's audiences. The former implied this was a weakness, and the latter seemed to compensate for this perception by describing Werrenrath's "strong, resonant, and manly tenor voice."[94] This derisive attitude toward the women in audiences fails to acknowledge the significant role they played in supporting concerts of instrumental music.[95] It is, however, further evidence that almost as soon as the genre of the song recital was established, it was associated with women, and high-quality performances and repertoire, as well as men's participation, did not prevent this association from carrying negative connotations.

Throughout Werrenrath's 1881 series, Emil Liebling (1851–1914) of Chicago provided the piano solos and Robert Thallon (1852–1910) the accompaniments. Thallon, who had studied at the Leipzig Conservatory, was an organist at the Plymouth Church, and he often collaborated with Werrenrath. The *New York Times* review of the encore recital that followed the official series is particularly unusual because it commends Thallon's piano accompaniment during Urich's "Barcarolle." In most other cases Thallon is only referenced in passing and Liebling's solos are simply listed.[96] This lack of appreciation for the accompanists in song recitals was typical of the period, and it was perpetuated in the reviews of Werrenrath's subsequent series, when he collaborated with Hermann O. C. Korthener, a well-respected local pianist.

Werrenrath's second 1881 series included songs by Grieg and two lieder cycles. Whereas the first recital featured *An die ferne Geliebte*, Werrenrath distributed the songs of *Die schöne Müllerin* across the series. In 1870 at St. James Hall in London, Stockhausen had taken a similar approach with Schubert's cycle, dispersing the songs across six recitals. Whereas Werrenrath gave the pieces in the context of song recitals, Stockhausen performed them during Charles Hallé's piano recitals.[97] Of Werrenrath's series as a whole, one critic echoed reviews of earlier lieder singers, writing: "These concerts are a source of the greatest pleasure to people of cultured taste and only by such are they appreciated."[98] Throughout the 1880s, and to a lesser extent in the 1890s, similar assessments that audiences for this type of recital were part of the musical cognoscenti became a well-worn trope in reviews of the recitals given by the other exponents of the lied, including Henschel and Max Heinrich. That is to say, the programming strategies that Werrenrath and others employed, such as combining lieder with a few lighter songs or folksongs, usually did not attract a diverse audience. These types of remarks also accord with the descriptions of lieder as high art that were common in the preceding decades.

Although Werrenrath frequently returned to composers whose works he had performed in Chicago, he also added others. His first 1881 series included Handel's "Deeper and Deeper Still" (from *Jephtha*, 1751), Jean-Baptiste Faure's "Bonjour Suzon," two songs by the Danish composer Niels Gade (1817–1890), and seven Scandinavian ballads.[99] In 1889 he sang Loewe's "Die Uhr" (op. 123, no. 3) and "The Bell Ringer's Daughter" (op. 112a), which he had rarely, if ever, sung before.[100] Some recitals featured a greater number of simpler songs than others. The last recital of the 1884 series was devoted to European folksongs, and the third recital of the 1889 series presented numerous lighter selections, including songs by Erik Meyer-Helmund (1861–1932).[101]

In addition to these series, Werrenrath presented stand-alone recitals devoted to folksongs from various European countries. Whereas other recitalists, including Raymond Ritter, also presented folksongs, performing Scandinavian folksongs was a part of Werrenrath's brand. In addition to his own heritage, his selection of this repertoire might have been influenced by hearing other singers in Europe; in particular, Swedish folksongs were part of Lind's concerts and marketing. He also presented programs devoted to settings of Robert Burns. Burns had attracted the attention of numerous German Romantic artists, including Schumann, but it is highly likely that Werrenrath's interest was sparked by a closer source. The father of Thallon, one of Werrenrath's colleagues, was a great admirer of Burns, and this might have influenced Werrenrath's creation of recital programs devoted to the Scotsman.[102]

Throughout the 1880s Werrenrath also gave solos during other types of concerts. He appeared in oratorios at the Springfield (Massachusetts) Festival in 1881 and 1883, as well as in a few Brooklyn Philharmonic concerts under Thomas; in one instance, he contributed to the performance of the Good Friday Spell from the third act of *Parsifal*. In 1884 he toured California with a German opera company, performing in *Der Freischütz*, and later in the same year he appeared during the Pappenheim Opera Company's productions in San Francisco and Utah. He also participated in the 1889 tour of the Scandinavian Festival, which included midwestern states such as Minnesota and Wisconsin. These types of activities, however, ceased in the 1890s, when Brooklyn papers primarily referred to him as a church singer and teacher.

After Werrenrath's death in 1898, brief obituaries appeared in papers as far away as Scotland, and while some of the longer ones were quite positive, a few of the local notices observed that after quickly coming to prominence in the United States, his fame diminished during the 1890s.[103] By this time he had been overshadowed by other concert singers, most notably Henschel and Heinrich. Many later references to Werrenrath were in the context of publications about his son, the noted operatic baritone Reinald. Histories of music in the United States published at the turn of the century rarely acknowledged Werrenrath's 1879 lieder series, let alone its innovations. Still, this series influenced Henschel and Heinrich. As the following chapters recount, both men met Werrenrath prior to presenting their first series of song recitals.

* * *

Americans settled on the title "song recital" before Germans established *Liederabend* as the standard nomenclature for similar types of performances. Although singers probably knew of contemporary performances in Europe, their development of song recitals featuring lieder was in large part influenced by the culture of specific cities and opportunities provided by institutions such as normal schools and the Hershey School. Some of the earliest recitals were facilitated by members of Dwight's and Thomas's extended network, and they were viewed as contributing to the network's efforts to elevate American concert life by introducing audiences to German repertoire. In varying degrees, they were like earlier chamber concerts that programmed lieder in that they often were shaped by instrumentalists and writers rather than the singers. Just as Dwight had promoted singers and lieder performances in Boston, so too Mathews promoted the genre through his work at various schools. Along similar lines, Wolfsohn's hand in shaping Werrenrath's first recital series in some ways mirrors Dresel's influence on singers in Boston. After their initial recitals, however, singers such as Hiltz and Werrenrath determined their own style of programs and career paths. At the same time as song recitals emerged, there was an increased effort to educate a wider range of amateur music lovers about the lied by means of public lecture recitals by the likes of Mathews and B. D. Allen, publications such as Ferris's article, and historically shaped programs like those by the Ritters and Osgood. Despite these efforts, it seems that audiences preferred programs comprising a diversity of styles to those dedicated to lieder, and that some audiences and performers preferred lieder sung in English, rather than German. Responses to some of the early recitals indicate that they were categorized as belonging to the woman's sphere, and while critics praised the lied and the women who performed them, some also denigrated the women in the audiences—an irony perpetuated throughout the century.

3

The Henschels' Polyglot "Vocal Recitals"

In 1880, when he made his first trip to the United States, George Henschel was greeted as a star, having established a reputation singing solo roles in oratorios and lieder on the Continent and in London, where he had recently settled. His principal purpose in coming to the United States was to sing solo roles in oratorios, but he quickly expanded this project to include giving vocal recitals and promoting his own compositions, an endeavor that included the sale of sheet music released by US publishers. Whereas Jenny Lind in the 1850s had realized Americans were not ready to hear lieder, Henschel was able to capitalize on the growing interest in lieder that singers in Boston, New York, and Chicago had created. Before presenting his first recitals in the country he met many of these musicians and, like August Kreissmann and George Werrenrath, he collaborated with many others who were promoting classical instrumental music. By the end of the 1880–1881 concert season he and his new American wife, his former student Lillian, née Bailey, had established "vocal recitals." During these recitals the couple gave solos and duets, with George accompanying himself and Lillian. Critics in New York clamored that "no such satisfactory interpreter of the German *Lied* has been heard here as Mr. Henschel."[1] But ironically, although Henschel's performances of lieder were emphasized in reviews, the couple's trademark recitals, which they developed in the following years, also included French, Italian, and English songs. This stylistic and linguistic diversity was key to their success. Ultimately these events contributed to solidifying the song recital as an edifying and entertaining concert genre, and they likely influenced the fad for polyglot recitals that emerged during the 1890s.

The couple lived in Boston during Henschel's 1881–1884 tenure as the first conductor of the Boston Symphony Orchestra. Like those of Damrosch and Thomas, Henschel's symphony programs comprised classical repertoire, in particular, works by German composers such as Beethoven. The couple's recitals similarly focused on serious repertoire. In Europe Henschel had collaborated with Brahms, and he shared the aesthetics and performance practices of Brahms's circle, which included the violinist Joseph Joachim (1831–1907). The tenets of this circle and the reverence audiences paid to their performances paralleled the aspirations of Henry Lee Higginson, the founder of the Boston Symphony, as well as those of Dwight and his network. Although the Henschels returned to England in 1884, they continued to concertize in the United States through 1901, and during the following years Henschel continued to teach American singers in both the United States and England and to promote his compositions and publications.

The Early Careers of George Henschel and Lillian Bailey

Whereas many of the earlier advocates of the lied, including Fanny Raymond Ritter and Kreissmann, learned their repertoire while living in the United States, Henschel arrived with a command of a significant body of repertoire and a distinguished record as a performer. He had quickly risen to fame in Europe in large part through his association with Joseph Joachim and Brahms. Born in Breslau, Henschel studied piano and singing at the Leipzig Conservatory. He then pursued further studies in voice and composition at Joachim's Königliche Hochschule für Musik in Berlin.[2] He met Brahms, one of Joachim's closest friends and colleagues, at the 1874 Lower Rheinish Music Festival in Cologne and subsequently sang numerous solo roles in oratorios under the composer's baton. During the 1870s, in both informal settings and public concerts, Brahms accompanied Henschel in performances of his own lieder as well as ones by other composers.[3] Through Brahms and Joachim, Henschel also met and collaborated with Julius Stockhausen and Clara Schumann.

After successful performances in London in 1877, Henschel decided to settle there, though he continued to perform on the Continent. In England he sang lieder and solo roles in oratorios and concerts in collaboration with colleagues of Brahms, including Joseph Joachim, Clara Schumann, and Hans Richter (1843–1916), one of his former teachers in Leipzig. As with his concerts on the Continent, most of his public performances of lieder took place during multi-genre programs that also included choral, orchestral, and chamber compositions or piano solos.

In contrast to these mixed-genre concerts, Henschel's 1877 "morning concert" and 1878 "vocal recital" were dominated by solo songs, complemented by only a few instrumental numbers. The first concert featured twenty-four songs, an unusually high number for the time. Arranged in a loose chronological order, it included works by Carissimi, Handel, Pergolesi, Haydn, Beethoven, Schubert, Schumann, Loewe, Chopin, Franz, Rubinstein, Brahms, and Henschel himself.[4] As the press noted, a recital consisting of one singer presenting classical repertoire was still unusual in Europe. The printed program's inclusion of the names of the poets who wrote the songs' texts was also considered a novelty.[5] Henschel's second recital did not attract a large audience; one reviewer attributed this to the fact that the repertoire was not popular. This critic also implied this type of event was still new and potentially problematic in that "even some lovers of high-class music might have shrunk from the monotony of a single male voice."[6] A reviewer of an 1878 "pianoforte and vocal" recital in which Henschel collaborated with the pianist Ignaz Brüll (1846–1907), another of Brahms's colleagues, was similarly greeted with the reservation that a concert given by two men without someone with a "soft voice and flowing robes" might tire an audience.[7]

Nonetheless, in general the critical responses to Henschel's performances in England were highly positive, with one reviewer placing him in the direct line of the great bass-baritones Johann Baptist Pischek and Josef Staudigl.[8] In the United States, *Dwight's Journal of Music* reported on Henschel's triumphs in London and his reputation as an interpreter of the lied. This journal also described Lillian Bailey's accomplishments and noted that she was studying with Henschel.[9]

Even before her studies in Europe, Bailey had established a reputation as a rising young star in the United States. Born in Columbus, Ohio, she trained in Boston under Erminia Rudersdorff and Charles R. Hayden, her uncle, both of whom were venerated singing teachers.[10] Beginning in 1876, while still a teenager, she performed a small number of lieder in concerts with some of Boston's highly admired instrumentalists. They included Arthur Foote and B. J. Lang, as well as the pianist Madeline Schiller (ca. 1843–1911), a former student of the Leipzig Conservatory who had previously given recitals with Clara Doria. In New York, Bailey sang an aria by Meyerbeer and Schubert's "Gretchen am Spinnrade" (D. 118) and "Heidenröslein" (D. 257) during one of Leopold Damrosch's 1877 Saturday Symphony Matinees. In other appearances she sang arias by Handel, a repertoire that pleased American concertgoers and was favored by Europeans, including Henschel.[11]

After a brief period of study with Pauline Viardot-Garcia in France during 1878 and further study and performances with Henschel in London, Bailey returned to the United States in 1880 to fulfill major engagements. These included a performance at the Worcester Festival with such distinguished singers as Myron W. Whitney (1836–1910) and Annie Louisa Cary (1841–1921).[12] Bailey was so admired in the Boston area that she was contracted as one of the soloists in the Handel and Haydn Society's performance of *Messiah* that marked the opening

74   CHAPTER 3

of the newly rebuilt Tremont Temple. She also contributed solos during the twenty-seventh anniversary concert of New York's Arion Society and concerts by Philadelphia's Arion and Orpheus Clubs.[13] In the following months she also appeared in numerous chamber and orchestral concerts with Henschel, as well as in his recitals.

In the days after their first New York recital, George and Lillian announced their engagement; their wedding took place in Boston in March 1881.[14] Although previously referred to as Miss Bailey or Lillian Bailey, after her marriage the press always called Lillian Mrs. Henschel or Mrs. George Henschel, as was the custom at the time.[15] Initially, programs and advertisements listed her as assisting her husband, but by the end of the 1880–1881 tour she was consistently given equal billing. Although she gave a number of independent performances during this tour, after she married she mostly confined her performances to the couple's recitals and to other concerts that involved her husband. This narrowing of focus was not discussed in the press.

The First "Vocal Recitals," 1880–1881

During his initial months in the United States, Henschel came in contact or collaborated with numerous musicians who were promoting classical instrumental music and lieder. In September 1880 he was introduced to a group of New York musicians during a social gathering at the house of Robert Thallon, a pianist who accompanied Werrenrath in Brooklyn and other lieder singers in New York. The guests included Leopold Damrosch and his wife Helene (who on occasion sang lieder during chamber concerts).[16] During the evening, lieder were sung by Henschel, Bailey, and Werrenrath.[17] Werrenrath had given his series of Chicago song recitals the previous season, and the assumption can be made that at some point he discussed them with Henschel. During the following months Henschel collaborated with other musicians promoting lieder and classical music when he performed in oratorios and during chamber and orchestral concerts: They included B. J. Lang, Jules Jordan, William Sherwood, and members of the Mendelssohn Quintette Club in Boston; Carl Wolfsohn in Chicago; and Damrosch and Theodore Thomas in New York.

At the end of 1880, Henschel, with Lillian assisting, began presenting performances that he titled "vocal recitals," as opposed to the label "song recitals" that US singers were using. The first of these followed his performances of solo roles in Mendelssohn's *Elijah* and Berlioz's *Damnation of Faust*.[18] Between December 7, 1880, and February 21, 1881, the couple presented four recitals in New York and three in Boston. In New York, Thallon provided most of the accompaniments, but Henschel played them in the Boston recitals and in most of the couple's subsequent appearances, typically performing from memory.

Although there were other singers who accompanied themselves, Henschel's piano accompaniments were viewed as part of the novelty of the couple's recitals.[19] Henschel had not presented a series of recitals before, and Walter's first series of *Liederabende* in Vienna would not take place until the following June. At the time, most New York and Boston concertgoers were probably not aware of Werrenrath's Chicago recital series, and this is likely why the *American Art Journal* claimed that Henschel's vocal recitals were a new idea.[20]

These events commanded greater attention than many previous lieder performances, but they nevertheless attracted an elite audience. Because of his reputation, Henschel was able to fill large halls and command higher ticket prices than other lieder performers. The recitals were held in Meionaon Hall and Tremont Temple in Boston and in Steinway Hall in New York, all of which seated more than a thousand. Tickets for the New York series were priced at five dollars, with individual seats costing a dollar fifty.[21] In contrast, tickets for Werrenrath's three recitals in Brooklyn cost a dollar each or two dollars for the series. Henschel's prices, which stayed fairly constant throughout his career, were also higher than those for popular entertainments. For instance, tickets for Emma Abbott's opera company at the Brooklyn Park Theatre ranged from fifty cents to a dollar.[22] Whereas all of Werrenrath's recital series were held in the afternoon, the Henschels' series in Boston and New York included evening and matinee performances. Reviews confirm that Henschel's audiences, like those of earlier Boston chamber concerts featuring lieder, consisted of discriminating musicians, and the New York *Sun* suggested that Henschel would do best to address himself to musicians rather than to "mere pleasure seekers."[23]

In terms of their conception, Henschel's programs both resembled and contrasted with those of Werrenrath. Both men's programs were primarily comprised of lieder, with a few piano solos for contrast, but they differed in that Mrs. Henschel's higher voice provided a timbral contrast, and the couple performed duets as well as solos. Also unlike Werrenrath's programs, Henschel's often began with a few Baroque and Classical numbers, including arias by Handel. In addition to providing stylistic and linguistic contrasts to lieder, the ornaments that characterize many of Handel's arias enabled vocalists to demonstrate techniques that lieder did not require.

Henschel did not organize the programs for his initial US recitals in a uniform way, and he emphasized lieder more heavily than in many of his later recitals. The couple had performed their repertoire in Europe, and many of their numbers, including Schumann's "Ich grolle nicht" (op. 48, no. 7) and "Die beiden Grenadiere" and Rubinstein's "Der Asra" had already been sung by US singers. Despite Lillian's familiarity with Boston musicians, the couple did not perform any lieder by Franz during their initial recitals in that city, though they did give two of his songs in New York. In general, it seems they did not

76   CHAPTER 3

share the admiration that Boston musicians such as Dresel and Osgood had for this composer.

A few of the lieder on the Henschels' programs, most notably those by Brahms, had rarely been performed in the United States. During the New York series, Lillian gave Brahms's "Es träumte mir" (op. 57, no. 3) and George sang "Wie bist du, meine Königin" (op. 32, no. 9) and three lieder from the *Magelone Romances*: "So willst du des Armen," "Wie soll ich die Freude, die Wonne denn tragen?" and "Wie Froh und Frisch" (op. 33, nos. 5, 6, and 14). All of these songs had been published during the preceding decades. Brahms's European publisher Simrock arranged for editions to include English translations; however, the songs had rarely, if ever, been performed on US stages. The reviewer for the *Musical Courier* considered the lengthy, technically demanding songs from the *Magelone* cycle to be "lacking in genuine musical interest to the majority of listeners, although they were excellently sung."[24] In contrast, the *New York Times* claimed these numbers "were perhaps the most artistic triumph" of the recital.[25] At the time, Thomas was advocating for Brahms's orchestral and large choral works, performing pieces such as the Variations on a Theme by Haydn (op. 56) in multiple cities. But the mixed responses to Henschel's performances of the composer's lieder were typical of the US reception of the composer's other works, and also of the reception of Brahms's lieder in Europe.[26]

Henschel's fourth recital program in New York contrasted with the others in that it was dominated by his own compositions. While some of these songs might well have received their American premieres during this recital, a few of Henschel's works were already circulating in the country. His song "Jamie or Robin?," which was dedicated to Lillian prior to the couple's engagement, was published by Church in Cincinnati in 1880, the year after it had been published in England.[27] This simple, sweet song with its tale of a "lassie" pondering whether she should love Jamie or Robin demonstrates Henschel's interest in appealing to women making music in their homes. In contrast, many of his lieder had already been released in English and German editions by Brahms's market-savvy publisher Simrock. Whereas these works carried opus numbers, the lighter songs for the domestic market did not. The New York recital opened with six songs from Henschel's cycle *Acht Lieder aus Scheffel's Trompeter von Säkkingen* (op. 25) and closed with his *Serbisches Liederspiel* (op. 32). Comprising ten songs for one to four voices, the latter cycle had received multiple performances in Europe. In the New York performance, the Henschels were assisted by Miss Louise Homer (contralto, 1871–1947) and Hayden (Lillian's former teacher). One critic praised the simplicity and elegance of some of Henschel's songs, the "vigor" of others, and noted that they were the products of an "accomplished musician." He also, however, observed a lack of originality.[28] Nevertheless, throughout the following decades Henschel's vocal works were taken up by Americans. During 1881 American publishers issued some of his English songs, which were briefly but warmly reviewed.[29] Of these, the lullaby "O Hush Thee My Baby," which was released by Ditson, had the type of text that was usually associated with women, and it was sung by Mrs. Henschel in later recitals. The Henschels rarely presented another program devoted entirely to George's songs,[30] but they frequently included a few of these works in their standard programs, with Mrs. Henschel singing them more frequently than did her husband. A wide range of other singers also performed them, from the popular opera star Johanna Gadski (1872–1932), who sang his "Morning Hymn" during her 1916–1917 tour, to members of women's clubs as far afield as Anaconda, Montana.[31]

Although Henschel's initial US recital programs were dominated by lieder, they included a variety of other repertoire. In addition to songs from earlier centuries, Henschel sang an air from Jules Massenet's *Le roi de Lahore* (1877) and "Vulcan's Song" from Gounod's *Philémon et Baucis* (1859–60, rev. 1876), both of which were sometimes performed by other concert singers. All the recitals also included a few piano solos. During the second New York recital Sherwood contributed substantial, technically demanding solos, performing Bach's Chromatic Fantasia and Fugue in D minor (BWV 903) and Schumann's Fantasie in C major (op. 17), which was not well known to the audience. In contrast, Henschel played two of his own smaller pieces during the first two Boston recitals. In addition, during the second recital, he was joined by B. J. Lang in a performance of the two-piano *Hommage à Handel* (op. 92) by Ignaz Moscheles (1794–1870), a composer with whom Henschel had studied in Leipzig.

Henschel's performances on this first tour were so successful that the *American Art Journal* placed a reproduction of Alma Tadema's portrait of him on the cover of its April 2, 1881, issue.[32] The New York recital series inevitably led to comparisons with Werrenrath's first Brooklyn recital series, which began around the same time as Henschel's series ended. Some of the reviews of Henschel's recitals suggest they were to some extent society events, a continuation of the antebellum notion that concert attendance promoted the acquisition of artistic sensibility and conferred or reinforced elevated social standing. In contrast, a review of Werrenrath's encore recital stated the attentive audience was there "for no other reason than musical interests."[33] The *American Art Journal* praised the artistry of both men and credited them with introducing "a class of entertainment of the highest order."[34] This type of comment echoes reviews of earlier Boston singers, such as Kreissmann, that positioned lieder as high art.

During the months following the Henschels' initial series of recitals, the couple gave recitals in Brooklyn, Providence, Rhode Island, Buffalo (where some of their friends resided), at Wells College, and in Washington, DC, where they were joined by the renowned Hungarian pianist Rafael Joseffy (1852–1915). Throughout these recitals they repeated repertoire they had given in Boston and

78   CHAPTER 3

New York, in addition to which Mrs. Henschel also performed a small number of songs by French composers, including Widor's "Lia è Morta" (op. 32, no. 1) and one of Viardot-Garcia's arrangements of a Chopin mazurka.[35] In Chicago, Henschel (without his wife) performed during a concert by the Beethoven Society and gave a song recital with Wolfsohn.[36] After a successful tour, the couple traveled to London in May 1881, returning to the United States the following fall.

The 1881–1884 Boston Sojourn

Henschel conducted the Boston Symphony Orchestra from 1881 to the end of the 1883–1884 concert season. During each of these three seasons, the orchestra performed all of Beethoven's symphonies as well as numerous works by Brahms, Schubert, and Schumann. Henschel's focus on German composers resembles that of Thomas and Damrosch. Like them, however, he also conducted works by other composers, including Berlioz, Rossini, and Saint-Saëns, and, in 1884, he gave the premiere of George Chadwick's Scherzo in F. His selections aligned with Dwight's and Higginson's efforts to promote serious classical repertoire, and the programs of his song recitals did likewise.[37] With his wife, Henschel gave a series of four vocal recitals during each concert season, as well as numerous individual recitals in public and private venues. Continuing their outreach to women, they gave matinee and evening performances each year. George also sang solo roles in oratorios and concerts in Boston and other cities, and his wife occasionally sang solos, including lieder, during the symphony's concerts.

The couple's 1881–1882 recitals reprised numbers they presented during their first US tour, including excerpts from *Die schöne Müllerin* and Henschel's *Serbisches Liederspiel*. But there were also other works, including vocal quartets from Brahms's lilting opp. 52 and 65 *Liebeslieder*, during which the couple was joined by well-known locals, Carrie Carper and Jules Jordan.[38] While conductor of the Boston Symphony Orchestra, Henschel led more performances of orchestral works by Beethoven, Mendelssohn, Schubert, and Schumann than those by Brahms, though he did give the Boston premiere of Brahms's *Alto Rhapsody* (op. 53) and the American premiere of the composer's Piano Concerto no. 2 (op. 83). But while a number of scholars have cited Henschel's reputation for performing Brahms's songs and have asserted that he played an important role in disseminating these works in Europe,[39] after the 1882 performance of the *Liebeslieder* the couple's US recitals featured fewer songs by this composer. Although their recitals were prominent features of Boston's musical season, Henschel's work with the orchestra was far more important and taxing. He was thirty when he accepted the position, and he had little experience as a conductor. The pressure to present high-quality orchestral works and performances, and to instill discipline in the players, possibly placed limits on how much new repertoire the couple could add to their recitals. Moreover, although he stayed informed of the publication of new songs by Brahms, he may have been reluctant to program them. He had received mixed responses to his performances of Brahms's songs during his first US recitals and was aware of more recent critiques of the composer's orchestral music.[40]

By the end of 1883 the Henschels had created a standardized format for their programs, and, unlike most of their previous recitals, it did not include instrumental numbers. Some American recitalists followed this practice, but many Europeans during the 1880s and 1890s continued to employ instrumental numbers to contrast with the songs. Most of the Henschels' programs featured a wider variety of styles and languages than did their initial New York recitals. Such programs were likely intended to appeal to audiences and critics opposed to hearing only German repertoire, and also to avoid charges of monotony. Henschel was not alone in considering the importance of variety on a program. That possibility permeated reviews in Europe as well as the United States, and even in the early 1890s Eduard Hanslick, one of Vienna's most influential critics, suggested that the inclusion of an aria might address concerns of monotony.[41]

Figure 3.1 provides two programs from 1884 that give a sense of the ways the Henschels varied the repertoire of their recitals while maintaining the same overall structure.[42] Most of their programs included about twenty-one numbers, with duets punctuating the beginning, middle, and end. Critics frequently reported audiences' enthusiastic responses to the duets, and they praised the blending of the two voices.[43] The couple often triumphantly concluded recitals with the coloratura duet from Donizetti's *Don Pasquale* (1843), "Pronta io son purch'io non manchi." While most critics and audiences warmly responded to this number, Frederick Gleason (in Chicago) observed that this style tended to reveal the weaknesses of the two voices compared to those of first-class opera singers and that Henschel's pronunciation of Italian was not the best.[44]

The couple reprised many of the works on the programs shown in figure 3.1. They seemed to have viewed the Chicago program, which included fewer lieder than the Boston one, as appropriate for audiences less experienced with lieder than those in Boston, because they gave very similar ones in numerous other locales.[45] The Boston program is somewhat unusual because it includes so many lieder from Schubert's cycles. In contrast, the couple's subsequent programs usually included lieder by a greater variety of composers.[46] Whereas the more upbeat songs from *Die schöne Müllerin* were enjoyed by at least one critic and the audience,[47] even in Boston the somber songs of *Winterreise* evoked little appreciation. Nevertheless, the critic from the *Boston Evening Transcript* was pleased by these songs. He noted that singers were passing over Schubert and performing songs by Schumann and Franz, and when they did sing Schubert they selected his "trivial" numbers, as opposed to those on the program, which the critic viewed

Chicago

Duet from *Giannina e Bernardone* Mr. and Mrs. Henschel	Cimarosa
Sacred Song "Wait Thou Still"	J. W. Frank (1630)
Vittoria	Carissimi
Creation's Hymn	Beethoven
"Air," *Jean de Paris* Mr. Henschel	Boieldieu
"Lusinghe più care," *Alessandro*	Handel
Canzonetta "Nina"	[attributed to] Pergolesi
Rheinisches Volkslied Mrs. Henschel	Mendelssohn
Duet: Gondoliera (Ms.) Mr. and Mrs. Henschel	Henschel
Two "Müllerlieder" [i.e. *Die schöne Müllerin*]	Schubert
Der Asra	Rubinstein
Air from *Le Roi de Lahore* Mr. Henschel	Massenet
Lullaby	Weber
Four Lieder im Volkston Mrs. Henschel	Henschel
Duetto from *Les Voitures Versées* Mr. and Mrs. Henschel	Boieldieu

Boston

Two duets –Pamina and Papageno's Duet from *Die Zauberflöte* Mr. and Mrs. Henschel	Mozart
"Là ci darem," *Don Giovanni*	
Six songs from *Die schöne Müllerin*	Schubert
Wandering	
Whither?	
Acknowledgment to the Brook	
The Inquirer	
Pause	
Jealousy and Pride Mr. Henschel	
Airs. "Ô malheureuse Iphigénie," *Iphigénie en Tauride*	Gluck
"Amor commanda," *Floridante*	Handel
"Non sò più," *Le nozze di Figaro* Mrs. Henschel	Mozart
Duet: from *Le nouveau seigneur de village* Mr. and Mrs. Henschel	Boieldieu
Five songs—from *Winterreise*	Schubert
The Linden Tree	
The Raven	
Last Hope	
The Wayside Inn	
The Organ Grinder Mr. Henschel	
Song: L'abeille	Widor
"Comment, disaient-ils"	Liszt
"Non, je ne veux pas chanter" Mrs. Henschel	Isouard
Duet: Gondoliera (Ms.) Mr. and Mrs. Henschel	Henschel

FIG. 3.1. Representative "vocal recitals" by the Henschels in 1884. Recital on Monday, May 5, 1884, at 8:15 p.m. in Hershey Hall, Chicago. Advertisement housed in Frederic Grant Gleason Collection of Music Scrapbooks, Box 32, vol. 2, p. 132, Newberry Library, Chicago. Recital at Boston's Meionaon Hall, Tuesday, February 5, 1884, 3 p.m. "Mr. and Mrs. Henschel's Recitals," *Boston Evening Transcript*, February 6, 1884, [1].

as representing Schubert's "truest greatness."[48] This is one of the few published indications that listeners discerned different types of lieder and that audiences and singers were sometimes deterred by the more introspective ones.

Whereas George typically performed a selection of lieder during the second half of a program, Lillian's selections were often more varied, including French, Italian, or English numbers. In general, she gave a few lighter songs such as her husband's songs in folk style. Sometimes her songs were labeled as Old French or Old Scottish, but she rarely presented the types of popular folksongs such as "Comin' thro' the Rye" and "Within a Mile of Edinboro'" that other stars, including Adelina Patti, routinely programmed. The placement of these numbers on the second half of the program is similar to many of George's Boston Symphony Orchestra programs, which placed short, lighter numbers such as piano solos or lieder in the second half. But whatever the merits of her songs, Mrs. Henschel was appreciated by audiences, and at times, as in her performance of her husband's "To My Turtle Dove" in New York in 1884, audiences called for encores.[49]

As Henschel's tenure with the orchestra was concluding in the spring of 1884, the couple gave their regular series of recitals in Boston and undertook a farewell tour, presenting recitals in Buffalo, Chicago, and Cincinnati, as well as three in New York. The editors of Boston's *Musical Herald*, while reminding readers of the great service Kreissmann had performed in introducing Boston to lieder (and having done so with little remuneration), saluted Henschel for his efforts in elevating the city's taste in vocal music.[50] On returning to Europe, the couple established a tradition of giving an annual recital series in London. They had already presented two recitals in that city's Prince's Hall in 1883, and although these events did not attract a great deal of attention, they were more positively reviewed than Henschel's recitals in 1877 and 1878. Critics praised the educational aspect of programs exhibiting so many styles, and their descriptors of rare and "quite a curiosity" confirm that few singers in England had begun to give these types of vocal recitals.[51] They also indicated that the absence of instrumental solos was a further novelty. Although the couple's subsequent recitals were greeted with greater enthusiasm, during the late 1880s and early 1890s singers in England did not adopt song recitals comprised of art songs with the same zeal as did those in Boston.

Critical Reception

From their earliest performances in the United States to their last appearances in 1901, critics extolled the Henschels' performances in the most glowing terms. Reviews of the couple's first recitals proffered praise for specific aspects of Henschel's voice, and to a lesser extent that of Lillian, but later ones offered less technical information. The prevailing attitude was that the degree of perfection exhibited by the couple was so well known that accolades did not need to be reiterated.

The characteristics of George's performances that US critics lauded were also important elements in European performances by instrumentalists such as Brahms, Clara Schumann, and Joseph Joachim. These artists were important representatives of the *Werktreue* tradition of performance, in which performers were perceived as staying faithful to a composer's score rather than presenting idiomatic interpretations and unnecessary virtuosic displays.[52] Tropes of *Werktreue* and the observation that Henschel's performances were models for students were already present in a review of his fourth New York recital in the 1880–1881 season:

> His voice may not be wholly sympathetic, and it may be possible to pick flaws in his style, but one cannot help admiring the thoroughly musician-like and finished character of his work, nor refrain from honoring him for his honesty of purpose and entire self-subordination. Apart from the mere pleasure that his singing has given, he has rendered a real service in showing our singers with what simplicity and directness song music should be sung—a lesson of which most of them stood badly in need.[53]

In other reviews, ideas of honesty and simplicity were termed the "purity of his method."[54] This approach was associated with "the severe, almost classical school,"[55] in which performers placed "interpretation before all personal display."[56] Another *Werktreue* characteristic that was repeatedly praised concerned performances in which Henschel so perfectly captured a composer's meaning that he seemed "as much at ease in the songs as though he had composed them himself."[57] Although *Werktreue* musicians were venerated for performances that were perceived as adhering to the scores, Henschel, like his colleagues, freely altered rhythms and introduced rubato, vibrato, and portamento for expressive purposes. Like Stockhausen and Amalie Joachim, who were also associated with Brahms and adhered to *Werktreue* principles, Henschel avoided overly theatrical gestures. The Schumanns likewise preferred lied singers who were not as theatrical as opera performers, but nevertheless some lieder, particularly dramatic ones, require singers to draw on the types of techniques employed in opera, though it was expected that they be used with greater subtlety.[58]

Many of the early reviews noted flaws in Henschel's voice but concluded that the praiseworthy aspects of his performances more than compensated for these. The *New York Tribune* published one of the most detailed enumerations of Henschel's faults, including a lack of a clean attack of notes and a nasal or choking sound.[59] In contrast, others praised his enunciation, phrasing, and control, as well as his voice's power, great compass (at both ends of his range), and the consistency of color across the range. After one of his first chamber music concerts in Boston, where he sang Handel's "Revenge, Timotheus Cries" (from *Alexander's Feast*, 1736) and Schumann's "Die beiden Grenadiere," a reviewer enthused: "He sings in a free, manly style, with no affectation or manner."[60]

Descriptors such as "manly" and "virile" appeared in other reviews of Henschel's performances as well as in those concerning other baritones, including Franz Remmertz, Max Heinrich, and David Bispham. References to virility were more common in reviews of concert singers than in those of opera singers. Such descriptions were likely employed as a way of negating the feminine connotations that were often associated with music in general, and with song recitals in particular.[61] In 1884 the San Francisco *Argonaut* claimed that female singers were better suited to recitals than were men. This perception became so well established in the late nineteenth-century American mindset that it would be repeatedly satirized in the press.[62] In contrast, the *Argonaut*'s conceit that this type of recital posed challenges to men was somewhat unusual:

> The experiment [of giving song recitals] has been less hazardous in feminine hands, however, than it would necessarily prove under masculine auspices. To please, in what is at its best a monotonous undertaking, the singers' most telling qualities must be maintained throughout, while their style and expression are constantly varied; and the latter part of this arduous task certainly falls with far heavier weight upon a man than upon a woman. She is helped out in a thousand little ways by the charm of her dress, and her inborn gift of histrionic power.[63]

In contrast to descriptions of George that invoked masculinity, accounts of his wife's performances employed terms portraying her as a model of gentility. For instance, an 1880 reviewer in the *New York Tribune* noted effusively that her singing was "kind, graceful, dainty, delicate, refined and full of sentiment and tenderness."[64] The word "sweet" occurred in so many reviews of her performances that in 1882 we read, "It is rumored that the phrase 'Mrs. Henschel sang with much sweetness' is 'kept standing' on the galleys of various newspaper offices."[65] There were, however, other observations that were more insightful, and, in particular, her performances of Liszt's "Die Lorelei" (S. 273) were often praised for their intensity and drama.[66] In general, her musicianship, exquisite phrasing, and delivery of the text were viewed as highly commendable.

Mrs. Henschel's repertoire of lighter numbers, some of which were described as "delicate" or "tender," might have contributed to the critics' gendered responses, and the occasions on which George showed gallantry or deference to his wife might have done likewise. Yet there was an additional way in which the couple contributed to this gender differentiation. Frequently Mrs. Henschel performed songs with a female narrative voice or ones that portrayed women in socially condoned ways. In particular, her performances of Weber's "Lullaby,"

84   CHAPTER 3

a number from *Oberon* (1826) that was also known under the title "Softly Now the Light of Day," was often greeted with calls for an encore. (This song was well known in the United States, where a variety of different arrangements and transcriptions circulated.) Whereas other women recitalists in the United States and Europe, including Amalie Joachim and Gertrude Franklin (ca. 1858–1913), sang settings of texts with a male narrative voice such as Beethoven's *An die ferne Geliebte*, Mrs. Henschel did not usually do so. Similarly, although men whose singing careers preceded or followed Henschel's, including Max Heinrich, performed lieder employing a female narrative voice, Henschel did not. Ultimately, during much of the twentieth century, the Henschels' practice became the norm.

In addition to his singing, Henschel's piano playing was consistently praised for its beauty, expressiveness, and perceived freedom, and as such as a model for other accompanists.[67] Only a small number of reviews, however, called their readers' attention to the piano's role in illustrating specific ideas in the songs' texts, such as the mill wheel in Schubert's "Wohin?" (D. 795, no. 2) or, more perceptively, "the psychological aspects of the subject" in Loewe's ballads.[68] Similarly, Howard Malcom Ticknor (1836–1905) was one of the very few critics who reported on Henschel's transitions: "The musical ear was again delighted by the art of his modulations from the key of one song to that of the next in sequence."[69] Such playing was perceived as improvising, though given how often Henschel performed the same songs, after a time such passages were no doubt well honed. Similar preludes were performed by other artists in Europe, though because of their ephemeral nature this aspect of lieder performances cannot be systematically studied.[70]

The 1887–1901 American Tours

From 1887 to 1901 the Henschels regularly returned to the United States. Whereas song recitals had been a novelty when the couple presented their first series in 1880–1881, during these later years recitals proliferated. In the spring of 1887 in Boston, for instance, there were recitals by the Henschels, Max Heinrich, and Anton Schott (1846–1913), a heldentenor who also gave recitals in Europe, as well as by a number of well-known local singers. Subsequently other cities witnessed a similar profusion of recitals. That the Henschels continued to return to the United States at the height of the concert season and that they filled large venues in major cities is a testament to the quality of their performances and programs (and perhaps also to savvy management). Most of these tours were scheduled during the first half of the year, usually March to May. Some also included performances of solo roles in oratorios, as at the Springfield festival in 1892, while others included solos during orchestral or chamber concerts. In Boston the couple usually presented a series of recitals, but the numbers of recitals in other cities fluctuated, not only from city to city but also from one year to another. An 1897 recital in Boston's Steinert Hall was particularly unusual because it was billed as "Mrs. Henschel's Recital." Although this is one of the few US recitals for which she is listed in this manner, Lillian headlined a few collaborative recitals in England. This matinee, which might have been designed to attract her women friends and admirers, did not significantly differ from the couple's joint recitals: She gave many of the same songs, and her husband accompanied her.[71] The number of cities where the couple appeared fluctuated. The tours in 1887, 1889, and 1896 primarily included major East Coast cities where the couple had performed before, though in 1889 they also performed during a Boston Symphony Orchestra concert in Chicago. The 1896 tour centered on the US premiere of George's Stabat Mater op. 53 (1894), when he led the Oratorio Society of New York with Lillian and Marguerite Hall (1862–1925), one of his former students, among the soloists. In contrast, the 1892 tour was the most extensive to date, including at least forty recitals in fifteen cities on the East Coast and in the Midwest.[72] The 1897–1898 and 1901 tours were even more extensive, with the former including their first performances in California and the latter their first time in Washington State. All of the tours were organized by well-known agents, with the 1897–1898 one being managed by Henry Wolfsohn (d. 1909), who also represented other stars including the singer Lillian Blauvelt (1873–1947) and the pianists Fannie Bloomfield Zeisler (1863–1927) and Moriz Rosenthal (1862–1946).

During their tours, reviewers, in particular those in Boston, treated the Henschels as old friends.[73] It was therefore appropriate that one of the couple's last appearances on an American stage was during the debut recital of their daughter Helen (1882–1973) in Boston. In 1901 Helen's performances in the homes of Boston women and before a women's club (where she accompanied herself) led to requests for a public recital. On March 30 she made her official debut in Association Hall. This recital was a family affair, with George accompanying the two duets sung by his wife and daughter, and family friends Foote and B. J. Lang playing a piano duet.[74] Precisely twenty-five years earlier Foote had been part of the concert during which Helen's mother made her Boston debut. In the 1901 event Helen gave lieder, "Old French songs," Foote's well-known "Land o' the Leal," and one of her father's parlor songs, "Sing Heigho." This last song had been published in the United States and England in 1880, her mother often performed it, and it was among the songs by Henschel that were programmed by members of women's clubs. The day after Helen's performance, her father's Stabat Mater was performed by the Cecilia Society with her mother singing one of the leading roles. This concert, in Symphony Hall, also featured Henschel's "Morning Hymn," arranged for chorus and orchestra (op. 46, no. 4) and his *Serbisches Liederspiel*, during which he accompanied the singers. It formed the capstone of the Henschels' US careers and demonstrated George's multi-pronged approach to music making and revenue streams in the country. He sang, conducted, and played the piano, and some of his large-scale works, art songs, and short parlor songs were performed. Furthermore, his influence as a teacher was reinforced by performances by two of his students, Charles W. Clark of Illinois (ca. 1866–1925) and Leo Liebermann (1888–1972) of New York.

The Henschels returned to England in May 1901. The following November, the musical world was shocked to learn of Mrs. Henschel's sudden death. George stopped singing in public for almost ten years, but he continued to visit the United States. In 1902–1903 he was in the country when Helen was on her first American concert tour. During this trip, his Requiem, which was inspired by his wife, was given by the Cecilia Society in Boston, with Helen performing the soprano solo, and he taught at the New England Conservatory.[75] Henschel returned in November 1904 to teach at the New York College of Music and to promote his recollections of Brahms in lectures at various clubs and universities in the East.[76] The pecuniary aspect of his tours is also demonstrated by his 1905 tour, during which he conducted a few numbers during a concert of the Boston Symphony Orchestra and Church issued his album *Fifty Songs*, which consisted mainly of works in English, but also a few in German and French. This year marked the start of his affiliation with New York's new Institute of Musical Art, where he taught for a few months of each year through 1907. In that year Henschel married one of his students at this school, the singer Amy Louis (1873–1956).[77] In England, he resumed his career as a lieder recitalist in 1909. He also sang on radio broadcasts from 1928 to 1930 and made a number of recordings of lieder, including some of those by Schubert, Schumann, and Loewe that he had performed in the United States.[78] In 1931, during his last visit to the United States, at age eighty-one, he conducted the opening concert of the Boston Symphony Orchestra's fiftieth season.

Beginning with their first recital series in 1880–1881, the Henschels presented both daytime and evening performances. Although reviews did not provide demographic information about the audiences, it is highly likely that those for daytime concerts were dominated by women, as was the case with matinee symphony concerts and Werrenrath's Brooklyn recitals. Some of the couple's recitals were hosted by women's music clubs, but the number of such appearances cannot be ascertained because some club events were not open to the public and were not reported in the press. This was particularly the case with clubs during the 1880s, when most had not established a public visiting artist series. Although the Henschels likely performed before women's clubs in New England and New York during this decade, their first widely advertised public recital to be hosted by a club was in 1892 for the Amateur Musical Club of Chicago, one of the most influential women's clubs in the country. This club's visiting artist series had already hosted concerts by the American violinist Maud Powell (1867–1920), instrumentalists who were internationally applauded such as Moriz Rosenthal and Fritz Kreisler (1875–1962), and widely admired singers including Marguerite Hall and Max Heinrich.[79] The Henschels' recital took place in a larger venue than those used for the other vocalists in the club's series: Central Music Hall, which seated about two thousand. In the following years the couple performed for numerous other clubs, including the Tuesday Musicale (Rochester, New York), the Tuesday Afternoon Club (Akron, Ohio), and the Schubert Club (St. Paul, Minnesota). That Henschel was positively received by club women is evidenced by members' performances of songs and duets by him, some of which took place in clubs, like the Philharmonic Society (Nashville) that the couple did not visit.[80]

Throughout their tours, the Henschels' audiences consisted of two groups: members of society and educated music lovers, including students and professionals. A promotional piece in 1889 was skeptical of the motivations of the social set, asserting that some of the "society people" among the Henschels' New York and Boston audiences "know that it is the correct thing to go whether they are much for music or not."[81] Reports of musically educated audiences appeared in numerous papers, and it was not only locally known musicians or students who attended. In Chicago in 1896, for instance, audience members included the internationally renowned singers Maria Brema (1856–1925) and Henry Plunket Greene (1865–1936), both of whom were on tour with their own highly successful recitals.[82] Whereas a Boston paper in the early 1880s commented that the recitals were attended by "fine audiences which are attracted only by something exceedingly *recherché*,"[83] during the 1890s an increasing number of press notices claimed the recitals could be enjoyed by all.

Although ticket prices ensured that audience members were almost certainly restricted to the middle and upper classes, an 1897 report of a San Francisco recital implied the Henschels had broad appeal. "They are artists in miniature, artists who have developed boudoir musical talents to a point of delicacy and distinction that is simply phenomenal. They rob the concert stage of that pompous gloom, which, perhaps more than anything else, stands between it and a popularity such as is given to the theater. The most laic listener in California last night could not but have taken comfort from the fragrant atmosphere that surrounded these artists in their work."[84] Descriptions of the couple's charming, unassuming personalities and repartee with each other, stages sometimes decorated like drawing rooms, and Henschel's seemingly improvised piano preludes all likely contributed to the projection of ease and informality.[85]

This staged intimacy, however, belied the couple's highly structured approach to concertgiving. In addition to their systematically organized programs, their performances were so well honed that the expressive nuances in the recordings that Henschel made of Schubert's "Der Leiermann" (D. 911, no. 24) in 1914 and 1928 are remarkably uniform.[86] The perceived ease of the couple's performances likewise concealed their studied craft. One critic perceptively hinted at this dichotomy of unaffected performances and the labor required to create such technical perfection, writing that Mrs. Henschel's training and "exquisite taste" resulted in singing that "seems to be the spontaneous creation of nature rather than the ultimate product of a studied art."[87] More broadly, although the appearance of informality and the drawing room façades might be interpreted as contradicting Levine's concept of the development of a sacralized concert hall, this was not the case. The couple's repertoire, George's occasional impatience with loud or late audience members, and his *Werktreue* approach to performance make clear that their performances aligned with the establishment of the high art that Dwight and his colleagues in the 1850s and 1860s advocated.[88] Moreover, the reverence that most audiences accorded the Henschels, as well as to performances by Amalie Joachim and Lilli Lehmann in Europe, indicate that many recitals at the end of the century likewise adhered to Levine's theories.[89]

The Tour Programs

The programs for the couple's tours followed the model they had established in 1883–1884 (as shown in figure 3.1). In general, US recital programs comprising numbers sung in German, French, Italian, and English were increasingly common during the 1890s. The inclusion of songs sung in English was important: Reviewers sometimes complained when programs did not include such numbers, and in other instances they reported the audience preferred the numbers performed in English.[90]

The Henschels produced program booklets for most recitals, but these accomplished little in the way of educating audiences. The booklets, which usually featured a headshot of the couple (figure 3.2), contained the program and translations of the texts, as well as the lyrics of the English-language songs. Unlike some of the "Books of Words" that they produced in England, the programs usually did not include the original texts of the songs.[91] Background information about the composers or the songs was not provided, either. Critics occasionally praised these pamphlets (which were somewhat unusual in the 1880s, but common in the 1890s), but, as with programs by earlier artists, the names of the poet or the librettist and those of the translators were not always given. Moreover, despite the translations, some audience members were likely not able to grasp the subtleties of lieder. In reviewing Henschel's 1881 recital in Chicago, Gleason observed that an audience appreciated the "swing" of Rubinstein's "Der Asra" but seemed not to appreciate the "sentiment and musical treatment" of Brahms's "Minnelied" (op. 71, no. 5) and "Unüberwindlich" (op. 72, no. 5).[92] The Henschels'

FIG. 3.2. Illustration on the title page of the program booklet for the Henschels' third recital at Meionaon Hall, Boston, 1892. Courtesy of the Boston Symphony Orchestra Archives.

seeming failure to improve their audience's understanding of individual songs or of the genre of the lied in general is not only disappointing, it also speaks to an elitist attitude that is somewhat at odds with the views of commentators who suggested that their events were educational.

Throughout their American tours the couple tended to favor lieder by Schubert and Schumann, but they also regularly performed ones by Brahms, Dvořák, Franz, Grieg, Jensen, Liszt, Loewe, and Rubinstein. Henschel, like many other recitalists, did not always program Loewe's ballads, but his dramatic renditions of these works, and in particular, of Loewe's version of "Erlkönig" (op. 1, no. 3), frequently earned the critics' praise.[93] The couple occasionally programmed lieder by Mendelssohn, but they kept to well-known ones such as the ubiquitous "Auf Flügeln des Gesanges." Although Wagner's lieder were performed by other recitalists, the programs that have been located suggest that Henschel did not sing them, though he occasionally gave well-known excerpts from this composer's operas, including *Tannhäuser*.[94] The couple also ignored lieder by later German composers such as Hugo Wolf and Richard Strauss. In general, they presented repertoire that other singers were also programming and frequently repeated songs they had given during their Boston sojourn. They added a few recently composed songs by Dvořák and Brahms to their later programs, however, and in particular Lillian added songs by Brahms such as "Das Mädchen spricht" (op. 107, no. 3) that are characterized by a female narrative voice.

During the 1890s Lillian's repertoire expanded more than that of her husband. This is perhaps understandable in that George had a multifaceted career that encompassed conducting, composing, and teaching in addition to the couple's recitals. Many of the songs that Lillian added in the 1890s were not lieder, but rather French songs by Chaminade, Gabriel Fauré (1845–1924), César Franck (1822–1890), and Ambroise Thomas (1811–1896). Some of these songs might well have been included in recognition of their growing popularity. This was likely the case with "L'été" (1894) and "Si j'étais jardinier" (1893) by Chaminade, a composer whose songs and piano works were performed by amateur and professional singers throughout the country and were particularly appealing to women audiences and music makers. Indeed, she had a very strong following among members of women's clubs.[95]

The French songs that Mrs. Henschel added to her repertoire did not, however, reflect the wealth of new songs being performed by Americans. The development of the French romance and *mélodie* and the significant increase in Boston musicians' interest in this repertoire are demonstrated by Gertrude Franklin's recital of French songs in 1890. Franklin had studied with de La Grange in Paris sometime prior to 1881. Some of the songs on her program were being performed by numerous other Americans; they included Léo Delibes's (1836–1891) "Regrets" and the Bolero from *Coppélia* (1870), Édouard Lalo's (1823–1892) "L'esclave," and Massenet's "Enchantement" (a newly published rendition of a song from *Hérodiade*, 1881, rev. 1883–84). Franklin also performed a song by Francis Thomé (1850–1909), a Creole pianist and composer who was the son-in-law of de La Grange and also a student of Ambroise Thomas. An earlier performance of three of his songs by a member of Cleveland's Fortnightly Musical Club indicates that, although these works were not being widely programmed on public recitals, they were already in circulation by the time of Franklin's recital.[96] In contrast, other composers on the program were scarcely known. Reynaldo Hahn (1875–1947), a pupil of Massenet and Gounod, specialized in *mélodie* and was a popular salon singer in Paris, but at the time of Franklin's recital, his career was just beginning to blossom. By the end of the century, however, Hahn's songs were sung throughout the country, and the two on Franklin's program, "Si mes vers avaient des ailes" and "Rêverie," were among those that circulated in sheet music. Both of Franklin's 1890 recitals also included songs by Augusta Holmès (1847–1903), whose career was followed by US newspapers and whose songs were taken up by other recitalists and members of numerous women's music clubs.[97]

Other than a few numbers by Arthur Goring Thomas (1850–1892) and traditional songs from the British Isles, George Henschel's songs accounted for most of the couple's English-language repertoire. Unlike other recitalists, they seldom programmed songs by Americans. This is particularly surprising given that Mrs. Henschel had worked with Foote before her marriage, and her performance of Foote's "Go, Lovely Rose" is cited in an advertisement of the score.[98] Furthermore, the couple socialized with numerous American song composers, including Clara Doria (who now went by her married name of Rogers), during their stays in Boston, and, when in England, Henschel occasionally conducted instrumental works by Americans. Works by women composers were regularly performed in Boston recitals, and songs by the likes of Margaret Ruthven Lang (1867–1972) and Amy Beach were performed by members of women's clubs across the country. Not only did the Henschels ignore this trend, the only European woman whose songs they occasionally programmed was Chaminade, and only Lillian sang her songs.

Henschel's American Legacy

In November 1880, before his first American recital, the Boston *Musical Record and Review* reprinted a description of Henschel's artistry. Although it was based on the baritone's appearances in Europe, it resonates with the reviews of his US performances. "[Henschel] seems to have made it his mission to bring good music to the nearer knowledge of the public. . . . To listen to him is like taking a lesson because it is to listen to musicianship of the first order."[99] Comments like this, and the numerous reviews that praised the Henschels for presenting many "artistic pearls,"[100] demonstrate that George's performances paralleled the efforts of Thomas and his network to elevate American concert programs and inform audiences. When he arrived in the United States Henschel benefited from the efforts of earlier musicians to develop audiences for lieder and song recitals. In contrast, in the United Kingdom, the couple "were the single greatest force in introducing art song and the song recital in the nineteenth century."[101] While the Henschels were not the first advocates of the lied in the United States,

92   CHAPTER 3

Henschel's European reputation enabled the couple to reach larger audiences than had the earlier lied singers. In this way, their success opened the way for other singers to cultivate the field of "intelligent and artistic song recitals."[102] An important factor in the couple's success, however, was their recognition that Americans preferred a blend of songs in contrasting styles and languages and that including a few numbers in a lighter vein was a near necessity.

Students of both singing and accompanying were often exhorted to attend the Henschels' recitals, and a reporter from Oakland claimed that the "manner" of local singers showed immediate improvement after the couple's 1897 recital in that city.[103] Henschel taught in a number of cities during his American concert tours and, after Lillian's death, taught in Boston and New York. But the extent of this activity is impossible to measure, in part because of the dearth of documentation. The press notices that cite Henschel as the teacher of specific American singers usually do not state whether the lessons occurred in the United States or in England, nor how long a given singer studied with him. For instance, notices indicate that Grace Hiltz and Medora Henson (ca. 1862–1928) studied with Henschel during his tenure with the Boston Symphony Orchestra, but given the performance schedules of both women, it is likely that the period of tuition was quite brief, perhaps only a few months. When the Henschels returned to London in 1884 numerous Americans followed them. Some students, such as Clark in Chicago, achieved regional prominence as concert singers but then turned to teaching, and in all likelihood passed on concepts they learned from Henschel to a new generation of American singers.

Henschel was venerated as a coach who specialized in the interpretation of songs and oratorios, and singers such as the famed African American tenor Roland Hayes (1887–1977) and the Irish tenor John McCormack (1884–1945) sought him out when studying the art of interpreting lieder.[104] Similarly, one of the few publications that mentions Henschel's approach to teaching briefly indicates that most of his students learned basic techniques from other pedagogues. Ironically, Henschel's few pedagogical publications mention only one or two lieder, instead focusing on vocal techniques and sound production.[105] They do not discuss the type of expressive rhythmic and tempo alterations that characterize his recordings.

Despite the Henschels' success in the United States, the limitations of their work should not be ignored. During his first series of recitals, George risked alienating audiences by promoting unfamiliar works, specifically complex lieder by Brahms. In contrast, in the following years the couple was not so adventurous, programming mainly works they had successfully presented on previous occasions or that other singers had introduced. Despite the accolades they received for the educational aspects of their programs and performances, the couple seems to have made little effort to educate general audiences about the historical or cultural significance of lieder and made only limited attempts to explain the depth of meaning of individual lieder. That there was a mercenary angle to their tours was noted by Florence French in 1901, though, to be sure, her rhetoric was judged to be unduly harsh.[106] Americans such as Gertrude Franklin, Heinrich, and Bispham needed to experiment with programming as a way of distinguishing themselves in what became a packed field of song recitals, and also to address increasing critiques of German repertoire and the proliferation of new songs by American composers. In contrast, the Henschels had so successfully established their brand that they could make a profit without responding to competitors or cultural changes.

* * *

Through their exquisite musicianship, the Henschels raised the standard of concert singing in the United States, just as they raised the standard of lieder singing in England.[107] While George's influence as a teacher continued into the twentieth century, the influence of the couple's recitals was strongest during the 1880s, when they contributed to solidifying the song recital as a concert genre and to establishing programs featuring lieder but also surveying historical repertoire and repertoire in contrasting languages and styles.

4

Max Heinrich's "Classical Song Recitals"

From the late 1880s through the 1890s Max Heinrich drew acclaim for song recitals where audiences listened "with bated breath" as he transformed "the simplest ballad into a classic by his exquisite art."[1] According to one tribute, "his whole life he worked ardently to spread the gospel of the German lied. He was a *Liedersinger* by divine right."[2] But when Heinrich arrived in the United States at the age of twenty, success was far from assured. He spent his early years in Philadelphia's German immigrant community, eking out a living as a piano teacher and freelance singer. After a successful audition with Leopold Damrosch, Heinrich rose to fame performing baritone solo roles in oratorios. Beginning in 1884 he parlayed this fame into promoting "Classical Song Recitals" comprised almost entirely of lieder. He initiated these before song recitals were fashionable, and contemporaries lauded his efforts to introduce lieder to American audiences.[3]

Although his recitals frequently included more lieder than Henschel's did, Heinrich modeled himself on Henschel.[4] Both men performed from memory, their recitals often incorporated a woman singer, and they accompanied themselves and their collaborator. But other lieder singers, including Franz Remmertz and George Werrenrath, also influenced Heinrich. He collaborated with these men when performing solo roles in oratorios and concerts conducted by Damrosch and Theodore Thomas. Through these singers and conductors, Heinrich, like Henschel and other German immigrants before him, became affiliated with the network of musicians who subscribed to the ethos of cultural uplift and who established lieder as part of American concert life, and his recitals and advocacy of the lied fully aligned with their efforts.

Sudden Fame

Heinrich was born in Chemnitz, Saxony, on June 14, 1853. In 1865, after serving as a choirboy, he began a period of study with Karl Emanuel Klitzsch (1812–1889), a composer, organist, and associate of Schumann's in Zwickau. From 1869 he studied opera at the Dresden Conservatory.[5] He left Germany at the age of twenty to escape military service, arriving in the United States on July 23, 1873. He initially settled in Philadelphia, where he married Anna (Annie) Schubert on December 31, 1874. Schubert came from a family of German immigrant musicians, and from 1872, after the death of her parents and uncle, she supported her five siblings by giving voice, guitar, and piano lessons.[6] By 1887 the couple had seven children: Julia, Carl, Edith, Frances, Annette, Florence, and Emil August. James Huneker (1860–1921) was befriended by Heinrich during these early years. Subsequently, he recalled the Heinrich household as noisy and chaotic, and he vividly portrayed Heinrich's unbridled personality and some of his escapades.[7]

Heinrich earned a living teaching piano and singing in German beer halls and local houses of worship, including Rodeph Shalom Synagogue on Broad Street, where Annie also sang. He occasionally sang in local operas and oratorios, as well as in local *Männerchor* concerts and chamber soirées organized by Charles H. Jarvis (1837–1895). (Jarvis, like the German instrumentalists in Boston, was known for promoting serious chamber repertoire.) From 1877 Heinrich worked as a piano teacher at the Judson Institute, a women's college in Marion, Alabama, where his wife also taught. He continued to make appearances in Philadelphia, however, and the family returned to that city sometime around 1881 or 1882. Heinrich resumed his former teaching and performing, but as he would later recall, opportunities to sing in chamber concerts were infrequent and not well paid.[8] Popular arias and songs by Abt, Lortzing, Marschner, Mendelssohn, Mozart, and Weber dominated his repertoire through 1882. In addition, he occasionally sang such well-known lieder as Schumann's "Du Ring an meinem Finger," "Frühlingsnacht," and "Ich grolle nicht," as well as songs by Schubert. The few brief reviews of these early appearances praised Heinrich's artistry and dramatic expression.[9]

In order to improve his financial situation, Heinrich sought an audience with Damrosch in New York. Based in part on his sight-singing abilities, Damrosch immediately hired him as a soloist in oratorios and orchestral concerts.[10] Heinrich's March 1883 performance of the title role in Mendelssohn's *Elijah* was extolled by numerous reviewers: "His singing of the famous prayer, 'Lord God of Abraham,' was a triumph, with such musical dignity, moving expression, and purity of voice was it uttered."[11] Reports of this performance were published as far afield as St. Louis, and almost all later biographical articles mention it. This

96   CHAPTER 4

success led Heinrich to continue performing the aria "It Is Enough" from this oratorio throughout his career. Aside from the composer's popularity and the beauty of the music, its message, with its promise of hope in the face of unbearable burdens, had near universal appeal, and numerous other artists sang it.[12] The success of his 1883 performance also led to further opportunities to perform solos in oratorios under Damrosch and Thomas as well as to Heinrich moving his family to New York. From 1883 through 1887 he sang solo roles in at least thirteen different oratorios, including the American premieres of works such as Bruch's *Achilleus* and Liszt's *Legend of Saint Elizabeth* (1857–1862).

Heinrich's national reputation was also enhanced by performances in numerous orchestral concerts, at May festivals, and at national *Saengerfeste* in locations such as Buffalo (1883) and Milwaukee (1886). At these events he appeared on stage with the likes of Lilli Lehmann and Emma Juch, and he appeared with similarly popular stars, including Remmertz, in concerts that Thomas conducted. During the Thomas Orchestra's 1884–1885 tours, when audiences often numbered well over two thousand, he appeared in cities such as Boston, Cincinnati, Kansas City, San Francisco, and Washington, DC. But as a supporting artist, Heinrich only performed a few numbers in each concert. These included arias by Spohr and Bizet that he had been singing since his early years in Philadelphia, as well as popular excerpts from Wagner's operas such as "Song to the Evening Star" from *Tannhäuser*.[13] He also sang an orchestral version of Schumann's "Die beiden Grenadiere," which Remmertz had given during earlier performances with Thomas.

Although many of Heinrich's appearances during the early 1880s did not include lieder, they provided opportunities for him to meet more established singers such as Werrenrath and Remmertz, who were known for their lieder performances. Remmertz, who had a particularly strong following among the German immigrant population, was already an established star when Heinrich arrived on the scene. Aside from performing solo roles in oratorios and during orchestral concerts, he was a popular performer at concerts given by the Arion Society and Liederkranz in New York, where he often performed lieder. Remmertz was the preferred concert baritone, and perhaps because of his artistic and financial success in this field he did not develop song recitals or advocate for the lied in the same manner as Henschel or Heinrich.

While Remmertz's domination of the bass roles in oratorios and concerts somewhat limited Heinrich's opportunities in these fields, the success of Henschel's and Werrenrath's song recitals presented Heinrich with an alternative career path. The first evidence of direct contact between Henschel and Heinrich dates from 1883. At a Boston Symphony Orchestra concert with Henschel at the piano, Heinrich performed Schubert's "Liebesbotschaft" (D. 957, no. 1) and "Rastlose Liebe" (D. 138). His performance was so successful that one critic claimed that Heinrich had established himself as a favorite of Boston audiences and that future appearances were anticipated.[14] No documentation has come to light that indicates whether Heinrich heard Werrenrath's or Henschel's recitals, but given that these two men collaborated with the same group of musicians as did Heinrich, and that their recitals were advertised in New York papers and music journals, at the very least he would have known of them.

The Heinrich and Henson Classical Song Recitals

Following the conclusion of Henschel's contract with the Boston Symphony Orchestra and his return to Europe at the close of the 1883–1884 concert season, Heinrich positioned himself as the principal advocate for the lied. At the end of 1884 he began presenting programs focusing on this genre. He coordinated these recitals with his more financially rewarding appearances in oratorios and concerts, and while most of them were open to the public, he also presented programs in private settings.[15] His initial song recitals in Chicago, Milwaukee, Philadelphia, and New York were titled "Classical Song Recitals," perhaps to contrast with the Henschels' "Vocal Recitals" but also to emphasize the style of the repertoire. Either in the interest of keeping costs down or to follow the format of the Henschels' 1883–1884 recitals, he did not include instrumental solos and he performed all the piano accompaniments. Furthermore, also like Henschel, he collaborated with another singer. Throughout his career almost all of Heinrich's collaborators were women, and during the period 1884–1887 most of these women had also appeared with him in orchestral concerts or oratorios. Working with another singer enabled Heinrich to rest his voice, and he likely selected women in order to provide a contrasting timbre. There is no evidence to suggest that at this stage Heinrich was appealing to women concertgoers; indeed, unlike Henschel, at first he seldom scheduled matinees.

Heinrich's first partner was the soprano Medora Henson, a daughter of a well-known minister in Philadelphia, who had established herself in Chicago. In 1882 she was one of the soloists in a concert of Wolfsohn's Beethoven Society during which Henschel also performed,[16] and, subsequently, she briefly studied with him in Boston. While she appeared in chamber concerts in Chicago and surrounding cities and towns in Illinois and Wisconsin, her work with Heinrich appears to have been the first time she presented a significant number of lieder.

In 1884 Henson and Heinrich were among the soloists in a performance of *The Creation* in Milwaukee, where they were described as "prime favorites" of the locals.[17] At the start of the following concert season they gave two song recitals at the four-hundred-seat Weber Hall in Chicago and then repeated them at the Academy in Milwaukee. Despite the potential of attracting the German populations of both cities, newspaper advertisements indicate that the recitals were geared to Anglo-American audiences: The song titles printed in the Milwaukee paper were given in a mixture of German and English, and those in the Chicago papers were given in English. According to one of the Milwaukee papers, the recitals were for "lovers of pure and undefiled music," and a subsequent review concluded, "The whole recital appealed to refined musical intelligence and artistic susceptibility."[18] Comments such as these are reminiscent of descriptions of earlier performances of lieder, including the Henschels' recitals, and they again confirm that such programs were addressed to educated musicians and the upper social classes, or those aspiring to join them.

Unlike Henschel's or Werrenrath's programs, Heinrich's were devoted to Schubert and Schumann lieder. Like some of Werrenrath's, they also departed from both Henschel's and contemporary European practices in terms of the sheer number of lieder: The first recital comprised twenty-four, and the second twenty-one. Nevertheless, while reviewers acknowledged these unusual qualities, some were concerned that such programs ran the risk of monotony.

A lengthy review of the first Chicago recital took care to note the challenges of devoting an entire recital to just two composers, and those that all lieder performers faced, the interpretive demands of the genre, and the technical demands placed on both singer and pianist. That done, the reviewer criticized the performances of both Heinrich and Henson, which suggests they were yet to attain the type of polish and expressiveness that they were later known for.[19] This event seems to have been the first time Heinrich had given a public song recital, and reports of earlier lieder performances do not indicate that he accompanied himself. It is possible, therefore, that he was still mastering both the vocal lines and piano parts of some of the pieces, and this would explain why he had not memorized all the music. The descriptor "preparatory concert," which was applied to Heinrich and Henson's following recital in Philadelphia, in December 1884, further supports this theory.[20]

Expanding on their Chicago and Milwaukee programs, Henson and Heinrich presented a series titled "Classical Song Recitals" at both the Academy of Fine Arts in Philadelphia and the small concert hall of the newly opened Metropolitan Opera House on the corner of 39th Street and Broadway in New York. Tickets for these four evening recitals cost the same in both cities: one dollar per concert or three dollars for the series. This was the same price as Werrenrath's Brooklyn recitals, but lower than those of the Henschels. The *Musical Courier* printed the programs for the first two New York recitals (see figure 4.1), which align almost completely with the descriptions in newspaper reviews of the corresponding Philadelphia recitals. These reviews also suggest that the performers followed the pattern they established in their midwestern series, with Heinrich mostly singing in German and Henson in English. Press descriptions of the third and

Recital 1

Four songs from *Winterreise* — Schubert
  Gefrorne Tränen
  Das Wirtshaus
  Täuschung
  Gute Nacht
              Heinrich

Schlummerlied — Schubert
Die junge Nonne
Alinde
Suleikas zweiter Gesang
              Henson

Three songs from the *Spanish Songbook* — Jensen
  Tango vos, el mi pandero
  Ribericas del Rio
  Ventecico murmurador
              Heinrich

Aus meinen grossen Schmerzen — Franz
Im Sommer
Abends
Vergessen
              Henson

Leis' rudern hier, mein Gondolier! — Schumann
Wenn durch die Piazzetta
Gruss [Aus den östlichen Rosen]
              Heinrich

Frauenliebe und -leben
              Henson

FIG. 4.1A. The first Heinrich-Henson recital in New York, 1885. Concert Hall of the Metropolitan Opera, Saturday, January 31, at 8 p.m. "Song Recital," *Musical Courier* 10 (1885): 86.

Recital 2

Geheimes   Schubert
Der Tod und das Mädchen
Frühlingsglaube
Sehnsucht
                     Heinrich

Selections from "Songs from Wilhelm Meister"
    Kennst du das Land?
    Nur wer die Sehnsucht kennt
    Heiss mich nicht reden
                     Henson

Greisengesang
Pax vobiscum
Lied des gefangenen Jägers
                     Heinrich

Selections from Robert Burns   Schumann
[*Myrthen*, op. 25]
    Hauptmanns Weib
    Hochländisches Wiegenlied
    Wie kann ich froh und munter sein? [Weit, weit]
    Im Westen
                     Henson

Ich grolle nicht
Am leuchtenden Sommermorgen
Ich wandre nicht
                     Heinrich

Lied der Braut
Dein Angesicht
Mondnacht
Aus alten Märchen winkt es
                     Henson

Mentre ti lascio   Mozart
                     Heinrich

Aria from *La Reine de Saba*   Gounod
                     Henson

Duet from *Rose of Sharon*   A.C. Mackenzie
                Heinrich and Henson

FIG. 4.1B. The second Heinrich-Henson recital in New York, 1885.
Concert Hall of the Metropolitan Opera, Saturday, March 7, at 8 p.m.
"Song Recital," Musical Courier 10 (1885): 149.

fourth recitals indicate that they were of similar length to the first two, but they do not supply complete programs. The third New York recital was slightly curtailed because Henson was unable to sing; Heinrich, however, sang more pieces than initially planned.[21]

While the programs drew on repertoire from the Chicago and Milwaukee recitals, none of them precisely replicated the earlier programs, though Schubert and Schumann dominated (see figure 4.1). The excerpts from the former's *Winterreise* and *Schwanengesang* (which Heinrich sang during the fourth New York recital) along with the hymn-like "Pax Vobiscum" ("Peace be With You," D. 551) and Schumann's "Leis' rudern hier, mein Gondolier" and "Wenn durch die Piazzetta" (a.k.a. the Gondolier Songs, "Zwei Venetianische Lieder," op. 25, nos. 17 and 18) would form the backbone of Heinrich's recitals throughout his career. Whereas Heinrich's repertoire overlapped with Henschel's, he sang far more songs by Schumann. Although this might have been a conscious attempt to differentiate himself from Henschel, Schumann was Heinrich's favorite lied composer.[22] Unlike their programs for their first series, those for Philadelphia and New York included lieder by a range of composers. Heinrich presented selections from Jensen's op. 21 *Spanish Songbook* and Beethoven's "Adelaide," and both singers performed works by Franz. Henson also gave songs by Rubinstein, including "Du bist wie eine Blume" (op. 32, no. 5). Other professional singers were already performing many of these songs, and most were available in English-language scores. In particular, "Murmelndes Lüftchen" (op. 21, no. 4) became one of the most frequently sung of Jensen's songs in the United States, and Heinrich continued to perform it throughout his career. Overall, the repertoire of the series demonstrated Heinrich's range, encompassing dramatic ballads, introspective plaints, and lighter vignettes.

Whereas the midwestern recitals did not include any duets, in Philadelphia the two vocalists performed Rubinstein's "Der Engel" (op. 48, no. 1) and Henschel's "O That We Two Were Maying."[23] These duets were likely chosen because they were already well known to audiences. In contrast, a duet from Mackenzie's *Rose of Sharon* (1884), which they performed at least once in New York and at least twice in Philadelphia, was less familiar. Heinrich was one of the soloists in the American premiere of Mackenzie's oratorio, which the New York Chorus Society gave the day before his last New York recital.[24]

Notwithstanding the contrasting moods and styles of the songs and duets, and the contrasting timbres of Henson's and Heinrich's voices, the programs' focus on lieder placed unusual demands on audiences. In contrast, Henschel's programs offered greater variety in terms of language and genre, and his wife frequently sang a few lighter numbers. Similarly, Werrenrath frequently varied his recitals by including a few popular numbers or folksongs. Heinrich's programs also eschewed early eighteenth-century arias, including popular ones by Handel,

102   CHAPTER 4

which Hiltz and Henschel performed. Ironically, some of the songs in Heinrich's programs that were not lieder, most notably the Mackenzie duet and the aria from Gounod's *La Reine de Saba* (1862), were viewed as out of place. Moreover, Heinrich and Henson were advised that in the future they should not attempt songs in Italian or French.[25] Perhaps this deficiency in languages contributed to Heinrich's decision to continue to sing mostly lieder whereas, in later years, his contemporaries offered an increasing amount of French repertoire.

Reviews in Philadelphia and New York were generally positive; however, they contrasted in length and nuance. According to one writer the first recital in Philadelphia, which was said to have been given to a full and enthusiastic hall, resembled "the unrestraint of a private drawing room entertainment." This reviewer stressed the novel aspects of the program and the insightful interpretations of the singers, and in so doing alluded to the local audience's limited knowledge of the lied: "It must have been felt by all present that these selections, particularly from the Schubert and Schumann works, gave us new thoughts and feelings, took us farther into the inner life of these musical benefactors of the world than we have been before." Whereas Schubert's "Ständchen" ("Serenade") and "Der Wanderer" and Schumann's "Widmung" and "The Two Grenadiers" were commonly heard, the "vast multitude of lieder" by these men were little known, and thus "how much did this concert add to our knowledge!"[26] This critic appeared to be quite knowledgeable, because he observed the poor quality of the English translations that Henson sang and praised the "exquisite" piano accompaniment of Schubert's "Young Nun" (D. 828)—a dramatic lied that Henson performed with "striking effect." His few comments regarding the audience's reactions highlighted lieder that had pleased numerous preceding audiences and would continue to delight. Henson's performance of "The Ring" and "Lost Happiness" from *Frauenliebe* drew hearty applause and, anticipating reactions by later audiences, Heinrich's "so fine, so true, so tender" performance of one of Schumann's Gondolier Songs had to be repeated—the only encore for that night. Philadelphia audiences had not experienced as many performances of lieder as had those in New York, and the Henschels were yet to present one of their vocal recitals there. Therefore, Heinrich's recitals were a revelation. Such was their success that Heinrich and Henson gave at least two additional recitals in that city.[27]

The reviews in New York praised Heinrich's artistry, and like the reviews of the Henschels, they noted the recitals' educational value and observed that although neither singer had a perfect voice, both gave remarkably expressive performances that moved the audiences. Like the Milwaukee press in 1884, the *New York Tribune* referenced the elite audiences who had the knowledge to appreciate high art and lieder.[28] The *New Yorker Staats-Zeitung* had a similar description, and it concluded that because Heinrich (who had been performing lieder for German organizations in that city) was already known as an ingenious lied singer no further words were necessary. Henson's voice, however, elicited a mixed reaction: On one hand the reviewer recognized that it had been well trained, but on the other he complained of its brittle, harsh qualities, and wrote that on occasion she sang flat.[29]

The *Staats-Zeitung* critic was less than pleased with Heinrich's accompanying, suggesting that he needed to be more discreet and in the future lower the piano's lid. In contrast, the *Musical Courier* praised his accompaniments. This critic, like later writers, commended the delicacy of his touch and drew attention to the difficulty of the piano parts in Jensen's songs.[30] Nevertheless, he hypothesized that Heinrich's seated position at the piano negatively impacted his tone production.[31] Although there were a few criticisms of Heinrich's accompaniments in later recitals, this particular objection seems to have been a favored point of view of this journal because it had lobbed the same criticism at Henschel.[32]

As with the reviewers of the Henschels' recitals, the New York critics only mentioned a few songs by name. One writer briefly noted the audience's appreciation of Henson's performance of Schumann's eerie love song "Dein Angesicht" (op. 127, no. 2) and Heinrich's rendition of the well-known, dramatic "Ich grolle nicht."[33] The critics did not discuss any of the songs in depth, but, rather, one remarked on their "downright tunefulness."[34] These remarks conform with reviews of other performances that also reflect the audience's preferences for lyrical melodies, love songs, and dramatic works. In most cases, the audiences could grasp the main points of the texts of these songs without a knowledge of poetic imagery or German culture.

Despite the audiences' appreciation of the performances, a critic for the *New York Times* voiced reservations about New Yorkers' attitude toward the genre of the lied:

> It is to be regretted that these affairs should not have had more liberal encouragement than has been accorded them. They have been both pleasant and instructive, and ought to have been very numerously attended. The public of the metropolis, unhappily, is subject to crazes, and just now its leaders clamor for nothing less than trilogies, symphonies, and concertos of the most advanced pattern and bewildering influences. Like the English weakness for "dirty greens" in pictorial art, the craving of the hour is for the vast, the unfathomable, and the incomprehensible.[35]

This resistance, which was also observed in reactions to other recitals and was implied in a review of one of the Henschels' 1883 recitals, is particularly surprising given the city's large German population and its participation in many other aspects of the city's musical life.[36] But audiences preferred larger genres such as operas and symphonies, a penchant that Henry T. Finck (1854–1926),

104   CHAPTER 4

the critic at the *New York Post*, later described as "jumbomania."[37] Nevertheless, other singers began presenting song recitals, and Anton Schott gave his first American recital just five days after Heinrich's first New York series ended.

Anton Schott

A comparison between Heinrich's programs and those of Anton Schott reveals the scope of Heinrich's accomplishment. After a military career, Schott quickly rose to fame in Europe as an opera singer. He first appeared in America in 1884, performing the title role in Wagner's *Tannhäuser* under Leopold Damrosch in New York. Although he returned to Europe after Damrosch's death in 1885, he made numerous subsequent tours to the United States, appearing in operas, concerts, and song recitals. The programs for his song recitals on both continents were closer to the European model of the late 1870s than to Henschel's and Heinrich's in that there were instrumental solos during both halves of the program and fewer solo songs.[38]

In contrast to Heinrich, with his evening recitals, in 1885 Schott gave three afternoon recitals, a schedule that likely pleased his women fans, many of whom were among the growing number of women flocking to Wagner's operas. During the first he gave Beethoven's demanding *An die ferne Geliebte* (figure 4.2) and, as might be expected from an opera singer specializing in Wagner, "Siegmunds Liebeslied" from *Die Walküre*. In contrast to Heinrich, Werrenrath, and Henschel, Schott reprised songs from one recital to another within a series, and, also unlike the others, he included a few lighter, more popular German songs by Abt and Stark. His first program resembles one he had given in Leipzig in October 1883; it included the same composers as well as the Beethoven cycle and violin solos. In the program printed by Steinway Hall, the titles of the songs were given in German and English. But although Schott had argued in favor of the Metropolitan Opera Company's singing German operas in English translation,[39] he usually did not sing lieder in English during his song recitals.

All in all, Schott's programs were far less impressive than Heinrich's. In his solo recitals Heinrich performed at least eighteen lieder, and in his joint recitals, which included over two dozen works, he sang more than half the songs on the program and played all the accompaniments. The reviewers did not mention these differences, but they did voice criticisms. The *New York Times* acknowledged Schott's appeal to the audience, particularly in the performance—in English—of Lohengrin's farewell, which Schott gave during his second recital. But this reviewer also asserted that the tenor did not demonstrate the skills or subtlety necessary to be a good lied singer.[40] The *New York Herald* shared this opinion, considering Schott's performance to be monotonous and spoiled by poor intonation. The *New Yorker Staats-Zeitung* was likewise critical, conclud-

An die ferne Geliebte	Beethoven
Violin Solo, Air Varié	H. Vieuxtemps
Jeanne Franko, violin	
Die böse Farbe	Schubert
Frühlingstraum	
Ständchen (Hark, Hark! The Lark)	
Intermission	
Reiselied	Mendelssohn
Schilflied	
"Siegmunds Liebeslied," *Die Walküre*	Wagner
Violin Solos, *Albumblatt*	Sam Franko
Obertass (Mazurka)	Henryk Wieniawski
Jeanne Franko, violin	
Schöne Fremde	Schumann
Die Lotosblume	
Wanderlied	

FIG. 4.2. Anton Schott's first New York song recital, Tuesday, April 21, 1885, 3 p.m. Ferdinand Quentin Dulcken (1837–1901), piano. Steinway Hall Programs, Music Division, New York Public Library.

ing that the only impressive thing in the performance of the Beethoven was the ending. This reviewer claimed he was not influenced by Schott's behavior in seeking to gain control of the Metropolitan Opera Company while Damrosch was on his deathbed. The same could not be said of the *Herald* reviewer, who began by noting the "unpleasant impression" of Schott that this episode had created.[41]

Schott returned to the United States at the start of 1887, when, in addition to appearing at the Metropolitan Opera, he gave recitals in New York, Boston, Chicago, and Washington, DC, where some of his appearances were before the Richard Wagner Society. By this time Heinrich had established himself as a lieder performer in these cities, and song recitals in general had gained a firmer footing in the concert season. As in 1885, Schott appeared before enthusiastic audiences, with one New York critic noting the pleasure he had given the women who attended one of his matinees.[42] Although some reviewers were still critical, many others were positive and praised Schott's dramatic numbers. The *New York Times* reported full houses and abundant applause, and it assessed Schott as "unquestionably one of the most agreeable lieder singers whom this public has had the pleasure of hearing recently."[43] In contrast, the *Musical Courier* complained of

106   CHAPTER 4

monotony and problems with intonation and questioned the audience's fervor; in addition, the *Tribune* queried some of Schott's interpretations.[44]

Schott also appeared during a concert of the Liederkranz that was attended by more than one thousand people, including not only members of that society but also those of the Brooklyn Germania and Hoboken German Club. He sang Schumann's "Die beiden Grenadiere" and Joseph Fischer's rousing "Hoch Deutschland, herrliche Siegesbraut" multiple times in response to calls for encores.[45] The latter was rarely if ever programmed by other lieder recitalists in the United States, though Schott frequently sang it. He was popular with German communities, and, like Remmertz, he performed lieder during events sponsored by numerous German choruses. Aside from appearing with the Arion Society and Liederkranz in New York, he appeared with the Liedertafel in Rochester, New York, the Germania Männerchor in Chicago, and the Arion in Milwaukee. Unlike other recitalists in the United States, occasionally he advertised a recital as a *Liederabend*. He proudly wore his military medals during recitals, and at the end of his recital in Washington, DC, which was described as a "brilliantly fashionable" affair, the secretary of the German Legation presented him with a laurel wreath in the German colors.[46]

Despite their warmth, the reviews of Schott's 1887 recitals lack the type of praise for insightful interpretations of lieder that became increasingly commonplace in reviews of Heinrich's performances in the 1890s. Moreover, whereas Schott seems to have had a reputation for singing sharp, Heinrich's intonation was rarely criticized. Nevertheless, by and large critics did not draw direct comparisons between the men, and though Schott's 1887 Boston recitals took place during the same weeks as the Henschels' and on at least one occasion they were mentioned in the same article, critics also did not compare them.[47]

Heinrich's 1887 Collaborative Recitals

Throughout 1886 Heinrich performed in numerous oratorios and at Milwaukee's much-publicized Saengerfest. He also contributed Schubert and Schumann lieder to concerts given by the Mendelssohn Glee Club in New York and the Buffalo Philharmonic Society in Queen's Hall, Montreal. During the following year he gave an increasing number of recitals, many of which were in Boston and the surrounding area. While working in Boston he followed other singers in giving a few matinees. Yet catering to audiences primarily comprised of women does not seem to have been his main concern because earnings from recitals supplemented his income from concerts and oratorios, and recitals were scheduled around his performances at these larger events.

In addition to solo recitals, he presented numerous recitals with collaborators. Ella Earle (1863–1939) sang with him in recitals in New York, Baltimore, and

Montreal.[48] In Boston, Mrs. F. J. Kirpal (Margaretha Kirpal, born ca. 1859) joined him for two programs in March, and Charlotte Walker (d. 1919) performed with him during three recitals in the following November and December. Walker also collaborated with him in a recital in Philadelphia. Prior to their joint recitals, each of the three women had previously appeared with Heinrich in at least one oratorio performance. The most significant of these was the American premiere of Liszt's *Christus* (1866–1872), during which Heinrich and Earle performed with the New York Oratorio Society.[49] At the time of their joint recitals, none of these women had Heinrich's stature, and only Walker (whose voice was described as too large for a small hall and too heavy for the repertoire) would subsequently maintain a national-level profile, albeit in the field of opera.[50]

While recitals featuring lieder were proliferating in Boston, New York seems to have retained some degree of disinterest in this mode of concertizing. Although one reviewer considered Heinrich and Earle's recital a welcome contrast to the usual operatic and symphonic concerts, he observed that others were still less enthusiastic, for "it is a well known fact that the New York musical public, highly educated as it is in the serious forms of symphonic music and the Wagnerian music drama is comparatively ignorant about good German lieder singing."[51]

Heinrich's 1887 joint recital programs had much in common with his series with Henson, and both Earle and Kirpal performed some of the same songs Henson sang. This suggests Heinrich had considerable influence over his collaborators' repertoire, which is perhaps to be expected because he played all the accompaniments. Heinrich likewise reprised selections of Schubert's and Schumann's songs, but on occasion he added new repertoire. In his New York recital with Earle, for instance, he sang three numbers from Hugo Brückler's (1845–1871) *Trompeter von Säkkingen* (published in 1872). Notable for their difficult piano parts, these works were not often sung by other performers. In the following years, however, Heinrich reprised them on numerous occasions, probably because he appreciated their ballad style. He also began performing songs by Brahms, including "Von ewiger Liebe" (op. 43, no. 1). Although in recent times this song has been interpreted as a woman's statement of undying love and is usually sung by a woman, in the nineteenth century it was also performed by men. During the 1890s it became quite well known, whereas Brahms's three "Heimweh" songs (op. 63, nos. 7–9), which Heinrich also gave in 1887, did not achieve such renown. Perhaps this lack of interest was because their introverted nostalgic texts, portraying the yearning for a bygone youth and home, though typical of German Romanticism, did not interest American audiences as much as dramatic love songs such as "Von ewiger Liebe."

Heinrich's collaborators also introduced works that his previous recitals did not include. For instance, Kirpal sang works by Eduard Lassen (1830–1904),

108   CHAPTER 4

Xavier Scharwenka (1850–1924), and Arthur Goring Thomas. Lassen, a Belgian-Danish composer who worked primarily in Weimar, composed songs in a variety of styles from folk-like to through-composed. Numerous other professional singers programmed his works, and his simpler numbers, like those by Scharwenka, gained currency in the United States through sheet music produced for the domestic market.

Despite the growing number of Boston recitalists performing lieder, a reviewer from the *Boston Herald* advised Heinrich to diversify his programs to please audiences "not given over to the absorbing love of German music which rules the hour."[52] This type of anti-German sentiment, which had also greeted one of Henschel's earlier recitals, was echoed in a review (perhaps by the same writer) of a recital by a local singer, William J. Winch, that similarly did not include songs in English. A week later, however, this critic was mollified by Winch's performance of songs in English by Margaret Ruthven Lang.[53]

The *Boston Herald* reviewer, however, was probably not concerned only about the dominance of the German language in Heinrich's recitals. It is likely he also sought the type of variety in musical styles that some of Boston's other recitalists proffered. For instance, Gertrude Franklin, with whom Heinrich had appeared in Gounod's *Redemption* in 1884, was developing a reputation for interesting programs that included works by contemporary American and French composers. Her March 1886 recital was lauded for its inclusion of songs by Chadwick, Foote, Osgood, James H. Rogers, and Benjamin Woolf, some of which had yet to be published. It also featured French songs such as Paul Lacombe's "Un Bal d'Oiseaux."[54] Later that year, her performance of Rossini's *La Regata Veneziana*, a cycle of three songs that one critic claimed were new to Boston audiences, was greeted with calls for an encore.[55] Franklin was well known in Boston, and unlike Heinrich had already collaborated with the Ditson publishing company. In 1881 it released sheet music of thirteen songs she performed, all with her image on the cover. In addition to Grieg's "Forest Wanderings," they included works by English, German, and French composers, all given in English versions. The only lieder, however, were Schumann's "Lotus Flower" and Taubert's "Bird Song," which Lind had popularized.

Perhaps in response to the criticism of his programs, Heinrich and Walker's third Boston recital had slightly more diversified repertoire. Walker gave numbers by American composers that reportedly were sung for the first time in Boston: "The Forsaken" and "On a Night in Spring" by Bruno Oscar Klein (1856–1911), and "Venetian Serenade" and "Daffodils" by Jules Jordan.[56] Heinrich was probably aware of the growing interest in compositions by Americans. He and Walker were among the soloists in Horatio Parker's *King Trojan* (1885) when it was performed during one of Frank Van der Stucken's (1858–1929) pathbreaking All American concerts in New York in 1887. The next year, Heinrich gave

Edgar S. Kelley's (1857–1944) "My Silent Song," "Love's Fillet," and "Love and Sleep" (op. 6, nos. 1, 2, and 4) during a concert with the Mendelssohn Glee Club in New York, perhaps a somewhat surprising choice given that this was a German organization.[57] In contrast, at this time he usually did not sing American songs in his own recitals.

Critics consistently acknowledged Heinrich's high ranking in the field of the intellectually demanding German lied.[58] While his recitals were well received, most reviews are very short and do not give details about audience reaction to individual songs. In contrast, Louis Elson was particularly critical, writing that Heinrich was "a good musician, but rather too guttural and spasmodic to suit my taste. I did not like his performance of the 'Erl King,' or the 'Wanderer.' They were too distorted, and, as I studied the one with August Kreissmann, and have often heard Staudigl give the other, I have a reliable standard in the matter."[59] Elson, who frequently reminded readers of his pedigree, was one of the most demanding critics of lieder singers, but the validity of his criticisms of Heinrich's technique is confirmed by a few other later writers. In general, Elson preferred the more polished Henschel (though he occasionally detected flaws in his performance as well). Around the time of Heinrich's Boston recitals, Henschel was back in the country and giving recitals in Boston to significantly larger audiences than those for the recitals by other singers (including Heinrich and Schott), who sometimes had difficulties filling halls.

By early 1888 Heinrich had reached a plateau. He was considered one of the country's best concert singers, but he was always on the lookout for new adventures. Observing that several colleagues were concertizing in England, at the end of May 1888 he decided to take his family and settle there.

England, 1888–1891

In England Heinrich contributed to orchestral and chamber concerts and presented his own recitals in collaboration with other singers and instrumentalists. He quickly acquired numerous engagements, including singing lieder during orchestral concerts led by the revered conductor August Mann (1825–1907). The other soloists for these types of concerts were among the most prominent musicians performing in England, including Joseph Joachim, Fanny Davies (1861–1934), who was a student of Clara Schumann, and Adelina Patti. Heinrich sang excerpts from Wagner's operas in concerts led by Hans Richter, and he joined Lillian Nordica and the esteemed tenor Edward Lloyd (1845–1927) in a performance of Berlioz's *Damnation of Faust*, which was also led by Richter. In contrast, most of the collaborators in his initial chamber programs were colleagues he had worked with in the United States such as the violinist Ovide Musin (1854–1929) and Walter Damrosch (1862–1950).[60] In addition to perform-

110   CHAPTER 4

ing, Heinrich taught at the Royal Academy of Music, at the Hyde Park Academy of Music for Ladies, and in his private teaching studio.

During one of his earliest recitals in England, at Balliol Hall, Oxford University, Heinrich presented the type of solo program he had been giving in America: He sang eighteen lieder to his own accompaniment.[61] In the following years he gave six series, each comprising three recitals, but these programs conformed more closely to the format of European programs and included instrumental numbers. Most were held in Steinway Hall in London, but a few were in Princes' Hall; some began at 3:00 p.m. and others at 8:30 p.m. His collaborators included Emanuel Moór (1863–1931), a Hungarian pianist and composer who worked in New York in 1887;[62] Lena Little (1853–1920), an American contralto; Benno Schönberger (1863–1930), an Austrian pianist and composer; Willy Hess (1859–1939), a violinist; and, during the final (sixth) series in 1891, his wife. After his second series of recitals, and likely in response to one critic who concluded that Heinrich's accompanying impaired his performance and viewed his work as merely an imitation of Henschel's,[63] Heinrich was often accompanied by Schönberger. Nevertheless, he continued to accompany collaborators such as Lena Little.

Critics initially viewed Heinrich's recitals as welcome novelties, which is somewhat surprising because the Henschels were also presenting their recitals in London, and on occasion in the same month as Heinrich's. Yet Heinrich's emphasis on lieder clearly differentiated his recitals from those of the Henschels. Despite some concerns about Heinrich's upper register, the *Daily News* praised the baritone for avoiding the songs frequently chosen by other vocalists and noted the audience's warm response.[64] Others reiterated these ideas, with the *Monthly Musical Record* sometimes providing a description of the current state of lieder performances in England that indicates there were far fewer song recitals consisting of lieder than in Boston. On one occasion the critic for that journal wrote:

> An expansion of this kind of very charming entertainment, largely represented in Germany by eminent vocalists such as Amalie Joachim, Hermine Spies, Thekla Friedländer, Rosa Papier, Gustav Walter, Mierzwinski, Theodor Reichmann, Bulss, Forsten, and others, would be a ready means for acquainting our audiences with many hidden treasures of vocal art. But do our audiences care for such treasures? The comparatively scanty attendance and the exceptional favour which greeted the only English song, given by Herr Heinrich (as an encore), point to a negative answer.[65]

The *Musical World* wrote that Heinrich's performance of four songs from Brückler's *Young Werner's Rhine Songs* (*Gesänge Jung Werner's*, op. 2) was the first time they had been sung in England. In contrast, he had already given these songs in the United States. Similarly, Heinrich's selection of songs by Jensen, including "Alt Heidelberg, du feine" (op. 34), were also described by one writer as "little known." This critic likewise thanked Heinrich for performing three of the "least-known" of Schubert's songs, including "An Schwager Kronos" (D. 369).[66] Heinrich's recitals with Little and some of their joint appearances in orchestral concerts featured duets by Brahms, Schumann, Dvořák, and Cornelius, but they seem to have had the most success with duets by the British composer Goring Thomas, who dedicated "Night Hymn at Sea" and "Mein Herz, werde wach" to them.[67] In America during the 1890s Heinrich would sing some of these same pieces with his wife or his eldest daughter Julia.

Newspaper reports of Little's singing date back at least as far as 1872, when she performed in school events in her hometown of New Orleans. She moved to New York, but then, with a recommendation from Leopold Damrosch, traveled to Frankfurt to study with Stockhausen. Like some of his other students, she lived with the Stockhausen family and met his colleagues, including Clara Schumann, Brahms, and Rubinstein.[68] Her career reached its climax with performances in London. On some occasions she collaborated with Sophie Löwe (1848–1926), another former student of Stockhausen's, and the Henschels.[69] A review of an 1887 recital in which Little collaborated with the English composer and vocalist Liza Lehmann (1862–1918) and Fanny Davies indicates Little's standing in England: "Little has established a reputation as one of our most intelligent and most congenial interpreters of modern German song. Her beautiful and sonorous contralto is singularly well adapted to the profound feeling which has inspired such songs as Brahms's 'Gestillte Sehnsucht' and 'Geistliches Wiegenlied' [op. 91]."[70]

Little sang numerous songs by Brahms, and she might have been among the musicians who inspired Heinrich to increase his Brahms repertoire. In general, at the time Brahms's lieder were more widely performed on English stages than those in the United States. This is likely because of the influence of Brahms's associates working in England. Those that Heinrich came in contact with included Richter, Marie Fillunger (the companion of Clara Schumann's daughter Eugenie, 1850–1930), and Hans von Bülow (1830–1894). In addition, in June and July 1889 Hermine Spies (1857–1893), a woman whom some thought Brahms might marry, sang lieder during at least one of Richter's orchestral concerts and two recitals, one of which occurred during the same week as one of Heinrich's recitals.[71]

At the end of 1889 Heinrich and Schönberger gave a series of three recitals devoted to Schubert, Schumann, and Brahms, respectively. Whereas Heinrich gave seven songs during the Schubert program and eight during the Schumann, he gave twelve during the Brahms recital—a feat that impressed his admirers at the *Monthly Musical Record*.[72] Many of the songs by Schubert and Schumann, including the first three and last two from *Dichterliebe*, were not among those

112   CHAPTER 4

that Heinrich frequently performed. Likewise, most of the seven songs from Brahms's *Magelone Romances* and all five of the op. 105 were new to him.[73] The latter five had been published the previous year, in 1888, and when Henschel gave "Auf dem Kirchhofe" (op. 105, no. 4) in February 1889 in London his advertisements listed it as new.[74] Heinrich may have learned about this collection from this singer, but there were other friends of Brahms in London at the time who also knew these songs. In particular, Spies had premiered "Immer leiser wird mein Schlummer" (op. 105, no. 2) in Germany and sang others from the op. 105 set with Brahms accompanying. When Heinrich resettled in the United States in 1892, he continued to sing Brahms's works, including the dramatic ballad "Verrat" (op. 105, no. 5), but most of the songs from opp. 33 and 105, as with the selections from *Dichterliebe* and *An die ferne Geliebte* (which he performed in another series), did not become part of his standard repertoire. It is possible that he was able to explore these works because he was not his own accompanist and that once he returned to accompanying himself, they became too challenging.

British reviews from mid-1889 onwards classified Heinrich's style as declamatory. Although this descriptor had rarely been used by previous American critics, once Heinrich returned to the United States it appeared with increasing frequency, in both positive and negative appraisals. In England this declamatory style was usually viewed as undesirable, and in general, during 1890 reviews showed a tendency to be less receptive to the baritone. A review of Heinrich and Schönberger's last recital noted the small attendance, and the critic's decidedly mixed impression of Heinrich's voice echoes some of the reservations Elson had made in response to Heinrich's earlier Boston recitals: "Possessed of a remarkably fine voice and excellent intonation, as long as he holds himself in check the effect is everything that can be desired. His mezza-voce is admirable, but he displays a tendency to exaggerate in passionate passages, and then uses the vibrato too freely to be pleasant."[75]

After Lena Little returned to the United States in 1891, Heinrich needed a new woman collaborator, and during his next series of three recitals his wife contributed a few songs. Although she had sung in public in Philadelphia before their marriage, the recitals in London were likely Annie's first performances in a prominent venue of such a large city. While the Henschels provided the model for a husband-and-wife recital, it is more likely that the inclusion of Mrs. Heinrich was a financial necessity, in that Heinrich might not have been able or willing to pay another singer. She gave songs in English by William Sterndale Bennett (1816–1875), Brahms, Gounod, Amy Horrocks (1867–1916), Mackenzie, Schönberger, and Charles Villiers Stanford (1852–1924),[76] many of which she would reprise during the couple's later US recitals.

Although Heinrich starred in numerous recitals and appeared in a variety of chamber and orchestral concerts during 1889, he appeared in far fewer in the following years. Aside from a few song recitals and a brief appearance during one of Isaac Albeniz's concerts in 1891,[77] his main performances during 1890 and 1891 were in Richter's concerts, where he presented excerpts from Wagner's operas. He seems to have appeared in few oratorios and, in general, he never attained the same status as an oratorio singer in Europe as he had in the United States. His failure to obtain oratorio roles could be attributed at least in part to the domination of the admired baritone Charles Santley (1834–1922). A review of Heinrich's first English recital noted that it was an opportune time for him to be in London because Santley was leaving for an Australian tour.[78] But reviews of Heinrich's oratorio performances were often more critical than those of his lieder performances, with writers focusing on the limitations of his tone production.[79] Such criticisms were somewhat ironic because in 1880–1881 US critics had been underwhelmed by Henschel's performances of solo roles in oratorios, whereas earlier British reviews of his performances in the same works had been considerably more positive.

The mixed reviews and decreasing performance opportunities led Heinrich to return to North America. Already in April and May 1891, he performed lieder during a concert in Montreal and in recitals in Philadelphia and Boston. Although he appeared in concerts in England at the beginning of the 1891–1892 season, from February 1892 Heinrich performed an increasing number of engagements in the United States. In England he had amassed a debt of more than one thousand pounds, and the *Standard* listed his case among those in Bankruptcy Court.[80] Resettling his family permanently in the United States, Heinrich immediately obtained a staggering number of engagements singing in oratorios and concerts, as well as in his own recitals and those of his colleagues. During the second half of his career he drew on his experiences in England, reprising lieder and English songs that he learned there and including his wife in his recitals. His financial failure likewise hints at personal flaws that would impact his career.

* * *

By 1888, when Heinrich departed for England, the song recital, often without instrumental solos, was an established genre in US concert life. Heinrich built on Werrenrath's and Henschel's recitals, and like theirs, his performances complemented the efforts of Thomas and of Leopold Damrosch to improve American concert life by programming German repertoire. Heinrich's collaborative experiences in concerts with these conductors and singers were significant because they fostered, and perhaps also inspired, his interest in the lied. He made no mention of lieder when recollecting his early studies in Germany, his initial public performances in Philadelphia primarily comprised operatic solos, and Huneker's description of playing through lieder with him in his Philadelphia home in the years prior to 1883 suggest that at this stage he had not mastered a significant number of lieder.[81] Furthermore, before auditioning for Damrosch, much of his income came from teaching piano. Nevertheless, in the period 1885–1887 he established a reputation as one of the foremost exponents of the genre in the United States.

There is no evidence from his early years that Heinrich had any idea of infusing or uplifting the American concert scene with German works. Ambitions of this scope seem to have gradually coalesced during the period 1883–1885, after his pivotal performance in *Elijah* under Damrosch, and during the time he was meeting lieder singers such as Remmertz, Werrenrath, and Henschel and touring with Thomas's orchestra. Years later, in 1894, his observation that Schubert "expressed true, beautiful musical thoughts . . . and his melodies always appeal to the refined minds of people"[82] perfectly aligned with the attitudes of Dwight, Thomas, and the other musicians who promoted German repertoire. Moreover, by titling his initial recital series "*Classical* Song Recitals" and excluding light crowd-pleasers, he was aligning himself with these musicians' goals. Nevertheless, as the critical responses reveal, the recitals of his that were comprised exclusively of lieder were daring, and they challenged US audiences. That these types of programs were also unusual in Europe is demonstrated by the fact that while in London he conformed to local customs and gave programs containing instrumental numbers and fewer lieder. He paid similar attention to his environment when he returned to America. During the 1890s he varied his programs to respond to rising American nationalism, and he tapped into the growing audiences at women's music clubs.

5

Max Heinrich's Expanding Stylistic and Geographic Vistas

In 1887, lied composer and acerbic Viennese critic Hugo Wolf ranted, "Lieder recitals are slowly becoming epidemic. Everything that sings and sounds, and doesn't sound, wants to warble and crow from the platform."[1] The US song recitals given in 1887 by the Henschels, Max Heinrich, and Anton Schott, along with those by numerous local artists in Boston, suggest that the situation Wolf described was replicating itself across the Atlantic. But the subsequent years witnessed somewhat of a downturn in the number of song recitals featuring lieder. With the above-mentioned singers in Europe, there were few recitals by singers of international repute in 1888. Moreover, in Chicago, two of the organizations that had sponsored performances of lieder, Wolfsohn's Beethoven Society and the Hershey School of Musical Art, had folded. In 1889 the Henschels toured the East Coast, Oberlin, and Chicago, and in 1890 and 1891 Theodor Reichmann, a German baritone who was performing solo roles at the Metropolitan Opera, gave recitals in New York City, Buffalo, Chicago, and Cincinnati.[2] But there were few other recitals by singers of the same caliber. As a result, an editorial writer in the *Musical Courier* decried the absence of song recitals: "What has become of the Song Recital? Has that all powerful tyrant the piano recital crushed it out of existence, or are there so few well equipped vocalists among us that they fear the test of this delightful form of musical entertainment?"[3]

In contrast, the 1891–1892 season brought recitals by several American performers who had returned from studying or working in Europe. They included Wilhelm Heinrich and Lena Little, who, along with the German immigrant Heinrich Meyn (1863–1933), were among the growing number of singers working in the United States who had studied with Julius Stockhausen in Germany. In 1892 Max Heinrich was back in the country, and the Henschels, Amalie Joachim, and Harry Plunket Greene were also here on tour.[4] By the end of the decade, song recitals were proliferating throughout the country, and the most accomplished artists began adding cities on the West Coast to their itineraries. The growing number of highly trained singers giving recitals reflected the changing cultural practice of lieder performances in Europe, where the increasing professionalization of lieder singers had already been under way for some time.[5]

From the early 1890s song recitals were a regular part of the US concert season, and in Boston and New York, it was sometimes possible to hear multiple recitals by admired artists on a single day. March 5, 1891, for example, witnessed two recitals in New York, one by Lena Little and the other by Conrad Behrens, a Swedish bass who was performing at the Metropolitan Opera. Little's recital and some of the reviews reflected trends and issues that would remain relevant to recitals throughout the decade. One critic was largely positive, but his sexist response also indicates that some New Yorkers still had a negative view of the lied as an art form and that for some, the lied was still associated primarily with women: "Miss Little is manifestly a ballad, or, better, a lieder singer; and in what may be called in the happier sense of the term, the homely branch of the art song, she displayed yesterday real and valuable gifts."[6] Little sang thirteen songs in German, Italian, French, and English, with one critic praising her enunciation of each language and dramatic expression, as well as her voice's rich timbre. Although such polyglot programs were becoming increasingly common, some audiences preferred to hear English. In this case, Little's audience was said to favor Antonio Secchi's (1761–1833) "Lungi dal caro bene" not only because of its style, but also because it was sung in English: "It fell like balm upon ears wounded with the burrs and prickles of the foreign languages in which the previous songs had been sung," wrote the reviewer for the *Sun*.[7] The pressure for recitalists to sing lieder in English translation increased with the rise of American nationalism. Adding to this pressure, during the same time, recitalists including Max Heinrich began presenting lieder in midwestern and western venues where English was strongly preferred.

Heinrich's performances of lieder in English were just one new aspect of his recitals. During the zenith of his career, from 1893 to 1897, Heinrich capitalized on the dramatic rise in interest in song recitals, exciting audiences in a wide variety of venues in large and small cities across the country. Responding to competition from other recitalists and to the increase of nationalism, he performed new works by Brahms and Strauss as well as songs by Boston composers. He also departed from the format of his original Classical Song Recitals, which were almost exclusively comprised of lieder, by programming a few lighter popular numbers. Reviews from perceptive critics reveal that his highly nuanced performances, in which all manner of characters and emotions were brought to life, set him apart from other recitalists and captivated his audiences. In his later years, as his voice deteriorated, he concentrated his efforts on composing,

Max Heinrich's Expanding Stylistic and Geographic Vistas   117 teaching, and publishing scores of lieder with singable English translations and numerous performance annotations.

Heinrich, 1892–1916

In 1892 Heinrich settled his family in Boston. He likely chose this city because he recognized that it was America's musical center and was renowned for its high level of culture. Numerous commentators, including Huneker, observed that Boston—with its symphony orchestra, an array of highly trained instrumentalists and composers, a supportive public, and institutes of higher learning—continued to rival, if not surpass, New York as a cultural mecca.[8] Heinrich immersed himself in Boston's musical life, collaborating in numerous chamber and orchestral concerts, singing in B. J. Lang's choir at King's Chapel (where he joined a quartet that included Lena Little), and teaching. He also initiated an annual series of song recitals, many of which included performances by his wife. These were modeled on those he gave prior to his English sojourn in that he accompanied himself and his wife, and, unlike his recitals in London, there were no instrumental numbers.

Like many recitalists resident in Boston, Heinrich could also be heard in a wide variety of "at homes" held in private residences of the well-to-do, some of which entertained more than one hundred women and men.[9] While some of these entertainments resembled recitals, others involved multiple singers and Heinrich only provided a few numbers. He could also be heard in private homes in other cities, and in 1899 it was reported that his fee for such appearances was $250. Although this was an impressive amount, Emma Eames (1865–1952), a popular operatic star, was said to earn $1,000 for such a performance, and famous instrumental stars from Europe commanded even higher rates.[10]

Heinrich fulfilled numerous engagements with the Boston Symphony Orchestra during Emil Paur's tenure as conductor (1893–1898) and participated in the orchestra's 1893–1894 tours. During the period 1894–1896 he toured with the Boston Festival Orchestra, performing at their May Festivals in states such as Utah, Indiana, and Vermont. On these occasions he often sang excerpts from Wagner's operas or orchestral versions of one or two lieder, including "Die Allmacht" (D. 852), Schubert's ode to God's awesome power. A reviewer of the Boston Symphony Orchestra's 1894 performance at the Brooklyn Academy of Music concluded that his voice had "certainly improved" during his time in England: "He sings more broadly and more skillfully than he did and his effects are more dramatic. There is still something of his reediness of voice, but his upper notes have cleared and are sweeter and fuller."[11]

Heinrich was also a sought-after soloist for performances of oratorios in Boston and throughout the East Coast, the Midwest, and Canada. As in the 1880s, he

FIG. 5.1. Photograph of Max Heinrich in the 1890s used in advertisements for a performance in Springfield, Massachusetts. MS Thr 467 (Box 49) Houghton Library, Harvard University.

appeared alongside major soloists of great popularity, including Eames, Emma Juch, Lillian Nordica, and Myron W. Whitney. In many cases, he reprised roles he had given before going to England, but now he also performed solo roles in works by Boston composers. In 1894 he appeared in a Boston performance of Parker's widely admired *Hora Novissima* (1893), which was conducted by the composer, and in 1895 in Detroit, he sang in the same composer's cantata *The*

Holy Child (1893). The next year, in New Haven, he performed *Cahal Mor of the Wine-Red Hand: A Rhapsody for Baritone and Orchestra* (1893), which Parker had dedicated to him, and Chadwick's *Lochinvar* (1896), a work for baritone and orchestra, which the composer had likewise dedicated to him.[12] The audience at this festival performance numbered well into the thousands, as it did at similar performances at Springfield's May Festival, where he repeated *Lochinvar*. In his recitals and other concerts, Heinrich also performed solo songs by these composers.

Networking with Boston composers reinforced Heinrich's awareness of the growing interest in compositions by Americans. Since Van der Stucken's path-breaking concerts in New York in 1887, the number of All-American concerts, as well as ones devoted entirely to a single American composer, had increased. Douglas Bomberger has tied the proliferation of these types of concerts to contemporary debates and policies regarding trade protectionism and tariffs,[13] and Jessica Gienow-Hecht has similarly observed the relationship between concert life, the Second Industrial Revolution, and the growth of nationalism in both the United States and Europe. Throughout the 1890s numerous publications called for the programming of American music in all genres and for a decrease in German music. For instance, in an 1893 critique of a performance of a few lieder by Schubert, Warren Davenport (1840–1908), an influential Boston critic and voice teacher, opined: "Our concert public has been Germanized to death, nearly for years."[14] Nationalism and the concomitant backlash against German works influenced the programming of orchestral music, as scholars such as Gienow-Hecht have noted, and these trends impacted song recitals and the study of songs as well. The *Musical Courier* was among the journals that frequently carried articles promoting American composers and performances of their music. In 1895 it described a series of five lectures on the history of American song given by H. W. Greene of the Metropolitan College of Music. Beginning with psalm tunes and traversing through the Civil War, the series reached contemporary songs in the last lecture, which included works by New England composers.[15]

At the peak of his career, Heinrich faced a variety of challenges. Some of the changes that he made were attempts to keep his programs fresh and to enable him to compete with the increasing number of prominent singers who were giving recitals. Others were likely made because his voice had started to degrade. In 1897 he introduced his eldest daughter, Julia, to his recitals, and while he reprised demanding repertoire that he had not sung for a while and introduced new works, both he and Julia also added simpler popular pieces. During this time, however, Heinrich's behavior created serious problems. In May 1896 the *Hartford Times* observed that Heinrich appeared to be drunk when he broke down and left the stage during a solo in a performance of *Elijah*. (Other

120   CHAPTER 5

papers merely reported that he was ill and had been so all day.) Heinrich sued the paper for $25,000, claiming its report had caused his income to fall from $10,000 or $12,000 a year to $4,000 or $5,000 and the number of future bookings to drop dramatically. The 1897 trial lasted six days, and the packed courthouse heard numerous witnesses describe Heinrich's behavior before and during the performance. The jury exonerated the paper, and Heinrich was required to pay the costs of the case.[16]

It is possible that the type of undisciplined behavior revealed in press notices relating to the trial also led to the casual atmosphere of some of Heinrich's recitals and to erratic performances. Elson described one 1897 Boston recital as so relaxed that it resembled an "at home" that was more of a social event than an artistic endeavor, but he acknowledged that audiences nevertheless appreciated Heinrich: "It is reminiscent of salad days to most men," he wrote, "to attend one of these gatherings, where the singer lounges in, sits at the piano and trolls out his songs. . . . His audiences know this already, but they flock to his recitals because they are unpretentious, informal, and pleasant affairs of a thoroughly enjoyable kind."[17] Philip Hale, one of Boston's most astute critics, seemed to grow increasingly impatient with the baritone's faulty technique. Once an admirer of Heinrich's, he observed that during a performance of Brahms's *Vier ernste Gesänge* (op. 121) all the baritone's "most disagreeable mannerisms and vocal offenses" were on display.[18] Heinrich's inappropriate mannerisms were also mentioned in a few reviews of performances in other cities, but none of these reports explain the nature of these gestures. Perhaps some of them were the type of inappropriately theatrical large gestures that other lied singers, including Stockhausen, Henschel, and Lilli Lehmann, avoided.[19] But despite these unfavorable reports, other reviews continued to laud Heinrich's recitals, and even Hale praised later compelling performances.

In April 1899 Heinrich became an instructor at the Chicago Conservatory. The decision to take this position and move his family to Chicago was influenced by a variety of issues, including the fallout from the lawsuit, the decline in his voice, and his never-ending need to be in motion. In addition, he was facing increased competition in New York and Boston. David Bispham had returned to the United States in 1896, and his recitals were drawing a great deal of attention. Moreover, stars of the Metropolitan Opera as well as touring artists from Europe were giving far more recitals than ever before. At the same time as the press optimistically reported Heinrich's arrival in Chicago, however, the conservatory was experiencing a financial and organizational crisis. This likely caused Heinrich to lose money, and after September 1900 he was no longer listed as faculty.[20] That year brought another blow: His wife died on July 27.[21] Despite these challenges, Heinrich established himself as a venerated artist and as a teacher with a private studio in the Fine Arts Building. In addition to collaborating with local artists and occasionally performing solo roles in concerts by local choral organizations, he and Julia gave an annual series of recitals and continued to tour, with near-annual appearances in Boston as well as in venues to the west of Chicago that they had not previously visited. Although the reviews continued to be positive, by 1902 it was clear Heinrich's voice had deteriorated, and he officially retired in 1903. In practice, however, this meant a reduction in the number of recitals and a shift to composing, rather than a complete departure from the stage.

Drawing on the wealth of his experiences as both a singer and pianist, Heinrich set about composing melodramas and solo songs. Since 1901 he had been performing Richard Strauss's melodrama *Enoch Arden* (1897). With a spoken part and piano accompaniment that accentuated key moments in the narrative, melodramas were a wonderful option for dramatic singers whose singing voices were failing. In 1903 and 1904 Heinrich premiered his own works in this genre, *Magdalena; or the Spanish Duel* (op. 17), a setting of a love story by F. J. Walker that one reviewer described as well known, and *Raven* (op. 15), a setting of Poe's poem.[22] By this time numerous women had entered the field of elocution,[23] and Heinrich's works appealed to them as well as to members of music clubs who had heard or heard about his song recitals. His melodramas were taken up by women as far afield as Colville, Washington, and Honolulu, as well as by professional singers.[24] Nevertheless, Heinrich had limited critical success as a composer, and Hale's review of the melodramas was charitable at best. Despite its "vapid" text, he preferred the color and "piquant rhythms" of *Magdalena* to *Raven*, and he joined other Boston critics in concluding that Heinrich's music did not do enough to accentuate the emotional intensity of Poe's poem. Heinrich dedicated these melodramas to Bispham, and although Bispham performed them, he programmed Heinrich's songs more frequently. Heinrich wrote more than twenty songs, most in English and a few in German. *Musical America* published a tepid review of some of these works, which noted the influence of Schumann—a lieder composer whom Heinrich had always favored.[25] Julia Heinrich and Bispham performed Heinrich's works quite frequently, with Bispham favoring "Sonnet" and "Who Knows," and recording the latter. Other professional and amateur musicians likewise presented Heinrich's songs in a wide variety of settings, from major concert halls to schools of music and women's music clubs.

In 1904, after a series of appearances in recitals on the West Coast with Julia, Heinrich married the German philanthropist and celebrity Anna Held (1849–1941), who had established an artists' colony near La Jolla, California.[26] The couple's sudden engagement and hastily arranged marriage were chronicled in newspapers nationwide and satirized in a half-page cartoon in the funny pages of the *Chicago Sunday Tribune*.[27] By the end of the year Heinrich had relocated to

California, where he set about establishing himself as a teacher and performer, giving recitals in the couple's home and regional venues, as well as in concert halls in Los Angeles and San Diego. Nevertheless, Heinrich continued to tour, and by 1906 he and Held led separate lives, though they remained in contact.[28] Max resettled in Chicago, and then, in 1909, in New York. He gave his last solo recital at New York's Princess Theatre in March 1916.[29]

Heinrich's Programs and Expanding Repertoire

Although Heinrich was devoted to the lied, he recognized audiences' need for greater variety, and on his return from England in 1892 he began programming other well-known works, including the aria "Where'er You Walk" from Handel's *Semele* (1743). Unlike Henschel, he did not establish a standard layout for his programs, though he usually grouped songs by English and American composers in the second half, a practice that was adopted by other recitalists. Hale, who enjoyed playing the contrarian, later claimed this placement implied that singers had little commitment to the American works and that their best performances were saved for the European ones placed on the first half.[30] Although he was writing in 1918, to some extent his analysis could apply to Heinrich, who advocated for the lied with much greater passion than he did for other genres. The program for his second Boston recital of 1893 (figure 5.2) combined songs that he had frequently performed during the 1880s with ones by Brahms and English composers that he learned while in England. In contrast to his recitals in England, this one contained twenty-nine numbers (in addition to encores), which was typical of his programs during the height of his career. His later programs, however, often included fewer numbers.

The program shown in figure 5.2 lists most of the lieder by their German titles, but according to Hale, Heinrich sang some of the ones by Schubert in English. This pleased the critic, who, unlike other writers, acknowledged that although Germans were more affected by performances in their own language, English translations were preferable for "mixed audiences." Furthermore, he argued that although translations of poets such as Heine often lost their subtlety, a serviceable translation conveying the sense of the poem was enough for the "ordinary hearer."[31] Heinrich continued to perform most lieder in German, but on his return from England he often sang at least some of the more widely known songs, such as Schumann's Gondolier Songs, in English. Occasionally he sang a lied twice, once in English and once in German.[32] While a few of his earlier performances of lieder in English were criticized, by the end of his career Heinrich's ability to sing in English was said to be rarely surpassed by native English speakers.[33] He believed that if good translations were available, they should be sung because to fully appreciate a song, one must understand the words. To this

TUESDAY EVENING, FEBRUARY 7, 1893.

Programme.

1. DER NEUGIERIGE. (The Inquirer).
PAUSE.
TROCKNE BLUMEN. (Withered Flowers).
GUTE NACHT. (Good Night).
DIE POST. (The Post).
LIEBESBOTSCHAFT. (Love's Message).
SERENADE.
AM MEER. (By the Sea).
DIE TAUBENPOST. (The Carrier Pigeon).

Schubert

MR. HEINRICH.

2. ABSCHIED. (Farewell).
LOTUSBLUME. (Lotus Flower).
DIE BLAUEN FRUEHLINGSAUGEN. (Spring Violets.)

Franz

MRS. HEINRICH.

3. DUET: Noontide heat is soon passed o'er.   *Goring Thomas*

MR. & MRS. HEINRICH.

4. WIE MELODIEN ZIEHTES. (Melodious sounds surround me).
JMMER LEISER WIRD MEIN SCHLUMMER. (Faint and fainter grows my slumber).
VOLKSLIED. (Folksong).
AUFDEM KIRCHHOFE. (In the Churchyard).

Brahms

MR. HEINRICH.

5. DER NUSSBAUM. (The Almond Tree).   *Schumann*
MAINACHT. (A Night in May).
DAS MÄDCHEN. (The Maiden Speaks).
NACHTIGALLEN SCHWINGEN. (On the Wings of the Nightingale).

Brahms

MRS. HEINRICH.

6. WHERE'ER YOU WALK.   *Handel*
SONGS OF ARABY.   *Clay*
SPRING SONG.   *Mackenzie*
MY LOVE'S AN ARBUTUS.   *Vill. Stanforth*
A BOWER OF ROSES.   *Vill. Stanforth*
DER ARME PETER. (Poor Peter).
PROVENCALISCHES LIED. (Song of the Provence).

Schumann

MR. HEINRICH.

7. TWO DUETS.
WANDERER'S NIGHT SONG.   *Rubinstein*
LA CI DAREM LA MANO.   *Mozart*

MR. & MRS. HEINRICH.

Steinway & Sons Grand Piano used. Furnished by M. Steinert & Sons Co.

FIG. 5.2. Program, "The Second Song Recital of Mr. and Mrs. Max Heinrich," Tremont Temple, Boston, Tuesday, February 7, 1893, 8 p.m. Program held by the Historic Opera, Concert, and Theatre Programs Collection in the Jerome Lawrence and Robert E. Lee Theatre Research Institute of the Ohio State University Libraries.

end, he called for more high-quality poetic translations of lieder.[34] In contrast, there are only a few reports indicating that sometimes he spoke to audiences about the aspects of German culture that informed the original poems. Most of these instances concerned performances of ten of Jensen's *Lieder aus Joseph Victor Scheffels Gaudeamus* (op. 40) in which Heinrich's descriptions of the light-hearted texts of these drinking songs contributed to the entertaining aspects of his recitals.[35]

During the second half of the program shown in figure 5.2, Mrs. Heinrich sang three lieder by Brahms. This was somewhat unusual. She sang Brahms's songs less frequently than Mrs. Henschel, and it was more typical for her group of songs in the second half of a recital to be more varied. She often sang lighter works by English, American, or French composers, including "Églogue," "Regrets," or "Bonjour Suzon" by Delibes—a composer whose works Mrs. Henschel also performed and were circulating in sheet music. Sometimes she gave Haydn's "My Mother Bids Me Bind My Hair," which was frequently sung in Boston during the 1850s and 1860s, and even later stars such as Marcella Sembrich (1858–1935) occasionally programmed it. Such was its popularity that the *Ladies' Home Journal* recommended it, along with other clearly gendered songs such as Henschel's "I Once Had a Sweet Little Doll, Dears," as appropriate for mezzo-sopranos.[36] Julia Heinrich also sang French and American songs. Some of these were similarly light numbers such as songs by Chaminade and Nevin, whose songs were becoming increasingly popular with amateur women music makers and were also sung by numerous professionals.[37]

Heinrich's performance of songs by English composers reflected his time in that country, but it also addressed the preference of American audiences for songs in the vernacular and for light works that were more popular than many lieder. He reprised the songs by English composers in the program given in figure 5.2 numerous times, but he favored "Gipsy John" by Frederic Clay (1838–1889) and "Bird and Rose" by Amy Horrocks.[38] Since 1881 "Gipsy John" had repeatedly been performed in England, most notably by Charles Santley. This rousing ballad was an admirable fit with Heinrich's style, and it quickly became his signature tune, with critics often observing that it always pleased audiences. "Bird and Rose" was the only work by a woman that Heinrich frequently performed, though on occasion he also performed Horrocks's "To Her I Love." Born in Brazil to English parents, Horrocks was educated in London and appeared there as a pianist and composer at the same time Heinrich worked in that city. "Bird and Rose" was one of her more popular songs; other American singers performed it and, like "Gipsy John," US publishers issued it in sheet music. As with some of the lieder that audiences most appreciated, this song is characterized by contrasting sections and characters. From 1897 Heinrich often programmed excerpts from Alexander Campbell MacKenzie's cycle *Spring*

Songs (op. 44). Hale disparaged these works as "little better than the sheet-music platitudes that entertain bulbous and heavily fed British matrons."[39] Despite this cruel lampooning of the imagined listeners (an attitude that conforms with the disrespect that other critics sometimes accorded song recitals and the women in their audiences), Hale's comment implies that Heinrich's programs were addressing the preferences of amateur women music makers. That he was willing to adjust his programs in this way represents a distinct change from his Classical Song Recitals, which were said to be best appreciated by the musical intelligentsia. Moreover, his first recitals were held in the evening, and there is no indication he was attempting to attract women attendees, but now, in addition to programming at least a few songs that might have pleased them, he regularly gave recitals during the day.

In recognition of the growing interest in the American art song and, particularly, the work of his new colleagues, Heinrich frequently programmed lieder alongside songs by Boston composers. During their March 1896 recitals in Boston, for instance, Heinrich and his wife presented numerous songs by locals, including Foote's "On the Way to Kew," Chadwick's "Were I a Prince Egyptian" and "Gay Little Dandelion," MacDowell's "What's His Heart" (also known as "The Yellow Daisy," op. 31, no. 2) and "Sweetheart Tell Me" (op. 40, no. 2), and Clayton Johns's (1857–1932) "I Cannot Help Loving Thee." On some occasions these composers accompanied Heinrich's performances of their songs, some of which were yet to be published. Composers such as Chadwick also dedicated songs to the baritone. While such dedications contribute to documenting the relationship between Heinrich and the composers of the New England School, in general composers often dedicated works to prominent singers with the hope that the singer's performances would generate sales of scores. In addition to performing American songs in his own recitals, Heinrich gave them during collaborative chamber concerts and concerts dedicated to the instrumental and vocal works of a specific composer. The press's reactions to Heinrich's performances varied; in many instances, writers stressed the lieder more than the American songs. Less frequently they critiqued the new American works, occasionally observing whether and how the music related to the words. For Hale, Heinrich used his highly developed skills of interpreting lieder in performing the American songs.[40]

Although Heinrich performed four songs by a certain Regina Watson during a Chicago recital in which she played the accompaniments,[41] like Henschel, he does not seem to have sung works by Boston women (who were far better known than Watson). Judith Tick has described Boston in the 1890s as a cultural center in which women's contributions, including their activities as musicians, were fostered,[42] but women composers were not always accorded the same respect as their male colleagues. In 1893 one Boston critic briefly surveyed the careers of

126   CHAPTER 5

Lang, Beach, Helen Hood (1863–1949), and Clara Doria Rogers, but words of praise were negated by demeaning remarks that have no equivalent in reviews about men's works. The acknowledgment that Rogers's songs "are compositions of high character" was preceded by a comment pushing her back to the parlor: "Another Boston woman well known in social life, who essays musical composition, is Mrs. Henry M. Rogers of Beacon Street."[43] Nevertheless, by the end of the century songs by these women were being performed throughout the country and by various well-known Boston recitalists. The Heinrichs might have neglected these works because Max was short-sighted and could not envisage how they would enhance his career in the same way as his collaborations with Boston's male composers had.

While other artists in Boston introduced audiences to composers whose songs were not well-known, Heinrich tended to return to familiar lieder composers. Lena Little and Mrs. Emil Paur programmed songs by Mily Balakirev (1837–1910), Nikolai Rimsky-Korsakov, and the French-trained American Charles Martin Loeffler (1861–1935), but Heinrich added more songs by Schumann, Brahms, and Strauss to his repertoire.[44] Excerpts from Schumann's *Lieder-Album für die Jugend* (op. 79) numbered among the less challenging pieces that he began to program. Whereas these songs are rarely programmed in twenty-first-century recitals, they were welcomed by nineteenth-century audiences and they were performed by other acclaimed recitalists, perhaps because their lyrical portrayals of childhood appealed to the women in the audience who could perform them at home.

As he was adding the Schumann to his repertoire Heinrich learned more challenging lieder. He first gave Brahms's *Vier ernste Gesänge* during the Boston Symphony Orchestra's 1897 memorial concerts for the composer, who had died on April 3. The orchestra presented the Tragic Overture (op. 81), the Concerto for Violin and Cello (op. 102), and the Fourth Symphony (op. 98), and Paur, the conductor, played the piano accompaniments for the songs. Published in 1896, the *Vier ernste Gesänge* were the last lieder Brahms composed, and Bispham had given the American premiere of this cycle in New York the preceding January. In the months following his performance with the Boston Symphony, Heinrich, who sang in English, repeated the cycle in other Boston appearances and during at least three recitals in New York. In these and later performances he accompanied himself—a significant feat, given the demands these works place on both the vocalist and the pianist. As was typical of performances of Brahms's works in Europe and the United States, these soul-searching settings of biblical texts had a mixed reception. The *Boston Herald* described them as the "most effective opiate" and observed that the songs' legato lines were not a good match with Heinrich's style. Nevertheless, the audience "vigorously applauded."[45] According to the critic Emilie Frances Bauer, the songs only interested the "true musicians" in a Brooklyn audience, the others being "intensely bored."[46] In contrast, the *Brooklyn Daily Eagle* reviewer offered exuberant praise for Heinrich's program and castigated other musicians who confined themselves to repeating easier, popular songs as "fatuous vain lazy artists."[47]

Heinrich began programming Strauss's lieder in 1899. "Hoffen und wieder versagen" (op. 19, no. 5), "Allerseelen" (op. 10, no. 8), "Serenade" (op. 17, no. 2), and "Wie sollten wir geheim sie halten" (op. 19, no. 4) became part of his favored repertoire, and reviews of his performances, including ones in Chicago and California as well as another reporting on a recital for a women's club in Indianapolis, sometimes indicated they were unknown to local audiences.[48] In adopting these works, Heinrich was influenced by a Chicago tenor, George Hamlin (1869–1923), who rapidly rose to fame by presenting recitals comprised of songs from Strauss's opp. 10 and 27.[49] Heinrich began performing Strauss's *Enoch Arden* after Bispham gave it on the East Coast in 1900. In anticipation of his first public performance of this melodrama in Chicago, W. S. B. Mathews's journal published an overview of the work's text and its relation to the music, a type of introduction that was rarely provided for lieder.[50] Despite his piano skills, Heinrich usually performed this melodrama with someone else, often Julia, rendering the piano part. When Strauss and his wife Pauline Strauss de Ahna (1863–1950) undertook a highly publicized tour of the United States in 1904, the composer accompanied Heinrich's performance of *Enoch Arden* in Chicago and Bispham's performances in New York and Boston.[51]

The few detailed reviews of Heinrich's performances that single out specific works indicate that audiences often favored lieder by Schubert and Schumann, almost all of which had already been sung on US stages in the preceding decades and were available in English-language sheet music. This preference is also evidenced by programs for request recitals. For instance, in such a recital in Detroit in 1894, Heinrich gave Schubert's "Frühlingsglaube" (D. 686), "Trockne Blumen," and "Die Post" (D. 911, no. 13), all of which had been circulating in sheet music since the middle of the century. The tender lyricism of the first and the piano's imitation of the post coach in the last particularly pleased one reviewer.[52] This unusually perceptive critic recognized the introspective aspect of the line "all must change" in "Frühlingsglaube," but he did not mention whether the audience appreciated it. In contrast, many other reviews of Heinrich's performances give little or no indication of which lieder were audience favorites, and, excluding a few published in New York, Boston, and Chicago, they do not indicate whether the critic or the audience appreciated the subtleties of the texts.

Tours, Audiences, and Venues

Heinrich's song recitals took place in major halls such as the Meionaon in Boston (where the Henschels often performed) and before the growing number of women's clubs that sponsored visiting artist series. When he returned from Europe Heinrich immediately realized the possibilities these clubs afforded. In 1892 he gave a solo recital for the Amateur Musical Club in Chicago, and he returned to this club with his wife in 1894. Subsequently, he appeared before numerous other clubs throughout the Midwest both as a solo artist and with his wife or daughter Julia. Local presses not only extolled his performances but also praised the clubs. In 1901 one critic praised the Fortnightly Club in St. Joseph, Missouri, because Heinrich's performance was both enjoyable and advanced "musical taste and culture."[53] Such references to cultural uplift echo the many similar descriptions of performances of lieder as far back as the 1850s.

Heinrich usually appeared before audiences in prestigious halls in major cities, but, unlike Henschel, he also performed in a wide variety of other venues. In 1896 he presented a recital on Ladies Night (also referred to as a "pop concert") at the Athletic Club in Providence. This recital was so successful that the venue, a gym, was too small to seat everyone, and as a result, some of the men stood. The program consisted of well-known songs that were always well received, including Schumann's "Die beiden Grenadiere" and Clay's "Gipsy John," but, according to reports, the most successful number was Foote's "I'm Wearing Away."[54] This folk-style song was one of Foote's most popular works.[55]

Some of Heinrich's recitals in Michigan were similarly marketed to general audiences. In 1895 at Sault Ste. Marie he appeared at the Soo Opera House, where Mark Twain had lectured just a few weeks earlier.[56] In 1896 he gave an evening billed as a "Popular Song Recital" in the four-hundred-seat hall of Detroit's Schwankovsky music store. As in Providence, he sang a mixture of songs by German, American, and English composers, with "Erl King" being so well received that Heinrich earned two recalls.[57] His broad appeal is demonstrated by an enthusiastic reviewer of a well-attended recital hosted by a women's club in Saginaw, Michigan, who concluded: "It does not need a person well up in music or schooled in classical work to understand his singing and appreciate it."[58] Tickets for these summertime recitals ranged from twenty-five cents to seventy-five cents, "popular" prices that were designed to draw an audience. Yet Heinrich's participation in such events at the height of his career was likely motivated not by an interest in reaching more diverse audiences but, rather, by his constant need for revenue, which his sister-in-law alluded to in her recollections.[59] Many, if not most, of Heinrich's recitals in Michigan were facilitated by a manager by the name of Schultz who focused on booking recitals and oratorio performances in the region and by women's clubs.[60]

By the late 1890s, numerous organizations in the United States scheduled song recitals during their annual concert series. This was also the case in England, where song recitals sometimes outnumbered instrumental recitals.[61] Women's clubs from Maine to Oregon were sponsoring recitals with increasing frequency, and other music organizations in urban areas were doing likewise. The Art Society of Pittsburgh frequently scheduled song recitals during its concert series, and, during the 1896–1897 season, the Brooklyn Institute of Arts and Sciences initiated an annual series comprised entirely of song recitals.[62]

The Brooklyn Institute had previously hosted recitals, with Heinrich and Blauvelt giving two each during the 1895–1896 season. The new evening series, titled "Popular Song Recitals," complemented the Institute's series of orchestral and chamber concerts, as well as its lecture series. The song recitals were usually collaborative performances that included instrumentalists who presented solos. Heinrich and the soprano Eleanor Meredith gave the first recital in the new series with the highly admired violinist Geraldine Morgan (1867–1918).[63] The 1897–1898 recital series at the Institute featured Heinrich, the Henschels, Bispham, Juch, and Blauvelt, all of whom were engaged in multi-state tours. Bispham gave two recitals, and the Henschels performed an additional recital that was not part of the series. As conveyed by the series title, most of the songs performed in these recitals were well known, including Schubert's "Erlkönig," and many lieder, including Dvořák's *Gypsy Songs* (op. 55), were sung in English.

In 1898 Heinrich toured the West Coast for the first time. By then a few of his competitors had already tested out this region, with Anton Schott being the first of the well-known recitalists to do so. In 1895 Schott had toured Texas, and the next year, after returning from Mexico, where he had reportedly given twelve concerts and been honored by President Porfirio Diaz, he and his pianist, Arthur Fickenscher (1871–1954), toured California.[64] They gave at least five recitals in Los Angeles, five in San Francisco, one in Riverside, and another at Stanford University. Although the first recital in Los Angeles was not well attended, most of the reviews were positive, though they were not detailed. By this time Schott's voice had deteriorated, and sometimes he gave as few as five songs, with students or lecturers filling out the rest of the program. Nevertheless, the recitals were successful enough for Schott and Fickenscher to remain in San Francisco through 1899, with Schott establishing a teaching studio and appearing in numerous small venues, including women's homes. From January through June 1898 Schott gave at least six recitals in San Francisco and made numerous appearances in recitals and collaborative concerts in Portland, Oregon. Between his 1896 and 1898 recitals, the Henschels performed in San Francisco, Oakland, and Los Angeles.

From October 1897 to March 1898 the Henschels gave at least eighty recitals in the United States, including performances in California during late October and early November.[65] Although this was their first tour to the state, the local press had sometimes covered their previous US and European performances, and several local musicians had connections with the couple. At least one, Anna Miller Wood (1868–1934), had studied with Henschel, and other women were also singing his songs.[66]

Most touring vocalists and instrumentalists experienced difficulties concertizing in California. A woman from Portland, Oregon, writing about her experiences in the San Francisco–Oakland area around 1898, observed that the audiences loved opera (including German opera) and novelties, but except for Paderewski, instrumentalists, including Moriz Rosenthal and the violinist Eugène Ysaÿe (1858–1931), might cover the costs of their first tour, but not of their second.[67] Despite advance publicity and the success of Schott's song recitals and those by local performers, there was concern that the Henschels would have trouble filling halls. Oakland's reputation for low attendance at classical concerts by visiting artists was such that the Henschels agreed to accept a guaranteed fee. But much to everyone's shock the audience numbered twelve hundred, and the couple would have earned more had they relied on box office revenues.[68] Halls in San Francisco and Los Angeles, which also had seating capacities of over one thousand, were often similarly filled. The couple had planned only four recitals in San Francisco, but these were so well received that they gave at least eight, in addition to providing the entertainment for at least one private dinner party. Their two recitals in Los Angeles were viewed as "a meed of pleasure never before approached in the musical history of this city."[69] The success and publicity of the Henschels' recitals perhaps inspired the Heinrich family to visit the state.

Throughout the Heinrichs' 1898 recitals, including those in Colorado, California, and Oregon, reviews and advertisements of their performances frequently mentioned Henschel. These references, some of which seem to have been generated by Heinrich's (unnamed) agent, positioned Henschel as "an aristocrat, an artist of the elevated, the classic" and Heinrich as an artist who appealed to everyone. In contrast to Henschel, "Mr. Heinrich is a musician of universal sympathy . . . he has such magnetism, such a 'personal' air with the audience and hearty enjoyment of singing. He could make a music hall ballad as acceptable as a classic. . . . The public admires Henschel, but loves Heinrich."[70] These comparisons highlight the two men's different personalities, with Henschel's restraint and reverence for the work (that is, his *Werktreue* aesthetic) affording a striking contrast with Heinrich, whose outgoing personality was combined with great egotism and uninhibited (on some occasions technically imperfect) performances. Nevertheless, the men were equally praised for their consummate artistry as both vocalists and pianists.[71]

Although the Heinrich family's first recital in San Francisco was not well attended, they went on to give at least eight others and three lecture-recitals as well as singing classes. Nevertheless, one critic suggested that music teachers and singers had not attended in full force because they incorrectly assumed that it was not necessary to hear another recitalist after having been so favorably impressed by Henschel.[72] In addition to the San Francisco events, the Heinrichs gave at least one recital in Oakland and three in Los Angeles, where

Max Heinrich's Expanding Stylistic and Geographic Vistas 131 there were similar reports of less-than-optimal-sized audiences. As with some of the Henschel and Schott recitals, some tickets for a few of the Heinrichs' last performances were priced as low as twenty-five cents to draw more attendees. Despite this uneven reception, Heinrich returned to California numerous times.

Heinrich's tours enabled him to assess American audiences' growing appreciation of lieder. "Improved!" he exclaimed in 1898, elaborating:

> It is wonderful, the improvement! It was only about ten years ago that I began to give my recitals all over this country. Since that time a great appreciation of the best music has grown among your people. Nowadays when I sing in small cities, and even little towns, the people all come provided with the music on my programme. . . . Nowadays I give recitals of Schumann, Schubert, Franz, and even Brahms's songs in remote places to interested audiences; in these same places, even a few years ago, they would not listen to anything of the kind.[73]

Such was Heinrich's popularity that in 1904 he and Julia were induced, reportedly for $1,000 per week, to appear in vaudevilles for the Orpheum Circuit in Chicago, Denver, San Francisco, and Los Angeles.[74] The venues for these performances were significantly larger than many of the halls for their recitals, with most seating between fourteen hundred and two thousand people. The Heinrichs were listed as an "added attraction," along with more typical performers of this type of entertainment, including Varin and Turenne, who juggled double-edged axes, a trapeze artist called Charmion who had previously performed a striptease on a high wire, and Albert Trelor, who made an early body-building movie. Although some writers pinned their hopes on the Heinrichs' appearances elevating vaudevilles, other classical artists, including the violinists Camilla Urso and Eduard Reményi, had already turned to this popularist genre, and Julia had performed in a San Francisco vaudeville in 1902. During their 1904 appearances the Heinrichs presented their most entertaining repertoire in English, with Max giving one of Mackenzie's *Spring Songs*, Schumann's "The Two Grenadiers," and Clay's "Gipsy John."[75] Later classical singers, including Bispham, also turned to vaudevilles at the end of their careers and were similarly judicious in their programing of lieder. In contrast, lieder singers of modern times have never attained this type of popular status, and even popular-styled classical concerts have long since ceased programming the type of lieder that were performed at such events at the start of the twentieth century.

Critical Reception

Before 1889, critics in Boston had generally praised Heinrich's performances of lieder, though Elson was quite critical of his singing technique. On his return from England, Heinrich received much stronger reviews that extolled his interpretations, with those penned by Hale being unusually detailed. In describing Heinrich's voice he demonstrated that he was willing to overlook the baritone's technical deficiencies. According to Hale, Heinrich had "a peculiar and interesting vocal physiognomy," and his voice was not what is normally considered beautiful. Moreover, in "impassioned moments" he tended to break the rules of "vocal art": "He then spurns legato; he forces a tone: he abuses the portamento. And yet, when you have said all this, he is nevertheless one of the most talented and interesting singers now on the American concert stage. His talent occasionally is absolute genius, for he has the great gift of finding at once the kernel of a song, and making it prominent. At times, and without any exaggeration, he adds to his vocal interpretation, dramatic power so that it is as though the actor chose song instead of ordinary speech as the medium of expression.... Mr. Heinrich may give an interpretation that seems at first erroneous to the hearer, but the interpretation has its reason, and it is effective."[76] Critics across the country reiterated similar comments throughout the rest of Heinrich's career, with the declamatory and acting aspects of his technique gaining greater prominence as the quality of his singing voice declined.

In dramatizing lieder Heinrich was, in some respects, approaching the lied in a manner similar to some European singers. Although contemporaries of Schubert recalled him admonishing singers to perform lyrically and not to impersonate the characters in songs, Johann Michael Vogl (1768–1840), one of his close colleagues, was noted for such performances, and at the end of the century dramatic interpretations, some of which were declamatory, became more common. In creating such renditions European singers, including Ludwig Wüllner (1858–1938), sometimes altered the music's rhythms and phrases. According to commentators, Wüllner dramatically embodied the characters in the lieder he performed, and in so doing transmitted their spirit to the audience. His powerful performances were characterized by facial expressions and gestures with his arms that some believed went too far.[77] In the United States, Heinrich's fame as an interpreter of the lied mirrored that of Wüllner, but he was not influenced by him. Wüllner had only just begun his career as a concert singer when Heinrich was in England, and he first toured the United States in 1908, by which time Heinrich's career was ending. It is not known, however, whether Heinrich, while he was in England, had the opportunity to hear Raimund von Zur Mühlen, whose highly expressive performances were also lauded.

By 1899 Heinrich's voice was rarely described as lyrical. Nevertheless, his interpretations were still praised: "He talks many of his selections more than he sings them," a Wisconsin reviewer wrote, "but so admirable is this talking in dramatic truth and power, and so excellent is the piano accompaniment that the poetic meaning and content to the song are revealed in all completeness."[78]

Many of these types of evaluations echo earlier descriptions of Vogl's dramatic, declamatory performances of Schubert's songs in Vienna. As with Heinrich, Vogl "overstepped the permissible limits more and more as he lost his voice,"[79] and just as Vogl's admirers valued expression more than a beautiful voice, so, too, did later American fans of Heinrich. Critics recognized the ways Heinrich employed his declamatory style for dramatic purposes and compared it to that of Wüllner, but they advised students not to emulate it.[80]

In discussing Schubert's unusually dramatic "Gruppe aus dem Tartarus" (D. 583), Heinrich himself stressed the importance of creating "vivid and real" depictions of the text's ancient sufferers,[81] and critics repeatedly praised the verisimilitude of his interpretations. According to Hale, Schumann's "Hidalgo" (op. 30, no. 3) was "too often sung as though the hero was nothing but a duelist with an uneasy rapier and a passion for stocking cemeteries. Mr. Heinrich made him as fascinating in wooing and pinking as any of the characters of the elder Dumas."[82] This song, with its crisp repeated Spanish-style percussive rhythms, has all the braggadocio of the characters in some of the other songs that Heinrich favored, such as "Gipsy John." But the baritone did not confine himself to such works, and critics repeatedly praised his ability to convey a wide range of emotions and situations. Hale tied this versatility to Heinrich's mercurial personality: "To this man of singularly strong temperament no phase of life seems foreign. He could roar out the tavern-ditty of a toss-pot so that the hearer would be mad with thirst, and then tell in song of the tenderest affections or the holiest emotions without the hearer feeling a shock at the sudden transition; such is the authority of his art."[83] Writers in Europe similarly valued performances in which lieder singers appeared to draw on their own emotions and experiences, and in the United States critics applied this conceit to other genres as well.[84] When Heinrich performed Horrocks's "To Her I Love" a reviewer in Cleveland suggested that Heinrich's rendition of a fervent lover reflected his home life. Successful singers comported themselves in such a way that listeners might assume they were singing of their own experiences, but this was part of the act. It is highly likely that this Ohio critic's assumption was not well informed, as Huneker makes veiled hints that Heinrich was not a faithful husband.[85]

Audiences' appreciation of the verisimilitude of Heinrich's performances indicates that they were not merely appreciating the melody of lieder, as critics had sometimes claimed in earlier decades, but rather understood that the works depicted specific characters and emotions. The types of songs that were said to be heartily applauded or encored, however, had not changed. Audiences still preferred theatrical numbers which often had contrasting sections, such as Schubert's "Gruppe aus dem Tartarus," the pathos of numbers such as Dvořák's "Als die alte Mutter" ("Songs My Mother Taught Me" from *Gypsy Songs*), and songs with vibrant rhythms, such as the other songs in Dvořák's cycle.[86]

Heinrich's success in conveying the emotions and narrative of a lied in part rested on his ability to bond with his audiences. Elson observed that "he sings as if he were in a social drawing room . . . and there is a feeling of intimacy between singer and audience that constitutes one of the chief charms of the concert."[87] Numerous reports similarly praised Heinrich's relation to his audiences, and in particular the ways his gestures invited the audiences into the world of each song. In contrast, critics sometimes noted the ways the Henschels interacted with each other, but they did not mention the couple reaching out to their audiences.

Reviews praised Heinrich's expressive gestures and eyes. A critic in Detroit observed that "Mr. Heinrich is what many singers are not; he is an actor. He understands how to express with his face, as well as his voice, and almost with gesture, although seated at the piano, how to convey the most subtle shade of expression."[88] While playing the piano Heinrich turned himself to face his audience, and numerous reviewers observed the importance of his "glowing" eyes. In a performance of "Erlkönig," his expressive eyes "showed the observant listener that Heinrich was *living*" the events.[89] Although Henschel's eyes were not mentioned in reviews, other acclaimed singers, including Lilli Lehmann, did employ facial expressions to "visually" bring songs to life.[90]

Most critics were impressed with Heinrich's piano playing. An observer in St. Paul offered an unusually vivid description of its expressiveness: "Under his fingers, which seem to have witchcraft in them, the piano becomes a thing of life, singing, crying, moaning in response to the mood of its master."[91] This comment hints at the role the piano plays in conveying a lied's text, and although this is a crucial element of the genre, it is a topic that most critics overlooked. Occasionally a critic echoed earlier observations that Heinrich's singing was impaired by his playing, and Elson once remarked that the piano part was not accurately synchronized with Heinrich's singing, but few others had complaints.[92] Despite acknowledging his playing, only a few observers mentioned preluding, and those who did simply stated something to the effect that Heinrich ran "his fingers through a prelude."[93] Because of this lack of detail, it is not known whether Heinrich followed Henschel's practice of providing a piano segue from one song to another. The descriptions of the amazing speed with which he changed mood as he moved from one song to another suggests that he usually did not.

Whereas critics praised the skill and artistry of both Mr. and Mrs. Henschel, Mrs. Heinrich was understood to be her husband's supporting artist. Although she was acknowledged in advertisements and reviews, the programs that included a photograph of her husband did not include one of her. (Similarly, only one press release containing an image of Max and Julia has been located.) Hale wrote somewhat disparagingly that Mrs. Heinrich's "voice is agreeable, eminently womanly. She sings with skill and taste."[94] Despite this condescension

Max Heinrich's Expanding Stylistic and Geographic Vistas

and sexism, a tone that appeared in some of his other reviews of the singer, most other critics were quite pleased with Mrs. Heinrich's performances. Although she never attained the same artistry as her husband, her voice, like Mrs. Henschel's, was important in providing a timbral contrast, and her presence might have appealed to women audience members. But it is highly likely that, as in England, Max incorporated his wife and his daughter Julia into his programs instead of paying another singer.

None of the available sources disclose Mrs. Heinrich's views on her participation in her husband's recitals, and Huneker, who praised her musicianship, is the only observer to hint at the burden she must have carried while running the household and raising seven children.[95] Although Heinrich's sister in-law recalled a loving marriage and spoke of Heinrich in positive terms, she also referred to him as temperamental, a descriptor that occurs in a few other sources. Helen Keller (1880–1968), who met Heinrich during his final years, penned a critique of his personality which similarly suggests that he would have been challenging to live with: "His unrest, charm, and willfulness were temperamental, and the sources of his joy and his misery. More than most men, he seized for himself the privilege of doing as he liked, and others less audacious got out of the way of his magnificent impudence."[96]

Keller's description aligns with Heinrich's sister-in-law's recollection of the way he strongly discouraged Julia from pursuing a career in opera. Eventually, from 1905 Julia studied and performed in operas in Germany, but when World War I ended this work, her father pulled her back into his orbit. Despite a successful performance as Gutrune in the Metropolitan Opera's 1915 production of *Götterdämmerung*, he persuaded her to return to concert singing, and he often served as her accompanist. Her recital programs explored repertoire that contrasted with her father's, including French songs and lieder by Wolf, and while reviews were highly favorable, New York critics hinted that despite her skill she was not among the very top tier recitalists.[97]

Heinrich the Pedagogue

Beginning in the mid-1890s Heinrich began to promote his tenets of lieder performance in publications and lecture recitals, some of which were titled "intellectual singing classes."[98] In general, he was against any type of method teaching. Although he touched on technical matters such as diction, phrasing, breath control, sound production, and elocution, he was primarily concerned that singers completely understood and clearly enunciated the texts; to him, this relied on their intellect. He also recognized that singers needed to appreciate all aspects of the music, including the harmonies, and not just the melody. Earlier, Mathews had observed that this was a challenge to some singers, and

136   CHAPTER 5

particularly so because the beauty of Italian works, which many of them sang, rested on the melody.[99] One newspaper described Heinrich the pedagogue as "the celebrated finisher"; that is, like Henschel, he taught interpretation rather than vocal technique, and his publications support this description.[100] Heinrich's lecture recitals in Chicago centered on lieder by Schubert, Schumann, Brahms, Tchaikovsky, and Strauss. These were held during the day, and although the press did not supply detailed reports of the attendees, the few participants that are mentioned were women.[101]

Summarizing the wealth of knowledge accumulated throughout his career, Heinrich published *Correct Principles of Classical Singing* and a series of annotated editions of lieder. In a little more than fifty pages he offered advice on such issues as tone color and breath control, as well as discussions of how to interpret numbers from Handel's *Messiah* and each song in *Die schöne Müllerin*. As the positive reviews noted, Heinrich explored interpretation in greater depth than other contemporary singing manuals.[102] In discussing Schubert's songs, he pointed out faults often made by singers in matters of conception, phrasing, and diction, and offered advice on issues such as tempo, rhythm, and ornamentation. Drawing on his accompanying experience, he also gave suggestions for the pianist. The copious musical examples are heavily annotated with suggestions for performance, and the same types of annotations appeared in his performing editions of other lieder. As part of the book's marketing strategy, Heinrich introduced and accompanied Stephen Townsend's English-language performance of *Die schöne Müllerin* in Boston.[103] Similarly, their 1913 English-language performance of *Dichterliebe* was linked to Heinrich's publication of a performing edition of that cycle. At that same recital, Townsend also sang at least thirteen other lieder by Schumann, all of which were published in Heinrich's edition of Schumann songs.[104]

Heinrich published similarly styled anthologies of lieder by Brahms and Schubert, as well as a collection of fifty songs by various composers from Germany, the United States, and England. This anthology includes a wide variety of the numbers that Heinrich repeatedly performed, ranging from "Gipsy John" to lieder by Jensen and Brückler. The only woman to be represented is Amy Horrocks. In 1917, the year after Heinrich's death, his editions of Strauss's "Barcarole" (op. 17, no. 6) and "Wasserrose" (op. 22, no. 4) were also released by his publisher, Carl Fischer.[105] Each of the editions that Heinrich devoted to a single composer begins with a brief introductory essay about the composer and his songs. In addition, the Schumann and Schubert volumes include an essay titled "The Art of Lieder-Singing" that reiterates many points about the importance of the singer's intelligence that he presented in other outlets. Each song is then accorded a few sentences, noting some of the performance challenges or the work's main characteristics.

During the first two decades of the twentieth century numerous publishers issued albums of classical songs with singable English translations. Like early sheet music, these were produced for the domestic market. Ditson published anthologies of favorite songs by such esteemed singers as Julia Culp (1880–1970), Geraldine Farrar (1882–1967), and Elena Gehardt (1883–1961), all of which emphasized lieder. These volumes included a photograph of the singer and a brief signed preface by her or him, all of which seem to be targeted to women fans. None of these volumes addressed the performer in the way Heinrich did, and all of them employed translations by a variety of people, who likely did not collaborate with the corresponding singer.

In contrast, Alice Mattullath (ca. 1873–1949) supplied all the English translations in Heinrich's editions. How Heinrich came in contact with her is not known, but it is possible that Carl Fischer connected them because Mattullath contributed to some of his other publications. Her work was highly regarded, and she also created translations of numerous German and French songs that were sung by the likes of Culp and McCormack, as well as translations of texts of a wide variety of other types of works. McCormack praised her translations in Heinrich's Schumann edition and ventured that Schumann's "Singer's Consolation" ("Sängers Trost," op. 127, no. 1), which he was performing in the United States, would become more popular if it were more frequently sung in English.[106] Mattullath's English versions of the texts in the Schubert edition were likewise praised as "highly poetic and singable."[107]

There is considerable variance in the number and kind of performance annotations that Heinrich supplied for each song, with some having none and others having far more than is characteristic of contemporary scores of art songs. The scores do not include all of Heinrich's performance nuances, however; he probably used more rubato, rhythmic alterations, and changes in tone color than are marked.[108] Many of his instructions to use changes in dynamics to underscore important moments in the texts can be heard in later recordings by other singers. These annotations could certainly assist a novice, as could the accents that Heinrich sometimes employed to indicate important lines in the middle and lower registers of the piano parts. Yet the multiple crescendo and decrescendo signs applied during passages of repeated broken-chord figuration seem unnecessary (see example 5.1). These markings suggest that Heinrich was trying to put his imprint on every measure.[109] Accomplished pianists might employ subtle dynamic shadings in these types of figures, but Heinrich's signs could easily be misinterpreted by a novice as indicating large swells, especially if that person did not have a teacher. And this raises the question of who the intended purchaser was. Fischer published all of Heinrich's compositions as well as his lieder anthologies, but this company did not have the same type of outreach to amateur music makers as did Ditson. Indeed, Heinrich's emphasis

138   CHAPTER 5

EX. 5.1A. The Schumann *Gesamtausgabe* edition of "Der arme Peter, I" (op. 53, no. 3), mm. 39–51

EX. 5.1B. Heinrich's edition of Schumann, "Der arme Peter, I" (op. 53, no. 3), mm. 41–51

on the intellect implies that students needed a well-rounded education, including harmony as well as German poetry, and this might have been beyond the reach (or interest) of the type of consumer who purchased the anthologies of lieder marketed by other singers.

At the peak of his career, highly perceptive critics such as Hale observed that Heinrich's individualized, thought-provoking interpretations of lieder set him apart from other performers, and some of the annotations in the scores reflect such idiosyncrasies. This is the case with his score of Schumann's "Die arme Peter" (op. 53, no. 3), a set of three short lieder. Heinrich's performance earned Hale's praise for bringing out this work's "deep pathos."[110] Toward the end of the first song (example 5.1b), Peter mutters words of despair to himself. Some singers perform this phrase at a slightly softer dynamic level than the preceding ones, but Heinrich raises it to *mf*. Although this seems to contradict the poem's indication that Peter speaks softly, at least it has the merit of underscoring the character's distress at seeing the woman he loved marry another. Heinrich similarly uses loud dynamics in a few other songs to highlight important places in the text that the composer marked *piano*. One might consider these incidents as Heinrich unnecessarily dramatizing what were meant to be introspective moments, but perhaps he believed the loudness better alerted inexperienced audiences to their importance. Ironically, Hale praised the "innigkeit" of Heinrich's performance of "Die arme Peter," invoking the German concept of introversion that is intrinsically tied to the genre of the lied but rarely discussed by American newspaper critics of the time.

Heinrich's publications and lectures had the potential to reach more students than did his individual studio lessons. But records have not survived to document the dissemination of the editions, and, as with Henschel, it is impossible to account for all the people who studied with him.[111] A 1915 advertisement claimed he had taught Hamlin, Bispham, Albert Reiss, William Wade Hinshaw (d. 1947), Mme. Belle Cole ("England's greatest contralto"), Margaret Keyes of the Chicago Opera, and his daughter Julia.[112] There were, however, many others of lesser renown whom he coached or influenced.

* * *

Heinrich's reputation rested on his vivid portrayals of diverse lieder and his ability to use his passion for the genre to engage audiences. Huneker praised his expressive range and versatility: "Such an emotional range and feeling for swiftly changing moods I have never heard with the exception of Marcella Sembrich and Lilli Lehmann. And remember that he had no personal glamour, in the sense of good looks, as had these women singers; his bold hawk-like profile, and too narrow face, were not particularly attractive, had he not such brilliant eyes which mirrored his evanescent moods."[113] His expressive eyes were an im-

140   CHAPTER 5

portant aspect of the way he dramatized each song and made connections with his audiences. During the second half of his career, Heinrich took advantage of the growing interest in lieder (including that demonstrated by women's music clubs) and recognized the importance of acknowledging American nationalism and composers. The success of his outreach can be measured by one admirer's analysis: "It makes no difference to what kind of an audience he appears, whether it be metropolitan, self-sufficient, hypercritical, or provincial, easily-pleased, uneducated musically, that poetic, natural, almost childlike element in the man and his music strikes home to their sympathies and intuitive comprehension."[114] This statement, made in 1898, documents how much the concert scene had changed. Whereas the Bostonians of the 1850s and 1860s were pitching lieder to the musically educated, Heinrich reached wider audiences, in terms of both geography and musical taste or experience.

6

Villa Whitney White and Women's Music Clubs

In an 1898 anecdote, an inquisitive child asked what a song recital was—to which the child's uncle responded: "A song recital? Well, somebody sings all afternoon, and an audience of women talk through the whole performance."[1] Published on the "Page of Fun" section of a Detroit newspaper and reprinted in numerous papers across the United States, this comment satirizes both recitals and the women in the audiences. The fact that so many outlets published this item highlights two aspects of nineteenth-century culture: the ubiquity of song recitals and a flawed perception of such functions as social opportunities for women who cared little for the music.[2] In reality, women's music clubs strove to enhance the musical skills of members and to enrich their communities by supporting high-quality performances and repertoire presented by eminent artists. The public concerts that they sponsored included classical orchestral works conducted by stars such as Anton Seidl (1850–1898), as well as song recitals by the likes of Max Heinrich and George Henschel.[3] Rose Fay Thomas (1852–1929), wife of Theodore Thomas and one of the leaders in the establishment of the National Federation of Music Clubs, discussed the role clubs were playing in elevating musical culture during her address to the Woman's Musical Congress, which she hosted in Chicago in 1893.[4] This goal of cultural uplift had inspired many of the efforts of her husband and other advocates of German music, including performers of lieder.

The number of women who participated in music clubs dramatically increased during the closing decades of the long nineteenth century. In 1893 there were 42 known clubs, and by January 1898 there were at least 225. Similarly, membership in clubs increased. Whereas the Schubert Club in St. Paul started with a membership of 75, by 1914 it peaked at 1,232, "making it the second largest music club in the United States."[5] Women auditioned to gain membership in these clubs, most of which expected members to perform in club concerts. Many of these performances involved the piano, whether it be in performing solo works or in accompanying singers or instrumentalists. At the same time as club membership flourished so, too, piano sales increased at a faster pace than in any of the preceding decades.[6]

In addition to enhancing the musical life of their communities, women's music clubs influenced the development of performers' careers. One such performer was Villa Whitney White, a mezzo-soprano whose presentations for the Amateur Musical Club in Chicago drew national attention and led to numerous other engagements throughout the country. White was best known for her lecture-recitals on the history of German song, and she was acclaimed as one of the most accomplished presenters, entertaining and educating audiences with her resonant voice, intelligence, and enthusiasm. Although these events were promoted as lecture-recitals, White often sang so much repertoire that her presentations were viewed as song recitals, and she gave them in some of the same concert series in which the most distinguished international artists gave song recitals. Like Henschel, she was affiliated with associates of Brahms and Julius Stockhausen in Europe and with the advocates of classical chamber music in Boston. In contrast to satirical representations of club recitals, White presented challenging repertoire which was often new to club members, and she sang in German at a time when other artists sometimes sang lieder in English. Through her lectures, she introduced audiences to the poetry of the lied, and in doing so strove to provide the type of cultural context for the works that most other singers did not address.

Early Career

Unlike some of the earlier exponents of the lied, White was an American; her family had settled in New England during the seventeenth century. She began her career by performing lieder and eighteenth-century arias in chamber concerts in New England. In 1882 she made her New York City debut, singing three lieder by Mendelssohn and Reinecke in a concert in Steinway Hall for the Teachers' Association, and in 1886 she returned to that hall to contribute six songs, including three lieder by Brahms, to a recital by Mrs. W. H. (Mary) Sherwood (b. 1855), a well-known Boston pianist.[7] From 1885 to 1889 she was a member of the professional quartet at the Central Congregational Church in Providence, Rhode Island, and by the end of the decade she was also serving on the Boston Conservatory's faculty.[8] She collaborated in concerts with other prominent Boston musicians, including Arthur Foote, and she toured with the

Eichberg String Quartet, America's first women's quartet. The quartet members, who had trained at the Boston Conservatory and at Joseph Joachim's school in Berlin,[9] might have influenced White's decision to study in Germany.

In 1891 White began studying with Amalie Joachim, the ex-wife of Joseph Joachim.[10] Amalie had studied with Stockhausen and was a close friend of Brahms. She performed numerous lieder and solo roles in Brahms's choral works, sometimes with the composer accompanying or conducting. During 1892 Amalie and White presented recitals in the United States that were comprised almost exclusively of lieder. As the assisting artist, White usually performed a small number of solo lieder, and the two women also gave between two and six duets. This tour overlapped with one of the Henschels' tours. George had appeared in concerts with Joachim in Europe, and in 1892 he and his wife presented recitals at some of the same US venues as Joachim. In addition, all three artists appeared as soloists during a performance of Bach's *St. Matthew Passion* in Boston.[11]

Throughout Joachim and White's tour, reviews offered tentative praise of White, whom they regarded as a young student although she was thirty-three. In contrast, they acknowledged Joachim as the foremost interpreter of the German lied and praised her beautiful, powerful sound. Although a few newspapers echoed the Leipzig *Signale* in focusing on the mercenary aspects of the tour,[12] most critics were supportive and reported that Joachim's recitals were well attended. Joachim, however, struggled with poor health, and a few critics noticed that her voice was showing the signs of age.

In letters to her friend Clara Doria Rogers, Joachim indicated her fondness for White while also mentioning her student's limitations. Joachim described White's voice as delicate and lyrical. Nevertheless, she indicated that it could be developed into a more dramatic instrument and that White had a potential career in both Germany and the United States.[13] After the tour White continued to spend up to six months of each year studying with Joachim in Germany, during which time she mastered the repertoire for the lecture-recitals that she began presenting in the United States in 1893. Whereas some of the earliest reviews of her performances are somewhat uneven and speak of a small voice, those of the late 1890s describe a poised artist with a rich voice that was particularly beautiful in the middle range.[14] This artistic maturation is likely the result of Joachim's teaching and the experience of performing with her.

While visiting her sister Ella (Mrs. Charles A. Bucknam; 1855–1943) in Minneapolis,[15] White met Mary B. Dillingham (1858–1949),who became her main accompanist from 1893. Dillingham also became a close companion and on several occasions joined White in Europe. From 1895 to 1898 the two women presented widely publicized lecture-recitals throughout the United States, many of which were hosted by women's clubs. Most reviews of White's recitals conclude

144   CHAPTER 6

with a sentence praising Dillingham's sensitive playing, but she did not have an independent career as a soloist, nor did she accompany other prominent musicians.[16]

Club Appearances

In 1895 White performed a series of four lecture-recitals at the Amateur Musical Club. This club often focused on serious repertoire, and its season also featured four lectures on Wagner by Walter Damrosch. White's events were held during the day, but they were open to the public, and newspapers printed their programs. She presented "Folksongs from the 15th Century to Contemporary Times," "Song in the Form of Arias," "Ballads and Romances," and a program of fifteen songs by Schubert.[17] White had been honing these programs and others for at least two years. Prior to her club series, she had presented stand-alone recitals and various combinations of two or three programs in locations where she was already well known. These included private homes, women's colleges, and clubs in Minneapolis and New England. She also presented multi-program series for the Schubert Club in St. Paul, the Fortnightly Music Club in Cleveland, and Lake Erie College in Painesville, Ohio.

According to a report from Iowa, White's performances in Chicago created a "furore."[18] Catapulted to fame, she set about fulfilling engagements in public venues and private homes in numerous cities.[19] Such was the repute of the Amateur Musical Club that her performances for this organization were often cited in advertisements for recitals in other cities. Her 1896 appearances included a recital for the Mozart Club in Jamestown, New York, a club that explicitly strove to elevate musical taste and that had also hosted the Henschels.[20] In Chicago she gave three more lecture-recitals for the Amateur Musical Club and appeared before other women's clubs as well as in numerous private homes of society women.

News of White's success also reached New York. In 1896 she performed four lecture-recitals at the home of the prominent patron and social activist Mrs. Arthur (Josephine) Dodge (1855–1928). These programs included complex repertoire such as the entire cycle of *Die schöne Müllerin*, as well as a selection of Irish, Welsh, English, and Scottish songs. Dodge was the daughter of Marshall Jewell (1825–1883), a former governor of Connecticut, and these recitals were widely publicized in New York papers and in *Vogue*.[21] Dodge's home was also the venue for White's recital before the Thursday Evening Club, an art and literature study group populated by socialites.[22] In addition, Dodge and her associates were "patronesses" of White's recital of spring songs at the Mendelssohn Glee Club. In 1897 White performed before several hundred patrons at an event aiding Dodge's charity the Jewell Day Nursery.[23]

From 1895 to 1898 White appeared in at least forty-five cities and towns across twenty-two states. Unlike Henschel's and Heinrich's tours, in most locations she gave more than one recital per visit, and at approximately 70 percent of the locations she performed for women's clubs. Although her programs might have been of interest to German immigrants, she rarely if ever appeared before German clubs, but occasionally her performances at women's clubs were covered by the local German press.[24] She usually appeared in the visiting artist series of women's clubs, many of which also showcased preeminent instrumentalists such as the virtuoso pianist Leopold Godowsky (1870–1938). In addition to her lecture-recitals for these clubs, White was invited to luncheons and receptions where she was sometimes called on to perform. Although most club appearances were open to the public, there were some exceptions. In 1898 her main recital in Denver was for associate members of the Tuesday Musical Club and out-of-towners, but the following day she gave a public performance of children's songs.

During her tours White was heard by over thirty clubs, more than double the number of clubs where either Heinrich or Henschel performed during the same years. This disparity came about in part because Heinrich and Henschel were more established artists who at the time were not appearing in so many regional venues. Heinrich was still scheduling recitals around performances in oratorios and concerts, and until his last tours, Henschel relied on bookings in major cities, particularly on the East Coast. From a broader vantage point, the volume of White's bookings with music clubs anticipated practices in the first decade of the twentieth century, when major stars (including David Bispham) were more willing to perform for the growing number of clubs in smaller locations beyond the Eastern Seaboard. The number of people who attended each recital (which newspapers did not report) varied depending on the size and outreach of each club and the size of the venue. Artists such as White and Heinrich were heard in venues that could accommodate at most three hundred,[25] but they also appeared in larger spaces. For instance, White's 1896 recitals for the Amateur Musical Club took place in the eight-hundred-seat Steinway Hall, and a few of the Henschels' club performances were in halls accommodating around one thousand people.

Like Dwight and Thomas, music clubs strove to improve the musical life of their communities by means of concerts featuring classical repertoire. A St. Paul paper observed that the Schubert Club's efforts to raise the standard of "music and musical ethics" in that city could be no better served than by hosting three lecture-recitals by White.[26] Although Henschel's and Heinrich's recitals were lauded as a type of education, such comments were usually in the context of educating singers and pianists. In contrast, the pedagogical aspects of White's presentations were part of a broader outreach.

A wide variety of clubs, organizations, and institutions throughout the country—and not just those devoted to music or those for women—regularly hosted public lectures. While many of these lectures were warmly received, as early as 1879 a newspaper article subtitled "Mania for Instruction" derided the "*improvement* mania" of women's clubs and repeated an anecdote of a woman knitting during a parson's lecture.[27] In contrast, White's audiences were described as attentive. According to reviews, her personal warmth, speaking voice, and ability to tailor her remarks to the audience's level resulted in lectures that were as enjoyable as her singing. Among the lecture-recitalists touring the country, the mezzo-soprano stood apart for her informative and entertaining programs; she even pleased the New York press:

> In a somewhat recently exploited department of musical art there has been an epidemic of late. . . . Among the most successful of all aspirants for honor in this popular field is Miss Villa Whitney White. . . . These lectures are not only entertaining but most instructive. Miss White's manner is exceedingly attractive and charming, holding her audiences thoroughly interested at all times.[28]

Mathews, himself a creator of lecture-recitals, similarly distinguished White from other presenters: "Of singers there are many and of musical lecturers not a few, but the combined intellectuality and artistic endowment which is possessed by Miss Villa Whitney White is indeed rare."[29] In addition to providing the historical context of the composers and their works, White explained the meaning of the texts and how they related to the music.[30]

Though White's recitals were well received, she was sometimes subjected to the same type of gendered reviews that occurred in some critiques of Lillian Henschel's performances. In anticipation of her appearance during a fundraiser in support of the Helen E. Pelletreau Scholarship Committee at the Pennsylvania College for Women, a press release reported that White's talks were "said to be admirable, with nothing pedantic about them, but everything that is bright, clever and womanly."[31] Just as Mrs. Henschel's voice was frequently referred to as "sweet," the word "charming" occurs in so many reviews of White's performances that at times it seems patronizing.

Programs and Repertoire

White's repertoire encompassed more than 160 songs arranged into at least fifteen lecture recitals (figure 6.1). These were not fixed programs, however, and individual numbers could be changed or moved from one program to another. The titles of the lectures, at least as they were reported in newspapers, varied, and some did not clearly indicate the variety of songs White presented. For instance, the program often referred to as "Folksongs from the 15th Century

Volks-Lieder, Songs from the 15th Century to Our Time
The Song in the Form of the Aria from the Seventeenth Century Until After
    Beethoven (including *An die ferne Geliebte*)
Ballads and Romances
Songs of Franz Schubert
Songs of Robert Schumann
Songs of Johannes Brahms
Songs of Robert Franz
International Folksongs (including Italian, French, Scandinavian,
    and Finnish songs)
Folksongs of the British Isles (Irish, Welsh, English, and Scotch songs)
Children's Songs
Sacred Music: A Historical Program That Encompasses the Four Seasons
    in the Church
Modern Sacred Song and Aria
Schubert, *Die schöne Müllerin*
Brahms, *Magelone Romances*
People's Songs of America

FIG. 6.1. Villa Whitney White's lecture-recitals

to Our Time," or sometimes "History of German Song" or "History of German Folksong," began with early songs that were originally notated as monophonic melodies and concluded with nineteenth-century lieder. "Ballads and Romances" comprised lieder ranging from Reichardt to Loewe, Schumann, and Brahms. While White's programs did not have the linguistic diversity of those given by the Henschels, some had greater variety in historical styles and genres. Furthermore, White was praised for her versatility in conveying the songs' contrasting moods, styles, and expressions.[32] White presented four programs more frequently than any of the others; they were often advertised under such titles as "Folksongs from the 15th Century to Our Time," "The Song in the Form of the Aria from the Seventeenth Century Until After Beethoven," "Ballades and Romances," and "Irish, Welsh, English, and Scotch Songs." In contrast, she gave programs devoted to one composer (Brahms, Franz, Schubert, or Schumann) far less often, and these recitals took place mainly in Chicago and New England. In general, song recitals focusing on one composer were not particularly common. They tended to be reserved for celebrations of milestones such as the fiftieth anniversary of a composer's death, though more frequently such celebrations presented programs comprising a range of vocal and instrumental genres. Many of White's programs, such as the one shown in figure 6.2, included some of the best-known lieder in the United States, but those dedicated to one composer

148   CHAPTER 6

Amateur Musical Club...

Four Vocal Recitals showing the development of the German
Song from the Fifteenth Century to our time

ARRANGED BY
DR. HEINRICH REIMANN, OF BERLIN

GIVEN BY
MISS VILLA WHITNEY WHITE

FIRST RECITAL

Volks-Lieder, Songs from the Fifteenth Century to our time.

Saturday, February 23, 1895, at 11 A. M.

15 WASHINGTON STREET

PROGRAMME

1	Ich Spring in diesem Ringe (1452)	
2	Minnelied (1460)	
3	Die Linde in Thal (1549)	
4	Lindenlaub (1549)	
5	Abschied von Innsbruck (1475)	
6	Pommersches Volkslied (1560)	
7	Wächterlied (1535)	
8	Schwäbisches Volkslied (1570)	
9	Der Hirsch	
10	Spinnerliedchen	
11	Tanzlied (1601)	*Hans Leo Hasler*
12	Sagt, wo sind die Veilchen hin? (1782)	*J. A. P. Schulz*
13	a Die Sendung / b Das Zeichen (1765)	*F. H. Himmel*
14	Gute Ruhe (1810)	*P. von Winter*
15	Ständchen	*W. A. Mozart*
16	Ständchen	*B. A. Weber*
17	Heiden-Röslein	*Franz Schubert*
18	Auf Flügeln des Gesanges,	*F. Mendelssohn*
19	An den Sonnenschein,	*R. Schumann*
20	Wiegenlied	*Joh. Brahms*

FIG. 6.2. Program for Villa Whitney White's "Volks-Lieder: Songs from the Fifteenth Century to Our Time." Sponsored by the Chicago Amateur Musical Club at the Washington Street clubrooms, Saturday, February 23, 1895, 11 a.m. Courtesy of the Chicago History Museum, ICHi-182672–001.

sometimes embraced a few less frequently performed lieder such as Brahms's *Heimweh* lieder and Schubert's "Ganymed" (D. 544).[33]

White assembled most of her programs with the assistance of Heinrich Reimann (1850–1906), an organist, music historian, and librarian working in Berlin. Reimann had assisted Amalie Joachim in formulating programs tracing the history of German song, and he published anthologies of the scores she used for her performances, along with samples of four historical programs.[34] These programs and scores encompassed folksongs, songs in folk style, and art songs. Both Joachim and Reimann had clear pedagogical aims, and they positioned their work in opposition to the "mass dissemination of parlor music."[35] By prioritizing German works, they modeled the significance of song to the German people and contributed to the nation-building efforts begun by previous publications of German folksongs, including those of Ludwig Uhland (1787–1862).[36] Many of White's American audiences, however, would not have realized the ideological aspects of Reimann's work. In the United States, Reimann was probably better known for his compositions for organ and his 1898 monograph on Brahms, but there are sporadic references to his work on German song. Ernestine Schumann-Heink occasionally performed a seventeenth-century "Spinnerliedchen" from one of his anthologies, and English-language versions of some of his arrangements of German, Polish, and Spanish folksongs were published as sheet music by Ditson.[37] The New York critics Richard Aldrich (1863–1937) and Henry Finck, both of whom lectured on folksong, were familiar with Reimann's research, and Finck concurred with Reimann's thesis that folksong heavily influenced the development of art music. The Ritters had similarly advanced this thesis during their recital series in 1869, and White also adopted it in her lectures.[38] White's "Folksongs from the 15th Century to Our Time" is one program of hers that hewed very closely to Reimann and Joachim's presentations. Indeed, she and Joachim had presented a variant of this program, which included a few duets, in Providence in 1892.[39] Her "Song in the Form of the Aria," which culminated with Beethoven, also closely adhered to one of her mentors' model programs. Her programs of sacred songs, international folksongs, and folksongs from the British Isles likewise drew from Reimann's anthologies.[40]

White's emphasis on singing complete song cycles was influenced by Joachim, who performed numerous complete cycles in Europe. Though American recitalists had been slowly increasing the frequency with which they presented lieder cycles, even in the mid-1890s these works were not a standard part of most recitals. In contrast, White gave repeated performances of Beethoven's *An die ferne Geliebte*, Schubert's *Die schöne Müllerin*, Brahms's *Magelone Romances*, Cornelius's *Christmas Songs* (op. 8), and Alexander von Fielitz's (1860–1930) *Eliland: Ein Sang vom Chiemsee* (op. 9). Before 1880 *An die ferne Geliebte* was given numerous times in Boston, where August Kreissmann performed it during the 1850s and 1860s, but by the end of the century performances were far from common, with Anton Schott being the only professional singer who favored it. In contrast, White gave this cycle quite frequently, in part because it was included in her "Song in the Form of the Aria" program. She presented *Die schöne Müllerin* at least thirteen times in venues from New York to Los Angeles. According to press reports, her performances were the first time the complete cycle had been heard on stages in Minneapolis, St. Paul, and Portland, Oregon. While many singers, including Max Heinrich and Henschel, performed individual songs from this cycle, even as late as 1904 the *New Yorker Staats-Zeitung* cautioned that performances of the entire cycle would not appeal to concertgoers who sought variety for their money.[41]

Although these cycles by Beethoven and Schubert are now usually sung by men, other nineteenth-century women sang them. Indeed, Joachim performed them in Europe, and she sang them on numerous occasions during her US tour. Whereas Joachim also performed *Winterreise* and *Dichterliebe* in Europe, there is no evidence that White performed these cycles, though she regularly programmed at least three songs from the former, and early in her career gave "Ich grolle nicht" from the latter.

White also did not perform Schumann's *Frauenliebe und -leben*, which was sung by Joachim as well as other contemporary American women. White might have eschewed this cycle because its musical style did not appeal to her or she believed that her voice, with its rich low range, was not suited to the songs, but another important reason could be that their texts did not align with her lived experience. In contrast to the devoted wife and mother portrayed in Chamisso's poems, White was quite independent. She did not come from a wealthy family; instead, she supported herself. Whereas Mrs. Henschel's and Mrs. Heinrich's careers were in large part determined by their husbands, White embarked on her own path. Her career differed not only from those of married female performers but also from those of unmarried vocalists, such as Lena Little, and vocalists who married when their performance careers began to wind down, as Marguerite Hall did. Despite the qualms that White might have had regarding the poems' themes, other women who had successful careers and large voices performed Schumann's cycle. Schumann-Heink was among these artists, but, unlike White, she cultivated an image of a loving mother.[42]

After studying Brahms's settings of fifteen poems from Ludwig Tieck's *Wundersame Liebesgeschichte der schönen Magelone und des Grafen Peter von Provence* (1797) with Joachim in Germany during the summer following Brahms's death in April 1897, White sang all or the majority of the cycle in cities that had not witnessed such performances before, including Minneapolis; St. Paul; Chicago; Portland, Oregon; and South Hadley, Massachusetts, at Mount Holyoke College. Previously, Heinrich Meyn had given most of the cycle in

Boston in 1891, and in February 1897 David Bispham presented the entire cycle in New York. Unlike White, however, Bispham had the assistance of three other singers, and both he and Meyn included readings of excerpts from Tieck's work to provide the narrative context for each song. Although such readings are often included in modern performances, it was not a standardized way of presenting the cycle in the nineteenth century. Moreover, Brahms himself indicated it was not necessary, and he also had reservations about performing the entire cycle in a single recital. His colleague Stockhausen did this on one occasion, and similarly Amalie Joachim seems to have given it only once: in 1896, the year before she worked on the cycle with White.[43] Although most advertisements imply that White sang the entire cycle, she omitted one (unnamed) song in Portland and "War es dir, dem diese Lippen bebten" and "Muss es eine Trennung geben" (nos. 7 and 12) in Boston.[44] There do not appear to be any technical elements that would have prevented her from singing these numbers, but perhaps their texts, which describe the yearnings of Peter (the lover of Magelone), were beyond her comfort level.

Unlike the other cycles that White sang, Cornelius's *Christmas Songs* and von Fielitz's *Eliland* are rarely performed today, but they were given by White's contemporaries. White often ended her sacred program with Cornelius's cycle of six Christmas songs, which Joachim also performed. It seems to have been a signature work for White; she performed it as early as 1893 and sometimes combined it with folksongs from the British Isles or, less frequently, with von Fielitz's song cycle. *Eliland* was not in Joachim's repertoire; its composer achieved a following in part because Lilli Lehmann promoted his works.[45] Breitkopf & Härtel published the score in 1896, but by that time the songs were already being performed; Wilhelm Heinrich gave one of the first performances of this work in Boston in 1895.[46] Von Fielitz was a professor at the Stern Conservatory in Berlin, and perhaps White met him while she was in that city during 1896 or 1897. One reviewer described the ten-song cycle as "weird love songs," likely because the texts by Kaspar Stieler (1632–1707) tell of a monk's love for a young nun.[47] The cycle was taken up by numerous other professionals and amateurs in the United States, including Nordica and members of women's clubs.[48] In 1906 Meyn performed the cycle, accompanied by the composer, who was then an instructor at the Chicago College of Music.[49] Although White did not perform the cycle as frequently as she did Cornelius's *Christmas Songs*, she did reprise it in later years, including during a recital at a 1910 normal course in Portland, Oregon.[50]

Unlike Heinrich and Henschel, White sang numerous folksongs. As with the cycles, her interest in folksongs was influenced by Joachim and Reimann, but other lieder singers also highlighted this repertoire. In the 1890s, recitals devoted to a particular nation's folksongs reflected the increasing significance of folk culture as European countries, and in particular those in the East, sought to create a national identity.[51] Writers such as Henry Krehbiel and Louis Elson toured the United States lecturing on folksongs from various European countries, and such presentations were paralleled by a flood of related publications on both sides of the Atlantic.[52] In 1895 the Schubert Club of St. Paul devoted multiple sessions to folksong, including presentations on American Indian music by the ethnographer Frances Densmore (1867–1957) and one on German folksong by White.[53] These and many of the other recitals, lectures, and publications focusing on the folksongs of specific nations had a clear pedagogical mission. In contrast, recitals focusing on ballads and folksongs of the British Isles, notably those of Harry Plunket Greene, were often intended as entertainment for large audiences. Indeed, although White's British Isles lecture-recital was informative, it appealed to audiences because the songs were sung in English, and a few, including the Welsh tune "All Through the Night," were well known. A review of White's performance of this program for the Ladies' Musical Club in Burlington, Iowa, in 1896 reported that it "was chosen particularly to meet the taste of the public."[54] Whereas White frequently gave this program, she rarely performed her international folksong program, though whether this reflected her preference or that of her audience is not known.[55]

White sometimes began her program of folksongs of the British Isles with three of Helen Hopekirk's settings of texts by Robert Burns: "Jockie's Ta'en the Parting Kiss," "Highland Balou," and "O Whistle and I'll Come to You, My Lad." On other occasions, she gave Hopekirk's "Flow Gently, Sweet Afton," a setting of another Burns poem, as an encore. These seem to be the only songs by a woman that White performed, and they are the only works by an American composer that she regularly programmed prior to 1898. It is highly likely that White met Hopekirk when both were living in Boston, but White performed these songs not because the composer was a woman or an American but, rather, because they were appropriate to her program. While some of White's programs might have been able to accommodate a lied by Clara Schumann, perhaps one that Amalie Joachim had sung, their concentration on German songs precluded works by American composers. Clubs often encouraged their members to perform works by women and American composers, but they chose not to exert control over the repertoire presented by touring artists.[56]

White's program of children's songs was the antithesis of those featuring complex cycles. She sang this program in at least six cities, sometimes for children and at other times at fundraisers for children's charities. Although White chose not to marry and did not have children, she had a strong sense of family: She was one of eleven children, and her father had five children from a previous marriage. White remained close to her sisters, in particular Ella, Stella (1860–1934), and Charlotte (a professional cellist, who trained with Robert

Hausmann in Germany, 1871–1952), who were teachers, as well as another sister, Julia Roberts White Dalrymple (1863–1947), an author of children's books. Villa's 1898 children's program in Portland comprised thirteen songs, including three from Schumann's *Liederalbum für die Jugend*, four by Taubert, Eugene d'Albert's (1864–1932) "The Hilarious Thrush," and Wilhelm Berger's (1861–1911) "The Boy and the Kite."[57] Presenting an entire program of pieces addressed to children was unusual, but other professional singers, including Joachim and Heinrich, offered selections from *Lieder-Album für die Jugend*, and earlier singers such as Clara Doria Rogers performed Taubert's works. It is likely that these types of songs were thought to appeal to female music makers in the audience, because many of them are relatively simple to perform and their texts concern ideas associated with the woman's sphere. Other recitalists occasionally gave performances for students and youth groups associated with women's clubs. Schott, for instance, presented free recitals for schools in Portland and other West Coast cities. But whereas he performed his standard repertoire, including "Erlkönig" and "Die beiden Grenadiere,"[58] White crafted her program for children, and she spoke directly to them.

Oregon to Massachusetts, 1897–1898

During her West Coast tours, White established a strong base of friends and supporters in Portland, Oregon. Her first appearances there were before the city's Musical Club. This group had formed relatively recently, and in 1896, after holding concerts by local performers that attracted about eight hundred "guests," it established a visiting artists series. The 150 associate members funded this enterprise by guaranteeing they would each purchase two seats per concert.[59] The first artist to appear in the series was Fannie Bloomfield-Zeisler, a Chicago-based pianist who had recently returned from successful performances in Europe and, like White, had previously performed for the Amateur Musical Club. White gave her first recitals for the Portland club on March 31 and April 1, 1897. When she returned the following December to commence her West Coast tour, she prefaced her presentation by praising the club's contributions to the city's cultural life, as well as its high standards and "lofty purpose."[60]

Dillingham did not join White on her first trip to Portland; rather, a local woman, Mrs. Harry Hogue (Blanche Hersey; 1868–1953), provided the piano accompaniments. Hogue became a leader of the local Christian Science community, a faith that White and the women in her family avidly practiced.[61] It is likely that White's continued interest in Portland was due to this community as well as to the warm welcome she received from the Musical Club.

While in Portland, White presented at least five lecture-recitals for the club in addition to other performances. During her first visit she gave "History of

German Songs" and "Folksongs of the British Isles," and at the end of 1897 Schubert's *Die schöne Müllerin* and Brahms's *Magelone Romances*. The combination of two cycles on adjacent evenings would challenge the most accomplished singers, let alone audiences. Despite this, tickets were more expensive than was typical, priced at one dollar and fifty cents instead of a dollar.[62] After these successful recitals White briefly left Portland to perform for the Ladies Musical Club of Tacoma, Washington, a club that other prominent lieder recitalists of the time had not visited. In contrast to her Portland events, this one was poorly attended.[63] When she returned to Portland, she sang Cornelius's *Christmas Songs* following the Christian Scientists' Christmas Day service. This took place in the church's Auditorium Hall, with an audience including local musicians and church members. During the following days she presented von Fielitz's cycle before a special meeting of the Musical Club, and club members also attended her performance of children's songs before the Carl Reinecke Society.[64]

White was not the only lieder recitalist to have success in Portland; both Schott and Heinrich subsequently worked with the Musical Club. It presented a series of five recitals by Schott during the summer of 1898. Although these were initially going to be held in private homes, there was so much demand that they were moved to Foreman Hall. Schott performed his typical German programs, including works such as Beethoven's "Adelaide" and *An die ferne Geliebte*, along with excerpts from Wagner's operas.[65] Exuding the same charm that had conquered New York audiences, he offered the women tips on singing technique, including the admonition to throw away their corsets so they could produce a dramatic vibrato.[66]

Despite the great interest shown in both Schott and White, their Portland recitals were not marketed in the same way as the Heinrich family's recital in November 1898. The Musical Club booked the Heinrichs in the Marquam, a venue for popular entertainments such as operas and minstrel shows that seated about sixteen hundred. It was reported that the Heinrichs' audience filled the hall. An advertisement listed all the songs in the program using their English titles, and other promotional material emphasized the American songs.[67] The program included more songs by American and English composers than Heinrich usually gave, and the lieder were restricted to familiar audience favorites like "The Two Grenadiers," "Erl King," and Brahms's so-called "Cradle Song." In contrast, Heinrich's Los Angeles recitals included a greater number of lieder, and the related newspaper notices printed the song titles in both German and English.

As she had in Portland, White performed in California months before the Heinrich family's first recital there. She was heard in San Francisco, Oakland, Redlands, and Los Angeles in January 1898, and in most instances performed in the same venues as other prominent singers. Except for Oakland, where she gave one performance, she presented at least three recitals in each location, typically two evening recitals and one matinee. During these three-program series, White performed her "History of German Songs" program and *Die schöne Müllerin*. In San Francisco, her third recital comprised folksongs from the British Isles followed by von Fielitz's *Eliland*.[68] In contrast, in Los Angeles and Redlands, her third performance was a matinee presentation of her children's program. Although one advertisement indicated that her performances were akin to the Henschels', critics did not compare the singers.

White's recitals were widely advertised, with one paper in San Francisco printing a large sketch depicting her to accompany an advertisement for her performances at the California Theater (figure 6.3). Despite these efforts, attendance was uneven, as was the case with some of Schott's and Heinrich's California recitals. One Los Angeles critic condemned the small audiences at White's recitals, opining that the citizenry was hindering their education by staying away from such cultural events and that the city was becoming "a laughing stock at home and abroad."[69] In contrast, reviews of White's performances and programs were positive and typically reported appreciative audiences.

White's series in Redlands was presented by the Spinet, the oldest federated women's musical organization in California, formed in 1894.[70] Although a reception in honor of White attracted more than two hundred guests, attendance at her recitals was uneven.[71] Press notices for her California recitals do not mention other women's clubs. There was, however, an informal reception for White in Los Angeles hosted by Mrs. C. C. Carpenter, a leading socialite who belonged to at least one women's club.

After leaving California, White worked her way back to the East Coast, giving recitals for the Ladies' Literary Club of Salt Lake City, the Tuesday Music Club in Denver (where she appeared in the same visiting artists series that the Henschels had during 1897), and the Fortnightly Club in Lincoln, Nebraska. She returned to audiences where she was well known, including those in Hartford, Connecticut, at the Heptorean Club in Boston, and at Mount Holyoke College (an institution where she knew the president and had given multiple recitals during each of the preceding years).

While the Henschels', the Heinrichs', and White's California recitals were months apart, their spring 1898 recitals in Boston were more closely scheduled. From February 16 to April 13, Wilhelm Heinrich (who was not related to Max) and Julia Terry presented a series of six "chamber concerts."[72] These included a recital by Marguerite Hall, a joint recital by Gertrude Edmands (who had studied with Henschel in London; ca. 1863–1956) and Wilhelm Heinrich, and a concert in which Wilhelm Heinrich collaborated with the harpist of the Boston Symphony Orchestra, Heinrich Schuecker (ca.1867–1913) and the historian and pianist Louis Kelterborn (1891–1933).[73] The Henschels gave a recital in this series

156   CHAPTER 6

FIG. 6.3. "Miss Villa Whitney White at the California [Theater]," *San Francisco Chronicle*, January 2, 1898, 35.

in addition to other Boston appearances, which included at least six other recitals, private soirées, and a variety of multi-genre concerts. Max Heinrich, who had given numerous performances in Boston during the preceding months, also contributed a recital to the chamber series. In this event, he was joined by his wife and daughter Julia as well as by Wilhelm Heinrich. Max's recital took place on the same evening as White's lecture-recital, which was not part of the series. The recitals in the chamber series were held in the seven hundred-seat

Association Hall,[74] whereas White's was in Steinert Hall. This thousand-seat hall was the venue for previous recitals by major national and international performers, including Amalie Joachim and the Henschels, and it was one of the highest-profile venues on White's tour.

Although Wilhelm Heinrich and Edmands presented songs by composers living in Boston,[75] most of the other recitals in the chamber series combined lieder with a variety of other songs in contrasting styles and languages. Hall's program, for instance, ranged from Bach and Jomelli to Brahms, Henschel, and Liza Lehmann, and it included a selection of French songs as well as American ones by Arthur Farwell (1872–1952) and Victor Harris (1869–1943), her accompanist.[76] In contrast, White performed thirteen songs from Brahms's *Magelone* cycle. While the large audience was said to have been pleased, two critics did not appreciate the songs, though both had also previously disparaged some of Brahms's other compositions as boring. Nevertheless, they praised White's delivery, unaffected manner, and intelligence.[77]

Denver Meeting of the General Federation of Women's Clubs

Rather than resting on her success in Boston, White returned to the road, performing in Cleveland; Davenport, Iowa; and Paris and Louisville, Kentucky. This series of recitals culminated with a triumphant recital in Denver at the fourth biennial meeting of the General Federation of Women's Clubs in June 1898. For this performance, she was joined by Anita Muldoon (1866–1909), a singer from Louisville who briefly worked in Chicago when White was based there during the mid-1890s. By this time the federation encompassed about 595 clubs, and the conference was attended by representatives from forty-two states. This was the largest federation conference to date, and its size and the diversity of the program were attributed to Ellen (Mrs. Charles) Henrotin (1847–1922), the industrious president of the federation.[78] Although this organization's third biennial conference in 1896 in Louisville had included a lecture on the history of German lieder authored by Emilie Schipper (of Plainfield, New Jersey), White's event was the first widely advertised recital for such a conference.

Newspapers from New York to Los Angeles covered this conference, and many mentioned White's recital. Her program encompassed African American, Native American, and Creole songs, which were performed in their original dialects, as well as songs by Caucasian composers dating from 1770 to 1865 (figure 6.4).[79] White, influenced by her work with Reimann and by contemporary discussions in the United States, made the argument that African American, Native American, and Creole songs were being absorbed into the wider culture

Part 1 Melodies of the North American Indians, "Creole Melodies" and "Negro Melodies."

Part 2 The People's Music of America from 1770 until 1865.

Chester, Majesty	William Billings, 1746–1800
Windham	Daniel Read, 1757–1800
China	Timothy Swan, 1758–1842
Plainfield	Jacob Kimball, 1759–1840
Celestial Watering	Jeremiah Ingalls, 1762–1843
Coronation (1793)	Oliver Holden
Missionary Hymn	Lowell Mason, 1792–1872
Ortonville	Thomas Hastings
Federal Street	Henry Kimball Oliver, 1800–1885
Sweet Hour of Prayer	William Batchelder Bradbury, 1816–1868
Speed Away	Isaac Baker Woodbury, 1819–1858
Old Folks at Home	Stephen Collins Foster, 1826–1864
Nellie Was a Lady	
Gentle Annie	
The Shining Shore	George Frederick Root, 1820–1896
Hazel Dell	
Rosalie, The Prairie Flower	
Darling Nellie Gray	B. R. Hanby
Rock Me to Sleep, Mother	Ernest Leslie
Sweet Genevieve	Henry Tucker
War Songs	
Maryland, My Maryland	
The Bonny Blue Flag	
Marching Through Georgia	Henry C. Work
Battle Cry of Freedom	George F. Root
	Villa Whitney White

North American Indian Melodies
Hae-Thu-Ska Song
Hubae Wa-an (Sacred Pole Song)
Hae-Thu-Ska Song (Song of Dismissal, Chorale)
Hae-Thu-Ska Song
Wa-Wan Wa-an (Song of Approach)
Choral—Wa-Wan Wa-an (After Pipes Are Raised)
Omaha Prayer
Hae-Thu-Ska Wa-an (Dance Song)

Creole Slave Songs
Ah! Suzette, Pov' Piti Momzel Zizi, Criole Candjo
Villa Whitney White

Negro Melodies
The Jews That Took Our Saviour
Mourn Lak' a Turtle Dove
Ma' Baby Lo'es Shortnin' Bread
Round About the Mountain (A Funeral Hymn)
Canaan, Bright Canaan
The Lord Is With Us
Some Come Cripple (A Shouting Hymn)
Freely Go Marching (A Baptism Hymn)
Met Miss Betsy in de Road
Res' My Soul
No Hidin' Place Down Thar
The Gospel Train
[Encore: The Sun Shines in My Old Kentucky Home]
Anita Muldoon

FIG. 6.4. Villa Whitney White's lecture-recital for the Fourth Biennial Meeting of the General Federation of Women's Clubs in Denver, June 20, 1898, as reported in "Clubs," *Courier* (Lincoln, NE), August 20, 1898, 5.

and becoming folksongs. She concluded the program by leading the sixteen-hundred-strong audience in a chorus of "The Battle Cry of Freedom."[80]

White and Muldoon were contracted to appear by Eva Perry Moore (Mrs. Philip North Moore, 1852–1931).[81] Moore was president of the St. Louis Music Club from 1892 to 1903 and responsible for organizing the music programs for the Denver conference. She might have met White when the singer presented recitals for women's clubs in St. Louis in 1896 and 1897, and White's successful performances before so many women's clubs throughout the country made her an ideal choice for the federation's conference. Moore might also have met Muldoon when she performed in St. Louis in 1892 and 1893. It's more likely, however, that Muldoon was contracted to sing at Denver after her performance of some of the songs illustrating the lecture on German song at the federation's 1896 conference, which Moore and Henrotin attended, or that the program committee approached her on the recommendation of her friend Mildred J. Hill (1859–1916), an authority on African American songs.[82] Muldoon and White had not collaborated with each other prior to their recital in Denver, and they did not appear together after it.

Neither of these women's previous recitals included African American or Native American songs, and it is not known who formulated the theme of the Denver recital. Moore, who said she had been interested in folksongs for some time, introduced the session by explaining that the history of American folk-song lies in the diverse origins of its people,[83] an idea that had been circulating in the press for a few years, though it was not universally accepted. But the fact that Moore introduced White's session does not mean that she was solely responsible for its theme; Henrotin probably also influenced it. Both Ellen and her husband Charles played significant roles on the committees that organized the 1893 World's Columbian Exposition in Chicago, with Ellen serving as the vice president of the Woman's Branch of the World's Congress Auxiliary, which organized the programs during the fair and hosted the associated International Folk-Lore Congress.[84] Frederick W. Root (1846–1916), a revered singing teacher and composer in Chicago, organized the highly successful Concert of Folk Songs and National Music that was held during one of the evenings of the Folk-Lore Congress. Both this event and some of those at the exposition included performances and lectures about the types of American songs on White's later program. Ellen was an influential participant in several Chicago clubs, including the West End Club, where White performed in 1895. Given the press coverage of White's successes and her multiple appearances in homes of Chicago society women, Henrotin must have at least known of her, and perhaps she contacted White and/or Root to create the program for Denver.[85]

A program comprised of such diverse American songs had rarely if ever been given by a singer of White's status. There had been lectures devoted to each of the genres, however, and some of these included a performance of a few representative songs. Three such lectures were presented at the exposition's Musical Congress. The pathbreaking ethnologist Alice C. Fletcher (1838–1923) and her associate John Comfort Fillmore (1843–1898) explored songs of Omaha Indians; Krehbiel spoke on African American songs; and Elson discussed music of the Pilgrims and "national" songs.[86] White was in Europe during this event, but she might have learned about these sessions from Root, Henrotin, or Calvin Cady (1851–1928), her close friend, who attended the exposition. Like the rest of the congress, the concert that Root organized embraced music from many nations, and some of the performers had also appeared at the exposition.[87] The American selections included five Native American songs, three Creole songs, two spirituals sung by a quartet, and three patriotic songs. White's later program likewise embraced these types of songs and, like the 1893 program, her selection of songs composed by Caucasians opened with "Chester" by Billings and ended with the "Battle Cry of Freedom" (figure 6.4). White acknowledged Root as assisting her in creating this part of her program, and it's possible that he also pointed her to information and scores for the Native American and Creole songs she performed.

The Omaha Indian songs that White sang had been published, with Fillmore's European-style diatonic harmonies and performance instructions, in Fletcher's *Study of Omaha Indian Music*, and White quoted both Fletcher and Fillmore.[88] Although she sang in dialect, White indicated that she was not replicating the "nasal" timbre or tuning that she believed was typical of the original performers.[89] Two of the pieces, "Song of Dismissal" and "Song of Approach," had previously been performed by Francis La Flesche (1857–1932), an Omaha Indian and ethnographer, during Root's concert for the earlier Folk-Lore Congress.[90]

White's three Creole songs had been published in an article by George Cable in the *Century Magazine* in 1886, where "Criole Candjo" appeared in an arrangement by Krehbiel.[91] Cable also gave a presentation titled "Creole Folksongs" during the Folk-Lore Congress. White probably acquired the scores she used in 1898 from Root or Cable. Krehbiel's lecture at the 1893 exposition focused on African American songs, but he also referenced other types of songs, and the accompanying performance included one Creole and one Iroquois song.[92] He asserted that African American songs (including Creole ones) were American folksongs, and in so doing negated earlier authors who had expressed claims to the contrary.[93] White made similar arguments in her presentation. Whereas Krehbiel's session included a performance of "Nobody Knows de Trouble I've Seen," which was already known to many, Muldoon noted that she did not give familiar African American songs.

In an interview prior to the Denver lecture-recital, Muldoon echoed themes propounded by earlier writers, in particular, by those responding to the 1893 premiere of Dvořák's *New World Symphony*.[94] Some of her songs were given to her by Mildred Hill, an influential music historian and composer in Louisville and a member of the Louisville Women's Club.[95] In 1896 Hill accompanied Muldoon's performances of some of her children's songs, which were influenced by African American songs, and at one of the other concerts during the Denver conference Muldoon performed her "March On, Brave Lads, March On."[96] Hill's 1892 article "Negro Songs" was known to Krehbiel and Dvořák.[97] In the months prior to the exposition, Krehbiel had previewed his lecture recital "Folk-Song in America" in Louisville, and Hill played the piano accompaniments for the local singers who performed the songs he discussed.[98] Given Hill's prominence and her friendship with Muldoon, she likely influenced Muldoon's research; she might also have informed her of Krehbiel's research.[99]

Like Hill and Krehbiel, and also some of those who heard the Fisk Jubilee Singers and the Hampton Institute Singers perform spirituals, Muldoon believed that the songs of African Americans were American folksongs. While learning songs for her presentation she came to understand (like Hill) the importance of preserving old songs such as the ones she performed, because young African Americans were forgetting them and also forgetting how to sing them. Muldoon had heard Black servants singing when she was a child, and while researching her presentation she listened to other old Black musicians in Kentucky (as Hill had previously done).[100] Hill, in her publications, and Krehbiel, in his talk, mentioned the importance of sorrow and suffering in African American songs, but reports of the Denver recital give no indication that either White or Muldoon explained that the roots of these songs lay in the trauma of slavery. Although Muldoon sang in dialect, in her interview she stressed that she could not completely render the songs the way an African American would, a distinction that Hill had drawn in an 1895 article.[101] She also noted the difficulties in finding accompaniments that follow the songs' unusual harmonies, and for that reason she sang the songs unaccompanied. However, none of the reviews of the recital made any mention of this.

Muldoon concluded her part of the program with an enthusiastically received encore. But rather than singing another African American number she gave Stephen Foster's "My Old Kentucky Home." Today, this choice would be unacceptable because of Foster's association with minstrelsy and this song's inclusion in such shows, as well as the lyrics' derogatory reference to African Americans. Nevertheless, neither Muldoon nor her audience registered discomfort; indeed, this song was among those that Frederick Douglass had praised for their potential to "awaken the sympathies for the slave, in which anti-slavery principles take root, grow, and flourish."[102]

Given their lack of experience with American songs, White and Muldoon were not obvious presenters for this type of program. The federation could

162   CHAPTER 6

have hired Krehbiel, Elson, Fletcher, and Fillmore, all of whom gave lectures in other venues during 1898, but because the event took place in the evening it is highly likely they wanted entertaining performances rather than lectures, and they preferred women performers, and especially ones with connections to women's clubs.[103]

The Denver audience responded enthusiastically to both White and Muldoon. Reviews consistently described their performances and explanatory commentaries as engaging and as demonstrating their deep appreciation for the songs. Like other contemporary reports of people hearing songs from unfamiliar cultures, at least two reviews suggested that the audience had somewhat negative reactions to one of the Omaha Indian songs because the words could not be understood and, similarly, the words of one Creole song and some of the African American songs were described as "non-sensical."[104] Similarly, although Muldoon venerated the African American songs, she showed no appreciation for Native American music, which she described as "merely a succession of shouts and howls," and she devalued Creole songs because she believed they were derived from other countries.[105]

Despite its success, White and Muldoon did not reprise the complete Denver program in subsequent engagements. White's sister Evelyn (1867–1959) taught at Atlanta University, an African American institution founded in 1865 by the American Missionary Association, from 1891 to 1892, and White performed at a fundraiser for this institution in 1894. But despite this connection to a Black university and the research she carried out for the Denver recital, she did not continue to program diverse American songs.[106] Subsequent recitals that she titled "People's Songs of America" and "Development of American Folk Song" centered on repertoire by white composers that she sang in Denver. This focus is at odds with the inclusive theme of her Denver program. Moreover, the titles of these recitals and the title "People's Music," which White used for the second part of her 1898 conference recital, while typical of ones used by authors covering similar repertoire, implies that Native Americans and African Americans were not people. Nevertheless, this type of affront eluded even well-intentioned white performers and audiences of the time. In contrast, Muldoon occasionally presented African American songs in her later recitals, but she did not achieve the same type of national profile that White did. She mainly performed for women's clubs and local organizations in Kentucky, and most of these performances took place before her marriage in 1907.

The themes of White and Muldoon's Denver program were attracting increasing attention. Less than a month after their performance at the federation's conference, the National Congress of Music, which took place at the Trans-Mississippi and International Exposition in Omaha, featured lectures by Elson and Fletcher. Elson expanded on themes of his address to the 1893 exposition by giving greater attention to Civil War songs. During "Indian Music Day," Fletcher's and Fillmore's presentations were followed by a performance by La Flesche.[107] While the Thursday Musical Club (of Minneapolis) hosted a presentation by Densmore in 1895, similar club presentations about indigenous repertoire only became more common during the following decade, when Arthur Farwell lectured on this topic to clubs across the country.[108] Although the 1898 National Congress of Music did not consider African American music, a growing number of publications and scores were already drawing attention to this repertoire. Not all of these, however, were as scholarly as Krehbiel's and Hill's work, and some scores likely included corrupted versions of the songs. In 1886, for example, a short notice about music scores in the *Ladies' Home Journal* listed "plantation songs" along with such other genres as operatic and sacred songs as being readily available in cheap editions.[109] And in 1897 a newspaper advertisement for a recital by Jeanette Robinson Murphy (1865–1946), who performed programs of African American songs (many of which were before East Coast women's groups) and also researched the tunes' history, remarked on the "fad in the study of negro musical folklore."[110]

Although White and Muldoon's program did not attract the attention of East Coast music critics, it anticipated trends in recital programs of the following decades. Bispham and other prominent recitalists occasionally programmed a few spirituals and arrangements of Native American melodies, but there seems to be no connection between these later singers and White. Instead, some of these singers were influenced by Harry Burleigh (1866–1949) and by members of the Indianist movement. Around 1919 Nelda Hewitt Stevens (1888–1948), who had previously given programs of antebellum songs that included a few "plantation" numbers, created a program titled "Phases of American Music" that was similar in design to White and Muldoon's recital in that it included songs by indigenous, African American, and Caucasian composers. She presented this type of recital for the eleventh biennial convention of the National Federation of Music Clubs and in numerous other venues through the 1930s.[111] She might have known about the Denver program and, more likely, the research of Mildred Hill. Like Muldoon and Jeanette Murphy, she grew up in Louisville and had first learned African American songs by listening to servants, but she also carried out more extensive research than Muldoon. Some of the accompaniments of the Black songs she performed were created for her by Nathaniel Clark Smith (1877–1935) of the Tuskegee Institute.

New Opportunities

White did not maintain a demanding touring schedule after her presentation in Denver. She continued to sing lieder in chamber recitals in New England, however, and occasionally performed in Chicago. A confluence of issues contributed to her reduced performing schedule and her return to Boston. At about this time her pianist and companion, Mary Dillingham, returned to Minneapolis to teach piano; White's longtime mentor, Amalie Joachim, died on February 3, 1899; and around April 1899 White became the soloist at the Christian Scientist Church in Concord, New Hampshire, a position she held until approximately June 1903, when that community adopted congregational singing rather than using a soloist.[112] In 1899 White also took a teaching position at the Hartford Conservatory, where she had already established considerable influence and was a member of the Board of Managers. Such was her reputation that she attracted pupils, most of whom were young women, from around the country. As a teacher she considered poetry, rhythm, melody, harmony, and form to be more important than the vocal utterance itself, an approach that aligned with those of Heinrich and Henschel.[113]

Beginning in 1906, White taught with Calvin Cady in Boston and in Portland, Oregon. She had worked with Cady in Chicago and, through her influence, in 1897 the Musical Club of Portland began to sponsor summer normal schools for music teachers modeled on those Cady gave in Chicago. Josephine Large, a Chicago pianist and associate of Cady and White, led the club's first summer school, and Cady himself directed subsequent schools.[114] Although White continued to be based in New England, many of her performances were in Portland, where she appeared at these summer schools, in conjunction with Cady's other ventures, and in private homes of women patrons. By 1913 Cady and his wife had established a music school for elementary students in Portland, with both White and Large among its directors. White's most ambitious project in Portland was a 1913 series of lecture-recitals reprising eight of her earlier programs. Linda Ekman (d. 1963), a fellow Christian Scientist with whom she had started to collaborate in Boston around 1907, provided the piano accompaniments.[115] After 1916 Cady no longer hosted summer recitals but, rather, focused his energies on the Cornish School of the Arts in Seattle. By that time White was fifty-eight, and although she continued to teach, it seems she no longer performed professionally. At about the same time, she relocated permanently to Portland, where during the mid-1920s she presented music appreciation classes for the MacDowell Club.

* * *

White's career trajectory was not typical for professional singers, especially not for a woman. Unlike contemporary women singers with national reputations such as Marguerite Hall, White rarely performed in oratorios or appeared in concert with the most prominent vocalists. Nevertheless, her success enabled her to compete in the busy 1896–1898 concert seasons when numerous international song recitalists were touring. Her engaging explications of lieder texts helped her avoid the types of criticisms of Germanocentric programs that were occasionally lobbed at some of her contemporaries. Whereas other singers fully appreciated that the words and music were equally important in lieder, White conveyed this to her *audiences*. In this way, she performed a much greater service in informing Americans of the meaning and historical context of lieder than did Henschel and many other singers. White's performances—and women's music clubs in general—perpetuated the ethos that classical music could uplift concert life and society that had been promulgated by Dwight and Thomas.

White's accomplishments, however, highlight the circumscribed role of women in music in the 1890s. Despite belonging to a family of strong women, having sisters who had careers, belonging to a faith led by a woman, and becoming successful in her own right, White did not use her agency to advance songs by women. She certainly chose not to conform to society's expectations in many ways, but moving beyond canonic composers to perform works by women (or, for that matter, to reprise the Creole or Native American songs she gave at the 1898 federation concert) seems not to have interested her. In part this might have been because Joachim seldom performed lieder by women. In contrast, during the early decades of the twentieth century an increasing number of recitalists regularly programmed songs by women.

Although White did not have the same impact on US concert life as Henschel or Heinrich, her success exemplifies the great interest in the lied during the late 1890s and attests to the role of women's clubs in disseminating this genre. Whereas more prominent artists such as Henschel repeatedly returned to cultural meccas such as Boston, White's tours demonstrate that there were receptive audiences for the lied in smaller locales in other parts of the country and at a growing number of institutes of higher learning. Her performances at social events, including fundraisers for charities in New York, New England, Pennsylvania, and Minneapolis, likewise indicate that the lied was very much in fashion. In addition, her folksong programs were always warmly received, and her American programs aligned with the increasing attention paid to American composers during the early decades of the twentieth century. It is her historical lecture-recitals, including that for the 1898 Denver conference, and her performances of complete lieder cycles, however, that signify the willingness of women's clubs to engage with complex, unfamiliar repertoire. In some ways her emphasis on cycles and the diverse repertoire of her Denver presentation were ahead of their time; many other singers did not adopt these repertoires until the new century.

7

David Bispham and the
Heyday of Song Recitals

At the peak of the song recital's popularity avid fans packed halls to hear David Bispham. During a multifaceted career, he earned plaudits for erudite recital programs and dramatic renditions of lieder, as well as for promoting American composers and singing in the vernacular. Although music was discouraged by the Quaker faith of Bispham's family, the young man sang in a variety of groups in Philadelphia including Michael Cross's choir at the Holy Trinity Church, the Orpheus Club, and the Arion Singing Society of Germantown. Max Heinrich, a fellow Philadelphian, befriended the young Bispham, and on at least one occasion (in 1885) they performed solo roles in Bach's *St. Matthew Passion*.[1] After attending Haverford College, a Quaker institution, Bispham complied with his family's wishes and worked in their wool business. At the age of thirty, however, after devoting all his spare time to singing and acting with amateur organizations, he went to Europe to commence a career in music.

In England, Bispham studied with William Shakespeare (1849–1931), a venerated voice teacher who taught numerous English and American lieder singers.[2] In 1886 he studied with similarly influential teachers Luigi Vannuccini (1828–1911) and Francesco Lamperti in Italy.[3] By this time, he had already married Caroline Russell (1860–1943) and had a daughter, Vida; Jeanette, Leonie, and David were born in England. After performing in a variety of theatrical works in England's provinces, Bispham began to establish a reputation as a concert singer in London. In 1892 he made his Covent Garden debut, singing the part of Beckmesser in *Die Meistersinger von Nürnberg*. Building on the success he achieved in this production, he burst onto the American scene with performances in the same role at the Metropolitan Opera in New York in November 1896. The US press immediately paid attention, at times pointing out the novelty of an American-born star, and a Quaker at that. Newspapers across the country claimed his appearances in operas and concerts could earn him as much as $30,000 per year.[4] At the end of a career lasting just under thirty years, Bispham reported that he had amassed a repertoire of about fourteen hundred songs, which he rendered in more than eight hundred recitals. He also appeared in around fifty operas and over one hundred oratorios and cantatas.[5]

Bispham's unusually diversified career was shaped by his abiding devotion to the theater. Although he acted throughout his career, most of his professional work in the theater took place during his initial years in England and the last decade of his life in the United States.[6] His success as an opera singer likewise set him apart from the earlier advocates of the lied, who were predominantly concert singers. Bispham performed with the Metropolitan Opera company until April 1903, appearing in both New York and touring productions.[7] He sang solo roles in Wagner's *Die Meistersinger, Lohengrin, Tristan und Isolde, Tannhäuser, Der fliegende Holländer,* and the 1899 and 1901 productions of the *Ring* cycle, as well as in stand-alone productions of *Siegfried* and *Die Walküre.* Although he was best known for these performances, he also appeared in operas by Mozart and Verdi. In addition, he performed solos during many major choral festivals, including those in Birmingham, England, Worcester, and Cincinnati. In all these venues and during national festivals of German men's choruses, he often shared the stage with other distinguished soloists, including Nordica and Ernestine Schumann-Heink, and the performances were led by esteemed conductors such as Thomas.

On returning to the United States, Bispham immediately attracted a cult following. Throughout the subsequent years, newspapers noted his personal charm and alluded to his appeal to women. Though some observed that his physical appearance was not strikingly attractive, others viewed him as debonair, with one paper describing him as "mighty well done up" (figure 7.1).[8] When discussing Bispham's followers, a New York critic reported having heard women in an audience whispering "such sweet expressions as 'Oh, isn't he lovely?' [and] 'Ah, what a man!'" This description was reprinted in other papers, including one in San Francisco that observed: "At last the matinee girl and the woman hero-worshiper of New York have found an American to burn incense before instead of seeking out hirsute foreigners as the objects of their adoration."[9] Dashing conductors and instrumentalists were frequently idolized by adoring female fans, who were sometimes referred to as "symphony girl[s],"[10] but such comments were not made about either Heinrich or Henschel. Moreover, Bispham's appeal was not confined to East Coast women, as he quickly began to realize the potential rewards of appearing before women's clubs. At the end of 1897 he appeared before the "musically cultured" women of the Wednesday Morning Musical Club in Nashville in an informal recital in the private home of a socialite (and friend). A report of this performance in the social pages stressed Bispham's

168   CHAPTER 7

FIG. 7.1. David Bispham in 1897. Photograph held in the Philip Hale Photograph Collection, Boston Public Library.

artistic credentials, but first noted his pleasing appearance and charm.[11] The following year, a large photograph of Bispham was prominently placed above the title of an article about American male concert singers in *Godey's Magazine* (a publication for women), even though he was not discussed until three pages later, where we read that his "star has swum into our ken very suddenly and very brilliantly."[12]

In contrast to the preceding decades, from the late 1890s numerous opera stars presented song recitals. Bispham's programs were designed to set him apart from his competition, with the press frequently reporting that he performed songs other artists were ignoring. Initially he established a reputation for offering challenging, serious programs and, in particular, complete lieder cycles. In the final decade of his career, however, he immersed himself in promoting recitals in the English language and performing songs by American composers. Although other singers were involved in these campaigns, Bispham's leadership roles in well-publicized organizations, and the fact that the press considered him quotable, gave him a broader platform than most. Campaigns to promote singing in English and the works of American composers were intertwined with sociopolitical changes that, in part, were influenced by the growing tensions in Europe that culminated in World War I. By the time the United States entered the war Bispham's voice had started to deteriorate, but he continued to give the occasional recital until his death in 1921.

A "Craze for Singers"

In the closing decades of the nineteenth century, song recitals were near rampant in Germany and Austria, and in the United States they were also considered "much in vogue."[13] Bispham was one of the opera stars to capitalize on their popularity. After numerous successful recitals in Europe, Lilli Lehmann gave her first US recital in 1897, and she continued to give recitals until 1902.[14] Marcella Sembrich gave recitals during the period 1900–1917, and other stars of the Metropolitan Opera, including Johanna Gadski, Nordica, Schumann-Heink, and Anton Van Rooy (1870–1932), a former pupil of Stockhausen, were also active recitalists. Although these singers were among Bispham's chief competitors, many were also his colleagues and collaborators. That so many recitals were given by stars, locally renowned singers, and amateurs is a testament to the economic rebound in the United States after the recessions of the preceding years. This flourishing economy supported not only an expansion in the number of recitals but also continued increases in sales of pianos and sheet music and the further development of women's music clubs, all of which also contributed to the dissemination of the lied throughout the country.

The pecuniary aspect of song recitals was frequently reported in the press. In reviewing the 1898–1899 and 1899–1900 concert seasons in New York, Henry Finck concluded that the song recitals given by Lehmann, Nordica, Sembrich, and Schumann-Heink, which excluded arias, "yielded them three or four times as much as an evening at the opera."[15] Whereas the best seats at a Henschel recital usually cost $1.50, those for the joint recital by Nordica and Schumann-Heink in 1900 were $2.50.[16] The Apollo Club in Denver paid Bispham $600 for each

170   CHAPTER 7

of the three recitals he gave there in 1907–1908, though locations with smaller halls, such as Hays, Kansas, paid less.[17] In March 1913 Nordica was so successful in packing a Phoenix hall that the ticket revenue was reported to be $2,000.[18]

Recitals by opera stars, however, were not always ambitious musical endeavors. Nordica and Schumann-Heink's 1899 recital in New York was lambasted both for its uninspired medley of familiar lieder and songs by MacDowell and for the quality of the singing of both stars. Furthermore, the "fashionable" audience was castigated for applauding at the wrong times and being there more for "sight seeing" than listening.[19] As in earlier years, attendance at recitals carried a good deal of social cachet and reflected one's social standing and culture. Some audience members also attended to hear their favorite singer. On one occasion, a critic went so far as to say that there was such a "craze for singers" that the significance of the actual compositions was lost on the public.[20]

Lieder dominated many recitals, but there was not a standardized programming format. Polyglot recitals comprised of German, French, and English songs had been growing in popularity since the 1880s, and many reflected the development of French art songs by programming new composers such as Fauré.[21] Sembrich distinguished herself from other artists who were presenting polyglot programs by exploring songs in Russian and Polish. Some critics, however, complained that there were too many of these recitals and that many singers did not have the required pronunciation skills. They also observed that audiences took more pleasure in hearing songs in English.[22] As a result, some recitalists, including members of women's clubs, sang English translations of songs from a variety of countries.[23]

It is not clear whether singers or audiences related polyglot programs to the types of national operas developing in Europe or to wider sociopolitical movements. Nonetheless, in both Europe and the United States, these developments influenced the increasing number of pedagogical publications and lecture-recitals that highlighted national schools of music. Prominent New York music critics including William Henderson and Henry Krehbiel lectured and published on national schools of folksongs and art songs. Finck organized his 1900 monograph *Song and Song Writers* according to national schools, and while German composers dominated, he also considered composers who were Hungarian, Slavic, Scandinavian (Grieg), Italian, French, and American (MacDowell). Similarly, numerous song recitals continued the tradition of programming folksongs from various European countries.

Establishing a Place in a Crowded Market

When he returned to the United States to sing at the Met, Bispham also set about giving recitals and concerts in New York and Philadelphia, as well as in other nearby cities. Almost immediately he was confronted with competition from Lilli Lehmann. On the same day as his first New York recital, Lehmann appeared in the afternoon in Carnegie's main hall, while Bispham sang in the evening in the smaller Carnegie Lyceum.[24] The *Tribune* claimed that Lehmann's recital provided "a sensation" that was only comparable to the reaction to Paderewski's piano recitals.[25] Her program included only thirteen songs, five of which were Wagner's *Wesendonck Lieder*. Although this collection's "Träume," "Im Treibhaus," and "Schmerzen" had been sung numerous times in the United States, and the score of "Träume" was included in anthologies of popular lieder, singing the entire cycle was unusual. But this novelty did not prevent critics from viewing the program as uninteresting. In his recital, Bispham gave the American premiere of Brahms's *Vier ernste Gesänge*, which he had recently introduced to London audiences. While critics praised his efforts in presenting Brahms's complex songs, none of their compliments were comparable to their effusive response to Lehmann's performance.[26]

Bispham's initial recitals included more lieder than did Lehmann's program, though most also included performances by other singers and instrumentalists. His second recital, in which he was assisted by the Kneisel String Quartet and Corinne Moore Lawson (1865–1928), a much-admired soprano from Ohio, focused on songs by Schubert. The third combined *An die ferne Geliebte* with English, German, and Italian songs, and the fourth, which was hastily arranged in response to the success of the preceding three, comprised Brahms's *Magelone Romances*. In presenting three lieder cycles, Bispham positioned himself as an erudite contender in the cluttered market of song recitals. While the programs of his second and fourth recitals earned jabs from the critics for their unwavering seriousness, in most cases audiences were reported to have been elated.[27]

Bispham's emphasis on lieder cycles was a gamble because performances of complete cycles were just beginning to gain currency, and Brahms's technically challenging works were not simple audience pleasers. Although the *Magelone* cycle is usually performed by one singer, Bispham allocated some of the songs to collaborators. He sang the songs of the character Peter and read the narratives between the songs, Marguerite Hall gave the songs of Magelone, and she joined Bispham in singing the final song of the cycle, "Treue Liebe," in unison.[28] Two of Bispham's colleagues from the Met also participated: Lloyd d'Aubigné (1871–1922) sang the minstrel's song, and Marie Engle that of the sultan's daughter. Bispham claimed that this performance was the US premiere, although Meyn had already sung most of the cycle. Nevertheless, both performances were significant because they took place while Brahms was still alive and at a time when European singers usually programmed only a small number of selections from the cycle. Although some critics acknowledged the significance of Bispham's performance, Henderson cautioned that the "profoundly intellectual" love songs

172   CHAPTER 7

would not be widely accepted.[29] Three months later, in a recital marking the death of the composer, Bispham introduced the cycle to audiences in London and reprised the *Vier ernste Gesänge*. But here also both cycles were met with resistance, with one reviewer complaining that Brahms was best "absorbed in small doses."[30]

Bispham's interest in Brahms's song cycles was likely influenced by colleagues in London who were connected to the composer. These included the Henschels; Fanny Davies and Leonard Borwick (1868–1925), both former students of Clara Schumann; Marie Fillunger; Joseph Joachim; Hans Richter; and J. A. Fuller-Maitland (1856–1936), a noted English music historian who published a monograph on Brahms.[31] Bispham's dear friend and collaborator, the composer Liza Lehmann, also had contact with this network.

Just as his initial New York recitals established Bispham's authority as a lied singer, they also demonstrated his support of American composers. His first recital included songs by Dudley Buck, Chadwick, Foote, Reginald De Koven (1859–1920), Henry K. Hadley (1871–1937), and Hermann Hans Wetzler (1870–1943), with Hadley and Wetzler providing the accompaniments for their compositions. These songs distinguished Bispham's programs from those of Henschel and other opera soloists who were slower to integrate American songs into their repertoire. Although he continued to favor works by Hadley and Wetzler, his favorite American song was Walter Damrosch's "Danny Deever" (1897), a popular-styled ballad that the baritone premiered with Damrosch accompanying. His intensely powerful performances of this song frequently thrilled audiences and critics.[32]

While working in England Bispham sang works by English composers, but in the United States Liza Lehmann was the only English composer whose songs he frequently programmed. In at least two of his US recitals between 1896 and 1898 he sang Lehmann's "Myself When Young" from her song cycle *In a Persian Garden* (1896), a setting of texts from Edward Fitzgerald's (1809–1883) translation of *Rubáiyát* by Omar Khayyám (1048–1131). In twenty-two movements, this cycle comprises solos, recitatives, duets, and quartets. Bispham had been among the singers to participate in its premiere in England in 1896, when Lehmann played the piano part, and he joined three other singers in introducing it to New Yorkers. Lehmann herself credited the New York performances with generating overwhelming enthusiasm for the work.[33] At the end of 1898, Bispham and his collaborators took the cycle on a tour that encompassed Chicago, Dayton, and Cleveland and included women's clubs such as the Tuesday Musical in Detroit. Edward Dickinson published a lengthy description of the work in *The Musician*, which was extracted in *Werners*.[34] The cycle was so popular that one commentator remarked that the work created a "fad" that encouraged American composers to create similar cycles.[35] Ultimately it became better known in the United States

David Bispham and the Heyday of Song Recitals   173

than in the composer's own country. In the following years Bispham performed some of Lehmann's other works, but none were as successful.

Toward the end of 1897 Bispham created a theatrical piece about Beethoven that was performed as part of the opening celebration of the new ballroom in the Waldorf Astoria Hotel in New York. Bispham and Edmond Howard translated and adapted a German work by Hugo Müller (1831–1881) and titled it *Adelaide: The Story of Beethoven's Love*. This one-act drama, in which Bispham played the lead role of Beethoven (see figure 7.2), featured him singing "Adelaide" and also included performances of several instrumental works. The drama's premiere, to a packed audience of society women, received press coverage from Maine to California. During the following year performances took place in theaters in New York, Philadelphia, Boston, Chicago, and London. Bispham repeatedly reprised the work and in 1916 took it on an extensive American tour.[36]

In addition to headlining his own recitals and singing in operas, Bispham collaborated with other well-known artists in a variety of settings. He was one of the supporting artists in Sembrich's concert tour through the eastern states at the end of 1897. With their traveling orchestra, they performed Italian arias by such composers as Bellini and Verdi, as well as a few well-known lieder including Schumann's "Nussbaum."[37] In 1900 Bispham and Gadski took part in Walter Damrosch's transcontinental tour of lecture-recitals on Wagner's operas. In some cities, including San Francisco, all three artists also collaborated in a recital in which Gadski and Bispham sang a variety of solos, including lieder.[38]

In the following years Bispham usually gave solo recitals, though he continued to occasionally collaborate with other singers. Whereas Henschel and Heinrich (and other recitalists) responded to criticisms of monotony by appearing with singers who had contrasting types of voices, recitals were now so well accepted that this was not required. Bispham worked with numerous accompanists, but, as was the custom for the era, few reviews mention them. Harold Osborne Smith (1880–1955) and Harry M. Gilbert (1879–1964) were Bispham's longest-serving accompanists. Both had studied in Berlin and were in the early years of their careers when they worked with the singer. Smith began accompanying Bispham around 1902 and was his regular accompanist from 1904 to 1909. Gilbert worked with him during the period 1910–1913, and together they toured Canada, Australia, and the United States. Despite these collaborations, Bispham only made passing, albeit positive, references to both in his recollections. Some of his accompanists performed a small number of solo piano pieces during the recitals, and a few, including Arthur Whiting (1861–1936), played their own works. Most accompanists were men, though some women composers accompanied him in performances of their works. Adella Prentiss (later Hughes, 1869–1950), who became a highly successful concert manager in Cleveland, sometimes served as his accompanist during his 1898–1899 tours.

174   CHAPTER 7

FIG. 7.2. Bispham as Beethoven in an 1899 performance of *Adelaide: The Story of Beethoven's Love*. Autographed photograph dated 1899. From the collection of the Ira F. Brilliant Center for Beethoven Studies, San Jose State University.

When he first returned to the United States, Bispham was repeatedly extolled for performances of dramatic songs and for his technique and wide range. Some writers, however, critiqued his nasal, muddy sound production and questioned his enunciation.[39] Furthermore, the *New Yorker Staats-Zeitung* at first had reservations about his ability to interpret lieder, and others questioned his attempts to convey true pathos.[40] In 1898 Philip Hale reprinted an assessment of the baritone that had been published by John Runciman (1866–1916), a well-known critic in England. Its praise is particularly valuable because Runciman was known for an acidic writing style, and he enjoyed playing the contrarian. Here, however, he congratulated Bispham on the way the singer had painstakingly acquired the skills to move from singing in the English provinces to Covent Garden. According to Runciman, Bispham sang with beauty and power such that "no living singer puts more sheer brain power into his work, none sings with more apparent artlessness."[41] Hale seemed to endorse Runciman's opinions (as was often the case), but like several other early American critics, he encouraged Bispham to create more varied programs. Runciman's emphasis on Bispham's intelligence echoes the singer's self-made brand, and US reviewers employed similar descriptors.

On the Road

Initially, Bispham's recitals needed to be scheduled around his performances with the Metropolitan Opera and his summer engagements in London, which continued through 1907. But when he could not agree to the contractual arrangements that the Met's Heinrich Conried (1855–1909) proposed for the 1903–1904 season, he left the Met and began to give significantly more recitals. In addition to touring the United States and Canada, he also toured the eastern coast of Australia in 1913 (the same season that Nordica was there). Typically, he maintained a hectic pace of between 100 and 150 performances per year.

Like Bispham, all the leading opera stars toured, and often their recitals were included in the same concert series as his. This was especially the case when the same person managed multiple singers. In 1904, Loudon G. Charlton (d. 1931) represented Bispham, Gadski (whose contract at the Met had suddenly been cancelled), and the piano virtuoso Vladimir de Pachmann (1848–1933). All three appeared in some of the same concert series, including one sponsored by a women's club in Wichita, Kansas, as well as those in major cities such as New York. Similarly, while under Frederic Shipman's management in 1912, Bispham, Nordica, and the violinist William Morse Rummel (1882–1918) presented recitals in Michigan, Texas, and Arkansas as part of the All Star Artists' Course. In addition to solo recitals, they gave joint recitals for Houston's Treble Clef Club and the San Antonio Press Club.[42]

Despite the hazards and inconveniences of traveling, Bispham and his contemporaries covered considerable ground. In his recollections he described occasions when the low temperatures in train carriages led to ill health. According to Emilio de Gogorza (1872–1949), an American concert singer who had trained in Spain, concert managers did not arrange schedules that fostered the preservation of good vocal health.[43] Nevertheless, from October 1909 to June 1910 Schumann-Heink, for example, completed more than 113 engagements, traveling over 46,700 miles through Florida, Texas, and Canada, and in 1905 Bispham traveled some 41,000 miles.[44] Both singers used these types of statistics in their marketing and as a way to reinforce their reputations as hardworking stars. In all, Bispham performed in at least forty-two states, significantly more than earlier exponents of the lied such as Henschel. Unlike Heinrich and White, Bispham and his fellow opera stars toured multiple southern states. Whereas he was particularly well received in Charleston, South Carolina, his 1907 recital in Tampa Bay was not well attended, a fact that was bemoaned by a reviewer who repeatedly misspelled Schubert's and Schumann's names. This was Bispham's first visit to Florida, and plans for the recital had been instigated by the women of the Friday Morning Musicale.[45] During the first two decades of the new century all the major recitalists appeared in cities and towns beyond the state capitals, with music clubs facilitating many of these performances. For instance, prior to Gadski's and Bispham's 1911 recitals for the Music Club in Lima, Ohio, the town had hosted performances by Schumann-Heink, Nordica, and Sembrich.[46]

Repertoire

Whereas Heinrich was known for his moving interpretations of lieder, Bispham defined himself by his programs. He described his standard program as comprising four contrasting sets that resembled a four-movement symphony.[47] Like the format of the Henschels' programs, Bispham's layout accommodated a fair degree of flexibility, as the two programs shown in figure 7.3 demonstrate. The Iowa program, for a public recital sponsored by a woman's club, emphasized well-known lieder and lighter numbers. According to one reviewer, the songs from the British Isles were "possibly, best of all," and Bispham's tender performance moved the audience.[48] The lieder on this program had been pleasing US audiences for decades. These types of songs by Schubert and Schumann, as well as Handel's arias, were widely programmed by other singers, and Bispham frequently sang them for audiences he judged to be less receptive to unfamiliar lieder. In contrast, the New York program, which began a series of three recitals, included fewer well-known numbers. Bispham's dramatic renditions of Loewe's ballads thrilled audiences, and many of his 1906–1907 programs included two or more. The New York program given in figure 7.3 included four, in addition

Iowa, 1905		New York, 1907	
"O Ruddier than the Cherry"	Handel	"Piangerò la Sorte mia" (*Giulio Cesare*)	Handel
(*Acis and Galatea*)		Pur dicesti	A. Lotti
"Qui sdegno" (*Magic Flute*)	Mozart	Che fiero Costume	G. Legrenzi
Adelaide	Beethoven	The Deserted Mill	Carl Loewe
Der Wanderer	Schubert	The Innkeeper's Daughter	
Du bist die Ruh'		Tom the Rhymer	
Ich grolle nicht	Schumann	Edward	
Widmung		Mr. Bispham	
The Monk	Meyerbeer	Waltz—Caprice, "Man lebt nur einmal"	Strauss-Tausig
The Wedding Song	Carl Loewe	Mr. Smith [piano]	
Oh! For a Burst of Song	Francis Allitsen	Gelb rollt mir zu Füssen	Anton Rubinstein
Who Knows!	Max Heinrich	Es blinkt der Thau	
Danny Deever (by Request)	Walter Damrosch	Waldesgespräch	Adolph Jensen
		Wie glänzt der helle Mond	Christian Sinding
OLD SONGS–		Faded Spray of Mignonette	Ernest Schelling
All Through the Night	Welsh	Faery Song (MS.)	Kurt Schindler
Young Richard (by Request)	English	(Accompanied by the composer)	
Annie Laurie	Scotch	Ballad—Aghadoe (op. 34)	Howard Brockway
My Love, Nell	Irish	The Irish Kings (No. 4 of Celtic Studies)	Henry F. Gilbert

FIG. 7.3. Bispham's contrasting four-part programs: "Song Recital by David Bispham, Under the Auspices of the Harmonie Society," Burtis Opera House, Davenport, Iowa, Friday, December 1, 1905, 8:15 p.m.; "David Bispham's First Song Recital," Mendelssohn Hall, New York, Thursday, November 7, 1907, 3:00 p.m., Harold O. Smith, pianist. Both programs housed in the *MBD(UN-CAT) Bispham collection, Music Division, New York Public Library.

to which Bispham sang the composer's "The Wedding" as an encore.[49] In other years Bispham did not program so many works by Loewe. In general, this is indicative of his habit of emphasizing a particular composer for one season, then dropping him or her or occasionally programming only one of that person's songs in subsequent seasons.

Both programs ended with the types of songs that Bispham described as "ditties." These could either be Welsh, Irish, Scottish, and English folksongs or light American songs. The acknowledgment that he performed "ditties" confirms that song recitals were a fluid genre: Some programs consisted entirely of challenging classical repertoire, whereas others blended classical repertoire with a variable but still small number of more popular songs. These types of mixed programs were given by many stars in both the United States and England.[50] While modern programs are often created with a unifying theme, programs of the nineteenth century emphasized diversity, and at times this resulted in combinations of different genres that more recent performers and scholars might find disconcerting.

Lieder Cycles

In the years immediately following his first concert season in the United States, Bispham continued his dedication to lieder cycles, reprising ones he had already given and adding others to his repertoire. In doing so, he anticipated the trend of singers recording complete cycles, which emerged after World War II.[51] At the start of the twentieth century, however, Bispham could use such performances to distinguish himself from his colleagues. In December 1898 he paired Brahms's *Vier ernste Gesänge* with Schubert's *Die schöne Müllerin*, a cycle that he had not previously performed in full. This program, which he gave in Boston and New York, challenged both the performers and the listeners, and the critical response was quite mixed.[52] Despite Bispham's reputation as an intellect, he, like his colleagues, rarely provided audiences with program notes that explained the songs. For these recitals, however, Krehbiel's program notes explained the story of the protagonist in Schubert's cycle. The next year Bispham added *Dichterliebe* and Lehmann's latest cycle, a setting of Tennyson's *In Memoriam* (1899), to his repertoire. Critics panned both Lehmann's cycle and Bispham's performance.[53] Some praised his performances of the Schumann, but others considered that he was more successful and comfortable in dramatic works than in such intimate lieder.[54] In later years Bispham continued to sporadically reprise *Vier ernste Gesänge* and *Dichterliebe*, but he seems not to have reprised the Schubert until 1904.

Bispham's interest in cycles culminated in a series of four recitals titled "Cycle of Cycles," which he presented during the 1904–1905 concert season. The first recital consisted of *An die ferne Geliebte, Frauenliebe und -leben* sung by Marguerite Hall, and *Dichterliebe*; the second, *Die schöne Müllerin*; the third, *Winterreise*; and the fourth, *Vier ernste Gesänge* and the *Magelone Romances*. Hall sang four of the songs in the *Magelone* cycle, and, as in their 1897 performance, joined Bispham in singing "Treue Liebe." This season was the first time he had performed the entire *Winterreise*, but he had been including more of the individual songs from this cycle in his preceding recitals. Due to its length and despairing aura this cycle had received fewer complete performances than *Die schöne Müllerin*, and, as in Europe, there were also fewer performances of individual songs from the cycle.[55] Around this time, Bispham began to preface his performances with comments about some of the songs on his programs, and he provided introductions for both *Winterreise* and the *Magelone Romances*. As was typical for him, however, he diverged from the topic at hand to include personal recollections, and some critics claimed that some of the information he provided about the songs was inaccurate or misleading.[56]

The concept of creating a recital series devoted to cycles was not common, and Bispham's series served to solidify his reputation for creating demanding programs. It also became part of his marketing. Newspapers throughout the country reported on the series, and advertisements for some of his later recitals also mentioned it. But Bispham presented this series only in New York, Boston, and Chicago, and his other performances of individual cycles were likewise mostly confined to large cities in the East and Chicago. While Villa Whitney White performed cycles in towns and cities in the East, the Midwest, and the West Coast, Bispham and other artists had reservations about West Coast audiences. As late as 1910 Ludwig Wüllner performed Schubert's three cycles and *Dichterliebe* in a series of New York recitals but not during his West Coast ones.

In New York, Bispham's "Cycle of Cycles" faced stiff competition. Gadski's first New York recital was the day after Bispham's second, and Sembrich gave a recital two days later. Whereas Gadski's program, which was dominated by such well-known lieder as Brahms's "Von ewiger Liebe," was panned for its unimaginative program, critics praised Sembrich's.[57] Encompassing works in Italian, French, German, and English, Sembrich's recital began with eighteenth-century songs and moved on to well-known lieder by Schumann, Brahms, and Strauss and less well-known songs by Reger, Wolf, and Debussy.[58] Both of the women's recitals were held in Carnegie Hall, whereas Bispham's series was held in the smaller Mendelssohn Hall, a difference that reflects the market share for performances of cycles and also the star power of the women. The *New Yorker Staats-Zeitung* endorsed Sembrich's recital with more enthusiasm than any of Bispham's renditions of cycles, lavishly praising her and claiming she scarcely had a rival in expressive performances of lieder.[59]

180   CHAPTER 7

The technical challenges posed by the cycles are amplified when they are sung together. Bispham made the task even more difficult because he scheduled these recitals in conjunction with numerous other performances, leading critics to express a concern that he was singing too much.[60] In New York, his Brahms recital took place the day before he performed solo roles in Brahms's *Ein deutsches Requiem* and Bach's Cantata 140; three days later, he read Byron's "Manfred" during a concert of Schumann's incidental music; and the day after that, he sang during a piano recital. While Bispham was lauded for the high quality of his series, especially compared to soloists who programmed only audience pleasers, critics in Boston and New York voiced a variety of reservations, including concerns that the cycles were too monotonous and too taxing for audiences.[61] One Boston critic also observed that the poetry of *Müllerin* was of little interest in the United States and that the German veneration of nature, which is inherent in these texts, was not obvious to Americans.[62] These comments confirm that audiences' understanding of the literary heritage of the lied had developed little since the genre had been introduced to US stages.

Bispham also performed song cycles written in English. In addition to Lehmann's, he gave Elgar's *Sea Pictures* (op. 37, 1899) with piano accompaniment and *Four Songs of the Hill* (1904) by Landon Ronald (1873–1938), a British accompanist, conductor, and composer with whom he had collaborated. But neither of these works became part of his standard repertoire. The success of *In a Persian Garden* likely led the young American Grace Wassall (d. 1919) to create *A Shakespeare Song Cycle* (1904), a collection of solos, duets, quartets, and one trio. In the 1904 premiere at Carnegie Hall and a subsequent performance in Chicago, the composer's hometown, Bispham and Gadski sang the main solos, assisted by Marguerite Hall and the tenor Kelly Cole.[63] In 1906 Bispham took Wassall's cycle on tour, traveling from eastern cities such as Allentown, Pennsylvania, to venues as far west as the Woman's Reading Club in Beaumont, Texas.[64] Although critics had mixed responses to the work, there was so much interest in it that Charlton (the tour's manager) limited the tour to twenty-four performances.

While honing the cycles, Bispham added other works to his repertoire, including melodramas and lieder. In 1900 he gave one of the first US performances of Strauss's melodrama *Enoch Arden*.[65] Like Max Heinrich, Bispham was quite fond of this work, and, more broadly, he was attracted to this genre because it enabled him to draw on his acting skills.[66] But while Bispham added other melodramas to his repertoire and performed them throughout the country, he did not market them as heavily as the lieder cycles. Nevertheless, this genre was popular, particularly with women who practiced the art of elocution. The *Ladies' Home Journal* asserted that Bispham popularized Rossetter G. Cole's (1866–1952) setting of Longfellow's "King Robert of Sicily," which the composer dedicated to him.[67]

Although *Enoch Arden* seems to have inspired Bispham to perform more of Strauss's lieder, he promoted his performances of Wolf's lieder more vigorously and claimed he introduced Americans to these works. Although a few singers had been sporadically programming Wolf's songs since at least 1896,[68] Bispham did bring new attention to them. In 1903, at a recital sponsored by the Brooklyn Institute, he departed from the typical well-known fare that this institute's recitals usually featured and sang Wolf's "Biterolf," "Wenn du zu den Blumen gehst," and "Auch kleine Dinge" (HWW 114, no. 3, 129, no. 16, and 159, no. 1).[69] During his New York recital the following January he gave ten songs by Wolf, but in other 1904–1905 recitals he gave groups of five. On these occasions the press often described the works as a "novelty," and in his recital in Washington, DC, Bispham addressed the audience, providing an overview of Wolf's life and untimely death. Here and in his recollections, he made erroneous claims, however, including the statement that many of Wolf's songs "seem to be the result of a mental abnormality."[70] Wolf's works did not become a permanent feature of Bispham's brand, but he continued to occasionally program them. In contrast, he did not embrace lieder by other recent composers such as Reger or Mahler.

Although critics occasionally lauded Bispham's performance of French songs, in 1906 one correctly observed that Bispham's French numbers were "thrown in for good measure."[71] During the 1907–1908 concert season, the baritone sometimes programmed a set comprising Debussy's "Chevaux de bois" (L 63a, no. 4, 1885), Hahn's "L'heure exquise" (1890), and Massenet's "Légende de la sauge" (from *Le jongleur de Notre Dame*, 1902), but Meyerbeer's "The Monk" (1834), an operatic-style scena with sections in contrasting tempi, was the French work he sang the most frequently. Similarly, Schumann-Heink and Gadski sang only a limited number of French art songs. In contrast, French opera singers such as Victor Maurel (1848–1923) and Charles Gilibert (1866–1910) developed fine reputations for performing French songs, which they included in their polyglot recitals.[72]

Songs by Americans

Since 1896 Bispham had occasionally performed American songs, but from around 1906 he became a passionate advocate for American composers. This represented somewhat of a volte-face because as late as 1905 he had opined that "as hard as it may be to say it, our composers are not the equals of the great masters of song and opera on the other side of the sea."[73] Nevertheless, by the end of his life he had performed songs and melodramas by at least fifty-nine contemporaries resident in the United States, at least ten of whom were women. The breadth of Bispham's selections of American repertoire contrasts with that of Heinrich, who favored songs by Boston composers such as Foote

182   CHAPTER 7

and MacDowell, but almost all the other major recitalists were also sampling the burgeoning number of new American songs.[74] Bispham's ability to re-create his artistic persona is emblematic of the type of malleability that Tunbridge has observed in other artists, including Schumann-Heink.[75] Indeed, Bispham's and Schumann-Heink's attention to branding anticipated the type of advertising that movie and popular music stars exploit today.

Bispham, who was described as "always alert and enterprising,"[76] was a shrewd businessman and an opportunist, and his new focus was probably not entirely altruistic. Having left the Met and milked performances of lieder cycles, he needed a new focus and marketing ploy. From late 1904 through 1905 there were scattered reports that he intended to retire from concert singing so that he could pursue theatrical work. Although these reports were denied, in 1906 he devoted most of his energy to producing and performing in Lehmann's new light opera *The Vicar of Wakefield* in London. This production received positive reviews, but the work had a limited run and Bispham did not fulfill his much-publicized plans of staging it in the United States.[77] However, throughout the remaining years of his career, and particularly in 1915–1916, he devoted increasingly more time to plays and musical theater.

Reviews of Bispham's post-1906 recitals continued to applaud the variety of his repertoire and his thrilling interpretations of dramatic ballads, but there were sporadic concerns about the uneven quality of his voice and a few suggestions that occasionally there were moments that were closer to speech than to singing. Perhaps, then, his shift in focus was influenced by his aging voice; though Bispham had been on US stages only since 1896, in 1907 he turned fifty. These concerns might have been amplified by competition from younger singers and by an increasing number of tours by some of the most lauded European lieder singers, including Elena Gerhardt (1883–1961) and Julia Culp. Also, if he was to maintain his reputation for seeking out new works, Bispham likely realized that he preferred singing American works to modernist ones from Europe, and that they were easier—and also more interesting to audiences.[78] In any event, his choice was made at an opportune time because a few years later it enabled him to position himself among the leading musicians responding to the intensifying nationalism that preceded America's entry into World War I. In 1907 the National Federation of Music Clubs established an American Music Department to promote American performers and composers, and in addition to performing before clubs Bispham, on at least one occasion, assisted with this organization's competition for new American compositions. In 1908 he became one of the vice presidents of the newly formed American Music Society; his friend Arthur Farwell was the president, and Walter Damrosch the musical director. His association with this society garnered him increased press coverage and glowing endorsements of his performances of American songs.[79]

Some of Bispham's recitals included works by or about African Americans and Native Americans. His recital at the White House in 1904 consisted largely of works by Americans he routinely programmed including Wetzler, MacDowell, and Henry Gilbert (1868–1928). But it began with a Zuni song, "Sunrise Call"; an Ojibway song, "Absence and Longing"; and the spirituals "Danville Chariot"("I Don't Want to Stay Here No Longer") and "Joshua Fit de Battle of Jericho," followed by a few lieder.[80] The placement of the Native American songs at the start of a program was particularly unusual because the second half of a program was the standard location for American repertoire. Bispham had already sung Harry Burleigh's arrangements of the two spirituals and "The Blackbird and the Crow" to London audiences in 1901, and he used "Joshua Fit de Battle of Jericho" as the concluding number in some of his 1902 US recitals. When recalling these performances, Bispham did not use the dialect in the titles given in Burleigh's 1901 *Plantation Melodies Old and New*.[81] This suggests that he likely did not sing in dialect, either.

Numerous other recitalists also took up spirituals and other settings of African American texts, some of which were also written in dialect. But when Burleigh wrote "Mammy's Li'l Baby" (1903) and dedicated it to Schumann-Heink, he and his wife, Louise Alston (who wrote the lyrics), standardized the text, which had originally been written in dialect.[82] The extent to which recitalists used dialect or studied African American music is unclear. In 1920, by which time Bispham was no longer programming such works, Nelda Hewitt Stevens charged that prominent singers and composers "strangled" the spirit of African American songs by distorting their harmonies and failing to study the musical style in the same way they studied the styles of composers such as Handel and Brahms.[83]

Bispham performed two settings of lyrics from (Maria) Howard Weeden's (1846–1905) *Bandanna Ballads* more frequently than arrangements of African American melodies. Weeden's poems memorialize southern Blacks who labored on plantations, and she accompanied them with her own illustrations of the corresponding characters (see figure 7.4). Such was the interest in this volume that the *Ladies' Home Journal* published a selection of the poems and portraits.[84] Several American composers set Weeden's poems; Bispham favored Sidney Homer's "A Banjo Song" (from the composer's 1910 op. 22, which set five of Weeden's lyrics) and Eleanor Freer's (1864–1942) "The Old Boatman" (op. 23, no. 1, 1909), which Bispham popularized, according to one critic.[85] "The Banjo Song" so pleased audiences that Bispham performed it in at least one vaudeville in San Francisco.[86] Subsequently, Paul Robeson recorded it to great acclaim.

Bispham performed "A Corn Song" (ca. 1896), a setting of the Paul Dunbar poem by the biracial British composer Samuel Coleridge-Taylor (1875–1912), in numerous East Coast and midwestern cities during his 1898–1899 tours. A few papers, some of which were published in cities where Bispham was not

184   CHAPTER 7

FIG. 7.4. Drawing accompanying "The Old Boatman" in Howard Weeden, *Bandanna Ballads* (New York: Doubleday, 1899), 39

performing, claimed that it was "not generally known that Coleridge-Taylor . . . was a fullblooded negro," whom Bispham had declared "the coming musical genius."[87] Bispham met this composer while working in London, where both were associates of Joseph Joachim. In his autobiography Bispham claimed that he had predicted Coleridge-Taylor would face more restrictions because of his race when he visited the United States than he experienced in England.[88] Nevertheless, there is no evidence that Bispham attempted to assist the composer. Excluding arrangements of spirituals, the only other song by a Black composer that Bispham sang was "An Exhortation" by Will Marion Cook. He programmed this song during his 1912–1913 recitals, including some of those he gave in Australia.[89]

While the media highlighted Bispham's advocacy of American composers, most of his recitals were not devoted exclusively to their works. Similarly, Bispham's marketing sometimes highlighted his performance of arrangements of African American songs by Burleigh and Native American tunes by Indianists such as Burton and Farwell, but many of his recitals in venues beyond major East Coast cities did not include that repertoire.[90] Although Bispham seems to have been somewhat more interested in advocating for these songs than were other leading recitalists such as Schumann-Heink, he did not do so as clearly as Burleigh, who gave recitals devoted to these types of works, as well as ones that combined lieder with multiple African American songs.[91] Moreover, there is no evidence that Bispham—or the press—discussed the place of these American songs in recitals otherwise comprised of lieder: Such repertoire was welcomed because variety continued to be the driving influence on programming.

Despite Bispham's praise for spirituals and for Coleridge-Taylor, he was not sympathetic to African American popular genres, and there are multiple reports that he deprecated rags. One Arkansas paper reported that while in Little Rock, Bispham described these songs as "made up of trashy tunes and degrading words," and it noted that there was an active campaign against the works that the Arkansas writer viewed as "evils" that needed to be "eradicated." In 1912, during a recital at Carnegie Hall, Bispham lamented "the prevalence of ragtime" and urged his audiences to "lend all their influence towards its abolishment." To him, the music did not "express a lofty, or at least an intelligent idea."[92] Bispham was not alone in expressing this type of appalling assessment; other major recitalists also did not program rags, and commentators in *Musical America* and the *Musical Courier* campaigned against rags and commercial music. Their elitist attitudes led them to interpret these genres as a threat to traditional music aesthetics and as symptomatic of the ways a consumer-driven marketplace threatened to degrade culture.[93]

Bispham's rants about rags are so fiercely worded that it is impossible to think they were not racially motivated. That he encouraged Bergh to set Vachel Lindsay's (1879–1931) poem *The Congo—A Study of the Negro Race* (1914), despite W. E. B. DuBois (1868–1963) having already criticized the racist aspects of the poem, gives credence to this conclusion.[94] A few other singers, including Dudley Buck, performed this cycle of three songs, but it did not attract a great deal of attention, though Ditson published it in 1918.[95]

Bispham's selection of American songs, like those of other singers, was influenced by personal connections. He often sang the works of friends and collaborators such as Henry Holden Huss (1862–1953). The score of Huss's "All the World's a Stage" (also known as "The Seven Ages of Man," op. 16, ca. 1898) claimed that Bispham sang the work more than four hundred times, but at least one critic was not impressed by the piece, observing that the piano part was more successful than the vocal line.[96] In other instances it seems Bispham's selections were based on expediency or generosity. In the case of a recital in

186   CHAPTER 7

Buffalo in 1907 he sang three songs by Rudolph Bismarck von Liebich, whose wife was instrumental in bringing Bispham to that city.[97] And some selections, perhaps including Lindsay's poems, might also have been influenced by what Walter Damrosch analyzed as Bispham's naïveté, "exuberant imagination," and fascination with the "extraordinary."[98] Bispham's interest in works that he considered exceptional, in that they were little known, likely deterred him from exploring popular Tin Pan Alley songs. Other major recitalists also did not take up this new, highly successful genre; however, recitals by less well-known singers did occasionally include a song by popular composers such as Victor Herbert.[99] (In general, Tin Pan Alley songs were more frequently programmed on mixed-genre concerts that included a band or orchestra than on recitals.)

Bispham advocated for the development of "high-class" American songs that, he claimed, would ultimately eradicate the "cheaper type of music."[100] While similar ideas were expressed by other writers, most of the American songs that Bispham and his contemporaries sang did not stand the test of time.[101] Although many of these works were not as popular as Tin Pan Alley songs, they were characterized by sentimental lyrics and an accessible style of music that sharply contrasted with emerging modernist works.[102] These pieces evade easy categorization as high art or popular music. In the nineteenth century American composers did not use titles or labels to distinguish between art songs and those intended for domestic music making by amateurs, and in some cases works they viewed as art songs attained the same type of success as parlor songs.[103] Nevertheless, the remarkable conformity in recital programs indicates that singers perceived differences between American songs that aspired to be art songs, more popular-styled songs (often by the same composers), and newly emerging commercial music.[104] While Bispham and his colleagues neglected rags and Tin Pan Alley songs, many of the American songs they selected were less complex than the lieder and *mélodie* that they programmed. Some of these were audience pleasers by composers who were also known for art music; they included Foote's "I'm Wearing Awa', Jean" and "Irish Folksong," Damrosch's "Danny Deever," Ware's "Boat Song," and Nevin's "The Rosary" and "Mighty Lak' a Rose."

Women Composers and Singers

Unlike Henschel and Heinrich, Bispham frequently programmed songs by women. In England in 1895 he was one of the collaborating artists in a vocal recital titled "Modern Women Composers,"[105] and his 1897 Brooklyn Institute recital featured many of the same composers. In Brooklyn he gave "The Devon Maid" by Beatrice Hallett, "To Daffodils" by Dora Bright (1862–1951), "Love Is a Babble" by Frances Allister, "Absent Yet Present" by Maud V. White (1855–1937), and "King Henry to Fair Rosamond" by Liza Lehmann.[106] He presented somewhat similar selections in some of his other recitals that year, but in the following years many of his programs included no more than one song by a woman.

While in England, Bispham also performed Clara Schumann's "Ihr Bild"/"Ich stand in dunklen Träumen" (op. 13, no. 1).[107] He likely learned of Schumann's works from her English students and collaborators. In New York, the contralto Antonia Henne had performed Schumann's "Liebst du um Schönheit" (op. 12, no. 4) in Steinway Hall in 1879. This work was published in an English-language version in 1885,[108] but few recitalists took it up. When Bispham sang "An einem lichten Morgen" (op. 23, no. 2), "Ich stand in dunklen Träumen," and "Liebst du um Schönheit" in Chicago in 1902, they were described as "unknown," though one Mrs. J. W. Hiner had performed the last two along with the composer's "Sie liebten sich beide" (op. 13, no. 2) during a meeting of the Amateur Musical Club in 1897.[109] Bispham subsequently reprised the three Schumann songs on his 1902 program during his 1904–1905 recitals, including one in Chicago where he sang works by Freer. He also included an English version of the score of "Liebst du um Schönheit" in his programs for women singers in his *Recollections* (see figure 7.5) and in his 1919 album *Celebrated Recital Songs*.[110] In both cases it is placed in the prominent second group of songs, which Bispham reserved for the most celebrated lieder composers, including Schubert and Robert Schumann. Nevertheless, Bispham promoted songs by Lehmann and American women more energetically than those by Clara Schumann.

Of the American women whose songs he performed, Bispham likely had the greatest impact on the careers of Carrie Jacobs Bond (1862–1946), Harriet Ware (1877–1962), and Freer. In 1905 he gave a recital in the Music Hall in Chicago that featured fifteen of Bond's songs. Bond had met Bispham on two previous occasions, but she was surprised by his intention to sing so many of her songs and his request that she accompany him. At the time, Bond's reputation was just beginning to grow, and critics praised Bispham's generosity in presenting the works of a composer who was not nationally recognized. Although Bond acknowledged his continued support and he performed her 1909 hit "The End of a Perfect Day," Bispham did not continue to promote her songs in such an aggressive manner. Still, she was able to use his performances in advertisements for her works.[111] Similarly, although Bispham participated in a recital dedicated to Ware's compositions,[112] the only song he incorporated into his standard repertoire was "Boat Song." In 1905 he programmed ten new songs by Freer in a recital in her hometown of Chicago, but in other venues that year he presented a smaller selection. As with the songs by American men, some of those by women were greeted with harsh reviews. An assessment following Bispham's performance of four of Freer's songs in New York panned the works, claiming

Men's Group		Women's Group	
"O, Ruddier Than the Cherry" (*Acis and Galatea*)	Handel	"My Heart Ever Faithful" (*Pentecost Cantata*)	Bach
"The Frost Scene" (*King Arthur*)	Purcell	To Florindo	Scarlatti
"At Last the Bounteous Sun" (*The Seasons*)	Haydn	Should He Upbraid (Shakespeare)	Bishop
"Now Your Days of Philandering" (*Marriage of Figaro*)	Mozart	I've Been Roaming (Soane)	Horn
Creation's Hymn (Gellert)	Beethoven	Marguerite at the Spinning Wheel (Goethe)	Schubert
The Wanderer (Lübeck)	Schubert	He, the Best of All (Chamisso)	Schumann
The Hidalgo (Geibel)	Schumann	Dreams (Wagner)	Wagner
May Night (Hölty)	Brahms	In Autumn (Müller)	Franz
Edward (Scotch Ballad)	Loewe	Lov'st Thou for Beauty (Rückert)	Clara Schumann
"When I Was Page" (*Falstaff*)	Verdi	"He Is Kind" (*Hérodiade*)	Massenet
At Evening's Hour (Verlaine)	Hahn	"Noblest of Knights" (*Les Huguenots*)	Meyerbeer
Autumnal Gale (Reichardt)	Grieg	"Oh, My Lyre" (*Sapho*)	Gounod
Secrecy (Mörike)	Wolf	"It Is Better to Laugh" (*Lucrezia Borgia*)	Donizetti
The Stonebreaker's Song (Henkell)	Strauss		
The Sea (Howells)	MacDowell	Orpheus with His Lute (Shakespeare)	Sullivan
O, Let Night Speak of Me (Bates)	Chadwick	The Blackbird's Song (Watson)	C. Scott
The Pirate Song (Stevenson)	Gilbert	The Maidens of Cadiz (De Musset)	Delibes
Sleep, Then, Ah, Sleep (Le Gallienne)	Branscombe	The Little Silver Ring (Baker)	Chaminade
Danny Deever (Kipling)	Damrosch	The Floods of Spring (Hapgood)	Rachmaninoff

FIG. 7.5. Model women's and men's recital programs in Bispham's *Quaker Singer's Recollections*, 350

that among other things they lacked originality, but it also observed that the audience "marvelled" at them.[113]

Bispham was not the only high-profile artist to program works by American women. Schumann-Heink, for instance, programmed and recorded songs by Bond, Margaret Ruthven Lang, Gertrude Ross (1889–1957), and Mary Turner Salter (1856–1938). (In contrast, the only song by a woman that Bispham recorded was Ware's "Boat Song.") While members of women's clubs frequently sang and lectured about songs by women during club meetings, Bispham and his colleagues gave these composers a much broader platform, and by giving their songs in major venues, they aided sales of sheet music.[114] Their performances reflected the dramatically increasing number of women who were writing and publishing songs, a trend that began in about 1890 and reached a peak around 1910. The numbers of new songs subsequently began to subside, with the sharpest declines occurring after 1920.[115] Most of the works by women that Bispham and his colleagues performed were not taken up by the following generations of singers, who largely ignored female composers. Although feminist musicology has brought new attention to Clara Schumann's works, those of Liza Lehmann are still little known, despite their quality. Many of the songs written by American men suffered the same fate, largely due to the downturn in amateur music making and the dominance of European and modernist works in concert halls. Until recently, songs by composers of the Second New England School tended to appear on programs tracing the history of American song, and songs by Amy Beach on those highlighting women. In contrast, the art songs that began to be produced in the middle of the century by the likes of Samuel Barber (1910–1981) and Marc Blitzstein (1905–1964) have earned greater respect.[116]

Despite programming women's songs and praising the work of women's clubs, Bispham was not always supportive of women. He warmly acknowledged the crucial role women's clubs played in creating recital venues in remote locations and the women's "artistic aims" and "business probity."[117] In contrast, some of his comments about women performers were demeaning. In describing his passion for melodramas, he asserted that women were ill advised to perform these types of works because they did not have the required vocal power. He claimed that they nevertheless performed melodramas more frequently than men because they were "carried away by impulse."[118] Bispham knew of women's interest in the art of elocution, and he frequently performed melodramas for their clubs. Instead of belittling their capabilities he could have learned more about their performances or offered tactful advice on how they could address the deficiencies he perceived (that is, if there were any real weaknesses).

Bispham had strong opinions regarding the relationship between the gender of a singer and that of the narrative personae in songs. Whereas White continued the European tradition of selecting repertoire almost regardless of its narrative voice, Bispham repeatedly argued that women should not sing pieces with a male narrative voice such as *An die ferne Geliebte.* Although he acknowledged that men inappropriately sang works with a female narrative voice, his harshest criticisms were targeted at women.[119] He asserted that there were plenty of appropriate pieces for women (including works that are not gendered) and held up *Frauenliebe und -leben* as a perfect example—that is, like the *Ladies' Home Journal,* he selected repertoire that provided models of women as loving wives and mothers.[120] In his recollections, Bispham presented model recital programs for men and women (figure 7.5). These programs included only three works by women: Chaminade and Clara Schumann are represented in the women's program, and a song by Gena Branscombe (1881–1977) appears in the men's. Bispham provided similar sample programs in his anthology *Celebrated Recital Songs,* in which he also created a model program that could be sung by either men or women; it included no songs by women. In general, given all the highly successful professional women he collaborated with, his advice to women singers is deplorable.

Singing in the English Language

Although Bispham gave a highly successful recital completely in English in 1898, he usually sang lieder in German and for years voiced reservations about singing in the vernacular.[121] From 1906 onward, however, he advocated for performances in English. By 1913 newspapers, probably influenced by his marketing, referred to him as the "apostle" for singing in English.[122] This change in approach might have been influenced by rising anti-German sentiment, but his tours were increasingly taking him to cities and towns beyond the East Coast, where audiences might have been less tolerant of songs in foreign languages. In 1908 a writer in Los Angeles suggested that audiences flocked to Bispham's concerts because they were sung in English, and in 1911 a promotional notice emphasized that a recital for the Des Moines Women's Club chorus would be in English (and include lighter numbers).[123] He heavily marketed his "all-English recital" programs, comprising lieder sung in translation and works written in English, and he often prefaced his performances by suggesting that singers give more attention to works in English.

Just as Bispham tended to latch onto and zealously promote repertoire first introduced by other performers, so, too, the idea of singing in English was not new. What was somewhat new was that Bispham linked the need to sing lieder in English to operas being performed in translation. Like earlier proponents of opera in the vernacular, he believed that singing in English would inspire American composers to set English lyrics.[124] He also adopted the argument of pedagogues such as W. S. B. Mathews that people should be *taught* to sing in English.[125]

David Bispham and the Heyday of Song Recitals   191

Bispham advanced his case in interviews, lectures, recitals, and even vaude-ville programs, as well as through leadership roles in organizations promoting opera in the vernacular.[126] In February 1911 he was among the initial organiz-ers of the Society for the Promotion of Opera in English and the Encourage-ment of American Music. Six years later, he became the vice president of the Society of American Singers, which aimed to realize his long-cherished goal of a permanent organization to support vernacular performances of comic opera. This organization, which was supported by other recitalists including Schumann-Heink, was also linked to contemporary war efforts in that officers and shareholders had to be US citizens.[127] After his death, the Bispham Memorial Medal was created to honor Bispham's contributions to opera sung in English. Each year from 1924 to 1955, the American Opera Society of Chicago awarded the medal to a US composer for writing an opera in English. The award was endowed by funds from Bispham's will and by Freer, a composer whose songs Bispham had performed.[128]

Closing Years

During the second half of his US career, Bispham's outreach activities en-compassed more teaching than in previous years. Beginning in about 1909 he gave "lecture-lessons" during the summer at his country house in Rowayton, Connecticut, and from 1918, as his performance career was winding down, he maintained a teaching studio in New York. Although Nelson Eddy's early lessons with Bispham have been noted, it seems he had greater impact through his role as a public advocate. Nevertheless, some of his more publicized endeavors did not come to fruition. As early as 1902 Bispham argued for the founding of a "University of Music" that, affiliated with existing schools of music, would foster America's talented performers, as well as host a national circulating library of scores in a wide variety of styles. He envisioned a school that would reach the "masses," in part by means of tours by its faculty.[129] While little came of these plans, Bispham's goals were somewhat aligned with those of the American Con-servatory of Music in Chicago, where he taught during the summers from 1919 to 1921. During the last of these summers, he gave a recital featuring lieder by Wolf and Strauss. This, however, was one of his last recitals; he died the follow-ing October.

Like many other artists of the day, Bispham was cognizant of the relation between song recitals and the sale of scores. Whereas Heinrich focused on pub-lishing lieder, most of Bispham's volumes encompassed a variety of repertoire and were likely created with a broader audience in mind.[130] His only album devoted to lieder, which contained just ten well-known works by Schubert and Schumann, appeared around the time of his first US recitals. The audiences' program booklet for some of his 1897 recitals noted which of the songs on the program were published in the album. In contrast, his 1908 album comprised a "representative" recital collection of thirteen songs that he frequently performed. It included only two lieder, Schubert's "Who Is Sylvia?" (D. 891) and Loewe's "Edward" (op. 1, no. 1). His 1919 album of forty-four numbers included a similarly diverse range of songs, but once again the only lieder were ones that were already well-known. The anthology begins with Bispham's remarks on Tchaikovsky's "Only a Yearning Heart," Schubert's "The Wanderer" (which he vigorously argued should not be sung by a woman), and Schumann's "The Two Grenadiers" (which he considered to be one of the greatest patriotic songs). Most of Bispham's brief commentary concerns performance techniques and expressive nuances. Although he explains the main characteristics of each song's protagonist and names the poets, there is no consideration of the cultural aspects of these poems, nor are there analytical remarks about Schubert's or Schumann's music. Because the anthology was published in 1919, it might have been too close to the end of the war to explore aspects of German culture. Yet it is doubtful that Bispham would have done so even if this was not the case, because it was not his style. Like his remarks to audiences, the paragraphs supplying background information for each song also include truisms and references to Bispham's own experiences that have little to do with the songs. Nevertheless, these commentaries are more informative than those in the anthologies in the series titled *The World's Best Music*, which were marketed to amateur women music makers and advertised in multiple issues of the *Ladies' Home Journal*. Moreover, some of the albums marketed as the favorite songs of singers such as Geraldine Farrar included a biography of the singer but nothing about the songs.

Despite his advocacy of American composers, Bispham's albums included few such works. James Francis Cooke's (1875–1960) "The Breath of Allah" was the only work by an American in the 1919 anthology, though it is possible that other selections were not included because of copyright limitations. There were no spirituals or Native American songs. In contrast, in her collection of international folksongs, *My Favorite Folksongs*, Sembrich included a Pawnee Indian and an Omaha Indian song, both with piano accompaniments by Harvey Worthington Loomis (1865–1930) and "Deep River" in an arrangement by William Arms Fisher (1861–1948, a student of Dvořák and director of publications at Ditson). Alma Gluck's *My Favorite Songs* also included Fisher's arrangement as well as his setting of Weeden's lyrics "Swing Low/Mammy's Lullaby" (op. 17, no. 2).

Bispham's publications did not attract as much critical attention as did Heinrich's; however, Bispham was considered marketable. In 1913 Witmark published *The Artistic Baritone: With Full Cover Picture and Biographical Sketch of David Bispham*, a volume of well-known light songs for their Artist Series, which included volumes by popular singers such as Enrico Caruso. Like the other volumes in the series, Bispham's comprised popular numbers such as "Drink to Me Only with Thine Eyes," "Erlking," and Mendelssohn's "I Am a Roamer Bold" (from *Die Heimkehr aus der Fremde*).

Bispham's recordings were more widely advertised than most of his anthologies of songs. At the start of the recording industry a few successful recitalists began to record lieder; Gadski and Schumann-Heink did so in 1903.[131] That recording companies were willing to devote their resources to lieder at the beginning of the recorded age is a testament to the genre's success. As a result of technological improvements, in about 1906 numerous other singers, including Bispham, also started to record. Aside from four lieder by Schubert, including "Erlkönig," and well-known Handel arias such as "O Ruddier Than the Cherry," most of Bispham's recordings were English-language ballads that he had repeatedly sung to adoring audiences, including "Danny Deever." In all he made about sixty-three recordings, most of which were for Columbia and date from 1906 to 1916.

During 1917 and 1918 Bispham gave few recitals but instead took part in numerous war efforts. One overview of the performing artists who were appearing at the troop training camps' Liberty Theatres, including Schumann-Heink and Douglas Fairbanks, singled out Bispham for particular praise, noting that he had "been indefatigable."[132] With Schumann-Heink and numerous other singers, he assisted in the promotion of the Liberty Bonds program.[133] Numerous US publications covered Bispham's project to raise money for the purchase of ambulances for wounded Italian troops, which was inspired by one of his daughters, who was married to an Italian officer.[134] Schumann-Heink was similarly praised for her wartime efforts. Three of her sons served in the American forces, and a fourth was killed fighting for the Germans. Bispham's only son, Lieutenant David Charles Bispham (1898–1917), was killed while serving in the Royal Flying Corps. Papers nationwide reported that, tragically, he died during a practice flight in London.[135] Bispham's patriotism continued after the war. As the chairman of the Standing Committee on Studios and Conservatories of the National Patriotic Song Committee, he urged teachers to ensure that students knew the words of the "Star-Spangled Banner."[136]

* * *

The concert scene at the start of the twentieth century was considerably different than that of the 1840s and 1850s, when lieder were just beginning to be introduced to US audiences. Song recitals comprised of art songs now held a central place in concert series throughout the country. Recitalists and publishers were well aware of women consumers: The recitalists appeared before women's music clubs and gave daytime performances in other venues, and publishers produced scores for music makers at home, many of which were billed as being favorite songs of the most successful singers. Yet the ideals of early advocates of lieder and of classical European instrumental music continued to be promoted. When campaigning for the establishment of an American University of Music, Bispham reflected the views of a growing number of white, middle-class musicians and advocates who were beginning to develop organizations based on the belief that "good" music (as opposed to jazz and rags) would enable the lower classes to become moral and cultured citizens.[137] In doing so he echoed and expanded on the similarly edifying and uplifting goals of Dwight and his colleagues of the 1850s and 1860s. With his typically naïve chauvinism, which prevented him from appreciating the richness of popular genres, Bispham envisioned a university that would inculcate the history of Western art music, and thereby "the influence of the charlatan would be kept within bounds" and "even the least attentive class of the population" would be "inspired with fresh courage to face the problems of life."[138] He praised early efforts to establish concert life in the United States, including those of Thomas and the Damrosch family. He also acknowledged others, including women's music clubs and writers such as Krehbiel, who upheld the importance of high art. To Bispham, lieder were a vital part of the classical canon and of the cultural uplift he championed

But ultimately, despite Bispham's reputation as a scholar and as someone who programmed works that were not frequently performed by other singers, he repeatedly sang the types of dramatic ballads and love songs that audiences in the United States and Europe favored. These preferences are also reflected in the programs of most of his contemporaries and in many of the score anthologies released by American publishers. Moreover, Bispham and his colleagues did not significantly advance Americans' appreciation of the literary traditions on which lieder were based or of how these songs differed from works originating in other countries. And while they contributed to raising the profile of American songs, interest in this repertoire evaporated in the following decades. Despite Bispham's commitment to so-called high art, he, and many of his contemporaries, realized that recital programs needed to include lighter, more accessible repertoire. Performers in the decades following the war ignored this tradition, however, and song recitals became the bastion of repertoire that continued to be perceived as high art. Although this ultimately resulted in recitals exploring a much larger range of lieder than the frequently programmed ones of Bispham's time, it has also contributed to a much greater chasm between lieder and popular song.

Epilogue
The End of an Era

In 1918 Henry Finck reminded his readers that the song recital was a relatively new phenomenon, with the most prominent opera singers only adopting the practice of presenting art song recitals just before the turn of the century.[1] But by complaining of the numerous mediocre recitals that had flooded New York's wartime concert season, he also signaled problems with the genre's long-term viability. After their introduction in the 1870s, song recitals were transformed from performances before professional musicians and well-informed music lovers to a ubiquitous concert genre serving audiences throughout the country in a variety of venues. But while recitals and sales of scores established and solidified the lied canon, the success of recitals could not be sustained indefinitely. The lied and the song recital rebounded after a lull in performances caused by World War I; however, they subsequently declined in popularity. This was due to multiple factors including the Depression and societal changes, which also impacted sales of pianos and sheet music, as well as membership in women's music clubs.

The successful integration of lieder into US concert life hinged on the promotion of German classical music, the development of song recitals, and women amateur musicians and patrons. Lieder initially found a place because they were integrated into the efforts of the musicians and critics who were promoting music that they considered to be serious or high art, and in particular German compositions. These advocates viewed such music as contributing to their efforts to raise the standard of concert life and to enhance culture and society in general. During the 1870s and 1880s singers and pianists who were part of this network developed the art song recital, a concert genre that was essential for the propagation of the lied because no other type of concert facilitated performances of numerous lieder. Many of the early recitals were given by women (who often were guided by male colleagues and teachers), and because some of the earliest recitals were held for music teachers (who were predominantly women), it is highly likely that their audiences were dominated by women. Women quickly became one of the most influential forces behind the dissemination of lieder; they avidly attended recitals, bought sheet music, and, through their clubs and roles in society, sponsored public and private recitals by professional musicians. From the early 1890s women's clubs became increasingly important agents in promulgating classical music as a civilizing force, and in doing so they contributed to the proliferation of song recitals emphasizing lieder.

During the 1850s and 1860s, social elites and the musically educated dominated the small audiences attending chamber concerts that programmed lieder. In contrast, members of the middle class increasingly attended the subsequent song recitals sponsored by normal schools, colleges, and an array of clubs and organizations. From the late 1890s lieder could be heard around the country, and some of the most widely appreciated lieder by Schubert and Schumann could be heard in a broad range of venues, which on occasion included vaudevilles and other concerts catering to the masses. From the start of the new century, star singers made gramophone recordings of lieder, and performers such as Julia Heinrich were employed by Edison and other major recording companies to tour the country, performing in stores so that potential buyers of both records and gramophones could compare live and recorded performances.[2] Most of these recordings were of canonical lieder such as Brahms's "Lullaby" and Schubert's "Erlkönig," that because of their popularity bridged the high-low divide.

Throughout the century interest in lieder was aided by the increase in amateur music making in homes, much of which was driven by women. The piano became a sought-after status symbol in the homes of socially aspiring families, and young women were given piano and voice lessons as part of the preparation for their roles as homemakers, wives, and mothers. Publications such as *Godey's Ladies Book* and the *Ladies' Home Journal* routinely carried articles about music, and at the peak of the popularity of song recitals some of these mentioned lieder and lieder composers; occasionally a story or anecdote modeling the appropriate behavior for a young women described someone singing or playing lieder by the likes of Schubert or Schumann.[3] From the 1850s the advocates of German music fostered the dissemination of lieder in English-language sheet music, and similar scores for home music makers were included in music magazines. At the turn of the century, in response to the increasing awareness of the genre, numerous publishers produced anthologies of lieder for amateurs. Despite America's entrance into the war, in 1917 Ditson released Finck's *One Hundred Songs by Ten Masters*. This is indicative of the firm position that the lied held in US music making, and, like the early recordings of lieder, it also contributed to solidifying the lied canon.[4] By this time, US publishers had also begun to release scores of songs by French, Russian, and American composers that were being performed in recitals with increasing frequency.

Canonical Song Composers

While song recitals were in vogue only for a relatively brief time, they had lasting effects. The most notable of these included the establishment of a lied canon, which paralleled that in Europe, and the concomitant US publication of scores, which provided greater (and lasting) accessibility to lieder and also to art songs from other countries. Music canons are established by performances,[5] but performances are dependent on scores, and both mediums played a role in the establishment of the lied canon in the United States. While criticism and scholarship also play roles in establishing a canon, in the nineteenth century US writers did not devote the same attention to lieder as did their German colleagues, and their articles and monographs, though valuable, had less impact on canon formation than did performances. The canonical status of the genre is no better illustrated than by the numerous encyclopedia-style multivolume series of scores that appeared at the end of the century. The titles of these sets usually implied that the songs were crucial to an informed music lover. This was the case with a Ditson series titled The Musicians Library, which began in 1903 and included over one hundred anthologies of songs and piano solos.[6] Whereas it encompassed anthologies of Russian and French songs, as well as folksongs from Europe and the United States, the volumes of lieder were more numerous. These volumes reinforced the canonical status of the lieder of Schubert, Schumann, and Brahms. Yet this status had only been attained gradually during the preceding decades. Writers of the 1860s and 1870s, for instance, documented the ways Schumann's works initially struggled in the United States. Mathews was pleased to report that by the mid-1870s this composer was no longer considered inferior to Mendelssohn. But though many now praised the beauty of Schumann's songs, other critics of the 1870s still had reservations, in particular, about the composer's ability to write sympathetically for the voice.[7] Brahms's lieder found a place in the canon even though as late as the mid-1880s Elson predicted that his songs would "not rank with the very greatest of German songs."[8] To him their artistry rested on harmonies rather than emotional power. He was not alone in this perception; a Berlin critic, for instance, observed in 1888 that Brahms's lieder demanded more of the listener and were less accessible than those by Schubert and Schumann.[9]

Some of the introductions to the anthologies in The Musicians Library acknowledged the secondary status of lieder by such composers as Franz, Grieg, Jensen, Liszt, Strauss, Tchaikovsky, and Wolf. The dissemination and significance of each of these composers, however, presents somewhat different issues. Despite the efforts of Otto Dresel in Boston in the 1850s and 1860s, in 1903 Apthorp acknowledged that Franz's songs had "not yet won real popularity," but he hoped this would not always be the case.[10] These lieder are still performed today, but they have not sustained the same level of attention as singers and scholars give to those by Schubert, Schumann, and Brahms. There are multiple reasons for this neglect, and most relate to Franz's status during the nineteenth century, rather than to the merits of the songs themselves. Having an introverted personality, Franz distanced himself from the leaders of German music, despite being praised by the Wagnerians, and because of this he failed to capture the attention of the many music historians and theorists who followed. That Franz did not compose large genres, and that many of his songs are fragmentary and rely on subtle nuances, has also contributed to this myopia. In contrast, Wolf, who was more heavily promoted by the Wagnerians, has been widely studied and performed, and most modern lieder scholars place his works at the head of the pantheon of lied composers with those of his three main predecessors. Because of their style and the difficulty of their vocal and piano parts, however, Wolf's lieder were not regularly programmed on US recitals until after 1903, by which time they were already well established in European recitals.

The editors of the Ditson anthologies, all of whom were prominent East Coast music critics, indicated that the works they selected represented each composer's "best" lieder, and a few alluded to the songs as being among those that were most frequently programmed in recitals. Many of the songs in this series had already been released as sheet music by Ditson, as well as by other publishers including Schirmer and Fischer. This was also the case with the songs by Beethoven, Chopin, Cornelius, Dvořák, Rubinstein, and Wagner that Finck included in his *Fifty Mastersongs by Twenty Composers*, which was also published by Ditson. In general, this publisher's decision to create such collections was based on its assessment of previous sales of sheet music.

Despite their connotations of permanency, canons respond to changing tastes and aesthetics. From the 1840s through the 1870s, Mendelssohn's songs were frequently performed and published, but from the 1880s onwards they were not among the most frequently programmed works, and Finck's *Fifty Mastersongs by Twenty Composers* did not include any. Reflecting the general perception in Europe and the United States, Elson considered Mendelssohn an "elegant, symmetrical and popular musician," but although he praised the composer's oratorios, he was less impressed with the songs, which he viewed as "graceful, delicate," but not "soulstirring."[11] A review of one of Schumann-Heink's 1909 performances of five (unnamed) Mendelssohn songs echoes Elson's assessment, implying that these works were rarely programmed because their sentimentality would not please audiences.[12] Similarly, other composers who were included in Ditson's series, including Rubinstein and Grieg, have long since fallen out of fashion in Europe and the United States, and likely for some of the same reasons Mendelssohn's songs did. Even during the nineteenth century only a few of these composers' lieder received repeated performances, and it was a rare event for a program to include more than one or two works by each man. As recitalists gradually reduced German repertoire during the war years, Grieg's works experienced somewhat of a renaissance in the United States, and in contrast to Ditson's other volumes, the Grieg volume was one of the few that aspired to introduce songs that were not well known. The interest in this repertoire was not sustained after the war, however.

The Musicians Library and most of the other anthologies of lieder did not include numerous other lieder composers whose works were sometimes programmed. European composers such as Brückler, von Fielitz, Henschel, Lassen, and Otto Lessmann (1844–1918), as well as German composers resident in the United States such as Oscar B. Klein, were mostly neglected, though recitalists in the United States in the 1880s and early 1890s had started to explore such composers. Similarly, an even wider array of composers whose songs were regularly performed in Vienna, including Richard Heuberger (1850–1914), Carl Reinecke (1824–1910), Karl Goldmark (1839–1915), and Jean Sibelius (1865–1957), were also neglected by US recitalists and publishers. These composers might have been overlooked because polyglot programs, including those that presented American composers, could only accommodate a limited number of lieder, and often the few spots available to them were given to canonic composers.

The reception of lieder in the United States operated on at least two levels. While some of the reasons for this variance are unique to the genre, in general, music lovers were not a unified community, with levels of skill and taste varying not only by region but also within urban areas.[13] To educated music lovers who appreciated German poetry, lieder appealed because of the intricate ways the music was structured and the ways it responded to the words. In contrast, many Americans had little to no knowledge of the sophisticated texts or of their association with German culture and history. Moreover, the spiritual aspect of German Romantic poetry that drew Dwight to lieder likely attracted only erudite concertgoers, perhaps because most of the performers did not educate their audiences. Heinrich was one of the few who emphasized the importance of the words; he did this so often that critics sometimes reinforced his stance in their reviews. But even his comments were generalizations, rather than exegeses of individual songs. Pedagogues such as Mathews, Elson, and Villa Whitney White provided a variety of audiences with at least a superficial understanding of the lied's position in German culture, and presentations created by members of women's clubs might have aspired to do this as well. Yet because of the dearth of documentary evidence such as scripts of lectures, the depth of their presentations cannot be assessed.

Lacking knowledge of German literary traditions, US audiences relied on the melodies and English translations of the texts. In a concert hall, listeners were moved by the performers' ability to convey the important emotional and narrative aspects of each song; those who did not possess knowledge of German poetry did not appreciate lieder any differently than the way they experienced songs from other countries. The union of the vocal line and piano part in portraying the meaning of a song is a defining characteristic of lieder. While some writers acknowledged this, reviews seldom referenced the piano part or the pianist. Indeed, Henschel's and Max Heinrich's piano playing was noted far more frequently than that of other accompanists because audiences and critics were so impressed by the way the men accompanied their own singing and that of their collaborators. Scores with simplified piano parts likewise reflect the perception that the piano part was less important than the melody.[14]

Rather than convincing audiences of the beauty of a large palette of lieder, many performers and publishers sometimes pandered to their tastes, resulting in a type of ossification of the canon. Recitalists continued to give programs dominated by the songs of Schubert and Schumann that had pleased crowds for decades, including ballads such as "Die beiden Grenadiere" and sentimental lyrical numbers such as "Widmung." Even in cultural hubs such as New York, singers tended to emphasize Schubert, Schumann, and Brahms more than other composers. Whereas they often presented a number of songs by each of these, they usually gave only one well-known song by each of the other composers on their programs.[15] This was the case with the programming of Tchaikovsky's "Nur wer die Sehnsucht kennt" ("None but the Lonely Heart," op. 6, no. 6), which is among the multivalent works that were considered both high art and popular, and with Grieg's "Ein Schwan" (op. 25, no. 2) and "Ich liebe Dich" (op. 41, no. 3).[16] Of course, many of these songs were also much loved in Germany and Austria, but the all-German programs in those countries enabled singers to perform a much greater variety of each composer's lieder. For instance, in the United States Cornelius's "Ein Ton" (op. 3, no. 3) was repeatedly sung, but in Vienna many more of his lieder were regularly programmed. Further, more recent live performers and recording artists have explored far more lieder by composers such as Tchaikovsky and Wolf than did recitalists at the turn of the twentieth century, in addition to which they perform lieder by women, including Fanny Mendelssohn Hensel (1805–1847). Nevertheless, although teaching students only canonical works is highly problematic, there is no evidence to suggest that repeated performances of canonical composers by nineteenth-century singers contributed to the decline of the song recital.

Despite the limitations of recital programs and the depth of audiences' appreciation, through performances and English-language scores, nineteenth-century advocates of the lied did succeed in canonizing lieder that are still studied and sung today. Moreover, the position of the lied alongside other classical genres, a status which is perpetuated in modern music history textbooks, was solidified by taste-making guides such as Henderson's monograph *What Is Good Music?*, which anticipated music appreciation textbooks.[17] Lieder were not consumed in a vacuum; further study of the reception of this genre by US writers would need to be coordinated with explorations of the reception of the composers' other genres, including their instrumental works, and despite landmark studies on the US reception of Beethoven, Schubert, and Schumann, this field of study is still developing.[18]

The Great War

World War I gradually impacted the success of both song recitals and the reception of lieder. Although the sinking of the *Lusitania* in 1915 led to increased animosity toward Germany, US concert life continued to feature German works. But once the United States went to war there were numerous highly publicized efforts to remove German repertoire, with the Metropolitan Opera being just one of the institutions that halted such performances. In addition to the shunning of Karl Muck (1859–1940) and Johanna Gadski's departure from the Met, German musicians such as Fritz Kreisler were forced to cancel concerts.[19] The volume of performances of German orchestral works was significantly reduced, and the pieces that were performed were carefully combined with an increasing number of works by French, Russian, English, and American composers.

As patriotic fervor increased, a writer for the *Musical Courier* asked that more singers perform songs by Americans rather than specializing in German genres. Although he greatly admired the lied he had concluded that not all lieder were of a truly exceptional quality and that songs by Americans could be equally if not more satisfying, noting "Carrie Jacobs Bond has given more pleasure to thousands with her 'Perfect Day' than many of Hugo Wolf's songs have given."[20] This statement represents an important reversal: Whereas critics in the 1850s exhorted singers to perform lieder because they believed they represented high art, this critic advocated for American songs, not only because of their artistic merits but also because of their accessibility. (That the American song he cited was composed by a woman is indicative of the status of women composers at the time, but the writer did not address this point.)

Because recitalists had already been programming American repertoire and songs from a variety of countries, they were well placed to reduce performances of lieder. Still, that only happened gradually. Julia Culp and Elena Gerhardt, for instance, continued to sing lieder in German as late as the early months of 1917. Similarly, an editorial in *Musical America*'s July 1917 issue was among the publications decrying the removal of lieder and the possible elimination of singing in German.[21] And in 1918, at a festival in Newark, New Jersey, Geraldine Farrar sang (in English) Franz's "For Music," Schumann's "Love's Secret Lost" (op. 40, no. 5), and Brahms's "A Thought Like Melody" (op. 105, no. 1).[22]

Yet Henderson's 1917 prediction that recitalists would likely discontinue singing lieder was accurate.[23] Many if not all of Schumann-Heink's 1918 recitals eschewed lieder, although she retained other works by Germans, including one aria by Bach sung in English and an aria from Handel's *Rinaldo* sung in Italian.[24] Similarly, during her 1918 tour of the Midwest, Farrar combined pieces by French, Russian, and American composers, along with one or two arias by Handel, which she sang in English. Like other singers she modeled American patriotism, beginning her recitals with "The Battle Hymn of the Republic" and ending with the "Star Spangled Banner," and on occasion she wore red, white, and blue hair ribbons.[25] In contrast, Bispham devoted less time to presenting recitals, instead focusing more on performing at events designed to raise the spirits of the nation or boost the troops' morale. He performed in large-scale popular events dominated by patriotic American music. At one of Sousa's New York concerts at the Hippodrome (which had a capacity of over five thousand) his numbers included "The Ride of Paul Revere" and "When the Boys Come Home."[26] In one of the few recitals he gave in 1918, the only lied was Schumann's "The Two Grenadiers," which was grouped with popular patriotic songs such as "Keep the Home Fires Burning."[27] Nevertheless, he continued to stage his play about Beethoven, during which he sang "Adelaide." Some performances were greeted with protests, but they were reported to be financially successful.[28]

While the United States was at war the number of recitals declined, and those that did take place featured songs by French, Russian, and US composers. In 1919 Bertram Taylor in Indiana observed that French repertoire had become "very popular" with concert singers because of the war.[29] However, interest in French songs had already been growing before the start of the war. Initially they were often used to bring variety to recitals emphasizing lieder, as was the case with the Henschels' recitals. Later, during the early decades of the twentieth century, singers from France, such as Victor Maurel, and those who had trained with French pedagogues made more significant contributions to disseminating French song, and in particular, the more recent examples of the *mélodie*. But although Mme. Emilie Alexander Marius (d. 1940), Mme. Emma Calvé (1858–1942), and Charles Gilibert gave a few recitals devoted to French song during the first decade of the twentieth century, such events did not gain currency until the war years.[30] Similarly, before the war Ditson had already published English-language scores of French songs. Philip Hale, who spent time in France and often advocated for French instrumental works, edited *Modern French Songs*, which Ditson published in 1904. Comprising sixty songs by twenty-seven composers, the two volumes included songs by Bizet, Debussy,

Fauré, Gounod, and Hahn. They also included songs by Chaminade and Holmès, both of whom had achieved quite a following among American women. In 1915 Ditson added Calvé's *My Favorite French Songs* to its series of song anthologies marketed by esteemed recitalists. It contained fifty-two numbers ranging from "old folksongs" to Debussy. By the time of the war some songs, such as Fauré's "Les Rameaux" and Debussy's "Mandoline" (L 43), were being presented by numerous recitalists (including those performing before women's clubs), but a canon of works was still developing; it is not clear that these two composers were more highly regarded than others such as Bizet or Delibes, whose songs had been programmed for decades.

Art songs by Russian composers had only begun to emerge and attract the attention of recitalists at the start of the twentieth century, and although performances increased during the war, ultimately this repertoire did not achieve the same status as did French art songs. During the second decade of the new century Schirmer released multiple volumes of Russian songs including not only English versions of lieder by Tchaikovsky and Rubinstein but also songs by the nationalists Glinka, Balakirev, Borodin, Cui, Mussorgsky, and Rimsky-Korsakov, some of which were excerpted from operas.[31] Recitalists programmed an increasing number of Russian songs during the war. For instance, Russians were represented on four of the five recital programs published in the February 18, 1918, issue of the *New York Tribune*. However, Éva Gauthier (1885–1958), a Canadian known for novel programs, was the only one of these singers who gave a program dominated by Russian works. She sang multiple songs by S. Ivan Taneyef (1856–1915) and Nikolai Medtner (1880–1951), as well as Stravinsky's *Japanese Lyrics* (of which she had given the US premiere in 1917).[32]

While war-time singers frequently sang American songs, they did not favor classical songs from the allied countries Italy and England as much as those from France and the United States. Occasionally they programmed Italian songs by Luigi Gordigiani (1806–1860) or Paolo Tosti (1846–1916), the latter of whom also wrote songs in French and English, or sometimes an aria from an Italian opera. Although folksongs from the British Isles and popular war songs by English composers such as "God Will Be with Our Boys Tonight" and "It's a Long Way to Tipperary" were programmed (and also recorded by stars such as McCormack), classical works were less common. Purcell's songs were performed more frequently than ones by later composers such as Coleridge-Taylor and Edward Horsman (1873—1918). In comparison, a much wider range of American songs were frequently programmed, including popular numbers such as "When the Boys Come Home." But despite the plethora of American songs that were performed and published before the end of the war, few of those by composers such as Chadwick and Salter are heard today.

Reversing Nineteenth-Century Trends

The wartime slump in performances of lieder, particularly noticeable in 1918, was already reversed in the early 1920s. Yet even before the war, critics occasionally had vented concerns that the vogue for lieder and recitals would not continue, and these issues, along with the 1929 stock market crash and subsequent depression, influenced more substantial declines in recitals that were not reversed. The conditions that enabled song recitals featuring lieder to thrive during the 1890s and the early 1900s were eroding, and the continued decline was influenced by permanent changes in society, technology, and commercial genres that changed the face of the performing arts.[33]

After the end of the war, singers quickly resumed giving lieder, but they sang in English. Singing in German was initially perceived as problematic, though a few performers began to do so as early as 1920. In 1922 lieder were so widely rehabilitated that when Elena Gerhardt toured she not only sang in German but also presented the complete *Winterreise*.[34] The wartime ebb and flow in the number of lieder performances and song recitals followed the same pattern as performances of German orchestral works by the New York Philharmonic Society and the Boston Symphony Orchestra.[35] Just as German orchestral works dominated most of the postwar decades, so too lieder dominated recitals, but the difference is that recitals and lieder subsequently dropped in popularity. Tunbridge has traced the story of the lied during the interwar years by focusing on performances in New York and London and on the importance of recordings and, to a lesser extent, radio broadcasts. She concluded that starting in the 1920s "lieder appreciation became an increasingly specialized affair; something in which one invested not only money but also time, retreating from company to listen attentively, score in hand."[36] Ultimately, recordings, and likely also the Urtext mentality, led to what is now considered the standard practice: singing lieder in German. Both of these trends—the private study of lieder and singing in German—are exclusionary and at odds with the practices of the nineteenth-century promoters of the lied, who were interested in creating audiences for the genre.

Despite the success of song recitals, critics had periodically voiced reservations. An 1893 review of the Heinrichs' performance before a woman's club in Worcester claimed that the word "recital" had "come to have a somewhat ponderous and ominous sound to the public ear," and, like other publications dating back to the early 1880s, it asserted that both voice and piano recitals ran the risk of monotony—a problem that also concerned Europeans.[37] Although there were numerous wonderful recitalists, during the first two decades of the twentieth century some critics implied that there were too many song recitals and that too many of the performances were subpar. In 1913, Henderson complained of singers' poor vocal technique, their failure to clearly discriminate songs of contrasting styles and moods, and their inability to enunciate clearly in multiple languages.[38] In 1918, Finck bemoaned the numerous recitalists who naïvely assumed they could achieve the same type of financial success as had stars such as Schumann-Heink. He also objected to the artistic standard of some of the songs that were being programmed instead of lieder.[39]

One of the key factors in the proliferation of the song recital, and in particular, of its adoption in locales beyond major metropolises, was the woman's club movement. Clubs hosted performances by both professionals and club members and fostered the development of amateur music making. During the twentieth century, however, the clubs' role in concert organizing was gradually usurped by a variety of (mostly male) concert organizers and organizations, and domestic music making declined. Although club membership peaked in 1930, during the financial crisis of the Great Depression numerous clubs folded. Later, the increase in the number of women in the workforce further eroded membership.[40] The reduction of amateur music making, which was not confined to clubs, can also be attributed to the development of technology. A growing number of people were listening to music on phonographs and radios, both of which enabled them to hear high-quality performances in the comfort of their own homes. The advent of these technologies also contributed to a decrease in piano sales. The drop in sales, which began after World War I and then rapidly increased because of the Depression, was a worldwide phenomenon. Whereas approximately six hundred thousand instruments were produced in 1910, fewer than a quarter of that number were produced globally in 1935. In the United States piano production peaked in 1923 but by 1929 it had already decreased, with the number of piano makers falling from 191 to 81.[41]

The declines in amateur music making and sales of pianos impacted the composition of American art songs, as did the burgeoning popular music industry. After a period during which the composition of American art songs flourished, the number of songs composed and published began to decrease as early as 1912, and did so more rapidly in the 1920s.[42] As with women's clubs and performances of lieder, this shift reflected the decreasing profitability of art songs that in part resulted from the increasing number of Americans who were listening to gramophone recordings and the radio rather than creating music. Men as well as women moved away from composing art songs. Some of the men turned to writing popular music, specifically Tin Pan Alley songs. But women did not have easy access to either Hollywood or Broadway, and as a result, many fewer of them continued to compose.[43] Although recitalists at the end of the twentieth century sometimes created programs comprising lieder and more popular genres such as songs from Broadway, recitalists at the start of the century, in some cases because of bigotry or fear of commercialism, rarely explored the possibility of programming new types of songs produced for the mass market.

Even before the war there were signs that the mechanisms by which lieder were integrated into US concert life were not going to stay in place. Levine observed that as early as 1903 terms such as "highbrow" were used derogatively,[44] and although Bispham believed lieder were high art, the press no longer promoted the genre by using such terms. The efforts of Dwight's network, women's clubs, and social reformers at the start of the twentieth century to use classical music (and predominantly German music) to improve society had mixed outcomes. Their efforts did result in the establishment of major orchestras and concert halls that are still in existence, though now under increasing financial pressures. But, lacking the *Bildung* ethos and nationalistic overtones of performances in Germany and Austria (which were described in the introduction), American performances of lieder did not have deeply rooted societal implications (though to be sure attendance at recitals was often an indicator of social class). At the turn of the century, some listeners, as today, were attending recitals for the social cachet or to hear their favorite singers—or those they had been told were outstanding or currently in vogue. Some might have been conscious of the philosophy of cultural uplift guiding the work of certain recitalists and concert organizers, but they were attending in order to be entertained. They were not there for moral enrichment, and the educational aspect of song recitals was confined to musicians who were able to evaluate performing techniques and those interested in learning new repertoire or gaining a historical perspective on the development of song.

In general, the goal of cultural uplift through classical music proved problematic. Theodore Thomas came to the realization that it was not possible to raise the level of music appreciation of the masses through symphony concerts, though he snobbishly believed that this was because of what he assessed to be the low intellectual level of workers and children.[45] Although social reformers of the 1920s and 1930s advocated for the teaching of classical music, invoking claims that "good music" was linked to ethical citizenship and social improvement, ultimately much of the resulting activity, such as music appreciation classes for children and adults and radio shows, addressed the socially aspiring middle classes. On a practical level, the lower classes were often locked out of classical concerts and recitals because of the cost.[46] Even membership in women's clubs necessitated a significant outlay in terms of purchasing an instrument, scores, the appropriate garb for attending events, and perhaps also lessons, as well as club fees and additional obligations such as the purchase of at least one ticket to each of the visiting artists' events. Moreover, low-priced "popular" concerts and recitals, including those conducted by Thomas, usually presented accessible repertoire that was already well known, rather than attempting to broaden audiences' tastes. In 1915 H. L. Mencken (1880–1956), with his characteristic pessimism, attributed the failure of the political and economic uplift that was reflected in contemporary literature to those who practiced "uplift as a means of eager self-seeking,"[47] and, to a degree, some of the musicians who espoused cultural uplift were also motivated by self-interest. Whatever their altruistic intentions, promoters of classical music attempted to impose their aesthetics and values on the wider society and, in so doing, ignored other types of music, in particular, music favored by the working classes and ethnic minorities.[48] Although song recitals embraced more varied repertoire than did many orchestral and chamber concerts, by ignoring increasingly popular commercial music genres they also participated in this exclusionary behavior.

The Future

While performances of lieder in London and New York during World War II and the strength of the scholarly discourse that subsequently developed and continues today speak to the genre's ability to survive in changing societal and musical landscapes, ultimately the lied and the song recital have not regained the type of visibility they attained in concert life circa 1900. Jennie Tourel (1900–1973) recalled giving successful song recitals throughout the United States during the 1950s, but in the following decades recital attendance continued to decline.[49] In 1984 Will Crutchfield, a vocal coach and critic for the *New York Times*, attempted to dispel the widespread notion of the death or decline of the song recital by listing all the New York venues hosting series of them, as well as the numerous acclaimed singers such as Elly Ameling (b. 1938) and Jessye Norman (1945–2019) who could fill concert halls.[50] Still, the recordings and tours of these artists did little to improve the situation in most areas of the country. Today, concert seasons in many cities outside New York do not regularly include a recital by a singer of national or international repute. Moreover, this decline is also evident in Europe.[51]

In 1997 speakers at "The Art of the Vocal Recital," a two-day forum hosted by the Marilyn Horne Foundation and the Juilliard School, repeatedly returned to the fate of the recital and to the question of the language of lieder performances. While audiences were reported as responding positively to lieder sung in English and Horne seemingly endorsed this practice, Christa Ludwig (1928–2021) disagreed, and the preference for German continues to this day.[52] The 2018 recording of *Winterreise* by British baritone Roderick Williams (b. 1965) and pianist Christopher Glynn is one of the few instances of a prominent English-language lieder performance.[53] But perhaps it is worth considering that numerous recitalists at the end of the long nineteenth century were able to achieve success throughout the United States in large part because they sometimes sang in English. (At the very least, subtitles could be more widely used, especially in YouTube videos.)

Singing lieder in English, however, is not enough. In 1884, a Boston critic asserted that singing English translations, as Mrs. Henschel had done in a performance of Liszt's "The Loreley," fail to convey the full import of the text.[54] Despite decades of music appreciation courses at US colleges, today Americans are likely to have no more knowledge of the lied than the listeners of this critic's time, and they are unlikely to be able to grasp the meaning of individual lieder without study or assistance. The German bass-baritone Thomas Quasthoff (b. 1959) has noted that this is also an issue in Europe, and he attributed the current difficulties of the recital and of lieder appreciation to the insufficient study of poetry in schools.[55] As in the nineteenth century, modern singers need to take more responsibility for filling these types of gaps. Entertaining explanations of individual songs, especially from the stage, could assist with this, but what is even more crucial, as Henderson argued in 1913, is for the singers to communicate to an audience the songs' meaning and to do so with sufficient power to stir their emotions.[56] Recent singers such as Thomas Hampson (b. 1955) and Ian Bostridge (b. 1964) have established reputations for doing exactly that.[57] Quasthoff, among others, follows much earlier recitalists such as Henschel in reminding singers that they cannot rely only on beautiful voices; they need to know how to interpret their works and how to use meaningful gestures to engage audiences.[58] But instead of taking the time to actively engage their listeners in the songs, too many performers seem to be happy to assume that their audience is comprised of educated musicians.[59]

Recently, Christopher Purdy astutely pinpointed one of the challenges posed by the type of soul-searching lyrics that characterize many lieder: "We as a public have become distrustful of introspection. TV, video, and film have made it easier for us to accept entertainment that is literally in our faces, leaving the emotional muscles necessary to fully enjoy a song recital under-utilized."[60] It is difficult to imagine a solution to such a significant cultural barrier, especially when so many listeners (including music students) are captivated by extroverted performances in such shows as *The Voice* and *America's Got Talent*. It is naïve to believe that recitals will be able to continue indefinitely with the traditional format characterized by few visual stimuli and formally attired artists, often hiding behind music stands, who make only limited attempts to connect to their audience and accompany their singing with a supply of stock gestures. Although experiments such as the planned animated film version of *Winterreise* might be intriguing, they also raise a variety of aesthetic concerns, and most lieder could not be easily adapted to this type of format.[61] Moreover, perhaps singers should consider the ways nineteenth-century performers created programs that were guided by variety, rather than rehash the complete cycles that were performed and recorded so frequently during the twentieth century.

The future, however, is not entirely bleak. An increasing number of festivals and summer schools promote lieder by hosting performances by acclaimed and up-and-coming professional recitalists, masterclasses for students, and a variety of related informative presentations for participants and the music-loving public. In addition, acclaimed singers host a variety of pedagogical events that are designed to attract young singers to the lied. But the majority of these are in Europe.[62] Perhaps such outreach projects, held in a greater number of US regional and local venues, would improve the current perception of lieder performances in the United States. In any case, in order to revitalize a broad interest in the lied any such projects would need to develop strategies to attract new audiences and not just aspiring singers.

The recent surge in interest in decentering the canon and diversifying programs has the potential to impact recitals. While this has already led to a greater number of performances and editions of lieder by women, it should also lead to a greater variety of genres and styles. In endorsing such diversity, David Patrick Stearns suggests that recitals might offer singers an alternative to the stereotype characters of operas.[63] Efforts to diversify programs include projects, such as the Cincinnati Song Initiative, that promote a broad range of songs and performers; the publication of editions of African American and Latin American songs; and advocacy groups such as Darryl Taylor's African American Art Song Alliance.[64] During 2020 and 2021, Hampson's commitment to expanding repertoire to include works by Black men and women was aided by his collaboration with Louise Toppin, a long-time advocate for the music of African Americans based at the University of Michigan.[65] It is too early to predict whether this will result in reviving the song recital. Although it is to be hoped that these groups have a more lasting influence than the performances of African American songs by Harry Burleigh and Roland Hayes at the start of the twentieth century and by Jessye Norman and Kathleen Battle (b. 1948) in the 1990s, there is a danger that, even with the power of social media, they might only reach people who are already invested in art songs and recitals.

* * *

In the twilight of their careers, Heinrich, Bispham, and Schumann-Heink each drew the applause of audiences at vaudevilles. It is hard to imagine a prominent lieder recitalist of the twenty-first century attracting such crowds. While Hampson, whose interest in exploring repertoire ignored by other singers and promoting American song composers is reminiscent of Bispham, and European recitalists such as Bostridge and Matthias Goerne (b. 1967) certainly have admirers, they have not captured the hearts of Americans in the same way lieder singers at the start of the twentieth century did.[66] Although diversifying the repertoire and highlighting popular songs might attract some new audiences, the key elements of Heinrich's success were his unbridled enthusiasm for lieder and his ability to create a rapport with his audiences—to make genuine eye contact with them and to meet them at their level. Perhaps his approach could inspire current performers to increase lieder's market share and to ensure the genre's survival beyond the halls of academia.

Appendix
Milestones in the Development of Song Recitals

1840	Joseph Philip Knight's classical song "concert" in Boston
1846	Johann Baptist Pischek's Abschieds-Concert of lieder in Vienna
1853	Georg Stigelli's "Lieder Concert" in Vienna
ca. 1853	August Kreissmann sings lieder in chamber concerts in Boston through to 1873
1856	Julius Stockhausen's first complete performance of *Die schöne Müllerin*, Vienna
1861	Stockhausen's first complete performance of *Dichterliebe*, Hamburg
1863	Kreissmann's first appearance in the Mason-Thomas chamber concerts, New York
1864	Stockhausen's first complete performance of *Die Winterreise*, Hamburg
1865	Stockhausen's first complete performance of *Frauenliebe und -leben*, Berlin
1866–1868	Karl Wallenreiter's performances of Schubert's and Schumann's cycles in Germany
1869	Fanny Raymond Ritter's "Historical Recitals of Vocal and Piano-Forte Music," New York
1872–1873	George L. Osgood's tour with the Thomas Orchestra
1875	Mrs. J. Hull's and W. S. B. Matthews's song recitals at normal schools in Watertown, New York
1876	Gustav Walter's first Schubert *Liederabend,* Vienna
	Osgood's performance of *Frauenliebe und -leben*
	Song recitals at a normal school in Wheaton, Illinois
1877–1878	George Henschel's first "vocal recitals" in London

1879	George Werrenrath and Carl Wolfsohn's song recital series, Chicago
	Grace Hiltz's first recitals in Chicago
1880	Jules Jordan's series of Schubert lieder cycles, Providence, Rhode Island
1880–1881	Henschel and Lillian Bailey's first vocal recital series, New York and Boston
1881	Walter's first series of *Liederabende*, Vienna
	Werrenrath's first recital series in Brooklyn
1881–1884	Henschel conducts the Boston Symphony Orchestra, gives annual series of vocal recitals in Boston
1883	The Henschels' first "vocal recital" with their standard type of program in London
1884–1885	Max Heinrich and Medora Henson's "Classical Song Recital" series in Chicago, Milwaukee, New York, and Philadelphia
1885	Anton Schott's first US song recitals, New York
1886	Gertrude Franklin's song recitals including French and American repertoire, Boston
1887	Hugo Wolf protests the "epidemic" of lieder recitals in Vienna
1888–1891	The Henschels' and Schott's East Coast and Chicago tours
1889	The Henschels' US tour
1891–1892	Lena Little, Wilhelm Heinrich, and Heinrich Meyn establish themselves in the United States
1892	The Henschels' US tour
1892	Max Heinrich settles in Boston
1895	Schott tours Texas and Mexico
1896	Schott establishes himself in California
1896–1897	David Bispham's first US song recitals, US premieres of Brahms's *Magelone Romances* and *Vier ernste Gesänge*
1897	Lilli Lehmann's first US song recitals
Oct. 1897– Mar. 1898	The Henschels' tour, including California
Dec. 1897– Jan. 1898	Villa Whitney White performs in Oregon and California
Nov. 1898	Heinrich performs in Oregon and California
	Harry Plunket Green's US recitals and ballad concerts
1898–1899	Victor Maurel's recitals of French and German songs
	Ernestine Schumann-Heink's song recitals begin
1899	Heinrich relocates to Chicago
1899–1900	Numerous reports of the US "vogue" for song recitals

1900	Marcella Sembrich's first US song recital, New York
	Schumann-Heink's and Lillian Nordica's first joint recital, New York
1901	The last Henschel song recital tour, including Washington State and California
1903	Heinrich retires
1904–1905	Bispham's "Cycle of Cycles" recital series
1906	Bispham begins promoting American songs and marketing "All English" recitals
1908	Ludwig Wüllner's first US recitals
1912	Julia Culp's first US recitals
	Elena Gerhardt's first US recitals
1916	Max Heinrich dies
1921	David Bispham dies

Notes

Introduction

1. A. L. J., "America Is the Place to Study Voice Culture, Says Max Heinrich," *Musical America* 11, no. 5 (December 11, 1909): 31.

2. "Six Books on Musical Topics," *Nation* 71, no. 1850 (December 13, 1900): 470.

3. Henschel was referred to both as George and Georg. All references in this book will use George.

4. Throughout this book Schumann refers to Robert Schumann. When Clara Schumann is referenced, her full name is given.

5. Nancy Reich, "Robert Schumann's Music in New York City, 1848–1898," 16, 22–23. Though she concentrates on the symphony, Jessica C. E. Gienow-Hecht provides one of the most sensitive examinations of the complex nature of the American adoption of German music in *Sound Diplomacy: Music and Emotions in Transatlantic Relations, 1850–1920*. See also Joseph Horowitz, *Wagner Nights: An American History*.

6. Nancy Newman, *Good Music for a Free People: The Germania Musical Society in Nineteenth-Century America*, 5.

7. The influence of nineteenth-century critics like Dwight and Mathews on the formation of musical taste in the United States parallels the efforts of critics in Europe. William Weber, *The Great Transformation of Musical Taste*, 102–6.

8. John S. Dwight, "Music a Means of Culture," 321–31.

9. Ibid., 326; and John S. Dwight, "The Intellectual Influence of Music," 615–16. For an exploration of Dwight's aesthetics, see Ora Frishberg Saloman, *Beethoven's Symphonies and J. S. Dwight: The Birth of American Music Criticism*. On Dwight's elitism and interest in raising the quality of the programs of instrumental concerts in Boston, see, e.g., Michael Broyles, *Music of the Highest Class: Elitism and Populism in Antebellum Boston*, 247–57, 263.

10. The role of music in the American uplift movement has been discussed by numerous scholars. Joseph Horowitz outlines its roots in German philosophies and discusses

some of the music critics who adhered to it in "Henry Krehbiel: German American, Music Critic," 165–87.

11. John Spitzer, "Review of Lawrence Levine's *Highbrow/Lowbrow*," 234–35.

12. Gienow-Hecht, *Sound Diplomacy*, 6; see also 12.

13. "Musical Review," *Dwight's Journal of Music* 1, no. 12 (June 26, 1852): 92–93.

14. W. W. Crane, "German Songs," 628. Katy Hamilton explores many of the issues involved with creating singable English translations of lieder texts in "Natalia Macfarren and the English German Lied," 87–110.

15. Armin W. Hadamer, *Mimetischer Zauber: Die englischsprachige Rezeption deutscher Lieder in den USA 1830–1880*, 235.

16. Unlike my study, Charles Hamm's book did not consider performances of German songs; he only considered the publication of scores. *Yesterdays: Popular Song in America*, 200, 194–195.

17. Richard Middleton and Peter Manuel, "Popular Music."

18. Derek B. Scott, "Music and Social Class," 545, 548; Hamm, *Yesterdays*, 76.

19. Lawrence W. Levine, *Highbrow/Lowbrow: The Emergence of Cultural Hierarchy in America*, 86, 93.

20. Hamm, *Yesterdays*, 194, 485–86; Hadamer, *Mimetischer Zauber*, 53. Like a small number of Schubert's other lieder, "Serenade" first appeared in the United States in French scores, though the performances examined for this study were in either English or German.

21. Elizabeth Ann Sears, "The Art Song in Boston, 1880–1914," 14.

22. Ann Ostendorf, *Sounds American: National Identity and the Music Cultures of the Lower Mississippi River Valley, 1800–1860*, 101–2.

23. "The Two Grenadiers" is listed as being popular in the United States in 1840 in Julius Mattfeld, *Variety Music Cavalcade 1620-1969: A Chronology of Vocal and Instrumental Music Popular in the United States*, 3rd ed. (Englewood Cliffs, NY: Prentice-Hall, 1971), 58.

24. Susan Youens, *Heinrich Heine and the Lied*, 176–212.

25. Roland Barthes, "The Romantic Song" (1976), 292.

26. Paul DiMaggio, "Cultural Entrepreneurship in Nineteenth-Century Boston: The Creation of an Organizational Base for High Culture in America," 33–50; Levine, *Highbrow/Lowbrow*, 115–46. Music scholars have critiqued Levine's conclusions, including Ralph P. Locke, "Music Lovers, Patrons, and the 'Sacralization' of Culture in America," 149–73, and Newman, *Good Music for a Free People*, 114–24.

27. Weber, *Great Transformation*, 35.

28. Several authors have discussed the lack of a clear demarcation between art songs and popular songs composed in the United States during the nineteenth century, and some have attempted to formulate a definition of art song based on the complexity of the music and the style of the texts. See, e.g., Hamm, *Yesterdays*, 323. More sustained discussions can be found in Sears, "The Art Song in Boston," 12–25, and Anthony Lien, "Against the Grain: Modernism and the American Art Song, 1900 to 1950," 9–18.

29. Beatrix Borchard, trans. Jeremy Coleman, "The Concert Hall as a Gender-Neutral Space: The Case of Amalie Joachim, née Schneeweiss," 140.

30. Walter Damrosch, *My Musical Life*, 323, 325.

31. Richard Crawford, *America's Musical Life*, 236–37; Adrienne Fried Block, "Matinee Mania, or the Regendering of Nineteenth-Century Audiences in New York City," 195–96. Already during the 1840s, the Germania Musical Society realized the potential power of women as patrons and developed marketing strategies to appeal to them. Nancy Newman, "Gender and the Germanians: 'Art-Loving Ladies' in Nineteenth-Century Concert Life," 289–309.

32. Crawford, *America's Musical Life*, 235.

33. Craig H. Roell, *The Piano in America, 1890–1940*, 4–5.

34. E. Chester, *Girls and Women*, 150.

35. Crawford, *America's Musical Life*, 220–21, 226, 232.

36. *Complete Catalog of Sheet Music and Musical Works* (n.p.: Board of Music Trade of the United States of America, 1870), 197–207.

37. In Europe, Amalie Joachim, for example, worked with the publisher Simrock. Borchard, "Concert Hall," 140. On the situation in England, see Simon McVeigh and William Weber, "From the Benefit Concert to the Solo Song Recital in London, 1870–1914," 182.

38. Linda Whitesitt, "Women as 'Keepers of Culture': Music Clubs, Community Concert Series and Symphony Orchestras," 67.

39. David Gramit, "The Circulation of the Lied: The Double Life of an Artwork and a Commodity," 301–14. Gramit also explores the emergence of the lied's canonic status.

40. Marcia Citron, *Gender and the Musical Canon*, 122–23.

41. Douglas W. Shadle, *Orchestrating the Nation: The Nineteenth-Century American Symphonic Enterprise*, 6–7.

42. [Gleason], "The Henschel Vocal Recital," *Morning News* (Chicago), April 28, 1884.

43. English translation in Otto Erich Deutsch, trans. Eric Blom, *Schubert: A Documentary Biography*, 758.

44. Natasha Loges, "Julius Stockhausen's Early Performances of Franz Schubert's *Die schöne Müllerin*," 212, 214.

45. Jennifer Ronyak, *Intimacy, Performance, and the Lied in the Early Nineteenth Century*, 5–9; Martin Günther, *Kunstlied als Liedkunst: Die Lieder Franz Schuberts in der musikalischen Aufführungskultur des 19. Jahrhunderts*, 234.

46. Wiebke Rademacher, "German Song and the Working Classes in Berlin, 1890–1914," 207–10, 215.

47. Natasha Loges and Laura Tunbridge, "Performers' Reflections," *German Song Onstage*, 270.

48. David Gramit, "Schubert's Wanderers and the Autonomous Lied," 153–54.

49. Susan Youens, "'Eine wahre Olla Patrida [*sic*]': Anna Milder-Hauptmann, Schubert, and Programming the Orient," *German Song Onstage*, 13.

50. Loges and Tunbridge, "Performers' Reflections," 263–64.

51. Crawford, *America's Musical Life*, 237.

52. Tunbridge, introduction to *German Song Onstage*, 2.

53. Günther, *Kunstlied als Liedkunst*, 344–46.

54. Anthony Tommasini, "Devising an Experiment to Save the Song Recital," sec. 1, 15.

Notes to Introduction   219

55. Loges, "Julius Stockhausen's Early Performances," 207.

56. The bibliography lists the archives and digital resources that provided much of the source material for this study.

57. Lien, "Against the Grain," 96.

58. With the exception of songs that were widely identified by their English titles, such as Schubert's "Ständchen"/"Serenade," most references to lieder in this book will use their German titles. The opus or catalog number will only be given the first time a song is mentioned; this information, however, is also available in the index.

59. See, e.g., Der Freyschütz, "Chicago" (April 3, 1875): 415–16.

60. Reports of performances of lieder are also available in a number of other sources, though they have the same types of limitations as those in newspapers and journals. These include George H. Wilson, *The Musical Yearbook of the United States*; Henry Krehbiel, *Review of the New York Musical Season*; and Vera Brodsky Lawrence, *Strong on Music: The New York Music Scene in the Days of George Templeton Strong, 1836–1875*.

61. Christopher Bruhn discusses Steinway's repertoire in "Taking the Private Public: Amateur Music-Making and the Musical Audience in 1860s New York," 260–90. Steinway's musical experiences and his association with New York's Liederkranz are chronicled in his diaries, which are available online at a site maintained by the Smithsonian Institution: https://americanhistory.si.edu/steinwaydiary/diary/. Although the biographies of the Damrosch family suggest they performed lieder at home, sources documenting such performances have not survived.

62. Natasha Loges, "The Limits of the Lied: Brahms's *Magelone-Romanzen* Op. 33," 302.

63. Dena J. Epstein discussed the challenges to studying the US production of scores in "Music Publishing in the Age of Piracy: The Board of Music Trade and Its Catalogue," 7–29.

64. Petra Meyer-Frazier, "American Women's Roles in Domestic Music Making as Revealed in Parlor Song Collections, 1820–1870," 16. The appendices list the songs in the volumes Meyer-Frazier researched.

65. Julia Wirth, *Julius Stockhausen: Der Sänger des Deutschen Lieder*; Beatrix Borchard, *Stimme und Geige: Amalie Joachim und Joseph Joachim*; Gabriele Gaiser-Reich, *Gustav Walter, 1834–1910: Wiener Hofopernsänger und Liederfürst*; Beatrix Borchard, *Pauline Viardot-Garcia: Fülle des Lebens*; Robin Terrill Bier, "The Ideal Orpheus: An Analysis of Virtuosic Self-Accompanied Singing."

66. Weber, *Great Transformation*, 152. Edward F. Kravitt, "The Lied in 19th Century Concert Life," 207–218; McVeigh and Weber, "From the Benefit Concert to the Solo Song Recital," 179–202.

67. Ronyak, *Intimacy, Performance, and the Lied*; Laura Tunbridge, *Singing in the Age of Anxiety: Lieder Performances in New York and London Between the World Wars*; *German Song Onstage*, ed. Natasha Loges and Laura Tunbridge.

68. Julia J. Chybowski, "Becoming the 'Black Swan' in Mid-Nineteenth-Century America: Elizabeth Taylor Greenfield's Early Life and Debut Concert Tour"; John Graziano, "The Early Life and Career of the 'Black Patti': The Odyssey of an African American Singer in the Late Nineteenth Century."

Chapter 1. Introducing a "Higher Class" of Song to American Audiences

1. Address by F. H. Underwood, "In Memoriam: August Kreissmann," 123.

2. Karen Ahlquist, *Democracy at the Opera: Music, Theater, and Culture in New York City, 1815–60*, 190–96.

3. "Musik in New York: 1849," in Rolf Weber, ed., *Land ohne Nachtigall: Deutsche Emigranten in Amerika*, 146.

4. On Thomas's views and role in elevating American concert life, see, e.g., Ezra Schabas, *Theodore Thomas: America's Conductor and Builder of Orchestras, 1835–1905*.

5. William Weber has observed that the words "miscellany" and "miscellaneous" were often used to describe these types of programs, and while those terms might carry negative connotations today, that was not the case during earlier centuries. Weber, *Great Transformation*, 14.

6. This correspondent claimed to write on behalf of the musically educated public, who, he acknowledged, included people from Germany. Progress, "Jenny Lind in Classic Music," *New York Tribune*, May 17, 1851, 6. The program of Lind's New York concert is given in "Amusements," *Evening Post* (New York), May 24, 1851, 1.

7. Louise and Otto Dresel (a German immigrant living in Columbus, Ohio, and unrelated to the musician of the same name in Boston), for instance, owned three volumes of Schubert's lieder. Molly Barnes, "The Other Otto Dresel: Public and Private Musical Identities in a German-American 'Forty-Eighter' and His Family, c. 1860–1880," 505–6. Amateur German musicians might have brought music with them when they migrated from Europe, but scores of German music were also imported and sold by US companies such as Edward Schuberth & Co. of New York.

8. Heike Bungert discusses the importance of *Männerchöre* in constructing a German American identity as well as the ways in which some of the music performed might have evoked nostalgic memories of the members' homeland. That she does not emphasize performances of solo lieder is a reflection of the choruses' priorities. *Festkultur und Gedächtnis: Die Konstruktion einer deutschamerikanischen Ethnizität, 1848–1914*; "The Singing Festivals of German Americans, 1849–1914," 141–79.

9. "German Liederkranz," *Evening Post* (New York), May 4, 1855, 2. For a similar sentiment see Bornonis, "From New York," 132.

10. Josef von Spaun, "Notes on My Association with Franz Schubert" (1858), trans. Rosamond Ley and John Nowell, as cited by David Gramit, "Schubert's Wanderers and the Autonomous Lied," 156.

11. Similarly, some of Schubert's lieder appeared in English-language scores before they were performed on stages in England. George Grove, *Beethoven-Schubert-Mendelssohn*, 222.

12. The following article was reprinted in multiple US publications: "Franz Schubert and Mayrhofer," *Southern Journal of Music* (Louisville, KY) 1, no. 1 (October 5, 1867): 1–2.

13. See, e.g., the scores at the end of *Musical Review and Musical World* 14 (1863).

14. Hitchcock was based in New York, but his scores were advertised as far afield as Texas. *Tri-Weekly State Gazette* (Austin, TX), March 1, 1869, 2.

15. This collection includes volumes created by women in East Coast cities. In contrast, binders from southern states rarely included lieder, though there does seem to have been a slight uptick in interest in Schubert's songs during the 1870s. This pattern of dissemination is mirrored by the later development of song recitals, with earlier recitals concentrated in the North. Karen Stafford, "Binders' Volumes and the Culture of Music Collectorship in the United States, 1830–1870," data at https://scholarworks.iu.edu/dspace/handle/2022/25306. Candace Bailey, *Unbinding Gentility: Women Making Music in the Nineteenth-Century South*, 73–74, 204, 207.

16. "The Little Golden Ring" (New York: Jollie, 1850). Ruth Solie explores the cultural work performed by Schumann's song cycle in "Whose Life? The Gendered Self in Schumann's *Frauenliebe* Songs," 219–40.

17. Crawford, *America's Musical Life*, 237.

18. Information about the programs of Thomas's orchestras and chamber concerts has been drawn from *Theodore Thomas: A Musical Autobiography*, vol. 2., ed. George P. Upton, and Music in Gotham, https://www.musicingotham.org.

19. Natasha Loges, "Detours on a Winter's Journey: Schubert's *Winterreise* in Nineteenth-Century Concerts," 33.

20. John S. Dwight, "The Concerts of the Past Winter," 50–51. While critics emphasized the art songs, the concert also included a duet by Bellini, a cavatina by Mozart, and songs and duets by composers such as Friedrich Heinrich Himmel (1765–1814) and Johann Wenzel Kalliwoda (1801–1866) who were popular and well respected at the time but whose lieder were not canonized in the same manner as Schubert's. An instrumental ensemble played a work by Haydn to open the first half of the concert and one by Mozart to open the second. The notices about the concert did not provide precise titles for the instrumental numbers. *Boston Post*, March 14, 1840, 3.

21. "Henry Russell," *Musical Magazine* 2, no. 33 (March 28, 1820): 102. This article claims that about 220 people attended Knight's concert.

22. One such critique, that of Henry C. Watson, is reported in Lawrence, *Strong on Music: The New York Music Scene in the Days of George Templeton Strong*, 1:146–47. Scholars have discussed the merits of operas sung in English translation, but they have not considered lieder. See, e.g., Katherine K. Preston, *Opera for the People: English-Language Opera and Women Managers in Late 19th Century America*, 193–94.

23. Horn served a term as the conductor of the Handel and Haydn Society in Boston. His career and his editions of "Adelaide" and "Erlkönig" are considered in Robert Stevenson, "Schubert in America: First Publications and Performances," 5–10.

24. "Concerts," *Musical Magazine* 2, no. 7 (March 28, 1840): 110–11. "Adelaide" was treated by contemporary writers as a lied, though its length and contrasting sections exceed the bounds of most lieder. Jennifer Ronyak explores its popularity in Europe and its generic identity in "Beethoven Within Grasp: The Nineteenth-Century Reception of 'Adelaide,'" 249–76.

25. Melissa D. Burrage surveys the development of Boston's musical life and the key role played by Germans in the first chapter of *The Karl Muck Scandal*. Germans continued to influence the scene through the end of the century. When Willy (or Willie) Henry (1865–1911), a son of a German immigrant who had settled in Illinois, moved to

Boston in 1884 to study singing, he adopted the German version of his name, Wilhelm Heinrich, in an attempt to better fit in with the community of German immigrants that he perceived as dominating the music establishment. Edith Lynwood Winn, *Wilhelm Heinrich, Musician and Man*, 70–71.

26. Broyles contrasted the overwhelming influence and significance of opera in New York with the importance of the Handel and Haydn Society and the subsequent emergence of instrumental music concerts in Boston. *Music of the Highest Class*, 301–5.

27. DiMaggio, "Cultural Entrepreneurship in Nineteenth-Century Boston," 36, 42.

28. Weber, *Great Transformation*, 128.

29. For information about the capacity of Boston halls, see Bill F. Faucett, *Music in Boston: Composers, Events, and Ideas, 1852–1918*, 13, and Paul Paige, "Musical Organizations in Boston: 1830–1850," 27–28.

30. Weber, *Great Transformation*, 124, 128.

31. Rohan H. Stewart-MacDonald, "The Recital in England: Sir William Sterndale Bennett's 'Classical Chamber Concerts,' 1843–1856," 117–19.

32. Katherine K. Preston, "Opera Is Elite/Opera Is Nationalist: Cosmopolitan Views of Opera Reception in the United States, 1870–90," 536.

33. W., "The Mendelssohn Quintette Club," *Boston Evening Transcript*, November 12, 1851, 1. Although some of the performers in the Quintette were German immigrants or children of German immigrants, others were born in America, and John Ryan was from Ireland. Richard M. Dowell provides brief biographies of the members in chapter 5 of "The Mendelssohn Quintette Club of Boston."

34. For an overview of Wolfsohn's accomplishments promoting instrumental music, see *Brainard's Biographies of American Musicians*, ed. E. Douglas Bomberger, 292–97.

35. This review begins by briefly tracing the development of chamber music concerts. "William Mason's and Carl Bergmann's Classical Matinees," *New York Musical Review and Gazette* 6, no. 25 (December 1, 1855): 400.

36. Concerts, Theodore Thomas Programs, box 226, Newberry Library, Chicago.

37. "Carl Wolfsohn," *North American and United States Gazette*, May 31, 1862, 2. Johannsen sang in operas in Frankfurt, New York, and Philadelphia before joining the faculty of the Boston Conservatory in 1870.

38. A New York critic, for instance, pleaded for more lieder to be performed during concerts and opined that during a performance of Schubert's "Der Wanderer" the singer, Philip Meyer, overused tremolo and portamento and took inappropriate tempi. "Eisfeld's Soiree," *Message Bird* no. 41 (April 1, 1851): 19.

39. [H. Perabeau], "Franz Schubert," 21.

40. Theo. Hagen, "Franz Schubert," 122–23.

41. John S. Dwight, *Select Minor Poems, Translated from the German of Goethe and Schiller*, xi.

42. David Urrows recounts Dresel's life and surveys his compositions in "Apollo in Athens: Otto Dresel and Boston, 1850–90," 345–88.

43. "Concerts of the Past Week," *Dwight's Journal of Music* 2, no. 15 (January 15, 1853): 118.

44. Newman, "Gender and the Germanians," 295–96, 307. Women had a clear pres-

ence in the audiences of early chamber concerts in England. Christina Bashford, "The Late Beethoven Quartets and the London Press, 1836–ca. 1850," 91.

45. "The Concerts," *Dwight's Journal of Music* 2, no. 13 (January 1, 1853): 102.

46. Levine, *Highbrow/Lowbrow*, 120–22, 134–35, 191.

47. Gramit, "Schubert's Wanderers and the Autonomous Lied," 156.

48. This survey did not consider repeat performances of individual works. "Music in Boston—Review of the Season, 1866–7," *Dwight's Journal of Music* 27, no. 6 (June 8, 1867): 47.

49. "Concerts," *Dwight's Journal of Music* 8, no. 24 (March 15, 1856): 190.

50. "Concerts of the Week," *Dwight's Journal of Music* 2, no. 17 (January 29, 1853): 134. Urrows, like Arthur Foote, concludes that Dresel influenced Dwight's understanding of music ("Apollo in Athens," 345). During one of his tours to Europe, Dwight met Franz, and subsequently he opined that Boston witnessed more performances of this composer's songs than did Europe; see "Chamber Concerts," *Dwight's Journal of Music* 20, no. 10 (December 7, 1861): 286–87.

51. Shadle discusses Dwight's limitations and the ways they hindered an appreciation of early American symphonies in *Orchestrating the Nation*, 122–30, 270–71.

52. Robert Schumann, "The Songs of Robert Franz," 1; Franz Liszt, "Robert Franz," 1–3, 10–11; A. W. Ambros, "Robert Franz," 193–94, 201–2, 209–10; August Saran, "Robert Franz and the German Volkslied and Choral," 86–87, 89–90, 97–98, 105–6, 113; "The Franz Fund Concert," *Dwight's Journal of Music* 33, no. 5 (June 31, 1873): 39. Other articles discussed Franz's editions of Baroque music; see, e.g., W. F. A[pthorp], "Is Robert Franz a Failure?," 173, 183, 190–91.

53. *Songs by Robert Franz*, 1st ser. (Boston: Ditson, 1865); "Concerts," *Dwight's Journal of Music* 25, no. 17 (November 11, 1865): 134. Dwight's translations of the texts of seven of Franz's songs were also printed in *Dwight's Journal of Music* 25, no. 21 (January 6, 1866): 161.

54. Stafford, "Binders' Volumes," 174–76.

55. *Gems of German Song: A Collection of the Most Beautiful Vocal Compositions* (Boston: Ditson, 1866).

56. *Otto Dresel: Keyboard Music*, ed. David Francis Urrows, reprints all twelve arrangements and discusses Dresel's works.

57. *Flower of Germany*, 2nd ser. (New York: Gordon, 1872).

58. The Franz scores included in the binders that Petra Meyer-Frazier studied were published by Tolman. Petra Meyer-Frazier, "American Women's Roles in Domestic Music Making," 321, 367, 467, 505, 548.

59. W. F. Rosier sang his own translation of Schubert's "Das Zügenglöcklein" ("The Funeral Bell") (D. 871) in a concert in Richmond (Virginia) in 1849. He also provided translations of the texts of a few songs in the *Gems of German Song* series, including that of Schubert's "Der Wanderer." Stevenson, "Schubert in America," 12.

60. Underwood, "In Memoriam: August Kreissmann," 123, provides an overview of Kreissmann's career. Kreissmann also composed, but this was not the strongest aspect of his career, and he does not appear to have performed his songs in public with any

sort of regularity. Yet his Schubertian "Du Geist der Wolke" ("Thou Spirit of the Cloud") was published in an English translation in Ditson's *Gems of German Song* series.

61. "Musikfeste, Aufführungen," *Neue Zeitschrift für Musik* 62, no. 36 (August 31, 1866): 307.

62. *Dwight's* includes a few glowing reports of the private performances and lively conviviality of this group. See, e.g., "The Orpheus Society," *Dwight's Journal of Music* 20, no. 6 (November 9, 1861): 255. Throughout her groundbreaking dissertation, Suzanne Snyder documents the revered place this group held in Boston and notes its participation in national festivals of *Männerchöre*. Suzanne Snyder, "The *Männerchor* Tradition in the United States."

63. This remark was part of a review of a concert by Camilla Urso during which Kreissmann performed. "Camilla Urso," *Dwight's Journal of Music* 22, no. 23 (March 7, 1863): 391.

64. "Musical," *Boston Traveler*, February 13, 1867, 2.

65. *New York Tribune*, February 25, 1852, 6. According to Nancy B. Reich, Schumann's "songs were rarely performed in New York from the 1850s through the 1870s, chiefly because of the huge popularity of opera." This also could be said, however, of performances of lieder in New York in general. Reich provides a list of Schumann's compositions performed in New York. "Robert Schumann's Music in New York City, 1848–1898," 16, 22–23.

66. "Songs by Heine," *Dwight's Journal of Music* 25, no. 20 (December 23, 1865): 153. *Songs by Robert Schumann* (Boston: Ditson, 1865) comprised fourteen songs, nine of which came from *Dichterliebe*.

67. "Concerts," *Dwight's Journal of Music* 20, no. 8 (November 23, 1861): 270.

68. Louis C. Elson, *The History of German Song*, 183.

69. "Concerts," *Dwight's Journal of Music* 16, no. 9 (November 26, 1859): 279. The family of August Fries, a member of the Mendelssohn Quintette Club, entertained each other with a performance of the Beethoven cycle. They reordered the songs and dispersed instrumental works between them. "A Double Feast of Beethoven," *Dwight's Journal of Music* 5, no. 1 (April 8, 1854): 7.

70. "Concerts," *Dwight's Journal of Music* 20, no. 8 (November 23, 1861): 270.

71. Program held by the American Antiquarian Society (no. 21651), available through Readex's *American Broadsides and Ephemera* (1749–1900).

72. "Ernst Perabo's First Matinée," *Dwight's Journal of Music* 29, no. 17 (November 6, 1869): 135; "Dramatic and Musical," *Boston Journal*, November 27, 1869, 1.

73. Loewe, "The Landlady's Little Daughter," translated and adapted by J. S. Dwight (Cleveland: Brainards, [1861]). Perabo published a piano transcription of Loewe's "The Secluded," and in 1870, he played transcriptions of two other ballads by this composer, "Der Totentanz" (op. 44, no. 3) and "Abschied" (op. 3, no. 1). "Ernst Perabo's Second Matinée," *Dwight's Journal of Music* 29, no. 23 (January 29, 1870): 183. Following Loewe's death, *Dwight's* carried a surprising number of articles about the composer, some of which derived from European publications; see, e.g., "Carl Loewe's Story of His Early Life," trans. Carl Loewe, *Selbst-biographie*, ed. C. H. Bitter (Berlin: 1870), *Dwight's Jour-*

Notes to Chapter 1   225

nal of Music 31 (1871): 73, 81–82, 89–90, 97–98, 105–6, 113–14; and "Two Biographies of Musicians," from Ed. Hanslick's review in the *Wiener Neue Freie Presse, Dwight's Journal of Music* 32, no. 12 (September 7, 1872): 297–98.

74. *New York Post*, April 22, 1863, 2, quoted at Music in Gotham, https://www.music ingotham.org/event/16653. The program of this concert was also printed in the *Neue Zeitschrift für Musik* 58, no. 25 (June 19, 1863): 219.

75. Levine views Thomas's programs, like Dwight's activities, as contributing to the separation of highbrow and lowbrow repertoire in US concert life. He mostly references Thomas's orchestral programs, however, and does not mention Thomas's programming of lieder. Levine, *Highbrow/Lowbrow*, 112–19.

76. "Amusements," *New York Times*, March 27, 1865, 4. Music in Gotham provides this and other reviews, but it does not correctly identify the songs: https://www.musicin gotham.org/event/59435. Kreissmann was scheduled to present lieder by Schumann and Franz during Thomas's Symphony Soiree on April 8, 1865, but he cancelled due to illness.

77. "New York, April 27," *Dwight's Journal of Music* 24, no. 3 (May 2, 1863): 23; italics in the original.

78. S., "Philadelphia, May 29," *Dwight's Journal of Music* 24, no. 6 (June 11, 1864): 256. The review does not indicate who accompanied Kreissmann, though it was likely Wolfsohn.

79. C. H. B., "Chicago" (April 26, 1879), 72.

80. Louis C. Elson, *European Reminiscences: Musical and Otherwise*, 266–70.

81. W. S. B. Mathews, *A Hundred Years of Music in America*, 606.

82. William Apthorp, *Musicians and Music-Lovers and Other Essays*, 5th ed., 219–20; William Apthorp, ed., *Fifty Songs of Robert Franz*.

83. Maurice Aronson, "Robert Franz in His Relation to Music and Its Masters," 455–62.

84. "Osgood, George Laurie," *The National Cyclopaedia of American Biography* (New York: James T. White & Co., 1892; rpt. 1897), 7:436; Louis C. Elson, *The History of American Music*, 251–52. These sources form the basis for John C. Schmidt, "Osgood, George Laurie," *Grove Dictionary of American Music*.

85. "Amusements," *Cleveland Leader*, August 14, 1872, 4.

86. "Theodore Thomas's Concerts," *Dwight's Journal of Music* 32, no. 18 (December 14, 1872): 351.

87. "The Concert To-night," *Democrat and Chronicle* (Buffalo), February 10, 1873, 4. "Local and Other Items," *Bangor (ME) Daily Whig & Courier*, December 14, 1872, 3.

88. This program is held by the Eastman School of Music's Sibley Music Library, Local History Ephemera.

89. [Attributed to George Upton], "Our Musical Season," *Chicago Tribune*, October 13, 1872, 4. Der Freyschütz (a.k.a W. S. B. Mathews), "Chicago" (1872), 333. Mathews's report positions the Thomas Orchestra's concerts as a high point in the city's recovery after the Great Fire of 1871.

90. "Musical," *The Ladies' Repository: A Monthly Periodical Devoted to Literature, Art and Religion* 33 (February 1873): 149. "Amusements," *Cincinnati Daily Gazette*, October 22, 1872, 4, and October 24, 1872, 4.

91. Thomas made orchestral arrangements for at least eight lieder by Beethoven, Schubert, Schumann, and Wagner, and he also conducted arrangements of lieder made by other composers, including Liszt. Theodore Thomas, *Selected Orchestral Arrangements*, ed. Paul Luongo; Paul Luongo, "An Unlikely Cornerstone: The Role of Orchestral Transcription in the Success of the Thomas Orchestra."

92. See, e.g., "Chamber Concerts," *Dwight's Journal of Music* 33, no. 26 (April 4, 1874): 207.

93. *Atlantic Monthly*, October 1877, 476–80.

94. Elson, *History of American Music*, 251.

95. "The Symphony Concerts" and "Chamber Concerts," *Dwight's Journal of Music* 33, no. 26 (April 4, 1874): 206–7.

96. Clara Kathleen Rogers (Clara Doria), *Memories of a Musical Career*, 403, 417.

97. Gounod's songs had started to appear in English-language US scores as early as the 1850s, and during the 1870s they were occasionally programmed on concerts and recitals given by students and faculty at institutions such as the Peabody Conservatory.

98. In a March 12, 1875, concert at Bösendorfer-Saal, for instance, Walter sang eleven songs by Schubert, Schumann, Brahms, Gounod, and Rubinstein, while Door contributed Schubert's D major Piano Sonata (D. 850) and around twelve character pieces by Theodor Kirchner. O. B., "Theater und Kunst," *Fremden-Blatt* 29, no. 76 (March 17, 1875): 5.

99. "Concerts," *Dwight's Journal of Music* 34, no. 1 (April 18, 1874): 214. See also "Concerts," *Dwight's Journal of Music* 33, no. 25 (March 21, 1874): 199; "Chamber Concerts," *Dwight's Journal of Music* 33, no. 26 (April 4, 1874): 207.

100. "Mr. Osgood's Second Concert," *Boston Daily Advertiser*, March 19 (morning), 1874, 2.

101. *Twenty Songs by Mendelssohn*, Musical Cabinet (New York: Boosey, 1876). Perhaps because of the cost or the small market share for lieder, covers of sheet music of lieder usually did not feature the type of realistic artwork of women making music in their homes that was featured on covers of scores of more popular mid-century songs. Petra Meyer-Frazier describes the covers of popular songs in *Bound Music*, 171–200.

102. "Miscellaneous," *Milwaukee Daily Sentinel*, May 15, 1876, 4; "Music and the Drama: Mr. Osgood's Concert," *Boston Daily Advertiser*, May 8, 1879, 1.

103. Laura Tunbridge explores the question of narrative voice and the performer in chapter 4 of *The Song Cycle*.

104. The program of the 1879 concert is given in my article "'For Any Ordinary Performer It Would Be Absurd, Ridiculous or Offensive': Performing Lieder Cycles on the American Stage," 114–15.

Chapter 2. Song Recitals and Song Recital Series

1. The term *normal school* refers to teachers' colleges, which were established in the United States during the 1830s. By the 1870s, normal schools and courses for music teachers (as well as for teachers of other subjects) were often held during the summer

months. Their activities were frequently reported in newspapers, where the schools were often referred to as "normals." George N. Heller and Jere T. Humphreys, "Music Teacher Education in America (1753–1840)," 49–58.

2. For Berlioz's impression of Pischek, see *Memoirs of Hector Berlioz*, 374–75.

3. "Pischeks Abschieds-Concert," *Wiener Zeitung*, April 21, 1846, 899. "Pischeks Abschieds-Concert von Wien," *Allgemeine Theaterzeitung* April 4, 1846, 322. Neither publication lists all the lieder that Pischek sang.

4. "Wien," *Fremden-Blatt* 7, no. 10 (January 12, 1853): 3.

5. Loges, "Julius Stockhausen's Early Performances of Franz Schubert's *Die schöne Müllerin*," 206–24.

6. "Dur und Moll," *Signale für die musikalische Welt* 24, no. 22 (April 1866): 400; 26, no. 3 (January 1868): 41; "Kurze Nachrichten," *Leipziger Allgemeine Musikalische Zeitung* 3, no. 1 (January 1868): 15; "Musikfeste, Aufführungen," *Neue Zeitschrift für Musik* 63, no. 49 (November 29, 1867): 435.

7. "Music and Musicians in Austria," *Harper's New Monthly Magazine* 64 (May 1882): 828.

8. Kravitt, "The Lied in 19th Century Concert Life," 211–12.

9. Rosamund Cole, "Lilli Lehmann's Dedicated Lieder Recitals," 226.

10. For an example of a review of one of these entertainments, see "Local and Provincial Intelligence," *Guardian* (London), March 27, 1844, 4.

11. See, e.g., "The Misses Malone Raymond," *New Orleans Crescent*, January 28, 1850, 2.

12. "Amusements," *World* (New York), December 6, 1864, 4. Notices and reviews of her concerts are given at Music in Gotham, https://www.musicingotham.org/event/76829 and https://www.musicingotham.org/event/65684. They include Lancelot, "Musical Correspondence," *Dwight's Journal of Music* 25, no. 4 (May 13, 1865): 29; *New Yorker Staats-Zeitung*, January 23, 1866, 4; and "Mme. Fanny Raymond Ritter's Concert," *New York Tribune*, January 26, 1866, 8.

13. William Steinway's performances of Schumann's lieder in his home and during social events suggest that during the 1860s there was a somewhat broader range of lieder by this composer being performed in some homes than in New York concert halls. See the Smithsonian Institution's digitization of Steinway's diary, https://americanhistory .si.edu/steinwaydiary/diary/.

14. The Ritters knew Kreissmann and on at least one occasion collaborated with him. In 1868 Kreissmann sang lieder during a concert that Ritter organized to showcase his own compositions. E. S. J., "Mr. F. L. Ritter's Concert in New York," *Dwight's Journal of Music* 28, no. 20 (December 19, 1868): 364–65.

15. Advertisement, *Watson's Art Journal* 10, no. 25 (April 17, 1869): 298.

16. "Mr. Ritter's Historical Recitals," *Watson's Art Journal* 10, no. 22 (March 27, 1869): 263; "Historical Recitals," *Watson's Art Journal* 10, no. 26 (April 24, 1869): 310. Frédéric Louis Ritter, *Music in America*, 358–60. Ritter possessed an extensive library of journals and books on music as well as scores. Tufts University Libraries currently holds much of his collection. See https://www.library.tufts.edu/tisch/berger/Ritter/index.htm. The Ritters also collaborated on other projects. For instance, Fanny provided the English

translations for the German texts that Frédéric set in his ten-lieder cycle *Hafiz*. "New Music," *Dwight's Journal of Music* 26, no. 12 (September 1, 1866): 303.

17. Ritter praised Schubert's lieder but preferred Schumann's instrumental pieces to the composer's lieder. *History of Music in the Form of Lectures*, 2:221, 231. Ritter accompanied his wife when she gave a pair of similar historical recitals in 1868 at Vassar College. "Vassar College," *Dwight's Journal of Music* 28, no. 8 (July 4, 1868): 271. The program for this series can be viewed at Hudson River Valley Heritage, https://hrvh .org/cdm/compoundobject/collection/vassar/id/2467/show/2464/rec/108.

18. "Historical Recitals," *Watson's Art Journal* 10, no. 26 (April 24, 1869): 311. As with the program for the 1868 recitals, this one does not include translations of the songs' texts. The four-page program may be viewed at Hudson River Valley Heritage, https:// hrvh.org/cdm/compoundobject/collection/vassar/id/2282/show/2280/rec/8.

19. "William Mason's Concerts," *Dwight's Journal of Music* 5, no. 25 (September 23, 1854): 198; "M. Fétis's Musical Testament," *Dwight's Journal of Music* 3, no. 26 (October 1, 1853): 206–7; "Bremen," *Dwight's Journal of Music* 23, no. 11 (August 22, 1863): 88.

20. "Classical Chamber Concerts," *Dwight's Journal of Music* 3, no. 3 (April 23, 1853): 23; "Musical Chit-Chat," *Dwight's Journal of Music* 10, no. 25 (March 21, 1857): 199; and 11, no. 2 (April 11, 1857): 14, 15.

21. The first program, with annotations, was reprinted in "Historical Recitals of Vocal and Piano-Forte Music," *Dwight's Journal of Music* 29, no. 1 (March 27, 1869): 7–8. The second and third programs were printed without annotations in "New York," *Dwight's Journal of Music* 29, no. 3 (April 24, 1869): 23–24.

22. Weber, *Great Transformation*, 35.

23. This conception of the influence of folk music also permeates the first volume of Ritter's *History of Music in the Form of Lectures*.

24. As cited in Günther, *Kunstlied als Liedkunst*, 349.

25. "New Haven," *Dwight's Journal of Music* 29, no. 23 (January 29, 1870): 183–84.

26. The report in *Dwight's* noted that Allen's series of talks were attended by a larger audience (perhaps of six hundred to eight hundred people) than would have been possible in Boston. Allen, a student of Dresel, presented numerous illustrated lectures and recitals. An organist, pianist, and conductor, he founded the Worcester Music Festival and taught at numerous institutions, including the New England Conservatory. "Worcester, Mass.," *Dwight's Journal of Music* 36, no. 15 (October 28, 1876): 327.

27. E. G., "Historical Concerts," *Old & New* 9, no. 3 (March 1, 1875): 371–77; "Historical Concerts," *Dwight's Journal of Music* 34, no. 20 (January 9, 1875): 367.

28. Fanny Raymond Ritter, *Woman as a Musician: An Art-Historical Study*; Petra Meyer-Frazier, "'Woman as a Musician': American Feminism in 1876," 2–3.

29. "The German Lied: Schubert, Mendelssohn, Schumann, Franz, etc.," *Dwight's Journal of Music* 30, no. 8 (July 2, 1870): 267.

30. George T. Ferris, "Four Great Song-Composers: Schubert, Schumann, Franz, Liszt," 193–96. Excluding the section on Liszt, this article was incorporated into Ferris's book *Great German Composers*.

31. On Brinkerhoff's performance of "Liebestreu," see "Theodore Eisfeld Classical Quartette Soiree," *Frank Leslie's Illustrated Newspaper*, February 13, 1858, 10.

32. For an advertisement describing these recitals that was printed in various newspapers, see "Clara Brinkerhoff," *Titusville* (PA) *Herald*, March 12, 1873, 2.

33. From the 1840s, Gustavus Geary used the term "vocal recital" for programs of popular songs such as Moore's *Irish Melodies*. He gave these recitals in Ireland, England, and America. Beginning in 1862, Mrs. Merest (d. 1886) presented "vocal recitals" in various English provinces. They included well-known arias by Handel, Haydn, Gluck, Méhul, Mozart, and Mendelssohn as well as her own ballads and a few piano solos. "Mrs. Merest's Vocal Recital," *Western Gazette* (Yeovill, England), July 30, 1864, 7.

34. In the United States, many "vocal recitals" included solo songs, a few piano solos, and recitations, but no lieder.

35. W. S. B. Mathews traces the history of normal schools from Lowell Mason's music teachers' conventions and the Normal Music Institutes he established with George F. Root (1829–1895) in the 1850s in "The 'Normal' Music School," 302–3. In "Prof. W. S. B. Mathews (1837–1912): Self-Made Musician of the Gilded Age," 50–58, James Wesley Clarke argues that Mathews influenced the incorporation of piano instruction into normals, but he does not mention song recitals or Mathews's participation in them.

36. For a brief biography in which Hull is described as a "magnificent" oratorio and church singer with a rich, expressive voice, see Mathews, *A Hundred Years of Music in America*, 708–9. Mathews frequently praised singers he knew or collaborated with.

37. "The First Song Recital," *Watertown (NY) Daily Times*, July 24, 1875, 3; Der Freyschütz (a.k.a. Mathews), "Binghamton, NY," 96.

38. [no title], *Watertown (NY) Daily Times*, July 27, 1875, 3; "Mrs. Hull's Song Recital," *Watertown Daily Times*, July 31, 1875, 3.

39. "The Song Recital," *Watertown (NY) Daily Times*, August 5, 1876, 3; "City and Vicinity," *Watertown Daily Times*, August 5, 1876, 3; *Watertown Daily Times*, April 13, 1877, 3.

40. Judith Tick uses census data to document the significant number of women music teachers in "Passed Away Is the Piano Girl: Changes in American Musical Life, 1870–1900," 326–27.

41. "Music: At Home," *Chicago Daily Tribune*, August 27, 1876, 9. Mathews played two piano solos during Jewett's recital and likely accompanied her. Program housed in Box 32 of the Frederick Grant Gleason Collection at the Newberry Library, Chicago.

42. Advertisement, *Musical Record* 61 (April 17, 1880): 464. Chamberlain previously gave at least one recital during Mathews's 1879 normal.

43. The printed program for Mathews's lecture-recital "Chopin, Schumann, Wagner" is held in the Frederick Grant Gleason Collection, Box 52, at the Newberry Library, Chicago, along with a handwritten list of the pieces to be performed during his lecture on Schubert and Mendelssohn. After Mathews left the Hershey School, Frederick Grant Gleason (1848–1903) presented illustrated lectures, some of which concerned lieder. Charles Brittan, another of Mathews's colleagues, also presented illustrated lectures on the history of song at other local schools.

44. It is highly likely that the normal school events were not the first performances to be called song recitals. None of the press notices concerning the recitals during the Watertown or Illinois normals states that song recitals were new, but an earlier usage of

this designation has not emerged. It is possible that other schools or studios were also using the title "song recital" or presenting similar recitals under another name. That these have not been revealed through digitized searches is likely because they were either not advertised in newspapers or the papers have not been digitized. However, students more often presented concerts or recitals mixing a significant number of instrumental works with solo songs and ensembles rather than ones emphasizing solo songs. It should also be recalled that, as the introduction noted, digitized searches are far from perfect, and they can miss relevant records. Searches for "song recital" were carried out multiple times, across multiple years, on at least three different newspaper archives and on Hathitrust. Although they located numerous piano recitals and performances of songs and recitations, they did not register song recitals before the mid-1870s. In contrast, these resources reveal a dramatic increase in reports of song recitals after 1880.

45. Aside from songs, this recital included a small number of solo works for violin and piano. "Soiree Musicale," *Wheeling (WV) Register*, February 8, 1881, 5.

46. From 1890 Norton taught at the Detroit Conservatory of Music. A later article, really a vanity piece announcing Norton's move to Homestead, Pennsylvania, claimed that "she was the first singer to introduce what is known as the recital-type of program, first employing that style in her first year of professional singing in San Francisco." *Pittsburgh Press*, June 7, 1925, 68.

47. G. A. D., "Musical," *Oakland (CA) Tribune*, October 4, 1884, 1; *Argonaut* (San Francisco), October 1884, quoted in *History of San Francisco Music*, vol. 7, *An Anthology of Music Criticism*, comp. Workers of the Writers' Program of the Works Progress Administration in Northern California, Sponsored by the City and County of San Francisco (1942, rpt. New York: AMS Press, 1972), 187–88. Although Pasmore gave recitals, he was better known as a composer and teacher.

48. "Musical," *New York Herald*, January 5, 1867, 8; "New York," *Dwight's Journal of Music* 36, no. 21 (January 5, 1867): 375; "Carl Wolfsohn's Second Matinee," *Evening Telegraph* (Philadelphia), December 11, 1866, 5. Pollack performed lieder in a few New York concerts as well as solos in German opera. He returned to Europe in 1869, after giving a farewell concert where he performed a few lieder. "Ignaz Pollack's Abschieds-Concert," *New-Yorker Handels-Zeitung*, March 25, 1869, 12.

49. [George Upton], "Music," *Chicago Tribune*, June 7, 1874, 6. This page also provides an overview of the concerts in Chicago during the 1873–1874 season, including several in which a few lieder were performed.

50. Florence French, comp., *Music and Musicians in Chicago*, 23.

51. [Attributed to George Upton], "Music," *Chicago Tribune*, June 6, 1875, 5. Most of the brief notices describing Stacey's performance imply that she sang all of *Dichterliebe*. Mathews, however, reported that she sang fifteen of the sixteen songs. Der Freyschütz, "Chicago," *Dwight's Journal of Music* (June 12, 1875): 40.

52. Der Freyschütz, "Chicago" (April 3, 1875): 415–16. Mathews had already penned an article that likewise advocated for Schumann's piano music. This article is germane to the present study because it indicates that he was familiar with the activities of Fanny Raymond Ritter. W. S. B. Matthews, "Robert Schumann, The Poetical Musician," 36.

53. French, *Music and Musicians in Chicago*, 23. The *Chicago Tribune* advertised and

Notes to Chapter 2   231

reviewed each of the Chopin recitals in turn, beginning on March 20, 1876 (p. 8) and ending on May 29 (p. 3). These articles provided the complete programs of each recital. The music critic at that time, who probably authored the reviews, was George Upton.

54. Frances Bennett, *History of Music and Art in Illinois*, 221–22.

55. "Musical: Series of Song Recitals," *Inter Ocean* (Chicago), February 22, 1879, 6; "George Werrenrath," *Musical Standard* 17 (December 27, 1879): 405–6. For an interview that chronicles Werrenrath's life see "George Werrenrath: His Career as a Singer and the Celebrities He Has Met," *Brooklyn Daily Eagle*, April 12, 1891, 19.

56. Before 1872, Sterling also sang in the choir of Brooklyn's Plymouth Church and gave numerous concerts at this church, most of which were collaborative events. She became one of England's most popular ballad singers. Derek B. Scott, *The Singing Bourgeois: Songs of the Victorian Drawing Room and Parlour*, 129–31.

57. Werrenrath and the Camp family are discussed in an illustrated biography of George's son Reinald Werrenrath (1883–1953), who achieved fame as an operatic and concert baritone. "An American Institution," *Musical Leader* 43 (1922): 582–83.

58. "The Werrenrath Concert," *Brooklyn Daily Eagle*, May 29, 1877, 3.

59. F. O. Jones, *Handbook of Music and Musicians*, 173.

60. "Song Recitals," *Chicago Tribune*, February 9, 1879, 10.

61. "Der und Moll," *Signale* 10, no. 6 (1880): 150. The complete program also included a few short piano solos; advertisement, *Bonner Zeitung*, February 28, 1880, 230. The article in the *Signale* referred to Joachim's event as a "Lieder-Concert," but the advertisement simply titled it "Concert."

62. For a discussion of the popularity of Mendelssohn's music in America see Joseph A. Mussulman, *Music in the Cultured Generation: A Social History of Music in America, 1870–1900*, 59–62.

63. "Feuilleton: Musik," *Wiener Abendpost*, February 1, 1882, n.p.

64. "New Musical Publications," *Boston Globe*, March 8, 1873, 1. An English version of "Ave Maria" was published in Ditson's 1881 *Gems of Foreign Song*. "Serenade" was sung in the United States as early as 1865, and was also known as "Sing, Smile, Sleep."

65. Hamm, *Yesterdays*, 485–86.

66. "Musical Notes," *Chicago Tribune*, April 7, 1877, 7.

67. A student who attended this event recalled that Ritter typically presented a lecture for each concert in which he gave the biographies of the composers, before talking about each piece that was to be played. "Home Matters," *Vassar Miscellany* 9, no. 4 (January 1880): 198–200.

68. "Gossip at Home," *Inter Ocean* (Chicago), March 1, 1879, 6.

69. Werrenrath's series is merely cited in C. H. B., "Chicago" (March 29, 1879): 47–48. Brittan's survey of the Chicago scene, which appears in "Progress of Music in the West," 10–11, appeared before the song recitals.

70. "Music," *Chicago Tribune*, February 23, 1879, 11.

71. A. G. L., "Newport R.I.," *Dwight's Journal of Music* 40 (September 25, 1880): 159. Although he continued to sing lieder, Jordan did not actively pursue a career as a recitalist. Instead, he became an admired choral director, composer, and pedagogue.

72. *Brainard's Musical World* 121 (December 1887), reprinted in *Brainard's Biographies of American Musicians*, ed. E. Douglas Bomberger, 146–47.

73. Even though Mathews worked with Hiltz, he also reviewed some of her performances, and on one occasion he described her as possessing "a rich soprano voice of great power and compass." Mathews, *A Hundred Years of Music in America*, 219–20 (see 229 for a portrait of Hiltz); "Musical Notes," *Chicago Daily Tribune*, August 4, 1879, 6; "Western Schools and Colleges," *Inter Ocean* (Chicago), August 2, 1879, 2.

74. The program supplies opus numbers for the Franz songs but not for the others.

75. J. C. F., "Musical Correspondence," *Dwight's Journal of Music* 39 (September 13, 1879): 151.

76. Numerous programs for concerts and recitals at the New England Conservatory from this period are available at archive.org. The Hershey School continued to host summer normal schools until at least 1883, and each year the faculty or pupils gave song recitals, some of which were devoted to lieder. For instance, in 1880 Gill presented a recital comprised of selections by Purcell, Arcadelt, Bach, Rubinstein, Schubert, and Schumann as well as *An die ferne Geliebte*.

77. In the programs for these recitals Hiltz appeared under her married name of Mrs. Grace Hiltz Gleason. Hiltz and Gleason were married on September 2, 1879. When they divorced in July 1883 Grace reverted to the name Hiltz. Both before and after their marriage Gleason reviewed Hiltz's performances positively.

78. On Osgood's performances see "Historical Concerts," *Dwight's Journal of Music* 35, no. 4 (May 29, 1875): 31; "Concerts," *Dwight's Journal of Music* 39 (May 24, 1879): 85. Osgood studied in Berlin at the same time as Hiltz's teacher Sara Hershey, though they worked with different voice instructors. It is not known whether the two met there or whether Hershey or Hiltz had direct contact with Osgood before assembling Hiltz's programs. The *Chicago Tribune*, in a very brief review of Hiltz's second recital, noted that many of the songs on this program "had not been heard here before." "Hershey School Concerts," *Chicago Tribune*, August 15, 1880, 10. The programs for Hiltz's recitals are housed in the Frederick Grant Gleason Collection, Box 52, Newberry Library, Chicago.

79. Hiltz also sang lieder and other solo songs and duets during some of Eddy's organ recitals. During the period 1877–1879 Eddy presented one hundred recitals, each with its own distinct program. Although arias by Handel were often included, most recitals presented a few lieder. These lieder were drawn from the work of seventeen composers. Most were by Schubert, Schumann, Franz, and Beethoven, but there were also ones by Jensen, Raff, Rubinstein, Lassen, Liszt, and the ever-popular Abt. Others included songs by Gounod, Arthur Sullivan (1842–1900), and Dudley Buck (1839–1909), composers whose songs were frequently programmed throughout the United States. The printed programs for these concerts included opus numbers for many of the lieder and the birth and death dates for almost all of the composers, a feature that *Brainard's* noted. Eddy's recitals included some of the same singers and a few of the same songs as Wolfsohn's recitals. *Brainard's Biographies of American Musicians*, 89. Hathitrust.org preserves the collection of programs for these recitals that had been owned by Eddy's foster daughter, https://babel.hathitrust.org/cgi/pt?id=nyp.33433082187794&view=1up&seq=7.

Notes to Chapter 2   233

80. Rudersdorff was a widely admired singer and teacher whose successful students included Emma Thursby (1845–1931). She and Thursby sang lieder during mixed-genre concerts, but neither of them was among the most influential advocates of the genre.

81. Mathews, *A Hundred Years of Music in America*, 220.

82. "The Letters," *Inter Ocean* (Chicago), April 22, 1882, 9.

83. An undated promotional brochure for Hiltz includes seven recital programs, most of which featured lieder. Most began with a few seventeenth-century numbers, and all indicated places where an instrumental number might be inserted. The dates of some of the favorable reviews of performances suggest that this pamphlet was created after Hiltz's return from Europe. She had sung many of the lieder, however, in her earlier US recitals. The number of songs in each recital ranged from eleven to twenty-six, with most having about sixteen. The placement of this brochure in the W. S. B. Mathews scrapbooks at the Newberry Library, Chicago, suggests it was produced sometime around 1884.

84. For an example of a recital at the Haymarket see "Amusements: General Mentions," *Inter Ocean* (Chicago), June 15, 1888, 4. The Indiana club recital was reported in "A Glittering Success," *Huntington (IN) Democrat*, June 16, 1892, 3.

85. *Brainard's Musical World* 121 (December 1887), reprinted in *Brainard's Biographies of American Musicians*, 147.

86. "Miss Grace Hiltz in the Parlors of Hotel Worth," *Fort Worth Gazette*, September 27, 1895, 7.

87. "The Song and Organ Recitals at Tremont Temple," *Boston Herald*, March 30, 1881, 4; "The Song and Organ Recitals," *Boston Journal*, April 4, 1881, 4. "Musical Lectures," *Buffalo (NY) Commercial*, November 13, 1883, 3.

88. Sylvan Pan, "Concert at Wells' College," 190; "Musical Lectures," *Buffalo (NY) Commercial*, November 13, 1883, 3.

89. In 1883 the Plymouth Church's quartet, including Werrenrath, was laid off because of the church's financial situation. Werrenrath then became the director of music at the Classon Avenue Presbyterian Church. "Plymouth Church," *Brooklyn Daily Eagle*, April 2, 1883, [4].

90. A description of the building gives the seating capacity of the auditorium as six hundred. See http://www.brooklynhistory.org/about/aboutbhs.html.

91. "Briefs and Semi-Briefs," *Musical Courier* 2, no. 8 (February 19, 1881): 144.

92. "Musik und Drama," *New Yorker Staats-Zeitung*, February 18, 1881, 8.

93. Tramp, "From Beechertown," *American Art Journal* 34, no. 20 (March 12, 1881): 385; "Werrenrath's Request Song Recital," *American Art Journal* 34, no. 22 (March 26, 1881): 430.

94. "Mr. Werrenrath's Concert," *New York Times*, February 26, 1881, 5. The use of the descriptor "manly" for lieder recitalists is discussed in Chapter 3.

95. Block, "Matinee Mania, or the Regendering of Nineteenth-Century Audiences in New York City," 193–216.

96. "General Mention," *New York Times*, March 18, 1881, 5.

97. "Musical Chat," *Music Trade Review*, November 5, 1881, 85; "Musical Notes," *New York Times*, November 30, 1881, 5. For Stockhausen's performances see the advertisements in the *Times* (London), May 16, 1870, 1. Werrenrath might have learned about

Stockhausen's earlier performances of cycles or even heard Stockhausen sing when both men were living in Hamburg during the 1860s. They probably did not overlap in London, however; Werrenrath's performances in London were a few years after Stockhausen's 1870 appearances.

98. "Mr. Werrenrath's Second Recital," *Brooklyn Union-Argus*, November 18, 1881, n.p.

99. "The Werrenrath Recitals," *American Art Journal* 34, no. 20 (March 12, 1881): 390–91. Jean-Baptiste Faure (1830–1914) was a French baritone and composer. Some of his other songs were performed in the United States around this time, and an English version of "Charité" (1869) was published by Ditson in 1881.

100. "The Werrenrath Recital," *Times Union* (Brooklyn), April 26, 1889, 4.

101. "Werrenrath-Kortheuer Recital," *Brooklyn Daily Eagle*, May 5, 1889, 6, and May 10, 1889, 5. Werrenrath was not the only concert singer to program works by Meyer-Helmund. During an orchestral concert at Steinway Hall in 1886 Lilli Lehmann sang this composer's "Mädchenlied" ("Mother Dear, Oh Be Not Angry"). The Steinway Hall program (housed in the New York Public Library, Music Division, *MBD [Steinway Hall Programme]) indicated that the score of this song, published by Schuberth & Co., was available for purchase in the lobby. This is a reminder that the commodification of music characterized by the coupling of the production of English-language scores and the programming of lieder in Boston concerts of the mid-century continued in other cities.

102. "Robert Thallon Residence," New York Chapter of the American Guild of Organists, http://www.nycago.org/Organs/Bkln/html/ResThallonR.html.

103. "George Werrenrath," *Brooklyn Daily Eagle*, June 5, 1898, 8.

Chapter 3. The Henschels' Polyglot "Vocal Recitals"

1. "Mr. Henschel's Second Vocal Recital," *Sun* (New York), January 5, 1881, 3.

2. For a brief biography and an overview of Henschel's lieder performances in London from 1885 onwards see Bier, "Ideal Orpheus," 27–50. Volume 2 reprints excerpts from many of the reviews of Henschel's performances in England.

3. The programs for Henschel's concerts with Brahms are given in Renate and Kurt Hofmann, *Johannes Brahms als Pianist und Dirigent: Chronologie seines Wirkens als Interpret*, 162–63, 167ff. See also George Henschel, *Personal Recollections of Johannes Brahms*.

4. "Herr Henschel's Morning Concert," *Academy: A Weekly Review of Literature, Science and Art*, n.s., no. 267 (June 16, 1877): 545. It is possible that Henschel presented somewhat similar programs in private homes, but descriptions of such performances have yet to come to light.

5. A report of Henschel's early years in London is given in "George Henschel," *Musical Times* 41, no. 685 (March 1, 1900): 155.

6. D. T., "Concerts Various," *Musical World* 56, no. 25 (June 22, 1878): 404.

7. "Concert of Mm. Henschel and Ignaz Brüll," *Examiner* (London), April 6, 1878, 26.

8. "Concerts," *Athenaeum* 2574 (February 24, 1877), quoted in Bier, "Ideal Orpheus," 1:128.

9. "Notes and Gleanings," *Dwight's Journal of Music* 39 (August 2, 1879): 127.

10. "Henschel, Lillian," *Musical Biographies*, volume 5 of *The American History and Encyclopedia of Music*, ed. William Lines Hubbard (Toledo: Irving Squire, 1908), 370. Hayden reportedly studied with George Henschel, but where and when is not indicated in his obituary: "Other Deaths," *Boston Daily Advertiser*, April 8, 1886, 1.

11. "Miss Lillian Bailey's Concert," *Dwight's Journal of Music* 36, no. 24 (March 3, 1877): 399; "Mme. Schiller's Recitals," *Boston Post*, May 9, 1878, 3; New York Public Library for the Performing Arts, *MBD (Steinway Hall Programme).

12. "Festival Notes," *Worcester (MA) Daily Spy*, May 12, 1880, 4.

13. Steinway Hall program of December 1880, New York Public Library for the Performing Arts, *MBD (Steinway Hall. Programme); "Musical Notes," *Times* (Philadelphia), December 17, 1880, 3.

14. "What Is Going on in Society," *Sun* (New York), December 19, 1880, 5; "Henschel-Bailey," *Boston Daily Advertiser*, March 10, 1881, 1. The Henschels were not the only married couple who performed lieder together. In the 1890s Arthur Nikisch (1855–1922), the conductor of the Boston Symphony Orchestra, occasionally accompanied his wife in performances of lieder, which sometimes led to comparisons with the Henschels. "A Musical Triumph," *Washington Post*, January 16, 1891, 6. Greta Rost Why (1888–1981) and her husband T. Foster Why (1884–1963) were also compared to the Henschels. Greta, a contralto, provided the piano accompaniments for herself and her husband. "Music," *Brooklyn Daily Eagle*, January 11, 1914, 48.

15. Except in paragraphs where both Lillian and George are discussed, this book will preserve the practice of referring to Lillian as Mrs. Henschel. Although the first name of women performers was consistently used for unmarried women, the manner in which married women were identified was somewhat variable. Most, like Mrs. Henschel, were not identified in the press by their first name. A few, however, including Fanny Raymond Ritter, continued to be referred to by their first name. Aside from being customary, the title Mrs. Henschel reflected the public's perception that she played a supporting (though important) role in her husband's career. Moreover, recital programs and media reports that the couple had control over would have used her first name had she requested they do so.

16. During the late 1860s Henschel sang under Damrosch's baton in Breslau, where their families lived. George Henschel, introduction to *Fifty Songs*, xi. It is highly likely that Helene Damrosch, a voice teacher, and her family also sang lieder as a pastime at home, but records of such activities have not survived.

17. "George Henschel," *Brooklyn Daily Eagle*, September 24, 1880, 3. During this first visit to the United States Henschel also sang at a number of other events in private homes.

18. Some American critics concluded that Henschel was better suited to "a parlor or chamber music concert" than to oratorios or large venues such as Steinway Hall. See, e.g., "Mr. Georg Henschel," *New York Times*, December 8, 1880, 5. Similarly, the surprisingly brief review in *Dwight's* of Henschel's first New York recital was more complimentary

than the review of his performance in *Damnation of Faust*: "New York, Dec. 13," *Dwight's Journal of Music* 40 (December 18, 1880): 208.

19. None of the reviews of Henschel's American performances discuss the placement of the piano. At least one review of a performance in England implies, however, that the instrument was placed so that the audience could see Henschel's face. Bier, "Ideal Orpheus," 1:142–45.

20. Apollo, "Apollo's Boston Chat," *American Art Journal* 34, no. 13 (January 22, 1881): 242.

21. Advertisement, *New York Times*, November 21, 1880, 11.

22. "Amusements," *Brooklyn Daily Eagle*, January 2, 1881, 1.

23. "Amusements: Mr. Henschel's Second Vocal Recital," *Sun* (New York), January 5, 1881, 3.

24. "Georg Henschel's Second Song Recital," *Musical Courier* 2, no. 30 (January 15, 1881): 45. See also "Georg Henschel's First Song Recital," *Musical Courier* 1, no. 45 (December 11, 1880): 690.

25. "Mr. Henschel's Vocal Recital," *New York Times*, January 5, 1881, 5.

26. Alison Deadman, "Brahms in Nineteenth-Century America," 65–84. I discuss the US reception of Brahms in "'The Brahms Question': An Anglo-American Fracas over *A German Requiem*," Paper presented at the Conference of the American Musicological Society, Boston, November 2019.

27. George Bozarth provides the bibliographic data for all of Henschel's compositions in appendix G of *Johannes Brahms and George Henschel: An Enduring Friendship*.

28. "Mr. Henschel's Fourth Recital," *New York Tribune*, February 11, 1881, 4.

29. See, e.g., L. C. E., "Review of New Music," *Musical Herald* 2, no. 8 (August 1881): 192. The artwork on the journal's cover reinforces the idea that music was the domain of women. Articles such as "How to Get a Husband" further indicate that women numbered among the readers of this journal. *Musical Herald* no. 264 (January 1884): 8. (Page 5 gives a review of one of the Henschels' New York recitals.) Although the journal was published by Ditson, it also carried notices about scores issued by other publishers.

30. For an exceptional program of Henschel's songs, see Howard Malcolm Ticknor, "Last Henschel Recital," 5.

31. Advertisement, *Morning News*, Wilmington (Delaware), January 1917, 6. The solo version of "Morning Hymn" was issued by Schirmer in 1904. "Butte Musical Club," *Anaconda (MT) Standard*, March 3, 1918, 6.

32. "Georg Henschel," *American Art Journal* 34, no. 23 (April 2, 1881): 441, 446.

33. "General Mention," *New York Times*, March 18, 1881, 5.

34. "The Werrenrath Recitals," *American Art Journal* 34, no. 20 (March 12, 1881): 390–91.

35. Whereas Widor's songs were not frequently performed in US concerts, Viardot-Garcia's 1848 arrangements of Chopin's mazurkas, with texts by Louis Pompey, received an increasing number of performances. Many women amateur and professional singers including Adelina Patti (1843–1919) performed them. It is likely that Mrs. Henschel performed "Aime-moi," an arrangement of Chopin's Mazurka op. 33, no. 2, which she had sung in Boston in 1878, before she studied with Viardot-Garcia. "The Henschel Concert,"

Notes to Chapter 3   237

Buffalo Morning Express and Illustrated Buffalo Express, April 22, 1881, 4; "Salem, Mass.," *Dwight's Journal of Music* 37, no. 25 (March 16, 1878): 200.

36. "The Henschel Recital," *Inter Ocean* (Chicago), April 23, 1881, 12.

37. Bozarth, *Johannes Brahms and George Henschel*, 72–85; Boston Symphony Orchestra Archive online database, https://archives.bso.org. Paul DiMaggio discusses the relation between Dwight, Higginson, and Henschel's symphony programs in "Cultural Entrepreneurship in Nineteenth-Century Boston," 308–10.

38. "The Henschel Recitals," *Boston Daily Advertiser*, January 10, 1882, 4.

39. J. A. Fuller-Maitland, *Brahms*, 62–63.

40. See, e.g., Henschel's quote of a negative review of Brahms's works in his recollections, *Musings and Memories of a Musician*, 286–87.

41. Eduard Hanslick, "Liederabende," *Aus dem Tagebuch eines Musikers: Kritiken und Schilderungen*, 355.

42. The operatic airs that Mrs. Henschel performed in the Boston program shown in figure 3.1 were identified with the assistance of the couple's repertoire list, which was included in a pamphlet comprising a collection of press notices assembled for promotional purposes. She rarely reprised these airs and the works by Liszt and Isouard in the same program. Frederick Grant Gleason Collection of Music Scrapbooks, Box 32, vol. 2, p. 131, Newberry Library, Chicago.

43. "The Henschels in Concert," *Boston Daily Globe*, January 30, 1884, 2.

44. "The Henschel Recital," unidentified publication, April, 1884, Frederick Grant Gleason Collection of Music Scrapbooks, Box 32, vol. 2, p. 425, Newberry Library, Chicago.

45. This recital, which was slightly shorter than other versions of this program, was added to the Henschels' itinerary after a successful concert during the preceding week that also included performances by the Chicago Quartet. "The Henschel Recital," *Inter Ocean* (Chicago), April 29, 1884, 3.

46. The titles of the songs from the two Schubert cycles listed in figure 3.1 were given in English in the *Boston Evening Transcript*, but it was Henschel's custom to sing these works in German. This recital was the third in a series of four.

47. "The Henschel Recitals," *Boston Daily Advertiser*, February 6, 1884, 4.

48. "Mr. and Mrs. Henschel's Recitals," *Boston Evening Transcript*, February 6, 1884, [1].

49. "Amusements," *New York Times*, December 12, 1883, 4.

50. Editorial, *Musical Herald* 5, no. 4 (April 1884): 86.

51. "Mr. and Mrs. George Henschel's Vocal Recital," *Era* (London), June 16, 1883, 14; Ferdinand Praeger and Joseph Bennett, "London (Prince's Hall): A 'Vocal Recital' Given by Herr and Frau Henschel," *The Musical Year 1883: A Record of Noteworthy Musical Events in the United Kingdom* (London: Novello, [1884]), 123–24. One source claims that Raimund von Zur Mühlen (1854–1931), a student of Stockhausen, gave a lieder recital in London in 1882, but documentation of such a recital has not come to light. *Baker's Biographical Dictionary of Musicians*, 5th ed., rev. Nicolas Slonimsky (New York: Schirmer, 1958), 1854.

52. I provide information about performances by Joachim and other members of

Brahms's circle in "Other Instrumentalists," 207–18; Karen Leistra Jones, "Staging Authenticity: Joachim, Brahms, and the Politics of *Werktreue* Performance," 397–436.

53. "Mr. Henschel's Fourth Recital," *New York Tribune*, February 11, 1881, 4.

54. "Notes and Gleanings," *Dwight's Journal of Music* 39 (August 2, 1879): 127.

55. "Henschel's Vocal Recitals," *American Art Journal* 34, no. 7 (December 11, 1880): 128.

56. "The Henschels," *Hartford (CT) Courant*, April 23, 1896, 7. In a brief description of Henschel's recordings of Schubert's songs, Natasha Loges describes his "disciplined and restrained approach to the score." "Singers," in *Brahms in Context*, 194.

57. "Mr. Henschel's Second Vocal Recital," *Sun* (New York), January 5, 1881, 3; "The Henschel Vocal Recitals," *Boston Daily Globe*, January 23, 1884, 2.

58. The question of gestures employed by singers is mentioned in a number of articles in *German Song Onstage*, ed. Natasha Loges and Laura Tunbridge. These include references to the Schumanns (63), Amalie Joachim (145), and Stockhausen (188).

59. "Mr. Henschel's Vocal Recital," *New York Tribune*, December 8, 1880, 4.

60. "Entertainments," *Boston Post*, November 12, 1880, 3. See also "Boston Symphony Orchestra," *Washington Post*, April 28, 1892, 4.

61. Kristen M. Turner, "Opera in English: Class and Culture in America, 1878–1910," chap. 3, especially 175–76. Mussulman briefly discusses the contrasting ways men and women were depicted in *Music in the Cultured Generation*, 63–66.

62. The types of people (mainly women and girls) who attended recitals, as well as singers such as Schumann-Heink and Gadski, were satirized in "At the Song Recital," *Musical America* 9, no. 2 (November 21, 1908): 14.

63. *Argonaut*, October 1884, quoted in *History of San Francisco Music*, vol. 7, *An Anthology of Music Criticism*, compiled by Workers of the Writers' Program of the Works Projects Administration in Northern California, Sponsored by the City and County of San Francisco (1942, rpt. New York: AMS Press, 1972), 187–88.

64. "Mr. Henschel's Vocal Recital," *New York Tribune*, December 8, 1880, 4. Henry Krehbiel was the critic at the *New York Tribune* at this time.

65. Proteus (Elson), "Music in Boston," 133.

66. "The First Henschel Concert," *Boston Post*, April 14, 1886, 5.

67. "Old Bay State Course," *Dwight's Journal of Music* 40 (November 20, 1880): 191.

68. On "Wohin?" see "Unqualified," *Akron (OH) Beacon Journal*, November 23, 1897, 3; on Loewe see [Mr. H. T. Fleck], "Loewe," *Musical Courier* 14, no. 25 (June 22, 1887): 402.

69. Howard Malcolm Ticknor, "Third Henschel Concert," 4.

70. Michael Scott briefly mentions the ways in which Henschel transitioned from one song to another. Unfortunately re-releases of Henschel's recordings, including those on YouTube, do not preserve these passages. Scott, *The Record of Singing: To 1914*, 55. Natasha Loges briefly references somewhat similar types of transitions during Stockhausen's complete performances of *Die schöne Müllerin* in "Julius Stockhausen's Early Performances," 215. Valerie Goertzen discusses the nineteenth-century tradition of these types of interludes in piano recitals, and in so doing cites Walter Dürr's conclusion

that Schubert expected preludes to be improvised to many of his songs, in "By Way of Introduction: Preluding by 18th and Early 19th Century Pianists," 309, n39.

71. "Mrs. Henschel's Song Recital," *Boston Globe*, December 18, 1897, 8. Most of the recitals that Mrs. Henschel headlined in England were in 1895, when George served as conductor of both the London Symphony Orchestra and the Scottish Orchestra of Glasgow. In these cases George did not accompany her, and she collaborated with other performers, some of whom contributed instrumental works.

72. "Sympathy of Mary," *Inter Ocean* (Chicago), January 17, 1892, 1.

73. See, e.g., Louis Elson, "Music Matters: The Henschel Recital," 8.

74. "Social Life," *Boston Herald*, January 6, 1901, 31; "Miss Henschel's Debut," *Boston Herald*, March 31, 1901, 8; "Preludes and Echoes," *Boston Daily Globe*, March 24, 1901, 23.

75. "Noted Musician Engaged," *Boston Globe*, September 21, 1902, 8.

76. These recollections were based on notes Henschel had taken when touring with Brahms in the 1870s. They were originally published in German shortly after the composer's death in 1897, and then in 1901 as George Henschel, "Personal Recollections of Johannes Brahms," 725–36. A few years later, they were published as a book that was widely advertised and excerpted in American newspapers: *Personal Recollections of Johannes Brahms* (1907); "Music and Musicians," *Times Union* (Brooklyn), March 24, 1906, 16.

77. "George Henschel Married," *New York Tribune*, March 17, 1907, 9.

78. There is general consensus that Henschel's voice was still in quite good condition at the time of his broadcasts and recordings. Appendix G of Bozarth's *Johannes Brahms and George Henschel* lists Henschel's recordings along with all of the associated bibliographic data. An accompanying CD includes Henschel's recordings of songs by Franck, Dvořák, Loewe, Schubert, and Schumann. Daniel Leech-Wilkinson discusses some of Henschel's recordings in *The Changing Sound of Music: Approaches to Studying Recorded Musical Performance* (London: CHARM, 2009), chap. 4, 19–22, and chap. 8, 34; https://www.charm.kcl.ac.uk/studies/chapters/intro.html.

79. During Powell's recital the New England baritone George E. Holmes sang three lieder by Henschel, "Mir ist's zu wohl ergangen," "Die Sommernacht," and "Nun schreit' ich aus dem Tore" (op. 25, nos. 1, 3, and 6), as well as songs by Nevin, Chadwick, and MacDowell. Programs housed at the Chicago History Museum, F38RL.A4Z Oversize.

80. "For Music Lovers," *Nashville (TN) Banner*, October 7, 1899, 13.

81. "The Henschel Recital," *Hartford (CT) Courant*, April 24, 1889, 8.

82. "Central Music Hall," *Inter Ocean* (Chicago), May 2, 1896, 6.

83. *Boston Sunday Times*, ca. 1884. Page 13 of a promotional pamphlet. Italics in the original. Gleason Collection of Music Scrapbooks, Box 32, vol. 2, p. 131, Newberry Library, Chicago.

84. Ashton Stevens, "Unostentatious Art," 9.

85. "Their Only Visit: Brief Chat with Mr. and Mrs. Georg Henschel," *Los Angeles Herald*, November 13, 1897, 10. Helen Henschel quotes her mother's description of the furnishings for a recital at a women's club in Harlem. The tone of this description strongly implies that the couple did not control the stage decorations. Notices from Buffalo indi-

cate that stagings there served as advertisements for local companies, a demonstration of the diverse ways in which recitals were monetized. Helen does not identify the exact location or date of the recital she described, and newspaper notices documenting this event have not been located. *When Soft Voices Die: A Musical Biography*, 46–47. See "The Henschel Recital," *Buffalo Morning Express and Illustrated Buffalo Express*, April 29, 1881, 4; *Christian Union* (New York), ca. 1884, quoted on p. 14 of the promotional pamphlet comprising excerpts from reviews of performances of the Henschels' recitals. Gleason Collection of Music Scrapbooks, Box 32, vol. 2, p. 131, Newberry Library, Chicago.

86. Leech-Wilkinson, *Changing Sound of Music*, chap. 8, 34, https://www.charm.kcl.ac.uk/studies/chapters/chap8.html.

87. "Mr. and Mrs. Henschel Sing," *New York Times*, March 20, 1892, 13.

88. The *Musical Courier*'s report that Henschel directly addressed a talkative woman in a Boston audience was reprinted in "Music and Musicians," *San Francisco Call*, January 27, 1898, 6.

89. *German Song Onstage*, 140, 187–88, 230.

90. "The Henschel Recital," *Boston Daily Globe*, April 14, 1887, 3; "The Henschel Recital," *Sun Herald* (Boston), April 10, 1892, 13.

91. Even in England, the booklet that accompanied the Henschels' performance of the quartet version of Brahms's *Zigeunerlieder* (op. 103), which included an introduction to the set, brief comments about each song, and music examples, was somewhat unusual for a performance of songs. In all likelihood these annotations were provided because this event was a concert that included instrumental music rather than a song recital. Saturday Popular Concerts, February 15, 1890. Program held by the Cambridge University Library.

92. [Gleason], "The Henschel Song Recital," May 1881. Gleason Collection, Clippings, Box 54, vol. 2, n.p., Newberry Library, Chicago. The name of the publication in which this review appeared is not preserved.

93. See, e.g., "Music," *Harper's Bazaar*, April 11, 1896, 29.

94. "Georg Henschel's Recital," *Boston Daily Globe*, January 10, 1882, 2.

95. Michele Aichele, "Cécile Chaminade as a Symbol for American Women, 1890–1920," 100–15.

96. On Thomé see "Musical Notes," *Chicago Tribune*, February 28, 1876, 3; "Music," *Plain Dealer* (Cleveland), April 2, 1899, 8.

97. Holmes, who was of Irish descent, changed the spelling of her name to Holmès. Nancy Sarah Theeman, "The Life and Songs of Augusta Holmès," 140–44, 151.

98. L. C. E., "Review of New Music," *Musical Herald* 5, no. 9 (September 1884): 242.

99. "George Henschel," *Musical Record and Review* 3 (November 13, 1880): 101.

100. "Gesangs-Recital," *New Yorker Staats-Zeitung*, January 20, 1898, 14.

101. Bier, "Ideal Orpheus," 1:133.

102. "The Henschel Concert," *Brooklyn Daily Eagle*, April 24, 1896, 7.

103. This report appeared in a women's social column. Meddler, "In the Swim," 6.

104. Tunbridge, *Singing in the Age of Anxiety*, 63. Initially, McCormack gave recitals consisting of operatic arias and ballads. Later, from around 1917, he turned his attention to lieder.

105. Perley Dunn Aldrich, "A Few Prominent European Teachers of Singing," 173–74. Henschel's publications are listed in the bibliography. His *Articulation in Singing* includes a few examples from lieder, but they merely demonstrate the articulation in one or two measures of a song. The only lied discussed at any length in *How to Interpret a Song* is Schumann's "Die Lotosblume" (op. 25, no. 7), and here the focus is on the somewhat problematic declamation in the first phrase. This publication also briefly mentions the necessity for singers to study theory, harmony, and counterpoint. Henschel's *Progressive Studies for the Voice with Pianoforte Accompaniment*, op. 49, provides exercises in sustained and florid singing.

106. L. H. C., "Music," *Los Angeles Herald*, March 3, 1901, 2.

107. Bier, "Ideal Orpheus," 1:129.

Chapter 4. Max Heinrich's "Classical Song Recitals"

1. "A Musical Treat," *Democrat and Chronicle* (Rochester, New York), January 28, 1899, 11.

2. "Max Heinrich," *Musical America* 24, no. 16 (August 19, 1916): 18.

3. *American History and Encyclopedia of Music*, s.v. "Heinrich, Max," ed. William Lines Hubbard, vol. 5, *Musical Biographies*, comp. Janet M. Green (New York: Irving Squire, 1910), 367.

4. Henschel and Heinrich collaborated in a small number of recitals in England and the United States, but they were not close, and there is at least one anecdote that described the antipathy between the two. [James Huneker], "The Raconteur" (1898): 24.

5. A one-paragraph biography of Heinrich appears in the supplement to Baker's *Biographical Dictionary of Musicians*, 669. Additional information about his early years appears in newspaper advertisements and interviews. See, e.g., "The Saengerfest," *Buffalo Commercial*, July 16, 1883, 3.

6. Annie's sister Emma, a harpist, wrote about her family's heritage and life, including Max's ardent courtship of her sister. Emma Schubert Brister, *Incidents*.

7. James Gibbons Huneker, *Steeplejack*, 1:148–54.

8. Robert A. Gerson, *Music in Philadelphia*, 126–27 and 299. Heinrich claimed that such performances paid only ten dollars each. "Max Heinrich and Dr. Damrosch," *Musical America* 9, no. 8 (January 2, 1909): 29.

9. "Amusements, Music, etc.," *Philadelphia Inquirer*, April 9, 1877, 3, and November 20, 1882, 3; "Classical Music," *Times* (Philadelphia), April 9, 1880, 2.

10. Interview with Heinrich: "The Musical Listener—Mr. Max Heinrich," *Etude* 46, no. 2 (February 1898): 41; http://etudemagazine.com/etude/1898/02/the-musical-listener---mr-max-heinrich.html. Heinrich later recalled that after his initial audition with Damrosch, the conductor found him a position at St. Chrysostom's Chapel in New York, which paid $1,000, and gave him a solo in an orchestral concert that paid $75. "Max Heinrich and Dr. Damrosch," *Musical America* 9, no. 8 (January 2, 1909): 29.

11. *Independent*, March 15, 1883, 10. This performance included other soloists such as Emily Winant and Margaretha Kirpal, who also performed lieder in various New York concerts. Heinrich would subsequently collaborate in song recitals with the latter.

12. Stephen Baur, "Music, Morals, and Social Management: Mendelssohn in Post–Civil War America," 100–101.

13. "Song to the Evening Star" was well received in part because it had been successfully disseminated as sheet music. Hamm, *Yesterdays*, 87, 199.

14. "The Symphony Concert," *Boston Herald*, October 28, 1883, 6.

15. Heinrich's song recital at Weber Hall in Chicago for invited guests on the evening after his performance in *Elijah* with the Apollo Club is one example of a private performance. "Notes Here and There," *Chicago Tribune*, November 22, 1885, 26.

16. "The Third Concert of the Beethoven Society," *Chicago Tribune*, April 21, 1882, 4.

17. Spex., "Milwaukee Correspondence," *Musical Courier* 9, no. 16 (October 15, 1884): 245.

18. "The German Lied This Week," *Milwaukee Sentinel*, August 31, 1884, 11; "Amusements," *Milwaukee Sentinel*, September 5, 1884, 4. "Henson-Heinrich Recitals," *Inter Ocean* (Chicago), August 31, 1884, 13, gives the programs for both recitals.

19. "Song Recitals and Light Opera," *Chicago Tribune*, September 7, 1884, 17.

20. "German Songs by Max Heinrich," *Philadelphia Inquirer*, December 8, 1884, 3. Heinrich and Henson also presented a sample of their repertoire during a Liederkranz concert in New York on November 17, 1884.

21. "Notes of the Week," *New York Times*, March 29, 1885, 9. Henson was also suffering from hoarseness during the fourth Philadelphia recital.

22. Although early reviews make superficial comparisons between the performances of Heinrich and Henschel, reviews from the late 1890s offer more insights, and these will be discussed in Chapter 5.

23. "Amusements, Music, etc.," *Philadelphia Inquirer*, February 9, 1885, 7, and March 14, 1885, 3.

24. "Amusements, Music, etc.," *Philadelphia Inquirer*, February 16, 1885, 3; "The Chorus Society," *New York Times*, April 17, 1885, 5.

25. "Song Recital," *Musical Courier* 10, no. 10 (March 11, 1885): 149; "Classical Song Recitals," *New York Times*, March 8, 1885, 7.

26. "Amusements, Music, etc.," *Philadelphia Inquirer*, January 12, 1885, 3.

27. "Amusements, Music, etc.," *Philadelphia Inquirer*, March 14, 1885, 3.

28. "Mr. Heinrich's Concert," *New York Tribune*, November 18, 1884, 6.

29. "Theater, Musik, und Kunst," *Sonntagsblatter der New Yorker Staats-Zeitung*, February 8, 1885, 4. After a brief marriage to the cornetist Walter Emerson and tours with the Boston Star Concert Company, Henson had a successful career in England. "Obituary," *Musical Times* 69, no. 1023 (May 1, 1928): 462.

30. "Song Recital," *Musical Courier* 10, no. 6 (February 11, 1885): 86.

31. "Home News," *Musical Courier* 10, no. 16 (April 22, 1885): 244. This page also reported that on the night preceding the song recital, Heinrich sang a few lieder during a fundraiser for the Vasar Gymnasium held at a private New York residence.

32. "Mr. and Mrs. Georg Henschel's Recital," *Musical Courier* 7, no. 24 (December 12, 1883): 346.

33. "Music and Drama," *Evening Post* (New York), March 9, 1885, n.p.

34. "Classical Song Recitals," *New York Times*, April 18, 1885, 4.

35. Ibid.

36. "Mr. and Mrs. Georg Henschel's Recital," *Musical Courier* 7, no. 24 (December 12, 1883): 346.

37. Henry T. Finck, *Song and Song Writers*, 19.

38. "Dur und Moll," *Signale* 62 (October 1883): 980. Later US recitals by other European singers, including Paul Kalisch (1855–1946), husband of Lilli Lehmann, and Theodor Reichmann (1849–1903), also retained the European format.

39. Turner, "Opera in English," 69.

40. "Musical and Dramatic Notes," *New York Times*, April 24, 1885, 5.

41. "Herr Anton Schott's Recital," *New York Herald*, April 24, 1885, 7; "Liederconcert," *New Yorker Staats-Zeitung*, April 22, 1885, 8. Schott's attempt to take control of the opera company was chronicled in the press. See, e.g., "Discord," *Cincinnati Enquirer*, February 20, 1885, 4.

42. "Home News," *Musical Courier* 14, no. 11 (March 16, 1887): 173. This writer also reported that Schott was assisted by the "pretty young pianist Miss Mary E. Garlichs."

43. "Herr Schott's Song Recital," *New York Times*, March 6, 1887, 2; "Herr Schott's Song Recital," *Sun* (New York), March 6, 1887, 11.

44. "Home Items," *Musical Courier* 14, no. 10 (March 9, 1887): 156. A report of another recital was more supportive than the one in "Home Items." See "Home News," *Musical Courier* 14, no. 11 (March 16, 1887): 173. See also "Herr Schott's Recital," *New York Tribune*, March 11, 1887, 4.

45. "German Liederkranz," *Musical Courier* 14, no. 10 (March 9, 1887): 156.

46. "Washington," *Musical Courier* 14, no. 24 (June 15, 1887): 387.

47. "The Concert Room," *Boston Daily Advertiser*, April 22, 1887, 8.

48. "Musical Matters," *Sun* (Baltimore), February 24, 1888, supplement 2; "Amusements in Canada," *Era* (London, England), Saturday, April 24, 1886, 17. At the end of April Heinrich and Earle were also the soloists for a performance of Mendelssohn's *St. Paul* with the Montreal Philharmonic Society. Preceding this concert, Heinrich gave two recitals in Montreal with the well-known Boston pianist Helen Hopekirk (1856–1945). Mrs. Page Thrower's Concerts [electronic resource]: Queen's Hall, Montreal (Printed ephemera, 1886), Hathi Trust Digital Library, https://babel.hathitrust.org/cgi/pt?id=aeu .ark:/13960/t54f2z57v;view=1up;seq=7. In October of that year, Heinrich and Earle performed the solo roles in *Damnation of Faust*. This performance celebrated the opening of the Music Hall in Buffalo; they were joined by members of the New York Symphony Orchestra under Walter Damrosch.

49. Earle sang lieder and solos in oratorios in numerous concerts in New York. She married fellow singer Theodore Toedt (1855–1920) in 1888 and subsequently performed less frequently. She taught voice in New York, both privately and at Juilliard.

50. After making a career for herself with appearances in operas and oratorios in America and England, in 1902 Walker married the portrait painter Edward de Komlosy and settled in Vienna. She returned to America in 1916. "Charlotte Walker," *Musical Courier* 79, no. 6 (August 7, 1919): 23.

51. "Mr. Heinrich's Recital," *New York Herald*, February 4, 1887, 4.

52. "The Heinrich Recitals," *Boston Herald*, November 29, 1887, 2. Programs for the Heinrich-Walker recitals, and also those for Heinrich's recitals with Kirpal, are housed in the New York Public Library, Music Division, *MBD (Un Cat) Max Heinrich.

53. "The First Winch-Whitney Vocal Recital," *Boston Herald*, December 8, 1887, 4; "Second of the Winch-Whitney Vocal Concerts," *Boston Herald*, December 15, 1887, 3. On Henschel's earlier recital, see "Vocal Recital at the Meionaon," *Boston Journal*, December 7, 1881, 6.

54. "Singing American Songs," *Boston Globe*, March 10, 1886, 4.

55. "The First of Miss Franklin's Song Recitals," *Boston Herald*, November 24, 1886, 8; "Miss Franklin's Second Recital," *Boston Daily Advertiser*, December 1, 1886, 4. It appears that most, if not all, the songs in the second recital were sung in English. Despite the popularity of Italian opera and the fact that these late songs of Rossini were published as early as 1835, they were not well known in the United States. The beauty of these works notwithstanding, singers wishing to program Italian works usually chose well-known arias from operas rather than Italian art songs, and none of the later major recitalists took up these songs.

56. Jordan, it may be recalled, had sung Schubert's lieder cycles during two series of recitals in 1880. Heinrich had appeared under his baton when the Arion Club of Providence, Rhode Island, gave the US premier of Dvořák's *Spectre's Bride* (1884) in 1885. G. H. Wilson, ed., *The Musical Yearbook of the United States*, vol. 5, *Season of 1887–1888*, 25. On the Dvořák see the listing in "Music and Dramatic Notes," *New York Herald*, November 19, 1885, 5.

57. Wilson, *Musical Yearbook of the United States*, 5:62. In his survey of concert life in America the New York critic Henry Krehbiel praised Van der Stucken for his pioneering efforts to promote the music of American composers. This series of articles covers performances of opera, oratorio, and orchestral music, but it does not discuss lieder or American art songs, an indication of their lowly status at this time. H. E. Krehbiel, "American Music," 121, 137, 155, 173.

58. "Mr. Max Heinrich's Song Recitals," *Boston Daily Advertiser*, March 23, 1887, 5; "Heinrich-Kirpal Recital," *Boston Herald*, March 23, 1887, 3.

59. Proteus (Louis Elson), "Music in Boston, Dec. 19, 1887," 10.

60. Heinrich and Musin were among the artists who performed at the fortieth anniversary concert of the New York Liederkranz. "German Liederkranz," *Musical Courier* 14, no. 2 (January 12, 1887): 21.

61. "Notes and News," *Oxford Magazine* 8, no. 8 (December 5, 1888): 130.

62. Advertisements and reviews for some of Moór's American appearances, including a performance of his piano concerto, were published directly adjacent to notices concerning Heinrich, raising the possibility that these two performers knew each other prior to their collaborations in England. See, e.g., "News of the Month," *Etude* 5, no. 3 (March 1, 1887): 38.

63. "Miscellaneous Concerts," *Monthly Musical Record* 19, no. 217 (January 1, 1889): 18; "Max Heinrich's Vocal Recitals," *Monthly Musical Record* 19, no. 221 (May 1, 1889): 115.

64. "Messrs. Heinrich and Moór's Recital," *Daily News* (London,), December 8, 1888, 3.

Notes to Chapter 4   245

65. "Various Concerts, etc.," *Monthly Musical Record* 19, no. 218 (February 1, 1889): 42. See somewhat similar ideas in "Miscellaneous Concerts," *Musical World* 69, no. 16 (April 18, 1889): 256.

66. "Mr. Max Heinrich," *Musical World* 69, no. 27 (July 6, 1889): 437; "Recent Concerts," *Saturday Review*, July 20, 1889, 74.

67. "Mr. Max Heinrich's Concert," *Observer* (London), June 30, 1889, 2.

68. "Concert at Grunewald Hall," *Times-Picayune* (New Orleans), November 14, 1877, 8; "Our Lena Little," *Times-Picayune* (New Orleans) July 10, 1886, 4.

69. "A Brahms Concert," *Times* (London), December 15, 1884, 4.

70. This recital also included songs by French and Italian composers, which the critic welcomed as an "antidote to too much German depth." This point of view had already started appearing in reviews of recitals in Boston. "Recent Concerts," *Times* (London), May 3, 1887, 3.

71. "Mr. Max Heinrich," *Musical World* 69, no. 27 (July 6, 1889): 421. Contemporary newspapers do not enumerate all the repertoire that Spies performed in England, but they do note that she sang works by Brahms and Henschel along with those by other composers. For an overview of the reception of Brahms in England that notes the colleagues of Brahms who were working in that country, see Hamilton, "England," 316–23.

72. "Max Heinrich and Benno Schönberger's Concerts," *Monthly Musical Record* 20, no. 230 (February 1, 1890): 42.

73. Heinrich sang numbers 2–5, 9, 12, and 14 from Brahms's *Magelone Romances*.

74. Henschel advertisement: *Daily Telegraph* (London), February 13, 1889, 1.

75. "Concerts, &c.," *Musical World* 70, no. 1 (June 14, 1890): 474.

76. Advertisements, *Times* (London), November 25, 1891, 1, and December 1, 1891, 1.

77. "Senor Albeniz's Concert," *Standard* (London), Wednesday, January 28, 1891, 3.

78. "Mr. Max Heinrich's Vocal Recital," *Pall Mall Gazette* (London), April 3, 1889, 5. The same paper also noted that Heinrich appeared in Richter's performance of Berlioz's *Damnation of Faust* in place of Santley. "The Last Richter Concert," *Pall Mall Gazette*, July 9, 1889, 6.

79. "Music in Manchester," *Musical Times* 29, no. 550 (December 1, 1888): 731.

80. *Commercial Gazette* (London), July 27, 1892, 37; *Standard* (London), July 22, 1892, 8.

81. Huneker, *Steeplejack*, 1:153.

82. "In Hotel Corridors," *Detroit Free Press*, November 26, 1894, 5.

Chapter 5. Max Heinrich's Expanding Stylistic and Geographic Vistas

1. "Lieder Recitals" (April 3, 1887), *The Music Criticism of Hugo Wolf*, 273.

2. In his 1887 tirade (see note 1), Wolf harshly critiqued one of Reichmann's European lieder recitals.

3. [Editorial], *Musical Courier* 20, no. 2 (January 8, 1890): 22.

4. Amalie Joachim's US tour is briefly described in Chapter 6.

5. Günther, *Kunstlied als Liedkunst*, 344, 358.

6. "Two Song Recitals," *New York Times*, March 6, 1891, 4; "Miss Lena Little's Concert," *World* (New York), March 6, 1891, 5.

7. "Miss Little's Concert," *Sun* (New York), March 6, 1891, 3.

8. *Musical Courier*, 1890; reprinted in James Gibbons Huneker, *Americans in the Arts: 1890–1920*, 141.

9. A few of these performances were documented in the social pages of newspapers. See, e.g., "The Social Side," *Boston Journal*, March 25, 1893, 7.

10. B. N., "Professional Parlor Exhibitions" [a report from New York], *Los Angeles Times*, December 10, 1899, Illustrated Magazine Section, 23.

11. "Boston Symphony Orchestra," *Brooklyn Daily Eagle*, February 10, 1894, 5.

12. "This Is Festival Week," *Daily Morning Journal and Courier* (New Haven), April 13, 1896, 5.

13. E. Douglas Bomberger, *"A Tidal Wave of Encouragement": American Composers' Concerts in the Gilded Age*, xiii–xvi, 13.

14. Quoted in Gienow-Hecht, *Sound Diplomacy*, 161. For a brief overview of the efforts to Americanize programming for orchestral concerts see 150–59.

15. "H.W. Greene on American Music," *Musical Courier* 30, no. 21 (May 15, 1895): 9.

16. The *Hartford Times* article is cited in numerous reports of the incident and subsequent lawsuit, including "Heinrich's Libel Suit," *New Haven Register*, November 30, 1896, 3. In contrast to other reports, "The Hartford Festival," *Daily Morning Journal and Courier* (New Haven), May 13, 1896, 1, simply reported that Heinrich was ill. The following articles chronicle aspects of the legal proceedings: "Max Heinrich's Libel Suit," *New Haven Register*, October 13, 1897, 5; "A Notable Libel Suit," *Chicago Tribune*, October 27, 1897, 6; and "Heinrich Loses His Suit," *Daily Morning Journal and Courier* (New Haven), October 20, 1897, 3. The case was also recounted in one of the obituaries for Heinrich: "Sued Hartford Paper for Libel," *Hartford (CT) Courant*, August 11, 1916, 2. Despite the incident in 1896, Heinrich and his daughter gave a successful recital in Hartford in November 1897. "Max Heinrich's Song Recital at University Hall," *Hartford Courant*, November 10, 1897, 3

17. [Elson], "Max Heinrich's Second Song Recital in Steinert Hall," *Boston Daily Advertiser*, December 8, 1897, 5.

18. Hale routinely criticized Brahms's compositions and thought more highly of the biblical verses of op. 121 than of the music. Philip Hale, "Symphony Night," April 11, 1897, *Dramatic and Musical Criticisms*, 6:110.

19. Cole, "Lilli Lehmann's Dedicated Lieder Recitals," 235.

20. "Chicago," *Musical Courier* 40, no. 23 (June 6, 1900): 27.

21. "Anna Schubert Heinrich," *Boston Evening Transcript*, August 4, 1900, 4. This obituary is one of the only times the press identified Heinrich's wife by using her first name; typically it called her Mrs. Heinrich. Indeed, most other notices of her death (which was reported in papers across the country) and advertisements for the couple's performances likewise referred to her as Mrs. Heinrich. Because of this usage and because she was always given second billing, this chapter will refer to her as Mrs. Heinrich, except in paragraphs where multiple family members are discussed. This aligns with the treatment of Mrs. Henschel, who had a more prominent role in recitals, in Chapter 3.

Notes to Chapter 5   247

22. "Hamlin Concert," *Chicago Tribune*, October 26, 1903, 9; Advertisement, *Philadelphia Inquirer*, January 31, 1904, 29.

23. Marian Wilson Kimber, *The Elocutionists: Women, Music, and the Spoken Word*, 18–21.

24. "News of the Week in Colville," *Colville (WA) Examiner*, March 7, 1908, [14]; "Central Union Women Plan Entertainment," *Pacific Commercial Advertiser* (Honolulu), May 9, 1915, 9.

25. A. W. K., "New Music—Vocal and Instrumental," *Musical America* 16, no. 21 (September 28, 1912): 24. A full-page advertisement lists many of Heinrich's published songs and melodramas: *Musical Observer* 14, no. 5 (November 1916): 64. The unnumbered page following the cover page of the October issue of the same journal lists some of the professional singers who performed his songs.

26. Held (not the actress of the same name) had been a nanny for the children of the son of President Ulysses Grant. She settled in San Diego when the family moved there in 1893. Her house, called the Green Dragon, was described in an article mentioning Heinrich that was printed in the *Ladies' Home Journal* and various newspapers: "In the Land of Bohemia," *Watertown (NY) Daily Times*, May 23, 1908, 9.

27. "Romantic Love Story of a Famous Chicago Singer," *Chicago Tribune*, November 20, 1904, [63].

28. "The Joyous Child: The Last Thirty Years," a typescript prepared by Havrah Hubbard in 1939, charts Held's life, including her time with Heinrich and his family. It notes that Held was quite an unorthodox person and the separation from Heinrich was mutually agreeable. This document and another typescript about Held's life titled "Old Green Dragon Days with Anna Held" (by Mrs. Denville and Olive Percival) are held by the Library of the University of California, San Diego, https://library.ucsd.edu/dc/object/bb8571489c.

29. The tactful reviews of Heinrich's last recital are excerpted in "Max Heinrich's New York Press Encomiums," *Musical Courier* 72, no. 15 (April 13, 1916): 9.

30. Philip Hale, "Roland Hayes at the Symphony," 14.

31. Philip Hale, "Drama and Music," 5.

32. In one recital Heinrich performed a spring song by Franz once in English and twice in German. [Elson], "Max Heinrich's Second Song Recital in Steinert Hall," 5.

33. "Another Concert," *New York Herald*, October 25, 1887, 6; W. S. B. Mathews, "Editorial Bric-a-Brac," *Music* 16, no. 1 (May 1899): 90–91.

34. A lengthy statement that Heinrich made in an interview is printed in "In Feasts of Music," *Chicago Tribune*, February 10, 1895, 37.

35. "Heinrich Song Evening," *Chicago Tribune*, December 13, 1901, 4.

36. "Musical Helps and Hints," *Ladies' Home Journal* 13, no. 10 (September 1896): 29.

37. Many of Nevin's works were highly successful in the domestic market and were programmed by amateurs at music clubs. Marketed to women, the scores were daintily decorated, and doilies were packaged with scores of his suite of piano pieces titled *A Day in Venice* (op. 25, 1898). Loesser, *Men, Women and Pianos*, 544–45. William Upton remarked on Nevin's popularity and his "fluent melody," but he asserted that the com-

poser "possessed no profundity of musical thought." *Art-Song in America*, 125. In a more favorable article for a woman's magazine, Rupert Hughes relates some of Nevin's songs to lieder by Schumann and Franz: "Music in America: I—Ethelbert Nevin," 527–30.

38. Throughout the years, advertisements for Heinrich's performances of Clay's song spelled the title as "Gypsy John," but most other sources, including published scores, used the spelling Gipsy.

39. Philip Hale, "Boston Concerts," 10.

40. Philip Hale, "Second and Last Song Recital of Mr. and Mrs. Max Heinrich in Steinert Hall," 7.

41. "Music of the Day," *Inter Ocean* (Chicago), January 24, 1902, 6.

42. Judith Tick, "Passed Away Is the Piano Girl," 343.

43. O. M. E. R., "Causerie from Boston: Women Musical Composers," *Worcester Daily Spy*, April 16, 1893, 4.

44. Philip Hale, "Mr. Loeffler's Songs," 7. Loeffler wrote songs in French and English. Sears provides a concise overview of these works and their reception, noting the difficulty of their instrumental parts as well as the eclectic style and influences that distinguished them from songs by other Boston composers: "The Art Song in Boston, 1880–1914," 218–25.

45. "The Symphony Concert," *Sunday Herald* (Boston), April 11, 1897, 7.

46. Emilie Frances Bauer, "Brooklyn," 27.

47. "Institute Song Recital," *Brooklyn Daily Eagle*, November 18, 1897, 7.

48. "Concerts of the Week," *Chicago Daily Tribune*, October 22, 1899, 44; Blanche Partington, "Huneker Asserts Strauss Is the Most Intellectual of the Living Musicians," 22; "An Enjoyable Concert," *Indianapolis Journal*, May 22, 1900, 8.

49. For excerpts from a variety of reviews of Hamlin's performances, see "The First Strauss Recital," *Musical Courier* 37, no. 17 (October 26, 1898): 13; and "George Hamlin's Strauss Recitals," *Musical Courier* 38, no. 9 (March 1, 1899): 39.

50. "Max Heinrich and Richard Strauss' 'Enoch Arden,'" *Music* 20 (November 1901): 396–402.

51. Pauline Strauss de Ahna sang twelve of her husband's lieder during the Chicago recital with Heinrich, and she sang another seven in a concert of his orchestral works given by Thomas's Chicago Orchestra with the composer conducting. "The Return of Richard Strauss," *Chicago Tribune*, April 10, 1904, 21. New York critics (whose opinions were published in Chicago papers) were not impressed by Strauss de Ahna's voice or interpretations, nor with her husband's accompaniments. At least one stated that the songs were better rendered by Americans. W. L. Hubbard, "Mme. Strauss as a Singer," 22. On Bispham's performances see "Strauss Song Recital," *New York Times*, March 2, 1904, 9; "Strauss Gives 'Enoch Arden,'" *Boston Herald*, March 29, 1904, 7.

52. "Heinrich Request Recital," *Detroit Free Post*, December 4, 1894, 5.

53. "Max Heinrich Recital," *St. Joseph (MO) Gazette Herald*, March 17, 1901, 5.

54. "Providence Social Gossip," *Boston Herald*, January 26, 1896, 22. The complete program was printed in "Providence Social Gossip," *Boston Herald*, January 19, 1896, 24.

55. Finck, *Song and Song Writers*, 233.

Notes to Chapter 5   249

56. "What Phillip Hale Says," *Sault Ste. Marie (MI) News*, July 27, 1895, 10.

57. Report from the *Detroit Free Press* reprinted in "The Heinrich Recital," *Sault Ste. Marie (MI) News*, July 25, 1896, 1.

58. "An Artistic Treat," *Saginaw Evening News*, February 19, 1895, 4.

59. Brister, *Incidents*, 32.

60. In 1897 Schultz replaced Heinrich with Perry Averill (1862–1935) as the only baritone he represented. Newspaper announcements of this change do not indicate whether this was because of Heinrich's alleged drunkenness in Hartford. "Amusements," *Jackson (MI) Citizen Patriot*, June 16, 1896, 6.

61. McVeigh and Weber, "From the Benefit Concert to the Solo Song Recital," 186–87.

62. "Some Institute Songsters," *Brooklyn Daily Eagle*, October 11, 1896, 8.

63. Heinrich had previously collaborated with both performers. During the preceding February, Heinrich and Meredith had been among the soloists in a performance of Berlioz's *Damnation of Faust* given in Chicago by the Apollo Chorus and led by Thomas. Morgan, a student of Joseph Joachim, had collaborated with Heinrich in 1892 in a recital for Rochester's Tuesday Musicale.

64. "The Musical Column," *Los Angeles Herald*, January 12, 1896, 14.

65. "The Henschels," *Musical Courier* 36, no. 11 (March 16, 1898): 40.

66. "Key and Bow," *Los Angeles Herald*, July 4, 1897, 14.

67. "Opera, Not Concert," *Oregonian* (Portland), November 11, 1900, 18.

68. "No Longer Is Oakland 'Jay': The Henschels Were Nearly Overcome by Their Reception," *San Francisco Call*, November 17, 1897, 11.

69. "The Henschels," *Los Angeles Herald*, November 12, 1897, 9.

70. "In the Musical World," *St. Paul (MN) Globe*, March 6, 1898, 10.

71. "The Heinrichs Give Their First Concert," *San Francisco Chronicle*, October 19, 1898, 10.

72. "San Francisco," *Musical Courier* 37, no. 18 (November 2, 1898): 45.

73. "The Musical Listener—Max Heinrich," *Etude Magazine* 46, no. 2 (February 1898): 41; http://etudemagazine.com/etude/1898/02/the-musical-listener---mr-max-heinrich.html.

74. "The Vaudevilles," *Inter Ocean* (Chicago), July 10, 1904, 26.

75. "Heinrichs Well Received: Raise Vaudeville Standard Bill at the Orpheum," *Los Angeles Herald*, September 6, 1904, 7.

76. Philip Hale, "Music: The First of Two Song Recitals by Mr. and Mrs. Max Heinrich in Steinert Hall," 6. The critic at the *Boston Evening Transcript*, likely Apthorp, had somewhat similar, though sometimes more critical, observations of Heinrich's performances. He also noted that some of Heinrich's unusual rhetorical readings, which resulted in unusual breaks in phrases, were seemingly improvised because they varied from one performance to another. "Mr. and Mrs. Heinrich's Recitals," *Boston Evening Transcript*, March 21, 1894, 10.

77. Edward F. Kravitt, *The Lied: Mirror of Late Romanticism*, 58–60, 177–78.

78. "Max Heinrich Recital," *Oshkosh (WI) Northwestern*, June 1, 1899, 7.

79. Eric Van Tassel, "'Something Utterly New': Listening to Schubert Lieder," 704–5.

80. "The Hamlin-Biden Recital," *Boston Herald*, January 31, 1902, 8.

81. Max Heinrich, "Interpretative Remarks," *Fifty Selected Songs by Franz Schubert*, n.p.

82. Philip Hale, "The Second Vocal Recital of Mr. and Mrs. Max Heinrich," 4.

83. Philip Hale, "First of Two Song Recitals Given by Mr. and Mrs. Max Heinrich," 7.

84. Kravitt, *Lied*, 177.

85. "Delighted Audience," *Plain Dealer* (Cleveland), February 7, 1896, 2; Huneker, *Steeplejack*, 1:150.

86. For examples of reports of reactions to these songs, see [Louis C. Elson], "Max Heinrich's Second Song Recital in Steinert Hall," 5; and "Mr. Heinrich's Recital," *Boston Herald*, December 8, 1897, 6.

87. Louis C. Elson, "Mr. Max Heinrich's Recital in New Steinert Hall," 8.

88. "Delightful Evening of Song," *Detroit Free Press*, February 20, 1895, 7. This recital took place in a private home.

89. "Friday Night's Concert," *Ann Arbor (MI) Argus*, February 20, 1894, 4. Italics in the original.

90. Cole, "Lilli Lehmann's Dedicated Lieder Recitals," 231, 235.

91. "Ovation to Max Heinrich: Minneapolis Turns Out to Hear Brilliant Artist," *Saint Paul Globe*, February 25, 1897, 2.

92. Louis C. Elson, "The Max Heinrich Recitals," 4.

93. "Entertainments," *Star Tribune* (Minneapolis), February 25, 1897, 2. A review of a performance of Wagner's "Evening Star" gave a more detailed description of Heinrich's improvising. "Delightful Evening of Song," *Detroit Free Press*, February 20, 1895, 7.

94. Philip Hale, "The First of Two Song Recitals," 6.

95. Huneker, *Steeplejack*, 1:149–52.

96. Helen Keller, *Midstream: My Later Life*, 272.

97. Brister, *Incidents*, 45, 49. For representative examples of the press's response to Julia's recitals, see "Julia Heinrich Is Heartily Welcomed," *Musical America* 9, no. 25 (May 1, 1909): 23; "A Song Recital," *New York Tribune*, April 22, 1909, 7. At the end of 1905 Max and his second wife joined Julia in Berlin, where they stayed for most of 1906. He seems to have spent most of this time socializing, but he did give a poorly attended recital in the Beethoven Saal. A translation of a polite review in the *Berliner Tageblatt* was printed in "Foreign Notes: Berlin," *New Music Review and Church Music Review* 56, no. 3 (July 1906): 1020.

98. Heinrich's articles, which are very short, are listed in the bibliography. His 1915 "Art of Singing" was reprinted in numerous outlets, and some of his ideas were similarly reiterated in various newspapers. One of these reprinted his critique of method teaching. "Max Heinrich on the Teaching of Singing," *Springfield (MA) Republican*, February 6, 1910, 24.

99. W. S. B. Mathews, "An American School of Singing," n.p.

100. "Social and Personal," *Evansville (IN) Courier and Press*, April 19, 1904, 6.

101. "Heinrich Lecture-Recital," *Chicago Tribune*, January 24, 1901, 7. Heinrich also gave these types of presentations in San Francisco and St. Louis. I am grateful to Marian

Wilson Kimber, who shared with me a copy of an advertisement for the St. Louis classes that was printed in the *Prospectus for 1900–1901 and 1899–1900 Year Book of the Union Musical Club of St. Louis,* a copy of which is located at the Missouri Historical Society Library and Research Center. This advertisement indicated that a half-hour private lesson plus two tickets for the lecture recitals cost $5.

102. "Recent Musical Books," *Pittsburgh Post Gazette,* March 30, 1911, 4. For additional reviews see "New Books," *Etude* 29, no. 1 (January 1911): 64; "Writes with Authority," *Boston Daily Globe,* November 26, 1910, 11.

103. "Recital by Mr. Townsend," *Boston Herald,* March 15, 1911, 8.

104. "Townsend Wins High Approval," *Boston Herald,* January 29, 1913, 4; "Schumann in English," *Musical America* 17, no. 14 (February 8, 1913): 39. Heinrich's anthologies of lieder are listed in the bibliography.

105. The front pages of the sheet music for "Barcarole" and "Wasserrose" carry an advertisement for *Richard Strauss: Selected Songs,* edited and revised by Max Heinrich, a series that was said to comprise these two songs in addition to fourteen others. However, it appears that this volume was not published.

106. D. L. L., "Secret of McCormack's Hold on His Audiences," *Musical America* 21, no. 17 (February 27, 1915): 17.

107. H. F. P., "New Music," *Musical America* 14, no. 13 (February 3, 1912): 28. See also "For Playgoers and Music Lovers," *New England Magazine* 46, no. 1 (March 1912): 25–26. The Brahms edition was also praised in A. W. K., "New Music," *Musical America* 21, no. 21 (March 27, 1915): 24. The Schubert anthology was praised as useful to performers in "Notes and Comment upon Musical Matters," ed. Olin Downes, *Boston Sunday Post,* June 1, 1912, n.p. The one negative review of the translations to come to light did not name Heinrich or Mattullath. Sigmund Spaeth criticized their English translation of lines in "Die beiden Grenadiere." He did not approve of translating "Sie liessen die Köpfe hangen" as "their hearts were depressed and aching" because it failed to reflect the drooping head, which Schumann's melodic descent depicts. He also censured the faulty declamation and lack of onomatopoeia when "Viel' Schwerter klirren und blitzen" is translated as "And swords clash and muskets rattle": "Translating to Music," 295, 296.

108. In describing Wüllner's technique, Kravitt asserts that singers at the turn of the century used much greater contrasts in vocal color than singers at the end of the twentieth century. Kravitt, *Lied,* 58.

109. The accents that Heinrich placed on the third beat of each measure of the piano part in example 5.1b were likely inspired by the accents that Schumann used in some of the preceding measures, though Schumann placed most of these accents between the staves, rather than on top of the highest pitch.

110. Philip Hale, "Mr. Max Heinrich's Third Recital in Steinert Hall," 7.

111. Fischer widely advertised Heinrich's editions, but the extent of their influence is impossible to measure because the company does not have records of sales or print runs. In an email communication from 2020, Glendower Jones, owner of Classical Vocal Reprints, reported that he sold about thirty-five copies of Heinrich's edition of *Dichterliebe* over the preceding twenty years. But purchasers might have been more interested in Heinrich's transpositions of some of the songs than in his annotations.

112. *New York Tribune*, October 10, 1915, 6.

113. Huneker, *Steeplejack*, 1:150.

114. "The Musical Listener—Max Heinrich," *Etude* 46, no. 2 (February 1898): 41.

Chapter 6. Villa Whitney White and Women's Music Clubs

1. "Song and Talk," *Detroit Free Press*, February 20, 1898, 14.

2. On a broader level, Ralph P. Locke discusses the satirizing and belittling of women patrons in "Paradoxes of the Woman Music Patron in America," 798–825.

3. Joseph Horowitz, "Laura Langford and the Seidl Society: Wagner Comes to Brooklyn," 164–83. Linda Whitesitt provides an overview of some of the clubs' most noteworthy achievements in "The Role of Women Impresarios in American Concert Life, 1871–1933," 159–80. A growing number of studies are delving into the activities of specific music clubs, but many of these (like Whitesitt's) emphasize instrumental music and ignore song recitals. Other studies have considered such wider issues as the role of women's clubs in relation to society's gender conventions. See, e.g., Karen Blair, *The Clubwoman as Feminist: True Womanhood Redefined, 1868–1914*.

4. Rose Fay Thomas's address was reprinted in "They Develop Taste," *Chicago Tribune*, July 8, 1893, 5.

5. James Taylor Dunn, *St. Paul's Schubert Club: A Century of Music (1882–1982)*, 15, 33.

6. Loesser, *Men, Women and Pianos*, 549.

7. Programs for both concerts are held by the New York Public Library for the Performing Arts, *MBD (Steinway Hall Programme).

8. John Chaney, archivist of the Central Congregational Church, Providence, Rhode Island (email December 2, 2016), confirmed White's position at the church. Mathews reported her position at the conservatory in *A Hundred Years of Music in America*, 466.

9. Sondra Wieland Howe, "Julius Eichberg: String and Vocal Instruction in Nineteenth-Century Boston," 151–52. The members of the Eichberg Quartet were Lillian Shattuck (1857–1940), Lillian Chandler (1869–1960), Abbie Shepardson (1832–1914), and Lettie Launder (b. 1857).

10. Newspapers identify a small number of other Americans who also studied with Amalie Joachim, though none of them achieved the same status as White. Throughout this chapter, unless otherwise stated, the name Joachim refers to Amalie.

11. "Handel and Haydn," *Boston Globe*, April 16, 1892, 4.

12. "Theatrical Notes," *Ironwood (MI) News-Record*, May 7, 1892, 6.

13. Letter from Joachim to Clara Rogers, December 19, 1892. MS Thr 470 (668): Clara Kathleen Rogers correspondence, bound (Subseries A), Houghton Library, Harvard University. Reprinted in my article "Amalie Joachim's 1892 American Tour," 7.

14. "Mrs. Sherwood's Recital," *New York Times*, January 14, 1886, 4; "Among the Musicians," *Pittsburgh Daily Post*, May 9, 1897, 12.

15. Ella Bucknam, a schoolteacher married to a prominent lawyer, was an active participant in Minneapolis's social life and was involved in a women's history club. None of White's performances in Minneapolis have been linked to a club, though many of her audiences were made up of society women.

16. Occasionally other eminent women singers collaborated with women pianists. During her tours in 1896 and 1897, Genevra Johnstone Bishop (1863–1923) usually performed with Nellie Cook. Schumann-Heink worked with the Minnesota pianist Katherine Hoffmann (b. 1878), who recorded with the contralto, as well as with other pianists, including Edith Evans.

17. White's programs, which merely list the songs to be performed, are among the programs of the Amateur Musical Club held by the Chicago History Museum, F38RL. A4P Oversize.

18. "Recital by Miss White," *Burlington (IA) Hawk-Eye*, January 28 (morning), 1896, 8.

19. To date the identity of White's manager (or managers) has not come to light. It is likely that White also had the assistance of contacts at women's clubs. Her 1892 tour with Joachim was managed by L. M. Ruben. A press release claimed he managed other prominent artists including the opera singer Conrad Behrens (1835–1898). "Mr. Ruben's Artists," *Musical Courier* 23, no. 15 (October 7, 1891): 390.

20. "Recitals of Folk Song," *Evening Journal* (Jamestown, NY), November 25, 1896, 8.

21. "Musicales," *Vogue*, March 5, 1896, iii

22. "The Spring Season," *New York Herald*, April 12, 1896, 10.

23. "For the Jewell Nursery," *New York Times*, April 25, 1897, 5.

24. For instance, a recital by White sponsored by three women's clubs in St. Louis was warmly reviewed in "Das deutsche Volkslied," *Westliche Post* (St. Louis), February 25, 1896, 8. Another German paper in that city reviewed her 1897 recital of eighteen lieder by Schumann. This was not one of the programs that she frequently presented, and this performance suggests that White perceived the St. Louis audiences as being more welcoming of a program comprised entirely of lieder by one composer than those in other cities. Whether this was due to the influence of the German community or the women's music clubs is unclear. "Frl. Whites letzter Gesangs-Abend," *Anzeiger des Westens*, March 19, 1897, 8.

25. "Miss White's Program," *Idaho Statesman*, December 3, 1897, 3; "Max Heinrich," *Courier* (Lincoln, NE), December 2, 1899, 2.

26. "St. Paul Music," *Saint Paul Globe*, January 27, 1895, 8.

27. "Boston: The Papyrus Club's Dinner for Their Literary Sisters; About Women's Clubs—The Mania for Instruction," *Chicago Tribune*, February 23, 1879, 12. Italics in the original.

28. "Amusements," *Sun* (New York), April 9, 1896, 5.

29. W. S. B. Mathews, as reprinted in "Musical Mention," *San Francisco Call*, December 12, 1897, 27.

30. "German Song and Story," *Morning Oregonian* (Portland), December 11, 1897, 9.

31. "In Society," *Pittsburgh Press*, April 11, 1897, 20.

32. "Social Affairs," *Inter Ocean* (Chicago), February 24, 1897, 8; "Society," *Pittsburgh Press*, May 4, 1897, 2.

33. In an 1895 recital White presented a variation of the program shown in figure 6.2. She ended with the same songs as this program did, but almost all the earlier repertoire was different. "Realm of Tone," *Penny Press* (Minneapolis), January 13, 1895, 2.

34. Heinrich Reimann, ed., *Das deutsche Lied: Eine Auswahl aus den Programmen der historischen Lieder-Abende der Amalie Joachim*. Like Joachim, Reimann taught at the Klindworth-Schwarwenka Conservatory. Borchard, *Stimme und Geige*, appendix: Repertoireauswertungen (located on the accompanying CD). The English translations of the song texts for Reimann's programs of historical concerts, which were provided by Mrs. John P. Morgan, suggest that these volumes had the potential to reach audiences in the United Kingdom and the United States.

35. Beatrix Borchard, "The Concert Hall as a Gender-Neutral Space," 143.

36. Philip V. Bohlman, *The Music of European Nationalism: Cultural Identity and Modern History*, 94–95.

37. "Greatest Contralto Is Schumann-Heink," *Salt Lake Tribune*, October 19, 1913, 40. An advertisement of Reimann's folksong arrangements accompanied the score of "May Song" ("Cancion de maja"), which was published in 1918. This score is held by the Sibley Music Library, https://urresearch.rochester.edu/institutionalPublicationPublicView .action?institutionalItemId=3843.

38. Finck, *Song and Song Writers*, 7. While White presented her Reimannian-style programs to many women's clubs, newspaper reports give no indication that either White's programs or Reimann's anthologies influenced later programs given by music club members. Researching the question of such influence is hampered by the lack of detailed reports of club presentations in newspapers and by the far-flung and incomplete records of club performances.

39. White had worked in Providence and still had many friends there, and, as a result, she sang more solo lieder in her recitals with Joachim than in the women's other recitals. They had planned to give two recitals, but these were so successful that they gave a third. The recital before the historical one comprised *Die schöne Müllerin* and a few duets, and the third recital presented a miscellany of nineteenth-century lieder, including ones by Brahms, Schumann, and Mendelssohn. "Song Recital," *Providence Journal*, March 5, 1892, 3; "Song Recital," *Providence Journal*, March 19, 1892, 3; "Lieder-Abend," *Providence Sunday Journal*, March 19, 1892, 2.

40. Reimann's anthologies are listed in the bibliography.

41. "Bisphams zweites Recital," *New Yorker Staats-Zeitung*, November 10, 1904, 14.

42. Paul R. Martin, "Schumann-Heink Receives Ovation," 17.

43. Loges, "The Limits of the Lied: Brahms's *Magelone-Romanzen* op. 33," 314–18; Borchard, *Stimme und Geige*, appendix: Repertoireauswertungen.

44. "German Song and Story," *Morning Oregonian* (Portland), December 11, 1897, 9; "Music and Drama," *Boston Evening Transcript*, March 19, 1898, 21.

45. Cole, "Lilli Lehmann's Dedicated Lieder Recitals," 230.

46. "Preludes and Echoes," *Boston Globe*, February 3, 1895, 16.

47. "Weird Love Songs," *Morning Oregonian* (Portland), December 28, 1897, 8.

48. "Fashionable Audience Thoroughly Entertained at the Kenton Club," *Courier Journal* (Louisville, KY), February 1, 1896, 5.

49. "Heinrich Meyn's Recital: Alexander von Fielitz Accompanies Some of His Own Songs," *Sun* (New York), January 19, 1906, 7. From 1905 to 1908 von Fielitz taught and conducted in Chicago; subsequently he returned to the Stern Conservatory.

50. During another recital at this normal course, White performed *An die ferne Geliebte* and "Adelaide." In both events she was accompanied by Josephine Large. "Music," *Sunday Oregonian* (Portland), July 24, 1910, sec. 4, p. 3.

51. Jim Samson's survey of nation-building efforts in Europe during the nineteenth century touches on folk culture, particularly in Slavic countries, but also stresses the roles of other genres, including opera: "Nations and Nationalism," 588–89.

52. Gienow-Hecht, *Sound Diplomacy*, 154.

53. "Music," *Saint Paul Globe*, October 6, 1895, 20.

54. "A Song Recital," *Burlington (IA) Gazette*, February 18, 1896, n.p.

55. In 1897 White gave her international folksong lecture-recital in a private home in Chicago. She probably drew her songs from Reimann's 1893 *Volksliederbuch*. "Social Affairs," *Inter Ocean* (Chicago), February 24, 1897, 8.

56. Whitesitt describes the limitations of the clubs' achievements and the ways they reinforced the male canon and traditional roles of women in "Women as 'Keepers of Culture,'" 67–68, 78–81.

57. "Children's Songs," *Sunday Oregonian* (Portland), December 26, 1897, 13.

58. "Notable Musical Treat," *Sunday Oregonian*, June 11, 1899, 24.

59. "Among the Musicians," *Sunday Oregonian*, January 12, 1896, 13; "Cluster of Stars," *Sunday Oregonian*, February 2, 1896, 5; "The Drama and Stage," *Sunday Oregonian*, September 27, 1896, 13.

60. "Weird Love Songs," *Morning Oregonian*, December 28, 1897, 8.

61. "Miss Villa Whitney White's Concert," *Morning Oregonian*, April 1, 1897, 5; Rolf Swenson, "Pilgrims at the Golden Gate: Christian Scientists on the Pacific Coast, 1880–1915," 229–63. White's mother, Lydia Whitney Roberts White (1832–1875), was among the earliest members of the Christian Science faith, and her sisters were also members. White sang a German "air" from 1673, arranged by Reimann, at the service dedicating Chicago's first Christian Science church. "In a Greek Temple," *Chicago Tribune*, November 15, 1897, 9.

62. "City News in Brief," *Morning Oregonian*, December 8, 1897, 5.

63. "A Unique Entertainment," *Seattle Post-Intelligencer*, December 16, 1897, 5.

64. "In Musical Circles," *Sunday Oregonian*, December 26, 1897, 13; "Weird Love Songs," *Morning Oregonian*, December 28, 1897, 8; "Songs for Children," *Sunday Oregonian*, December 19, 1897, 13.

65. "Portland's Musical Club," *Morning Oregonian*, May 29, 1898, 15. Schott returned to Oregon to give recitals in Astoria and Portland in 1899.

66. "Throw Off Corsets," *Sunday Oregonian*, June 5, 1898, 15.

67. "Max Heinrich Recital Programme," *Sunday Oregonian*, November 20, 1898, 15.

68. "Dramatic and Musical Review," *San Francisco Chronicle*, January 9, 1898, 5.

69. "Key and Bow," *Los Angeles Herald*, January 30, 1898, 20.

70. John Brown Jr. and James Boyd, *History of San Bernardino and Riverside Counties*, 1:211. Because of the continuing proliferation of music clubs, later recitalists, including Bispham, were able to perform before more clubs in California than did White.

71. "Redlands," *Los Angeles Herald*, January 20, 1898, 6; "San Bernardino County," *Los Angeles Herald*, January 24, 1898, 6; "Redlands," *Los Angeles Times*, January 24, 1898, 9.

72. Wilhelm Heinrich, a blind tenor and singing teacher who was well known in Boston, also organized recital series with a variety of collaborators in 1892, 1896, 1897, and 1903. Most of the programs were dominated by lieder.

73. "Vocal Chamber Concerts," *Boston Herald*, January 30, 1898, 31.

74. *King's Handbook of Boston* (Cambridge, MA: Moses King, 1878), 223.

75. "Miss Edmands and Mr. Heinrich," *Boston Journal*, April 14, 1898, 6.

76. Philip Hale, "Miss Marguerite Hall," 6.

77. Philip Hale, "Music in Boston" (March 30, 1898): 16; Philip Hale, "Miss Villa White's Singing," 8; "Miss White's Recital," *Boston Herald*, March 24, 1898, 6.

78. W., "The General Federation," *Evening Post* (New York), May 28, 1898, 16. Before serving two two-year terms as president of the National Federation of Women's Clubs (1894–1898), Ellen Henrotin co-founded Chicago's Friday Club, which focused on the arts and literature. From 1897 she was also a member of the Chicago Women's Club. See Mrs. J. C. Croly, *The History of the Woman's Club Movement in America*, 183–88.

79. None of the sources for the program provide English subtitles for the two Omaha Indian songs listed as "Hae-Thu-Ska Song," and as a result it is not possible to identify them. The program also omitted the names of the composers of "Maryland, My Maryland" and "The Bonny Blue Flag," perhaps because both were based on preexisting melodies.

80. "Clubs," *Courier* (Lincoln, NE), August 20, 1898, 5; Viola Price Franklin, "Echoes of the Biennial," 10.

81. Marian Wilson Kimber's study of Moore's career draws on material in Moore's scrapbooks, which are housed at the Missouri Historical Society Library and Research Center in St. Louis. These scrapbooks contain the program from White and Muldoon's recital. I am extremely grateful to Wilson Kimber for sharing a photograph of this document with me. The program was also printed in newspaper reports.

82. In an interview, Muldoon recalled that the conference program committee contacted her and requested that she be responsible for the African American part of the program. She confessed that prior to this invitation she had not researched these songs. This interview was published in the *Denver Times* and reprinted in "Musical Matters," *Courier-Journal* (Louisville, KY), June 16, 1898, 20.

83. "Folk Song of America." Marian Wilson Kimber kindly sent me a copy of this clipping from Moore's scrapbooks, held by the Missouri Historical Society Library and Research Cener, St. Louis. Neither the newspaper nor the date of publication is provided.

84. According to Edward T. James, "much of the credit for the strong feminist emphasis that characterized the Columbian Exposition" was due to Ellen Henrotin. She was intimately familiar with the presentations, putting in personal appearances at many and giving speeches. Edward T. James et al., *Notable American Women, 1607–1950: A Biographical Dictionary*, 2:182.

85. Root and White had not previously collaborated on a public performance, but given their reputations within the musical circles of Chicago they certainly would have known of each other. White appeared before the Amateur Musical Club in 1895 and 1896, when Root was the director of the club's chorus.

Notes to Chapter 6   257

86. The sessions were described in "Song Among Indians," *Chicago Tribune*, July 6, 1893, 4. Fletcher's, Fillmore's, and Krehbiel's presentations took place on the morning of July 5, and since Root presented a paper about teaching singing at the exposition during the following afternoon, he might have attended them. In the following years, Elson presented variants of his lecture in numerous cities. His research culminated in two books that expanded on his themes: *The National Music of America and Its Sources* and *The History of American Music*.

87. Helen Wheeler Bassett and Frederick Starr, eds., *The International Folk-Lore Congress of the World's Columbian Exposition*. The program for the concert is given on 426–36.

88. Alice C. Fletcher, *A Study of Omaha Indian Music*. Scholars have noted Fletcher's significance as well as the limitations of her assessment of the Omaha Indians' music and of Fillmore's arrangements. See, e.g., Crawford, *America's Musical Life*, 398–403; Michael Broyles, "Art Music from 1860 to 1920," 251–52; Hewitt Pantaleoni, "A Reconsideration of Fillmore Reconsidered," 217—28.

89. White's prepared remarks have not survived, but some of the newspaper reports recorded her main points. See, e.g., "Flower and Folk Songs," *Daily News* (Denver), June 25, 1898, 5. Marian Wilson Kimber's discussion of elocutionists' use of dialect places white women's performances of African American dialect in the context of their appropriation of a range of other dialects. Most of the performances she cites postdate White and Muldoon's lecture-recital. Wilson Kimber, *Elocutionists*, 109–49.

90. Bassett and Starr, *International Folk-Lore Congress*, 432. La Flesche also performed during Fletcher's presentation at the exposition. It is likely that White performed the same "Omaha Prayer" that he performed then.

91. George W. Cable, "Creole Slave Songs," 807–28. "Ah! Suzette" and "Pov' Piti Momzel Zizi" were arranged by Madame L. Lejeune.

92. Krehbiel also supplied the scores for the Creole songs that were performed during the Folk-Lore Congress's concert, and he advised the singer. Bassett and Starr, *International Folk-Lore Congress*, 435–36.

93. Krehbiel further explained his position in his 1914 *Afro-American Folksong: A Study in Racial and National Music*. This volume includes the three Creole numbers White performed. Krehbiel gave his exposition presentation in East Coast and midwestern cities from 1893 to 1897. Many of these included definitions of folksong and discussions of both European and American folksong. At least one report noted that not everyone agreed with Krehbiel's classification of songs by Blacks as American songs: "Entertainments," *Star Tribune* (Minneapolis), April 25, 1895, 6.

94. "Musical Matters," *Courier-Journal* (Louisville, KY), June 16, 1898, 20. Shadle explores these themes in relation to Dvořák in *Antonín Dvořák's* New World Symphony, 122–24.

95. She probably learned "Round About the Mountain," "Freely Go Marching," and "Some Come Cripple, Some Come Lame" from Hill, and it is likely that other songs also came from Hill. I am grateful to Josephine Wright for assisting me in locating these three songs in Krehbiel's *Afro-American Folksong* (63, 88, 158), where Hill is cited as the source. The provenance and authenticity for Muldoon's other songs cannot be traced.

258   Notes to Chapter 6

96. The federation formally adopted this song, whose lyrics were written by Anna J. Hamilton (1860–1922), as its patriotic song. It was said to be the only war song in which the words and music were written by women. Printed note accompanying White and Muldoon's recital program in Moore's scrapbook, Missouri Historical Society Library and Research Center, St. Louis. Hill also composed the melody to "Happy Birthday to You."

97. Hill signed her article as Johann Tonsor. Mildred Hill, "Negro Music," 119–22. Michael Beckerman discusses this article, Hill's life, and her contact with Dvořák in "'Rare in a Generation of Remarkable Women,'" 7–50.

98. "Folk-Song in America," *Courier-Journal* (Louisville), April 28, 1893, 7. Muldoon was living in Louisville at this time and might have attended this event. Hill attended the 1893 exposition in Chicago, where her sister Patty Smith Hill (1868–1946) was honored for her work with Louisville kindergarten children. Mildred's article "Unconscious Composers" (p. 1) indicates that she was familiar with topics discussed at the exposition's Musical Congress.

99. Hill attended at least one reception at the federation's conference in Louisville, and given Henrotin's participation in the organization of Chicago's exposition, she likely knew of Hill's work. White might have learned of Hill from Cady, who taught Hill sometime around 1892 and encouraged her composing.

100. Muldoon was born after the 1863 Emancipation Proclamation, but it is possible that her family's household help were former slaves. Her father Michael, an Irish immigrant, owned the Muldoon Monument Company, which reportedly made 90 percent of the Confederate monuments in the South after the Civil War. "Madison, GA's Historic Cemeteries," https://www.madisoncemeteries.com/copy-of-artisan-muldoon.

101. Hill, "Unconscious Composers," 1. Part of this article responds to Dvořák's much-cited 1895 article in *Harper's Magazine* that discusses the state of music in America. In so doing he suggests that American music is indebted to "all the races that are commingled in this great country" (433), a theme that seems to be reflected in Moore's statement about White and Muldoon's recital and comments attributed to White.

102. Frederick Douglass, *My Bondage and My Freedom*, 462. For a discussion of Foster's relation to slavery that positions his songs in relation to the commercial marketplace rather than as reflecting his personal politics and that considers this song, see Steven Saunders, "The Social Agenda of Stephen Foster's Plantation Melodies," 277, 279, 282–85.

103. Other performances at the conference, which were accorded less press coverage, were given by music club choruses or by women soloists. The program suggests that very few men were involved in these concerts. "Biennial Arrivals," *Daily News* (Denver), June 19, 1898, 5. This preference for women performers also informed the process of selecting artists to appear before some music clubs. Linda Whitesitt, "Women as 'Keepers of Culture,'" 68.

104. "The Slate Made Up: Folksongs," *Denver Post*, June 26, 1898, 9.

105. "Musical Matters," *Courier Journal* (Louisville, KY), June 26, 1898, sec. 3, p. 4. Hill might have influenced Muldoon's perceptions. In "Unconscious Composers," Hill claimed that Dvořák, who otherwise lauded Native American music, stated, "But then

Notes to Chapter 6   259

I was taken to hear some red men sing, and it was horrible." Hill appears to endorse this assessment. Beckerman was unable to locate the source of this quote or any similar statements by the composer. Beckerman, "'Rare in a Generation,'" 44.

106. The fundraiser, where White performed German folksongs, was held at the Jamaica Plain Unitarian parish house. "Local Varieties," *Boston Herald*, February 14, 1894, 6.

107. The National Congress of Music ran from June 30 to July 4. "Music," *Chicago Tribune*, June 5, 1898, 36. Women's clubs in Omaha invited women traveling to the Denver federation conference to attend the "Omaha Prelude" on June 18 and 19, which was also part of the Trans-Mississippi Exposition. This event, which was attended by about one thousand women, including Henrotin, featured various presentations that were not on music and an evening concert by the Thomas Orchestra. Martha Scott Anderson, "They're in Denver," 5.

108. Barbara Sue Lamb, "Thursday Musical in the Musical Life of Minneapolis," 145. Whitney Ann Henderson ("'History of the Ladies Musical Club,'" 115) documents presentations about Native American music for the Seattle Musical Club beginning in 1904 with Farwell's national tour lecture, "Music and Myths of the American Indian." According to her, Farwell promoted the research of Fletcher, La Flesche, Natalie Curtis (1875–1921), and Densmore. In 1917 Marcella Sembrich began programing an Omaha Indian song introduced to her by Densmore. Michael V. Pisani describes Farwell's lectures, his interest in American Indian music, and his related compositions in "Hiawatha to Wa-Wan: Musical Boston and the Uses of Native American Lore," 46–48.

109. Margaret B. Harvey, "Musical Studies," 12.

110. "A New Fad," *Worcester (MA) Daily Spy*, February 28, 1897, 5. Murphy's 1899 study includes transcriptions of five African American melodies. Jeanette Robinson Murphy, "The Survival of African Music in America," 660–72.

111. The conference, which was held in Peterboro, New Hampshire, was reported in various papers including the *Tampa Tribune* ("Many Interested in National Music Convention," June 28, 1919, 8). During her recitals, Stevens wore a different costume for each group of songs. She dressed in tribal garb of a Native American that had been made for her by tribal women for the selection titled "Aboriginal Tribal Indian Melodies." In contrast, she dressed as an upper-class white woman for the selection titled "Old Negro Melodies and Plantation Songs." While this choice might be viewed as preferable to the "mammy" costumes and blackface employed by others, it fails to acknowledge that the people who created and first sang these songs would not have had the finances for such clothing. *Musical Monitor* (Official Magazine of the National Federation of Musical Clubs) 10 (October 1920): 462.

112. Two of White's letters to the founder of Christian Science, Mary Baker Eddy (1821–1910), were published. "Letter to Mrs. Eddy" and "Christmas Greetings to Mrs. Eddy," *Christian Science Journal* 18 (1900–1901): 169–70, 694. In all, the Mary Baker Eddy Library of the Church of Christ Science in Boston holds thirteen handwritten letters from White to Eddy. I am most grateful for the assistance of Nancy Dalrymple, a relative of White's, who obtained copies of these letters. Many of White's colleagues and friends also practiced this faith. From around 1911, White's companion was Johanna Bruno (ca. 1857–1934), a fellow Christian Scientist whom she had met in Germany. Bruno is believed

260   Notes to Chapter 6

to have been one of the first German adherents to Christian Science in Berlin, and she subsequently became a healer (Clifford P. Smith, "Early History of Christian Science in Germany"). On August 5, 1897, while in Berlin, White wrote to Eddy describing Bruno's interest in the church (Mary Baker Eddy Library, TC#420). Bruno immigrated to the United States in 1911; during the boat trip from Belgium, she was accompanied by White. The two women lived together in Boston and then in Portland until the early 1920s. Numerous other contemporary musicians were Christian Scientists. Notably, although raised in a Quaker family, David Bispham became a Christian Scientist. "Mrs. Eddy's Cult to Change World, Asserts Singer," *Denver Post*, November 6, 1908, 11.

113. Villa Whitney White, "The Educational Value of Vocal Study from the Ethical View-Point," 176–79.

114. Flora Bauer, "Portland," 34.

115. [Advertisement], *Sunday Oregonian* (Portland), August 31, 1913, sec. 1, p. 4; "Music," *Sunday Oregonian*, September 7, 1913, sec. 3, p. 9.

Chapter 7. David Bispham and the Heyday of Song Recitals

1. "David Bispham Dies in His 65th Year," *New York Times*, October 3, 1921, 13. According to Bispham, both Heinrich and Henschel discouraged him from pursuing a career as a singer. However, Huneker contradicted this statement, claiming that Heinrich had coached both himself and Bispham and had recognized Bispham's promise. See Huneker's review of Bispham's *Quaker Singer's Recollections*, reprinted in Huneker, *Americans in the Arts*, 86. The *St. Matthew Passion* performance was led by Michael Cross. "Passion Music," *Philadelphia Times*, March 8, 1885, 3.

2. In 1900, with Bispham's encouragement, Shakespeare toured the United States, where his *Art of Singing* (1898) was reissued numerous times.

3. Bispham, *Recollections*, 49.

4. See, e.g., "The Week at Butte's Theaters," *Butte Daily Post* (Montana), March 20, 1897, 3.

5. Bispham, *Recollections*, 302–3, 347. Bispham was an avid recordkeeper. After his death, the New York Public Library Music Division acquired many of his papers and scores, but these materials were separated and placed in different parts of the collection. Although some of his press clippings, programs, photographs, and scores are available to researchers, his personal records documenting all of his performances were not catalogued and cannot be located.

6. The final chapters of Bispham's *Recollections* describe many of the theatrical productions he was involved in during his last years. He reported that, in all, he acted in twenty-five plays (282).

7. The Metropolitan Opera Archives hold records of Bispham's performances with this company: http://archives.metoperafamily.org/archives/frame.htm.

8. [Untitled anecdote], *Emporia (KS) Gazette*, November 4, 1909, 5; "Reception to David Bispham," *Music News* 7 (April 2, 1915): 35. The photograph shown in figure 7.1 can be accessed at https://ark.digitalcommonwealth.org/ark:/50959/vh53x540g.

9. "Music and Musicians," *San Francisco Call*, April 16, 1898, 6.

10. Gienow-Hecht, *Sound Diplomacy*, 137.

11. "A Memorable Event in Musical Circles," *Tennessean* (Nashville), December 26, 1897, 4.

12. Rupert Hughes, "American Concert Singers V," 402, 405–6.

13. Ivan Lavretsky, "New York Musical Season: Song Recitals," *Pittsfield (MA) Sun*, February 16, 1899, 6. For information about the situation in Europe see Kravitt, *Lied*, 20–22.

14. During previous tours, Lehmann's events were titled concerts and emphasized operatic arias rather than lieder.

15. Finck, *Song and Song Writers*, vi.

16. Advertisement, *New York Tribune*, January 25, 1900, 10.

17. "David Bispham to Sing in Hays," *Hays (KS) Free Press*, August 22, 1908, 1. Artists' fees had increased since the mid-1890s. In 1896 Heinrich's fee for a performance at the Fortnightly Musical Club in Cleveland was $300. Linda Whitesitt, "Women as 'Keepers of Culture,'" 68.

18. "Nordica Here One Year Ago," *Arizona Republican* (Phoenix), May 12, 1914, 9.

19. "An Extraordinary Exhibition," *Musical Courier* 40, no. 6 (February 7, 1900): 24–25.

20. "Music," *New York Times Illustrated Magazine*, April 9, 1899, 34. This performance was one of Nordica's first ventures into the recital scene.

21. Philip Hale, "Miss Little and Mr. Meyn," 5. Lena Little sang Fauré's "Au cimetière" (op. 51, no. 2) and "Clair de lune" (op. 46, no. 2) in Boston in 1892, the same year as the first US performance of the composer's Violin Sonata no. 1 (op. 13). Heather de Savage considers 1892 as the start of the American reception of this composer: "'Under the Gallic Spell': Boston's Embrace of Gabriel Fauré, 1892–1924," 258–59.

22. Whereas Hale, "Music in Boston" (1901): 5, complained of singers with faulty diction, a reviewer of a New York recital praised Hast's performances in German and English but nevertheless reported the audience's preference for the songs he sang in English. "Gregory Hast's Farewell Recital," *Musical Courier* 44, no. 5 (January 29, 1902): 39.

23. For a sample of a club performance in which songs from various countries were sung in English translation, see "Social and Personal," *Lexington (KY) Leader*, June 8, 1902, sec. 2, 4.

24. "Amusements," *New York Tribune*, January 10, 1897, 11.

25. [Attributed to Krehbiel], "Two Song Recitals," *New York Tribune*, January 13, 1897, 7.

26. "Music," *Athenaeum* no. 3602 (November 7, 1896): 644; "Lilli Lehmann's Recital" and "Mr. Bispham's Concert," *New York Times*, January 13, 1897, 5. See also "Lehmann's Song Recital" and "Song Recital by Mr. David Bispham," *Sun* (New York), January 13, 1897, 7.

27. "Second Bispham Recital," *Musical Courier* 34, no. 4 (January 27, 1897): 17.

28. Hall had collaborated with Bispham in London; she appeared in some of his first

recitals in the United States in 1896 and continued to appear in some of his other recitals at least through 1905.

29. [William James Henderson], "Mr. Bispham's Recitals: The Whole of Brahms's 'Die Schoene Magelone' Excellently Given at the Opera House," 6.

30. "St. James Hall," *Morning Post* (London), May 11, 1897, 3.

31. In London, Bispham collaborated with Fuller-Maitland and members of the Dolmetsch family in "Mr. David Bispham's Concert Consisting of Music of Olden Times," St. James Hall, December 10, 1895. Program preserved in the [Six Books of Words of Concerts Given by D. Bispham], British Library, Shelfmark d. 488.c.(3.), 1895. Bispham did not give such historical programs in the United States.

32. "Metropolitan Concert," *Brooklyn Daily Eagle*, February 14, 1898, 7; "David Bispham," *Democrat and Chronicle* (Rochester, NY), February 13, 1900, 11.

33. Liza Lehmann, *The Life of Liza Lehmann*, 77; "The Singers," *Musical America* 1, no. 11 (December 17, 1898): 14.

34. Edward Dickinson, "In a Persian Garden," 136–37.

35. "Song Cycles," *Etude* 19 (1901): 151.

36. "Events of the Week," *New York Times*, November 28, 1897, 14. Notices describing performances of the drama paid little attention to the play itself, though some referenced its sentimental character. One of the fiercest critiques of the quality of the writing appeared in London's *Musical Standard* and was reprinted in "News in General," *Buffalo Sunday Morning News*, July 17, 1898, 14.

37. "Return of Mme. Sembrich," *New York Times*, October 27, 1897, 7.

38. "Miscellaneous Concert Programme," *San Francisco Call*, March 14, 1900, 9.

39. The mixed responses of the critics are sampled in "Bispham Recital," *Musical Courier* 37, no. 25 (December 21, 1897): 16; [William James Henderson], "Mr. Bispham's Recitals: Third of His Series at the Carnegie Lyceum," 7. The critics writing in *Musical America* seemed to be harsher than others; see, e.g., John C. Freund, "The Passing Show," 11, and Warren Davenport, "Musical Boston," 29.

40. "Mendelssohn Hall," *New Yorker Staats-Zeitung*, December 16, 1898, 8; Louis C. Elson, "Interesting Song Recital by David Bispham," 4.

41. Philip Hale, "Music and Musicians," 26.

42. For an advertisement of the series, see *Times Herald* (Port Huron, MI), August 26, 1912, 6. Nordica and Bispham's joint recital in Houston was reviewed by Wille Hutcheson, "Amusements," 8. For notices about Nordica's and Bispham's individual recitals in Fort Worth see Kitty Barry, "Music Festival Big Success; Bispham to Return Here," 9.

43. "Musicians and Their Work," *Los Angeles Herald*, December 20, 1908, 109.

44. "Schumann-Heink Success," *Buffalo Sunday Morning News*, December 11, 1910, 8; "Of Music and Musicians," *Springfield (MA) Republican*, March 18, 1906, 20.

45. "David Bispham, the Artist," *Tampa Tribune*, December 10, 1907, 6.

46. "David Bispham Coming," *Republican Gazette* (Lima, OH), September 26 (morning), 1911, 8. The precise number of Bispham's appearances before clubs is unknown because his records are lost and many newspapers do not identify the hosts or sponsors of recitals.

47. Bispham, *Recollections*, 347–48.

48. "David Bispham at the Burtis," *Daily Times* (Davenport, IA), December 2, 1905, 20. Although neither the program preserved at the New York Public Library nor the review names the pianist, both state that an Everett piano was used, and the program gives Bispham's endorsement of this company—yet another way singers profited from recitals. Occasionally a newspaper advertisement carried somewhat similar endorsements. An advertisement for a local piano dealer claimed that its Steinway grand had been used at one of Bispham's concerts: *Idaho Statesman* (Boise), March 29, 1905, 5.

49. "Bispham's Recital," *Brooklyn Daily Eagle*, November 8, 1907, 12.

50. McVeigh and Weber, "From the Benefit Concert to the Solo Song Recital in London," 180.

51. Tunbridge, *Singing in the Age of Anxiety*, 168.

52. For excerpts from reviews of both performances see "Bispham Recital," *Musical Courier* 37, no. 25 (December 21, 1898): 16.

53. "Mr. David Bispham's Song Recital at Mendelssohn Hall," *New York Times*, December 8, 1899, 6.

54. For positive and negative reviews of Bispham's performances of *Dichterliebe* see, respectively, "David Bispham Delights Jordan Hall Audience," *Boston Journal*, October 26, 1904, 6; "Bispham Gives Song Recitals," *New York Press*, November 1, 1904, n.p.

55. Loges, "Detours on a Winter's Journey," 26. Wilhelm Heinrich and the contralto Louise Rollwagen (1854–1923) had performed *Winterreise* in Boston in 1892 and 1897; in both instances each sang half of the cycle.

56. Glenn Dillard Gunn, "Bispham's Third Recital," 6; "Last Bispham Recital," *New York Times*, December 1, 1904, 9. Victor Maurel also prefaced his performances with brief remarks about his repertoire. See Ivan Lavretsky, "New York Musical Season: Song Recitals," 1.

57. Nevertheless, Gadski pleased her large audience of admirers. "Mme. Gadski's First Recital," *New York Tribune*, November 11, 1904, 7.

58. "Mme. Sembrich's Song Recital," *New York Times*, November 13, 1904, 20.

59. "Frau Sembrich's Recital," *New Yorker Staats-Zeitung*, November 13, 1904, 38.

60. "Bispham's Recital," *New Yorker Staats-Zeitung*, November 22, 1904, 2.

61. "Bispham Closes Song Cycles," *New York Press*, December 1, 1904, 6.

62. "Mr. Bispham's Recital," *Boston Herald*, November 8, 1904, 8.

63. "People Talked About," *Leslie's Weekly* (New York) 99, no. 2568 (November 24, 1904): 481; "Society," *Chicago Tribune*, January 15, 1905, 25.

64. "The Shakespeare Cycle," *Allentown (PA) Leader*, January 3, 1906, 1.

65. The program notes for this performance of *Enoch Arden* were unusually detailed. They introduced the work and provided musical examples of its main themes and brief explanations of what they represented. Program held by the New York Public Library Music Division, *MBD (Un-Cat) Bispham.

66. "David Bispham Talks on Melodrama," *Inter Ocean* (Chicago), Magazine, March 12, 1905, 7. A series of photographs demonstrates the theatrical techniques Bispham brought to performances of Bergh's *Raven*. Edward Kravitt, "Theatrical Declamation and German Vocal Music of the Late Romantic Period," 176.

67. Margaret Gordon, "Entertainment Ideas for Teachers," 62. An article about melodramas in *Good Housekeeping* that highlighted Bispham's performances of *Enoch Arden* likewise demonstrates women's interest in this genre. Gustave Kobbé, "Reciting to Music," 218.

68. In an 1896 recital in Boston that was commended for highlighting works that were not well known, Eliot Hubbard gave four songs by Wolf. "Mr. Hubbard's Recital," *Boston Daily Advertiser*, December 1 (morning), 1896, 5. A local teacher in Iowa likewise gave three of Wolf's songs (during a recital in a private home) before Bispham took up this composer. "Saturday Musical Recital," *Davenport Morning Star*, June 14, 1901, 8. This suggests that the works were more widely disseminated in the country than Bispham acknowledged.

69. "Musical," *Brooklyn Times Union*, October 23, 1903, 2. In this recital Bispham collaborated with the contralto Louise Homer (1871–1947), another soloist at the Metropolitan Opera. She performed songs by Saint-Saëns and Lalo and five songs by her husband Sidney Homer (1864–1953), who accompanied her.

70. "The Bispham Recital," *Evening Star*, January 27, 1904, 16; Bispham, *Recollections*, 306.

71. "New York," *Pittsburgh Press*, January 6, 1906, 6.

72. Gilibert was a French singer working at the Metropolitan Opera. He performed in collaborative recitals in New York and Boston and often sang French works. In 1903 he recorded Fauré's "Les Rameaux" for Columbia.

73. "Famous Bispham Coming to Boise," *Idaho Statesman* (Boise), March 18, 1905, n.p.

74. J. Van Broekhoven lists many of the recitalists who were programming American repertoire in "American Songs," 19.

75. Tunbridge, *Singing in the Age of Anxiety*, 22–29. For more on Schumann-Heink see E. Douglas Bomberger, "'Was Ever Woman so Tortured and so Tried?': Ernestine Schumann-Heink and the German-American Experience in World War I," paper presented at the Conference of the Society of American Music, 2020; Bomberger, *Making Music American: 1917 and the Transformation of Culture*, 88–89, 129–30.

76. C. L. G., "Music," *Guardian* (London), May 12, 1897, 739.

77. Bispham frequently sang "The Mad Dog" from *The Vicar* in his subsequent recitals. Liza Lehmann, *The Life of Liza Lehmann*, 103–14. One of the articles denying reports of Bispham's retirement from recitals is accompanied by a list of dramatic works that were being planned for the singer. "David Bispham's Plans," *Philadelphia Inquirer*, October 17, 1904, 3.

78. In contrast, some younger artists explored new European works as well as pieces by Americans. In 1911 Alma Gluck's (1884–1938) Carnegie Hall recital program included works by Schoenberg, Balakirev, Paladilhe, Mahler, Anton Arensky (1861–1906), Alberto Bimboni (1882–1960), Henri Duparc (1848–1933), Charles Seeger (1886–1979), Erich J. Wolff (1874–1913), and Kurt Schindler (1882–1935). Carnegie Hall, Digital Archives, CH 1107091 and 1107093.

79. "Noted Musician Advocates American Music for Americans," *Los Angeles Herald*, April 28, 1909, 11.

Notes to Chapter 7   265

80. "White House Musicale: A Brilliant Affair," *Washington Times*, January 9, 1904, 7. A transcription and arrangement of the Zuni song "Sunrise Call" was published in Carlos Troyer's *Traditional Songs of the Zuñi Indians*. It is likely that Bispham gave the version of the Ojibway song "Absence and Longing" with harmonies and English words supplied by Frederick Burton (1861–1909). Krehbiel seemed not to be convinced of this version and could not find "anything of the Indian Spirit" in it. Henry Krehbiel, "Indian Melodies," 2. The cultural implications of the appropriations made by Indianist composers such as Farwell are discussed in Tara Browner, "'Breathing the Indian Spirit.'"

81. Bispham, *Recollections*, 295; "Mr. Bispham's Second Recital," *New York Times*, February 2, 1902, 10.

82. Jean E. Snyder, *Harry T. Burleigh: From the Spiritual to the Harlem Renaissance*, 258. Schumann-Heink's music collection and personal materials, including her score of "Mammy's Li'l Baby," are housed at the Special Collections of the Claremont Colleges Library. https://ccdl.claremont.edu/digital/collection/p15831coll6.

83. Nelda Hewitt Stevens, "Singers Desecrate Negro Music by False Interpretations," 47. Stevens's comments were reprinted in several newspapers.

84. "Bandanna Ballads," *Ladies' Home Journal* 17, no. 5 (April 1900): 9. Maria Weeden published under her middle name as Howard Weeden. Born in Huntsville, Alabama, she published numerous books of poetry. Her paintings of African Americans were exhibited in Berlin and Paris.

85. "Bispham in Race Across Continent," *Music News* 4, no. 35 (August 30, 1912): 20.

86. "David Bispham Gains Applause in Favorite Songs at Orpheum," *San Francisco Examiner*, April 13, 1914, 7. Bispham performed in the Keith and Orpheum circuit vaudevilles in 1913, 1914, and 1916. His vaudeville numbers consisted of selections from operas, including an excerpt from *I Pagliacci*, as well as popular ballads such as "Danny Deever" and "Drink to Me Only with Thine Eyes." On some occasions he performed a couple of lieder or the melodrama on Poe's "The Raven," which the composer Arthur Bergh (1882–1962) dedicated to him. Although critics were not impressed with his talk about American songs and singing in English, audiences appreciated his singing. "The Vaudeville Lure," *Sacramento Bee*, July 26, 1913, 21.

87. "The News Briefly Told," *McCook (NE) Tribune*, July 28, 1899, 3.

88. Bispham, *Recollections*, 287.

89. [Advertisement], *Sydney Morning Herald*, June 12, 1913, 2.

90. Compare an advertisement for a Bispham recital with the program that was given in a review. "American Songs," *Chattanooga News*, January 31, 1906, 6; "Great Baritone Receives Ovation," *Chattanooga News*, February 16, 1906, 6.

91. On Burleigh's adoption of Native American songs see "Of Interest to Society," *Yonkers (NY) Herald*, May 11, 1903, 3. For one of his programs combining lieder and African American songs, see "Music and Monday Club," *Courier-News* (Bridgewater, New Jersey), April 26, 1901, 1.

92. "Refuses to Play For 'Rag' Dances," *Arkansas Gazette*, August 24, 1913, 8. The statements Bispham made during his Carnegie Hall recital were reported in "American Music Isn't Bad," *Union-Banner* (Clanton, AL), February 8, 1912, 8. A reviewer of his

recital in Waco described the singer's aversion to rags as "applaudable": M. M. H., "The Bispham Concert," *Waco Morning News*, March 20, 1913, 2.

93. Matthew Mooney, "An 'Invasion of Vulgarity': American Popular Music and Modernity in Print Media Discourse, 1900–1915."

94. "David Bispham's Recital," *Brooklyn Daily Eagle*, March 17, 1919, 6; Walter C. Daniel, "Vachel Lindsay, W. E. B. Du Bois and *The Crisis*," 290–92. A. Walter Kramer ignored the poem's racism when he penned a highly positive review of the songs: "Arthur Bergh's New Cycle," 31. Excerpts of the review were reprinted in newspapers including "Set to Music," Daily *Illinois State Register*, September 13, 1918, 4.

95. "'An Hour of Music,' with the Students of Dudley Buck," *Musical America* 29, no. 17 (February 22, 1919): 35.

96. "Song and Violin Recital," *Brooklyn Daily Eagle*, December 23, 1898, 5. Bispham usually performed "All the World's a Stage" with piano accompaniment, though Huss also created an orchestral version. The work was not published until 1926, five years after Bispham's death. Huss's biographer suggested that this might have been to preserve Bispham's exclusive association with it. Gary A. Greene, *Henry Holden Huss: An American Composer's Life*, 61.

97. M. B., "Bispham in Buffalo," *Musical America* 6, no. 25 (November 2, 1907): 2.

98. Walter Damrosch, *My Musical Life*, 160.

99. For a recital that included Herbert's "Outlaw" and well-known lieder see "Mr. Gareissen's Second Recital," *Evening Star* (Washington, DC), April 21, 1905, 11.

100. "Music in New York," *Hartford (CT) Courant*, November 8, 1911, 19.

101. Max Heinrich and some of the other composers whose works Bispham sang are not listed in Judith E. Carman et al., *Art Song in the United States, 1759–1999: An Annotated Bibliography*.

102. Lien, "Against the Grain," 310–15.

103. According to Charles Hamm, this was the case with De Koven's "Oh, Promise Me" (1889): *Yesterdays*, 321–22.

104. When *Musical America* had twenty-six "leading concert artists" (including Bispham) list the ten songs by Americans that they most liked to sing, none of them listed Tin Pan Alley songs. Only a couple of singers listed light, popular numbers such as Nevin's "The Rosary," although they were often programmed. "Their Ten Favorite American Songs," *Musical America* 22, no. 24 (October 16, 1915): 3–5.

105. [Advertisement], *Morning Post* (London), May 9, 1895, 1.

106. "Notes of Coming Music," *Brooklyn Daily Eagle*, October 24, 1897, 21.

107. [Advertisement], *Morning Post* (London), June 25, 1892, 1.

108. New York Public Library, Music Division, *MBD (Steinway Hall Programme). In 1885 the Cincinnati publisher Church released a simplified English version of Clara Schumann's song under the title "Lov'st Thou for Beauty." Personal communication from Jonathan Kroeger, June 8, 2020.

109. "Easter Concerts," *Chicago Tribune*, March 31, 1902, [5]; "Amateur Musical Club," *Inter Ocean* (Chicago), January 12, 1897, 10.

110. Bispham, *Recollections*, 350; and *Celebrated Recital Songs*, viii.

Notes to Chapter 7   267

111. Carrie Jacobs Bond, *The Roads of Melody*, 135–42; Glenn Dillard Gunn, "Bispham in Splendid Voice," 4; "Music," *Chicago Tribune*, April 2, 1905, 29–30; "News of the Theaters," *Chicago Tribune*, April 3, 1905, 8.

112. "American Girl's Compositions Receive Hearing," *Musical America* 7, no. 22 (April 11, 1908): 4. The misogyny in this title is typical of the era and demonstrates the ways women composers were treated differently from the boys, despite their success.

113. "David Bispham to Sing," *Inter Ocean* (Chicago), November 26, 1905, 35; "David Bispham Discovers the Vocal Compositions of Eleanor Everest Freer," *Sun* (New York), December 27, 1905, 4. Schumann-Heink's performances of Mary Turner Salter's (1856–1938) "The Cry of Rachel" elicited a similar disparity between the audiences' enthusiasm and the critics' negative assessments of the quality of the music. See Marian Wilson Kimber, "Listening to Loss in 'The Cry of Rachel.'"

114. Finck and Foote observed that the popularity of songs was greatly influenced by concert singers. Finck, *Song and Song Writers*, 233.

115. Christopher Reynolds, "Documenting the Zenith of Women Song Composers," 673, 674, 685.

116. Peter Dickinson, H. Wiley Hitchcock, and Keith E. Clifton, "Art Song," 1:211.

117. Bispham, *Recollections*, 315.

118. Ibid., 282.

119. Ibid., 349; David Bispham, preface to *Celebrated Recital Songs*. Bispham's views are briefly reiterated in "The Gender of Songs," *Musical America* 31, no. 19 (March 6, 1920), 24.

120. See the selection of songs offered as appropriate for a mezzo-soprano in "Musical Helps and Hints," *Ladies' Home Journal* 13, no. 10 (September 1896): 29.

121. "Mr. Bispham's Recital," *Sun* (New York), February 22, 1898, 7; "Famous Bispham Coming to Boise," *Idaho Statesman*, March 18, 1905, 7.

122. "Lights Will Be Lowered as David Bispham Sings," *Dayton Herald*, January 21, 1913, 7.

123. "Musicians and Their Work," *Los Angeles Herald*, December 20, 1908, 109; "Concerning David Bispham," *Des Moines Register*, November 5, 1911, 4.

124. Kristen M. Turner, "'A Joyous Star-Spangled-Bannerism,'" 225.

125. Mathews, *A Hundred Years of Music in America*, 169. In the following years, several journals ran articles exploring various issues related to singing in English. See, e.g., Florenza D'Arona, "Is English a Musical Language?" Francis Rogers's "The Use of English in Singing" was endorsed by *Musical America* 9, no. 8 (1909): 16.

126. David Bispham, "Singing and the King's English," 261–62; "Foremost Exponent of English Song Undertakes Extended Vaudeville Tour," *Musical-Monitor and World* 3, no. 7 (March 1914): 182.

127. "Incorporate to Give English Opera Comique," *New York Tribune*, March 5, 1917, 11.

128. American Opera Society of Chicago, Bispham Memorial Medal, https://american operasocietyofchicago.org/bispham-memorial-medal.

129. "David Bispham Giving Summer Lecture Series" [in Connecticut], *San Diego Union*, August 15, 1909, 13; David Bispham, "Music as a Factor in National Life," 799.

130. *The Bispham Album of Classical Songs: Being Ten Songs by Schubert and Schumann* was briefly reviewed in the *Musical Times* and advertised on the back pages of some of the journal's 1898 and 1903 issues. "Reviews," *Musical Times* 39 no. 659 (January 1, 1898): 33. Bispham's albums of solo songs are listed in the bibliography. Bispham also published an anthology of popular choruses: *The David Bispham Song Book*.

131. Discographies of Gadski, Schumann-Heink, Bispham, and others are available at *Discography of American Historical Recordings*, https://adp.library.ucsb.edu/index.php.

132. "Through Our Own Opera Glasses," *Baltimore Sun*, July 14, 1918, 34.

133. "Valuable Aid Given by Many Famous Singers to Help Launch the Third Loan," *Boston Herald*, May 5, 1918, 17.

134. "Bispham," *Musical America* 26, no. 20 (September 15, 1917): 18.

135. "David Bispham's Son, War Victim," *Dayton (OH) Daily News*, November 11, 1917, 37.

136. "Teach Our National Anthem's Words," *Musician* 24, no. 1 (January 1919): 43.

137. Gavin James Campbell does not discuss Bispham or lieder, but he surveys the activities of the social reformers who voiced ideas similar to Bispham's. "'A Higher Mission Than Merely to Please the Ear': Music and Social Reform in America, 1900–1925," 259–86.

138. Bispham, "Music as a Factor in National Life," 799; see also 791 and 797.

Epilogue

1. Henry Finck, "The Song Recital," B-6.

2. In 1919, while on one of these tours, Julia Heinrich was killed at a railway station in Hammond, Louisiana. She was hit by a piece of debris that was launched into the air by a passing train. Due to the unusual nature of the accident, her death was reported in newspapers throughout the country. "Noted Singer Is Killed at Hammond," *Town Talk* (Alexandria, LA), September 18, 1919, 1.

3. Jean Forsyth, "A Singing Student in London," 389–90.

4. This collection included well-known songs by Schubert, Schumann, Franz, Rubinstein, Jensen, Brahms, Tchaikovsky, Grieg, Wolf, and Strauss.

5. William Weber, "The History of Musical Canon," 340.

6. Art Song Central lists some of the titles in The Musicians Library and includes hotlinks to digitized volumes. https://artsongcentral.com/2008/the-musicians-library -oliver-ditson/. The introductions to these volumes varied in content. Those by Finck provide the greatest amount of information about a composer's songs and their reception. Most others, however, give only a biography and succinct overview of the composer's songwriting style.

7. Mathews's article was excerpted in "Schumann's Music," *Chicago Tribune*, May 23, 1875, 3. Caroline Pettinos Hall's critiques of Schumann's songs are typical of those who were concerned about his writing for the voice; see her "Schumann's Songs," 10.

8. Elson, *History of German Song*, 208.

9. As cited in Beatrix Borchard, "The Concert Hall as a Gender-Neutral Space," 139.

10. William Foster Apthorp, *Fifty Songs by Robert Franz*, xvii. There was, however,

sufficient interest in Franz that Schirmer also published an anthology of his songs in its Golden Treasury of Music series, with Krehbiel supplying an introductory essay. Robert Franz, *A Collection of Sixty-Two Songs with Piano Accompaniment*.

11. Elson, *History of German Song*, 206. As Schubert and Schumann lieder rose in popularity and as singers began to explore French repertoire, England also witnessed a decline in the number of performances of Mendelssohn's songs and the publication of his scores. Melissa Evelyn Givens, "The Wings of Song Stilled: The Rise and Decline of Felix Mendelssohn's Lieder in London," 78–79.

12. "Schumann-Heink's Recital," *New York Times*, November 7, 1909, 13.

13. Daniel Cavicchi, *Listening and Longing: Music Lovers in the Age of Barnum*, 144.

14. This was the case with the score of Schubert's "Hark, Hark! The Lark!" that was published in Helen Kendrick Johnson, *The World's Best Music: Famous Songs and Those Who Made Them*, 3:785.

15. For an example of this type of programming, see Schumann-Heink's program for a recital at the Academy of Music for the benefit of the Union Protestant Infirmary. "Like Grand Opera Night: Madame Schumann-Heink's Recital a Great Success," *Baltimore Sun*, May 11, 1901, 7.

16. There was a similar ossification of arias by Handel such as "Where'er You Walk" and "O Ruddier Than the Cherry," which were also simultaneously popular and high art.

17. All the citations of songs in Henderson's section on song form are lieder (*What Is Good Music?*, 75–78). In addition, he asserted that "Schubert's art songs went side by side with Beethoven's symphonies in preaching the gospel of freedom from formalism and led the way to the forms of Schumann and Liszt" (65–66).

18. Michael Broyles, *Beethoven in America*; Stevenson, "Schubert in America"; Reich, "Robert Schumann's Music in New York City."

19. See, e.g., E. Douglas Bomberger, *Making Music American: 1917 and the Transformation of Culture*, esp. chap. 11; Horowitz, *Wagner Nights*, 196–301; Burrage, *Karl Muck Scandal*.

20. "Singing American Songs," *Musical Courier* 75, no. 19 (November 8, 1917): 20. According to this editorial, Americans who studied abroad were not trained to sing American songs, and this discouraged them from exploring this repertoire.

21. "Against Boycotting German 'Lieder,'" *Musical America* 26, no. 12 (July 21, 1917): 20. This article was reprinted in papers as far afield as Ardmore, Oklahoma.

22. "Happenings of Interest in the Concert World," *New York Daily Tribune*, April 28, 1918, sec. iv, 2.

23. W. J. Henderson, "Rising Tide of Sentiment Against German Music," 8.

24. "Idol of Soldiers Is Singer of Old," *Tribune* (Scranton, PA), April 12, 1918, 11. In some cases concert organizers told Schumann-Heink not to sing lieder, even ones in English. Bomberger, *Making Music American*, 184.

25. Mrs. David H. Barnes, "In Society's Realm," 19.

26. "All American Concert," *Times Union* (Brooklyn), February 5, 1916, 8.

27. This recital was at the Brooklyn Academy of Music. "Song Recital by Mr. David Bispham," *Brooklyn Life*, April 13, 1918, 5.

28. "Sabbatarians' Protest Has Amusing Results," *News-Journal* (Lancaster, PA), February 23, 1918, 5.

29. Bertram Taylor, "Matters of Musical Interest," 7.

30. "French Song Recital," *Boston Globe*, March 10, 1904, 3; "Mm. Marius's Recital," *New York Times*, January 13, 1903, 9; "M. Gilibert's Recital," *Hartford (CT) Courant*, March 24, 1908, 7.

31. Kurt Schindler, ed., *A Century of Russian Song from Glinka to Rachmaninoff*; Kurt Schindler, ed., *Masters of Russian Song*. Ditson's two-volume anthology *Modern Russian Songs* appeared after the war, and, as with the company's volume of Wolf's songs, it was edited by the English critic Ernest Newman.

32. "Programmes for the Week," *New York Tribune*, February 10, 1918, sec. 4, p. 2.

33. While noting the importance of the recording industry, David Gramit discusses the marginalized status of the lied at the end of the twentieth century in terms of multinational capitalism and globalization. "The Circulation of the Lied: The Double Life of an Artwork and a Commodity," 312–14.

34. "*Die Winterreise* Cycle Is Sung by Elena Gerhardt," *New York Tribune*, December 1922, 10. Laura Tunbridge documents performances of lieder primarily for the New York social set following the war and the parallel revival of the lied in London through such efforts as the London Lieder Club. *Singing in the Age of Anxiety*, 133–38.

35. Barbara L. Tischler, "One Hundred Percent Americanism and Music in Boston During World War I," 172–73.

36. Laura Tunbridge, "Singing Translations: The Politics of Listening Between the Wars," 67.

37. "Mr. and Mrs. Heinrich," *Worcester (MA) Daily Spy*, January 26, 1893, 1.

38. W. J. Henderson, "The Art of Farrar, Mary Garden and Julia Culp," sec. 7, p. 5.

39. Finck, "Song Recital," B-6.

40. Linda Whitesitt, "'The Most Potent Force' in American Music," 675–76.

41. Michael Chan, "The Piano in the Plugged-In World," 311; Roell, *Piano in America*, 200.

42. Lien, "Against the Grain," 276–84.

43. Reynolds, "Documenting the Zenith of Women Song Composers," 674; Reynolds, "Growing the Database of Women Songwriters."

44. Levine, *Highbrow/Lowbrow*, 235.

45. Thomas, however, did support concerts marketed to people who could only afford cheap tickets. Some of these programs included orchestral versions of Schubert's "Am Meer" (D. 957, no. 12) and Schumann's "The Two Grenadiers." Rose Fay Thomas, *Memoirs of Theodore Thomas*, 258–60.

46. Campbell critically examines the ideology of the reformers who advocated for the enriching power of what they called "good music," and the related teaching of music appreciation, which took advantage of newly produced recordings, in "'A Higher Mission Than Merely to Please the Ear,'" 259–86. Tunbridge also briefly considers music appreciation classes during her exploration of the challenges involved in broadcasting lieder performances on the radio. *Singing in the Age of Anxiety*, 72–74.

47. H. L. Mencken, "The Sawdust Trail," 152.

48. Campbell, "'Higher Mission,'" 274–76.

49. As cited by Christopher Purdy, "Whither the Song Recital."

50. Will Crutchfield, "The Song Recital Is Not Yet Dead," sec. H, 13, 16.

51. Thomas Quasthoff, in an interview by John Gilhooly at Wigmore Hall, London, on November 24, 2019: https://www.youtube.com/watch?v=etvcfwt89cc.

52. Anthony Tommasini, "Devising an Experiment to Save the Song Recital," sec. 1, p. 15; Loges and Tunbridge, "Performers' Reflections," 272. Despite Horne's efforts, in 2017 it was reported that she continued to refer to the song recital as an "endangered species." "Marilyn Horne Masterclass at Carnegie Hall," *Voce di Meche*, January 19, 2017, http://www.vocedimeche.reviews/2017/01/marilyn-horne-master-class-at-carnegie.html.

53. *Schubert Winter Journey*, recorded by Christopher Glynn and Roderick Williams. Translations by Jeremy Sams. Signum Classics, SIGCD531, 2018. https://www.chandos.net/chanimages/Booklets/SIG531.pdf.

54. *Boston Evening Transcript*. Page 6 of the promotional pamphlet comprising unsourced reviews of the Henschels' performances. The author might have been Apthorp, the paper's music critic at the time. Frederick Grant Gleason Collection of Music Scrapbooks, Box 32, vol. 2, p. 131, Newberry Library, Chicago.

55. Quasthoff, interview with John Gilhooly.

56. Henderson, "The Art of Farrar, Mary Garden and Julia Culp," sec. 7, p. 5.

57. See, e.g., a review of one of Bostridge's performances by Allan Kozinn, "A Tenor Whose Style Is Reminiscent of Piaf's," E5.

58. Thomas Quasthoff, Wigmore Hall masterclass, November 22, 2019, https://www.youtube.com/watch?v=SJLw2IFsxbQ (accessed October 23, 2021).

59. Some singers such as Susan Graham are experimenting with programming as a way to entice audiences to the lied. Tim Smith, "Songs of a Woman's Love and Loss, from a Stellar Messenger," E5.

60. Purdy, "Whither the Song Recital."

61. Elsa Keslassy, "MK 2 Leaps into 'A Winter's Journey' Made by 'Despicable Me' and 'Loving Vincent' Artists," *Variety*, February 19, 2020, https://variety.com/2020/film/global/berlinale-2020-mk2-leaps-into-a-winters-journey-made-by-loving-vincent-despicable-me-artists-exclusive-1203507625/.

62. Oxford Lieder: https://www.oxfordlieder.co.uk; Leeds Lieder Festival: https://leedslieder.org.uk/2022festival-programmes; The International Lied Festival Zeist in the Netherlands: https://ilfz.nl; Hampson's Heidelberg Lied Academy: https://www.heidelberger-fruehling.de/en/song-centre/projects/lied-academy/. An example of a training program in United States is Songfest: https://www.songfest.us.

63. David Patrick Stearns, "No Binoculars Needed," H4.

64. Cincinnati Song Initiative: https://www.cincinnatisonginitiative.org; The African American Art Song Alliance: https://artsongalliance.org and https://www.facebook.com/groups/artsongalliance/. Patricia Caicedo has published numerous books,

272   Notes to Epilogue

scores, recordings, and podcasts promoting songs of Latin America: https://www
.patriciacaicedo.com.

65. See Hampson's radio series "Songs of America," https://songofamerica.net/program/,
and his interview with Toppin in his Idagio series "Song and Beyond," February 3, 2021,
https://www.youtube.com/watch?v=ILhJx2ulV9g; see also Toppin's African Diaspora
Music Project, https://africandiasporamusicproject.org.

66. Richard Dyer, "Goerne Cuts an Independent Path," D3.

Bibliography

Digital Sources and Archives

This study is primarily based on digitized newspapers and journals that are provided by the services listed below (* includes US German-language newspapers; † provides access to European publications).

American Antiquarian Society Historical Periodicals Collection, https://www.american antiquarian.org/newspapers-periodicals
ANNO, Austrian Newspapers Online, http://anno.onb.ac.at†
Archive.org
British Newspaper Archive, https://www.britishnewspaperarchive.co.uk†
California Digital Newspaper Collection, https://cdnc.ucr.edu
Chroniclingamerica.loc.gov*
Early American Newspapers, 1690–1922, https://www.readex.com/content/early-american -newspapers-1690–1922
Gale Historical Newspapers, https://www.gale.com/primary-sources/historical-news papers†
GenealogyBank.com (Newspaper Archives)*
Hathitrust.org*†
Music in Gotham, https://www.musicingotham.org*
Newspapers.com*†
NYS Historic Newspapers, https://nyshistoricnewspapers.org
Old Fulton New York Post Cards, fultonhistory.com
Proquest Historical Newspapers, https://www.proquest.com/products-services/news -newspapers/pq-hist-news.html
Le Répertoire international de la press musicale, https://www.ripm.org*†
Sheet Music Consortium, http://digital2.library.ucla.edu/sheetmusic/

Archives and Libraries

Printed concert and song recital programs archived by the following institutions were also examined. Some of these are available from the institutions' websites.

Boston Conservatory
Boston Public Library
British Library
Cambridge University Library
Chicago History Museum
Chicago Public Library
Gesellschaft der Musikfreunde Archiv (Vienna)
Historical Society of Philadelphia
Historical Society of Washington, DC
Houghton Library (Harvard University)
Indiana Historical Society
Newberry Library, Chicago
New England Conservatory
New York Public Library, Performing Arts Division
Oberlin Conservatory
Ohio State University, University Libraries, Special Collections
Sibley Library, Eastman School of Music
University of Michigan
Wiener Stadt- und Landesarchiv

Publications from 1800 to 1921, the Year David Bispham Died

Most of the citations throughout the book are to newspaper, magazine, and journal notices. Because most of these notices are unsigned and very short (and therefore are only cited once), and because some have similar titles, they are not listed in this bibliography but, rather, cited in full in the notes. Notices in music journals that are likewise not signed are also not included in this bibliography.

Aldrich, Perley Dunn. "A Few Prominent European Teachers of Singing." *Music* 16, no. 2 (June 1899): 173–74.

Ambros, A. W. "Robert Franz." *Dwight's Journal of Music* 31 (1872): 193–94, 201–2, 209–10. Excerpted and translated from *Bunte Blätter: Skizzen und Studien für Freunde der Musik und der bildenden Kunst* (Leipzig: F. E. C. Leuckart, 1872).

Anderson, Martha Scott. "They're in Denver." *Minneapolis Journal*, June 21, 1898, 5.

Apthorp, William, ed. *Fifty Songs of Robert Franz*. Boston: Ditson, 1903.

———. "Is Robert Franz a Failure?" *Dwight's Journal of Music* 39 (October 25, 1879): 173, (November 8, 1879): 183, (November 22, 1879): 190–91.

———. *Musicians and Music-Lovers and Other Essays*. 5th ed. New York: Charles Scribner's Sons, 1908.

Aronson, Maurice. "Robert Franz in His Relation to Music and Its Masters." *Music* 8, no. 4 (February 1898): 455–62.

Baker, Theodore, ed. *A Biographical Dictionary of Musicians.* New York: Schirmer, 1905.

Barnes, Mrs. David H. "In Society's Realm." *Tulsa Democrat,* May 26, 1918, 19.

Barry, Kitty. "Music Festival Big Success; Bispham to Return Here." *Fort Worth Star-Telegram,* November 29, 1912, 9.

Bassett, Helen Wheeler, and Frederick Starr, eds. *The International Folk-Lore Congress of the World's Columbian Exposition.* Chicago: Charles H. Sergel, 1898.

Bauer, Emilie Frances. "Brooklyn." *Musical Courier* 35, no. 21 (November 24, 1897): 27.

Bauer, Flora. "Portland." *Musical Courier* 35, no. 16 (October 20, 1897): 34.

Bennett, Frances. *History of Music and Art in Illinois, Including Portraits and Biographies of the Cultured Men and Women Who Have Been Liberal Patrons of the Higher Arts.* Philadelphia: Historical Pub. Co., 1904.

Bispham, David, ed. *The Artistic Baritone: With Full Cover Picture and Biographical Sketch of David Bispham.* New York: M. Witmark, 1913.

———, ed. *The Bispham Album of Classical Songs: Being Ten Songs by Schubert and Schumann.* London: Forsyth Bros.; New York: Schuberth, 1897.

———, ed. *Celebrated Recital Songs.* Philadelphia: Presser, 1919.

———. *The David Bispham Song Book.* Philadelphia: John C. Winston, 1920.

———. "Music as a Factor in National Life." *North American Review* 175, no. 553 (December 1902): 786–99.

———. *A Quaker Singer's Recollections.* New York: Macmillan, 1920.

———. "Singing and the King's English." *Musical-Monitor and World* 3, no. 9 (May 1914): 261–62.

Bispham, David, and Hermann Klein, eds. *Bispham Song Album: A Representative Recital Collection.* Cincinnati: Church, 1908.

Bornonis, "From New York." *Dwight's Journal of Music* 6, no. 17 (January 27, 1855): 132.

[Brittan, Charles H.] "Chicago." *Dwight's Journal of Music* 39 (March 29, 1879): 47–48.

———. "Chicago." *Dwight's Journal of Music* 39 (April 26, 1879): 72.

———. "The Progress of Music in the West." *Dwight's Journal of Music* 39 (January 4, 1879): 10–11.

Broekhoven, J. Van. "American Songs." *Musical Observer* 3, no. 1 (January 1909): 19.

Burleigh, H. T. *Plantation Melodies Old and New.* New York: Schirmer, 1901.

Cable, George W. "Creole Slave Songs." *Century Magazine* 31, no. 6 (April 1886): 807–28.

Calvé, Emma. *My Favorite French Songs.* New York: Ditson, 1915.

Chester, E. [Harriet E. Paine.] *Girls and Women.* Riverside Library for Young People 8. Boston: Houghton, Mifflin, 1890.

Crane, W. W. "German Songs." *Appleton's Journal of Literature, Science and Art* 9, no. 216 (May 10, 1873): 627–29.

Croly, Mrs. J. C. *The History of the Woman's Club Movement in America.* New York: Henry G. Allen, 1898.

D'Arona, Florenza. "Is English a Musical Language?" *Musical Courier* 40, no. 26 (June 27, 1900): 8, and 41, no. 4 (July 25, 1900): 9–10.

Davenport, Warren. "Musical Boston." *Musical America* 1, no. 13 (December 31, 1898): 29.

Dickinson, Edward. "*In a Persian Garden.*" *Werners Magazine* 22, no. 2 (October 1898): 136–37.

Douglass, Frederick. *My Bondage and My Freedom*. New York: Miller, Orton & Mulligan, 1855.

Dvořák, Antonín. "Music in America." *Harper's New Monthly Magazine* 90, no. 537 (February 1895), 429–34.

Dwight, John Sullivan. "The Concerts of the Past Winter." *Dial* (July 1840), reprinted in John C. Swan, ed., *Music in Boston: Readings from the First Three Centuries*, 50–51. Boston: Trustees of the Boston Public Library, 1977.

———. "The Intellectual Influence of Music." *Atlantic Monthly* 26, no. 157 (November 1870): 614–25.

———. "Music a Means of Culture." *Atlantic Monthly* 26, no. 155 (September 1870): 321–31.

———. *Select Minor Poems, Translated from the German of Goethe and Schiller*. Boston: Hilliard, Gray, 1839.

Ehlert, Louis. "The German Lied: Schubert, Mendelssohn, Schumann, Franz, etc." Translated by Fanny Raymond Ritter. *Dwight's Journal of Music* 30, no. 8 (July 2, 1876): 267.

———. *Letters on Music, to a Lady*. Translated by Fanny Raymond Ritter. Boston: Ditson, 1870.

Elson, Louis C. *European Reminiscences: Musical and Otherwise*. Philadelphia: Presser, 1914.

———. *The History of American Music*. New York: Macmillan, 1904.

———. *The History of German Song: An Account of the Progress of Vocal Composition in Germany from the Time of the Minnesingers to the Present Age*. Boston: New England Conservatory of Music, 1888.

———. "Interesting Song Recital by David Bispham." *Boston Daily Advertiser*, December 14, 1898, 4.

———. "The Max Heinrich Recitals." *Boston Daily Advertiser*, February 17, 1892, 4.

———. "Max Heinrich's Second Song Recital in Steinert Hall." *Boston Daily Advertiser*, December 8, 1897, 5.

———. "Mr. Max Heinrich's Recital in New Steinert Hall." *Boston Daily Advertiser*, January 6, 1897, 8.

———. [pseud. Proteus]. "Music in Boston," *Church's Musical Visitor* 11, no. 5 (1882): 133-34.

———. [pseud. Proteus]. "Music in Boston, Dec. 19, 1887." *Musical Visitor* 17, no. 1 (January 1888): 10–11.

———. "Music Matters: The Henschel Recital." *Boston Daily Advertiser*, March 30, 1892, 8.

———. *The National Music of America and Its Sources*. Boston: L. C. Page, 1900.

Farrar, Geraldine, ed. *My Favorite Songs*. New York: Ditson, 1916.

Ferris, George T. "Four Great Song-Composers: Schubert, Schumann, Franz, Liszt." *Appleton's Journal* 1 (August 1876): 109–14, reprinted in *Whitney's Musical Guest* (Ohio), (September 1, 1876): 193–96.

———. *The Great German Composers*. New York: Appleton, 1891.

Finck, Henry T., ed. *Fifty Mastersongs by Twenty Composers*. New York: Ditson, 1903.

———, ed. *One Hundred Songs by Ten Masters*. Philadelphia: Ditson, 1917.

———. *Song and Song Writers*. New York: Scribner, 1900.

———. "The Song Recital," *Nebraska State Journal*, April 21, 1918, B-6. Originally published in the *New York Evening Post*.

Fletcher, Alice C. *A Study of Omaha Indian Music*. Salem, MA: Salem Press, 1893.

Forsyth, Jean. "A Singing Student in London." *Harper's New Monthly Magazine* 88 (February 1894): 385–91.

Franklin, Viola Price. "Echoes of the Biennial." *Nebraska State Journal* (Lincoln), July 10, 1898, 10.

Franz, Robert. *A Collection of Sixty-Two Songs with Piano Accompaniment, Preceded by a Biographical and Critical Essay by H. E. Krehbiel*. New York: Schirmer, 1907.

French, Florence, comp. *Music and Musicians in Chicago: The City's Leading Artists, Organizations and Art Buildings*. Chicago: French, 1899.

Freund, John C. "The Passing Show." *Musical America* 2, no. 4 (January 28, 1899): 11.

Fuller-Maitland, J. A. *Brahms*. 2nd ed. London: Methuen, 1911.

[Gleason, Frederick Grant]. "The Henschel Vocal Recital." *Morning News* (Chicago), April 28, 1884, Frederick Grant Gleason Collection of Music Scrapbooks, Box 32, vol. 2, p. 425, Newberry Library, Chicago.

Gluck, Alma, ed. *My Favorite Songs*. New York: Ditson, 1917.

Gordon, Margaret. "Entertainment Ideas for Teachers." *Ladies' Home Journal* 28, no. 7 (April 1, 1911): 62.

Gunn, Glenn Dillard. "Bispham in Splendid Voice." *Inter Ocean* (Chicago), April 3, 1905, 4.

———. "Bispham's Third Recital." *Inter Ocean* (Chicago), February 6, 1905, 6.

Hagen, Theo. "Franz Schubert" (translated from the German and reprinted by the *New York Musical World*). *Dwight's Journal of Music* 19, no. 16 (July 20, 1861): 122–23.

Hale, Philip. "Boston Concerts." *Musical Record and Review* no. 431 (December 1, 1897): 10.

———. "Drama and Music." *Boston Journal*, February 8, 1893, 5.

———. *Dramatic and Musical Criticisms*. Scrapbooks owned by the Boston Public Library. https://archive.org/details/bplscphscrap.

———. "The First of Two Song Recitals." *Boston Journal*, March 21, 1894, 6.

———. "First of Two Song Recitals Given by Mr. and Mrs. Max Heinrich." *Boston Journal*, March 17, 1896, 7.

———. "Miss Little and Mr. Meyn." *Boston Journal*, December 2, 1892, 5.

———. "Miss Marguerite Hall." *Boston Journal*, April 7, 1898, 6.

———. "Miss Villa White's Singing." *Boston Journal*, March 24, 1898, 8.

———, ed. *Modern French Songs*. Boston: Ditson, 1904.

———. "Mr. Loeffler's Songs." *Boston Journal*, December 1, 1897, 7.

———. "Mr. Max Heinrich's Third Recital in Steinert Hall." *Boston Journal*, January 26, 1897, 7.

———. "Music and Musicians." *Boston Sunday Journal*, December 18, 1898, 26.

———. "Music in Boston." *Musical Courier* 43, no. 23 (December 4, 1901): 5.

———. "Music in Boston." *Musical Courier* 36, no. 13 (March 30, 1898): 16.

———. "Music: The First of Two Song Recitals by Mr. and Mrs. Max Heinrich in Steinert Hall." *Boston Morning Journal*, March 21, 1894, 6.

———. "Roland Hayes at the Symphony: Singer Has Courage to Open Program with American Songs." *Boston Herald*, November 22, 1918, 14.

———. "Second and Last Song Recital of Mr. and Mrs. Max Heinrich in Steinert Hall." *Boston Journal*, March 24, 1896, 7.

———. "The Second Vocal Recital of Mr. and Mrs. Max Heinrich." *Boston Journal*, March 28, 1894, 4.

Hall, Mrs. Caroline Pettinos. "Schumann's Songs." *Sherman & Hyde's Musical Review* (October 1, 1875): 10.

Hanslick, Eduard. *Aus dem Tagebuch eines Musikers: Kritiken und Schilderungen.* Berlin: Allgemeiner Verein für Deutsche Litteratur, 1892.

Harvey, Margaret B. "Musical Studies." *Ladies' Home Journal* 3, no. 10 (September 1886): 12.

Heinrich, Max. "Are Singers, Like Poets, Born or Made?," *Musical America* 11, no. 8 (January 1, 1910): 16.

———. "The Art of Singing." Annual Musical-Education Section, *New York Tribune*, October 10, 1915, pt. 8, p. 19.

———. "Breath Control and the Singer." *Musical America* 11, no. 11 (January 22, 1910): 28.

———., ed. and annot. *Classic Song Album: Fifty Selected Songs of Old & Modern Masters.* Translated by Alice Mattullath. New York: Carl Fischer, 1914.

———. *Correct Principles of Classical Singing: Containing Essays on Choosing a Teacher; The Art of Singing, et cetera; Together with an Interpretative Key to Handel's "Messiah," and Schubert's "Die schöne Müllerin."* Boston: Lothrop, Lee & Shepard, 1910.

———, ed. and annot. *Fifty Selected Songs by Franz Schubert.* Translated by Alice Mattullath. New York: Carl Fischer, 1912.

———. "Max Heinrich on Singing Teachers." *Musical America* 11, no. 6 (December 18, 1909): 30.

———., ed. and annot. *Robert Schumann: Poet's Love.* Translated by Alice Mattullath. New York: Carl Fisher, 1912.

———, ed. and annot. *Sixty Selected Songs by Johannes Brahms.* Translated by Alice Mattullath. New York: Carl Fischer, 1915.

———, ed. and annot. *Sixty Selected Songs by Robert Schumann.* Translated by Alice Mattullath. New York: Carl Fischer, 1913.

———. "Voice Production (Tone Placing)." *Musical America* 11, no. 10 (January 15, 1910): 28.

Henderson, W[illiam] J[ames]. "The Art of Farrar, Mary Garden and Julia Culp." *Sun* (New York), January 9, 1913, sec. 7, p. 5.

———. "Mr. Bispham's Recitals: Third of His Series at the Carnegie Lyceum." *New York Times*, February 10, 1897, 7.

———. "Mr. Bispham's Recitals: The Whole of Brahms's 'Die Schoene Magelone' Excellently Given at the Opera House." *New York Times*, February 20, 1897, 6.

———. "Rising Tide of Sentiment Against German Music." *Sun* (New York), December 2, 1917, 8.

———. *What Is Good Music? Suggestions to Persons Desiring to Cultivate Taste in Musical Art.* New York: Scribner's, 1898.

Henschel, George. *Fifty Songs*. Cincinnati: Church, 1905.

———. "Jamie or Robin?" *Church's Musical Visitor* 9, no. 4 (January 1880): 10–12.

———. *Musings and Memories of a Musician*. New York: Macmillan, 1919.

———. "Personal Recollections of Johannes Brahms." *Century Magazine* 61, no. 5 [n.s. 39, no. 5] (March 1901): 725–36.

———. *Personal Recollections of Johannes Brahms: Some of His Letters to and Pages from a Journal Kept by George Henschel*. Boston: Richard G. Badger, The Gorhan, 1907.

———. *Progressive Studies for the Voice with Pianoforte Accompaniment*. London: Novello, 1892.

———. "Some Elementary Truths in Song Interpretation." *Etude* 35, no. 10 (October 1917): 645–46.

Hill, Mildred [pseud. Johann Tonsor]. "Negro Music." *Music* 3 (1892–93): 119–22.

———. "Unconscious Composers: The Characteristics of Street Cries." *Courier-Journal*, March 27, 1895, sec. 4, p. 1.

Hubbard, William Lines, ed. *The American History and Encyclopedia of Music*. Toledo: Irving Squire, 1908.

———. "Mme. Strauss as a Singer." *Chicago Tribune*, March 20, 1904, 22.

Hughes, Rupert. "American Concert Singers V." *Godey's Magazine* 136 (April 1898): 402–6.

———. "Music in America: I—Ethelbert Nevin." *Godey's Magazine* 130 (May 1895): 526–31.

[Huneker, James]. "The Raconteur." *Musical Courier* 36, no. 13 (March 30, 1898): 24.

———. *Steeplejack*. New York: Scribner, 1920.

Hutcheson, Wille. "Amusements." *Houston Post*, December 3, 1912, 8.

Johnson, Helen Kendrick, Reginald DeKoven, Frederic Dean, and Gerrit Smith, eds. *The World's Best Music: Famous Songs and Those Who Made Them*. New York: University Society, 1904.

Jones, F. O. *A Handbook of Music and Musicians*. Buffalo: C. W. Moulton, 1887.

Kobbé, Gustave. "Reciting to Music: A Home Entertainment," *Good Housekeeping* 44 (February 1907): 218–23.

Kramer, A. Walter. "Arthur Bergh's New Cycle *The Congo* Is Notable Addition to American Music." *Musical America* 28, no. 18 (August 31, 1918): 31.

Krehbiel, Henry Edward. *Afro-American Folksong: A Study in Racial and National Music*. New York: Schirmer, 1914.

———. "American Music." *Musical Courier* 14 (1887): 121, 137, 155, 173.

———. "Indian Melodies." *New York Tribune*, August 31, 1902, 2.

———. *Review of the New York Musical Season*. New York: Novello, Ewer, 1885–1890.

Lavretsky, Ivan. "New York Musical Season: Song Recitals." *Pittsfield (MA) Sun*, February 16, 1899, 1.

Lehmann, Liza. *The Life of Liza Lehmann*. London: T. Fisher Unwin, 1919.

Liszt, Franz. "Robert Franz." *Dwight's Journal of Music* 33 (1873): 1–3, 10–11 Excerpted and translated from *Robert Franz* (Leipzig: F. E. C. Leuckart, 1872).

Martin, Paul R. "Schumann-Heink Receives Ovation." *Indianapolis Star*, March 20, 1914, 17.

Mathews, W. S. B. "An American School of Singing." *Morning News*, May 17, 1884, Frederick Grant Gleason Collection of Music Scrapbooks, Box 32, vol. 2, pp. 127–28, Newberry Library, Chicago.

———. [pseud. Der Freyschütz]. "Binghamton, NY." *Dwight's Journal of Music* 33, no. 12 (September 20, 1873): 96.

———. [pseud. Der Freyschütz]. "Chicago." *Dwight's Journal of Music* 32, no. 16 (November 2, 1872): 333.

———. [pseud. Der Freyschütz]. "Chicago." *Dwight's Journal of Music* 34, no. 26 (April 3, 1875): 415–16.

———. [pseud. Der Freyschütz]. "Chicago." *Dwight's Journal of Music* 35, no. 5 (June 12, 1875): 40.

———. "Editorial Bric-a-Brac." *Music* 16, no. 1 (May 1899): 90–91.

———. *A Hundred Years of Music in America*. 1889. Reprint, New York, AMS Press, 1970.

———. "The 'Normal' Music School." *Dwight's Journal of Music* 32, no. 12 (September 7, 1872): 302–3.

———. "Robert Schumann, the Poetical Musician." *New York Musical Gazette* 7, no. 3 (March 1, 1873): 36.

Meddler. "In the Swim." *Oakland Tribune*, November 20, 1897, 6.

Mencken, H. L. "The Sawdust Trail." *The Smart Set: A Magazine of Cleverness*, August 1915, 150–56.

Murphy, Jeanette Robinson. "The Survival of African Music in America." *Popular Science Monthly* 55 (1899): 660–72.

Newman, Ernest, ed. *Fifty Songs by Hugo Wolf*. Boston: Ditson, 1909.

———. *Modern Russian Songs*. The Musicians Library. Boston: Ditson, 1921.

Osgood, George L. *Guide in the Art of Singing: Based on the Reliable Tradition of the Italian School of Vocalization and Practical Developments of Modern Science*. Boston: Ditson, 1874.

Pan, Sylvan. "Concert at Wells' College." *American Art Journal* 35, no. 10 (July 2, 1881): 190.

Partington, Blanche. "Huneker Asserts Strauss Is the Most Intellectual of the Living Musicians." *San Francisco Call*, March 30, 1902, 22.

[Perabeau, H.]. "Franz Schubert." *Dwight's Journal of Music* 1, no. 3 (April 24, 1852): 21.

Reimann, Heinrich, ed. *Das deutsche Geistliche Lied: Von der ältesten bis auf unsere Zeit*. 6 vols. Berlin: Simrock, 1895.

———. *Das deutsche Lied: Eine Auswahl aus den Programmen der historischen Lieder-Abende der Amalie Joachim*. Berlin: Simrock, 1892–1893.

———. *Volksliederbuch: Eine Sammlung ausländischer Volkslieder*. 3 vols. Berlin: Simrock, 1893.

Ritter, Fanny Raymond. *Woman as a Musician: An Art-Historical Study*. London: Reeves, 1876.

Ritter, Frédéric Louis. *History of Music in the Form of Lectures*. Boston: Ditson, 1874.

———. *Music in America*. New York: Scribner's, 1884.

Rogers, Clara Kathleen (Doria). *Memories of a Musical Career*. Boston: Little, Brown, 1919.

Rogers, Francis. "The Use of English in Singing." *Musical America* 9, no. 8 (1909): 14.

Saran, August. "Robert Franz and the German Volkslied and Choral." *Dwight's Journal of*

Music 35 (1875): 86–87, 89–90, 97–98, 105–6, 113. Excerpted and translated from *Robert Franz und das deutsche Volks-und Kirckenlied* (Leipzig: F. E. C. Leuckart, [1875]).

Schindler, Kurt, ed. *A Century of Russian Song from Glinka to Rachmaninoff.* Golden Treasury of Music. New York: Schirmer, 1911.

———, ed. *Masters of Russian Song.* New York: Schirmer, 1917.

Schumann, Robert. *Music and Musicians: Essays and Criticisms.* Translated by Fanny Raymond Ritter. New York: Schuberth, 1877.

———. "The Songs of Robert Franz." *Dwight's Journal of Music* 23, no. 1 (April 4, 1863): 1. Translation of a review of Franz's op. 1 in "Lieder," *Neue Zeitschrift für Musik* 19, no. 9 (July 31, 1843): 34–35.

Sembrich, Marcella, ed. *My Favorite Folksongs.* New York: Ditson, 1918.

Shakespeare, William. *The Art of Singing.* London: Ditson, 1898.

Spaeth, Sigmund. "Translating to Music." *Musical Quarterly* 1, no. 2 (April 1915): 291–98.

Stevens, Ashton. "Unostentatious Art." *San Francisco Call*, October 27, 1897, 9.

[Stevens, Nelda Hewitt]. "Singers Desecrate Negro Music by False Interpretations." *Musical America* 31, no. 20 (March 13, 1920): 47.

Taylor, Bertram. "Matters of Musical Interest." *Indianapolis Sunday Star*, November 2, 1919, 7.

Thomas, Rose Fay. *Memoirs of Theodore Thomas.* New York: Moffat, Yard, 1911.

Thomas, Theodore. *Theodore Thomas: A Musical Autobiography.* George P. Upton, ed. Chicago: A. C. McClurg, 1905.

Ticknor, Howard Malcolm. "Last Henschel Recital." *Boston Daily Globe*, March 31, 1889, 5.

———. "Third Henschel Concert." *Boston Daily Globe*, March 29, 1889, 4.

Troyer, Carlos. *Traditional Songs of the Zuñi Indians.* Philadelphia: Presser, 1904.

Underwood, F. H. "In Memoriam: August Kreissmann." *Dwight's Journal of Music* 39 (August 2, 1879): 123.

Weeden, [Maria] Howard. *Bandanna Ballads.* New York: Double Day & McClure, 1899.

White, Villa Whitney. "The Educational Value of Vocal Study from the Ethical Viewpoint." In *Studies in Musical Education: History and Aesthetics, 2nd ser. Papers and Proceedings of the Music Teachers' National Association at Its 29th Annual Meeting.* Columbia University, New York, December 27–31, 1907, 2:176–79. [Hartford, CT]: Music Teachers National Association, 1908.

Wilson, George H., ed. *The Musical Yearbook of the United States.* Boston: n.p., 1885–1893.

Winn, Edith Lynwood. *Wilhelm Heinrich, Musician and Man: A Tribute.* Boston: Thompson, 1914.

Publications, 1922–2022

Ahlquist, Karen. *Democracy at the Opera: Music, Theater, and Culture in New York City, 1815–60.* Urbana: University of Illinois Press, 1997.

Aichele, Michele. "Cécile Chaminade as a Symbol for American Women, 1890–1920." PhD diss., University of Iowa, 2019.

Bailey, Candace. *Unbinding Gentility: Women Making Music in the Nineteenth-Century South.* Urbana: University of Illinois Press, 2021.

Barnes, Molly. "The Other Otto Dresel: Public and Private Musical Identities in a German-American 'Forty-Eighter' and His Family, c. 1860–1880." *Nineteenth Century Music Review* 19, no. 3 (December 2022): 481–513.

Barthes, Roland. "The Romantic Song" (1976). In *The Responsibility of Forms: Critical Essays on Music, Art, and Representation*, translated by Richard Howard, 286–92. Berkeley: University of California Press, 1991.

Bashford, Christina. "The Late Beethoven Quartets and the London Press, 1836-ca. 1850." *Musical Quarterly* 84, no. 1 (2000): 84–122.

Baur, Stephen. "Music, Morals, and Social Management: Mendelssohn in Post–Civil War America." *American Music* 19, no. 1 (2001): 64–130.

Beckerman, Michael. "'Rare in a Generation of Remarkable Women': Mildred Hill, Dvořák, Black Street Cries and the Making of 'Happy Birthday.'" *Journal of Czech and Slovak Music* 28 (2019): 7–50.

Berlioz, Hector. *Memoirs of Hector Berlioz*. 1935. Annotated and translation revised by Ernest Newman. Reprint, New York: Dover, 1966.

Bier, Robin Terrill. "The Ideal Orpheus: An Analysis of Virtuosic Self-Accompanied Singing as a Historical Vocal Performance Practice." PhD diss., University of York, 2013.

Blair, Karen. *The Clubwoman as Feminist: True Womanhood Redefined, 1868–1914*. New York: Holmes & Meier, 1980.

Block, Adrienne Fried. "Matinee Mania, or the Regendering of Nineteenth-Century Audiences in New York City." *19th-Century Music* 31, no. 3 (2008): 193–216.

Bohlman, Philip V. *The Music of European Nationalism: Cultural Identity and Modern History*. Santa Barbara: ABC-CLIO, 2004.

Bomberger, E. Douglas, ed. *Brainard's Biographies of American Musicians*. Westport: Greenwood, 1999.

———. *Making Music American: 1917 and the Transformation of Culture*. New York: Oxford University Press, 2018.

———. *"A Tidal Wave of Encouragement": American Composers' Concerts in the Gilded Age*. Westport: Praeger, 2002.

Bond, Carrie Jacobs. *The Roads of Melody*. New York: Appleton, 1927.

Borchard, Beatrix. "The Concert Hall as a Gender-Neutral Space: The Case of Amalie Joachim, née Schneeweiss" (trans. Jeremy Coleman). In Loges and Tunbridge, *German Song Onstage*, 132–53.

———. *Pauline Viardot-Garcia: Fülle des Lebens*. Vienna: Böhlau, 2016.

———. *Stimme und Geige: Amalie Joachim und Joseph Joachim*. 2nd ed. Vienna: Bohlau, 2007.

Bozarth, George. *Johannes Brahms and George Henschel: An Enduring Friendship*. Sterling Heights: Harmonie Park, 2008.

Brister, Emma Schubert. *Incidents*. Privately published, 1936.

Brown, John, Jr., and James Boyd. *History of San Bernardino and Riverside Counties*. Chicago: Western Historical Association, 1922.

Browner, Tara. "'Breathing the Indian Spirit': Thoughts on Musical Borrowing and the 'Indianist' Movement in American Music." *American Music* 15, no. 3 (1997): 265–84.

Broyles, Michael. "Art Music from 1860 to 1920" In *The Cambridge History of American Music*, edited by David Nicholls, 214–54. Cambridge: Cambridge University Press, 1998.

———. *Beethoven in America*. Bloomington: Indiana University Press, 2011.

———. *Music of the Highest Class: Elitism and Populism in Antebellum Boston*. New Haven: Yale University Press, 1992.

Bruhn, Christopher. "Taking the Private Public: Amateur Music-Making and the Musical Audience in 1860s New York." *American Music* 21, no. 3 (2003): 260–90.

Bungert, Heike. *Festkultur und Gedächtnis: Die Konstruktion einer deutschamerikanischen Ethnizität, 1848–1914*. Paderborn: Ferdinand Schöningh, 2016.

———. "The Singing Festivals of German Americans, 1849–1914." *American Music* 34, no. 2 (Summer 2016): 141–79.

Burrage, Melissa D. *The Karl Muck Scandal: Classical Music and Xenophobia in World War I America*. Rochester: University of Rochester Press, 2019.

Campbell, Gavin James. "'A Higher Mission Than Merely to Please the Ear': Music and Social Reform in America, 1900–1925." *Musical Quarterly* 84, no. 2 (Summer 2000): 259–86.

Carman, Judith E., et al. *Art Song in the United States, 1759–1999: An Annotated Bibliography*. 3rd ed. Boston: Scarecrow, 2001.

Cavicchi, Daniel. *Listening and Longing: Music Lovers in the Age of Barnum*. Middletown: Wesleyan University Press, 2011.

Chan, Michael. "The Piano in the Plugged-In World." In *Piano Roles: A New History of the Piano*, edited by James Parakilas et al., 311–20. New Haven: Yale Nota Bene, 2002.

Chybowski, Julia J. "Becoming the 'Black Swan' in Mid-Nineteenth-Century America: Elizabeth Taylor Greenfield's Early Life and Debut Concert Tour." *Journal of the American Musicological Society* 67, no. 1 (2014): 125–65.

Cimarusti, Thomas. "The Songs of Luigi Gordigiani (1806–1860), 'Lo Schuberto Italiano.'" PhD diss., Florida State University, 2007.

Citron, Marcia. *Gender and the Musical Canon*. 1993; reprint, Urbana: Illinois University Press, 2000.

Clarke, James Wesley. "Prof. W. S. B. Mathews (1837–1912): Self-Made Musician of the Gilded Age." PhD diss., University of Minnesota, 1983.

Cole, Rosamund. "Lilli Lehmann's Dedicated Lieder Recitals." In Loges and Tunbridge, *German Song Onstage*, 223–43.

Crawford, Richard. *America's Musical Life: A History*. New York: Norton, 2001.

Crutchfield, Will. "The Song Recital Is Not Yet Dead," *New York Times*, September 2, 1984, H13, 16.

Damrosch, Walter. *My Musical Life*. New York: Scribner's, 1923.

Daniel, Walter C. "Vachel Lindsay, W. E. B. Du Bois and *The Crisis*." *Crisis* 86, no. 7 (August–September 1979): 290–93.

Deadman, Alison. "Brahms in Nineteenth-Century America." *Inter-American Music Review* 16, no. 1 (1997): 65–84.

Deutsch, Otto Erich. *Schubert: A Documentary Biography*. Translated by Eric Blom. New York: Da Capo, 1977.

Dickinson, Peter, H. Wiley Hitchcock, and Keith E. Clifton. "Art Song." *Grove Dictionary of American Music*. 2nd ed. New York: Oxford University Press, 2013, 1:208–12.

DiMaggio, Paul. "Cultural Entrepreneurship in Nineteenth-Century Boston: The Creation of an Organizational Base for High Culture in America." *Media, Culture and Society* 4, no. 1 (1982): 33–50.

Dowell, Richard M. "The Mendelssohn Quintette Club of Boston." PhD diss., Kent State University, 1999.

Dunn, James Taylor. *Saint Paul's Schubert Club: A Century of Music (1882–1892)*. Saint Paul: The Schubert Club, 1983.

Dyer, Richard. "Goerne Cuts an Independent Path." *Boston Globe*, July 13, 2001, D3.

Epstein, Dena J. "Music Publishing in the Age of Piracy: The Board of Music Trade and Its Catalogue." *Notes* 31, no. 1 (September 1974): 7–29.

Faucett, Bill F. *Music in Boston: Composers, Events, and Ideas, 1852–1918*. Lanham: Lexington, 2016.

Freitas, Roger. "Singing Herself: Adelina Patti and the Performance of Femininity." *Journal of the American Musicological Society* 71, no. 2 (2018): 287–369.

Gaiser-Reich, Gabriele. *Gustav Walter, 1834–1910: Wiener Hofopernsänger und Liederfürst*. Tutzing: Schneider, 2011.

Gerson, Robert A. *Music in Philadelphia*. 1940; Reprint, Westport: Greenwood, 1970.

Gienow-Hecht, Jessica C. E. *Sound Diplomacy: Music and Emotions in Transatlantic Relations, 1850–1920*. Chicago: University of Chicago Press, 2009.

Givens, Melissa Evelyn. "The Wings of Song Stilled: The Rise and Decline of Felix Mendelssohn's Lieder in London." DMA diss., University of Houston, 2012.

Goertzen, Valerie. "By Way of Introduction: Preluding by 18th and Early 19th Century Pianists." *Journal of Musicology* 14, no. 3 (1996): 299–337.

Gramit, David. "The Circulation of the Lied: The Double Life of an Artwork and a Commodity." In *The Cambridge Companion to the Lied*, edited by James Parsons, 301–14. Cambridge: Cambridge University Press, 2004.

———. "Schubert's Wanderers and the Autonomous Lied." *Journal of Musicological Research* 14 (1995): 147–68.

Graziano, John. "The Early Life and Career of the 'Black Patti': The Odyssey of an African American Singer in the Late Nineteenth Century." *Journal of the American Musicological Society* 53, no. 3 (2000): 543–96.

Greene, Gary A. *Henry Holden Huss: An American Composer's Life*. Metuchen: Scarecrow, 1995.

Grove, George. *Beethoven-Schubert-Mendelssohn*. London: Macmillan, 1951.

Günther, Martin. *Kunstlied als Liedkunst: Die Lieder Franz Schuberts in der musikalischen Aufführungskultur des 19. Jahrhunderts*. Stuttgart: Steiner, 2016.

Guzdski, Carolyn. "Saint-Saëns in New York." In *Camille Saint-Saëns and His World*, edited by Jann Pasler, 191–200. Princeton: Princeton University Press, 2012.

Hadamer, Armin W. *Mimetischer Zauber: Die englischsprachige Rezeption deutscher Lieder in den USA, 1830–1880*. Münster: Waxmann, 2008.

Hamilton, Katy. "England." In *Brahms in Context*, edited by Natasha Loges and Katy Hamilton, 316–23. Cambridge: Cambridge University Press, 2019.

———. "Natalia Macfarren and the English German Lied." In Loges and Tunbridge, *German Song Onstage*, 87–110.

Hamm, Charles. *Yesterdays: Popular Song in America*. New York: Norton, 1983.

Heller, George N., and Jere T. Humphreys. "Music Teacher Education in America (1753–1840): A Look at One of Its Three Sources." *College Music Symposium* 31 (1991): 49–58.

Henderson, Whitney Ann. "'The History of the Ladies Musical Club Is Like the Biography of a Great Man': Women, Place, Repertory, Race, and the Ladies Musical Club of Seattle, 1891–1950." PhD diss., University of Washington, 2018.

Henschel, George, ed. *Articulation in Singing: A Manual for Student and Teacher, with Practical Examples and Exercises*. Cincinnati: Church, [1926].

———. *How to Interpret a Song*. The Etude Musical Booklet Library. Philadelphia: Presser, [1929].

Henschel, Helen. *When Soft Voices Die: A Musical Biography*. London: Methuen, 1949.

Hofmann, Renate, and Kurt Hofmann. *Johannes Brahms als Pianist und Dirigent: Chronologie seines Wirkens als Interpret*. Tutzing: Schneider, 2006.

Horowitz, Joseph. "Henry Krehbiel: German American, Music Critic." *Journal of the Gilded Age and Progressive Era* 8, no. 2 (2009): 165–87.

———. "Laura Langford and the Seidl Society: Wagner Comes to Brooklyn." In *Cultivating Music in America: Women Patrons and Activists Since 1860*, edited by Ralph P. Locke and Cyrilla Barr, 164–83. Berkeley: University of California Press, 1997.

———. *Wagner Nights: An American History*. Berkeley: University of California Press, 1994.

Howe, Sondra Wieland. "Julius Eichberg: String and Vocal Instruction in Nineteenth-Century Boston." *Journal of Research in Music Education* 44, no. 2 (1996): 147–59.

Huneker, James Gibbons. *Americans in the Arts, 1890–1920*. Edited by Arthur T. Schwab. New York: AMS Press, 1985.

James, Edward T., Janet Wilson James, and Paul Boyer. *Notable American Women, 1607–1950: A Biographical Dictionary*. Vol. 2. Cambridge: Harvard University Press, 1971.

Johnson, Graham, and Richard Stokes. *A French Song Companion*. Oxford: Oxford University Press, 2002.

Jones, Karen Leistra. "Staging Authenticity: Joachim, Brahms, and the Politics of *Werktreue* Performance." *Journal of the American Musicological Society* 66, no. 2 (2013): 397–436.

Keller, Helen. *Midstream: My Later Life*. Garden City: Double day, 1929.

Koegel, John. *Music in German Immigrant Theater: New York City, 1840–1940*. Rochester: University of Rochester Press, 2009.

Kozinn, Allan. "A Tenor Whose Style Is Reminiscent of Piaf's." *New York Times*, April 14, 1999, E5.

Kravitt, Edward F. *The Lied: Mirror of Late Romanticism*. New Haven: Yale University Press, 1996.

———. "The Lied in 19th Century Concert Life." *Journal of the American Musicological Society* 18, no. 2 (1965): 207–18.

———. "Theatrical Declamation and German Vocal Music of the Late Romantic Period." *Seminar* 14, no. 3 (1978): 169–86.

Lamb, Barbara Sue. "Thursday Musical in the Musical Life of Minneapolis." PhD diss., University of Minnesota, 1983.

Lawrence, Vera Brodsky. *Strong on Music: The New York Music Scene in the Days of George Templeton Strong, 1836–1875.* 3 vols. New York: Oxford University Press, 1988–1995.

Leech-Wilkinson, Daniel. *The Changing Sound of Music: Approaches to Studying Recorded Musical Performance.* London: CHARM, 2009.

Levine, Lawrence W. *Highbrow/Lowbrow: The Emergence of Cultural Hierarchy in America.* Cambridge: Harvard University Press, 1988.

Lien, Anthony. "Against the Grain: Modernism and the American Art Song, 1900 to 1950." PhD diss., University of California, 2002.

Locke, Ralph P. "Music Lovers, Patrons, and the 'Sacralization' of Culture in America." *19th-Century Music* 17, no. 2 (1993): 149–73.

———. "Paradoxes of the Woman Music Patron in America." *Musical Quarterly* 78, no. 4 (1994): 798–825.

Loesser, Arthur. *Men, Women and Pianos: A Social History.* New York: Simon and Schuster, 1954.

Loges, Natasha. "Detours on a Winter's Journey: Schubert's *Winterreise* in Nineteenth-Century Concerts." *Journal of the American Musicological Society* 74, no. 1 (2021): 1–42.

———. "Julius Stockhausen's Early Performances of Franz Schubert's *Die schöne Müllerin*." *19th-Century Music* 41, no. 3 (2018): 206–24.

———. "The Limits of the Lied: Brahms's *Magelone-Romanzen* op. 33." In *Brahms in the Home and the Concert Hall: Between Private and Public Performance*, edited by Katy Hamilton and Natasha Loges, 300–23. Cambridge: Cambridge University Press, 2014.

———. "Singers." In *Brahms in Context*, edited by Natasha Loges and Katy Hamilton, 187–95. Cambridge: Cambridge University Press, 2019.

Loges, Natasha, and Laura Tunbridge, eds. *German Song Onstage: Lieder Performance in the Nineteenth and Early Twentieth Centuries.* Bloomington: Indiana University Press, 2020.

———. "Performers' Reflections." In Loges and Tunbridge, *German Song Onstage*, 262–80.

Luongo, Paul. "An Unlikely Cornerstone: The Role of Orchestral Transcription in the Success of the Thomas Orchestra." DM diss., Florida State University, 2010.

Macleod, Beth Abelson. *Women Performing Music: The Emergence of American Women as Classical Instrumentalists and Conductors.* Jefferson: McFarland, 2001.

Mattfeld, Julius. *Variety Music Cavalcade, 1620-1969: A Chronology of Vocal and Instrumental Music Popular in the United States,* 3rd ed. Englewood Cliffs, NY: Prentice-Hall, 1971.

McVeigh, Simon, and William Weber. "From the Benefit Concert to the Solo Song Recital in London, 1870–1914." In Loges and Tunbridge, *German Song Onstage*, 179–202.

Meyer-Frazier, Petra. "American Women's Roles in Domestic Music Making as Revealed in Parlor Song Collections, 1820–1870." PhD diss., University of Colorado, 1999.

———. *Bound Music, Unbound Women: The Search for an Identity in the Nineteenth Century.* Missoula: College Music Society, 2015.

———. "'Woman as a Musician': American Feminism in 1876." *Bulletin of the Sonneck Society for American Music* 24, no. 1 (1998): 2–3.

Middleton, Richard, and Peter Manuel. "Popular Music." *Grove Music Online*, 2001. https://www-oxfordmusiconline-com.

Mooney, Matthew. "An 'Invasion of Vulgarity': American Popular Music and Modernity in Print Media Discourse, 1900–1915." *Americana*3, no. 1 (Spring 2004). https://www .americanpopularculture.com/journal/articles/spring_2004/mooney.htm

Mussulman, Joseph A. *Music in the Cultured Generation: A Social History of Music in America, 1870–1900*. Evanston: Northwestern University Press, 1971.

Newman, Nancy. "Gender and the Germanians: 'Art-Loving Ladies' in Nineteenth-Century Concert Life." In *American Orchestras in the Nineteenth Century*, edited by John Spitzer, 289–309. Chicago: University of Chicago Press, 2012.

———. *Good Music for a Free People: The Germania Musical Society in Nineteenth-Century America*. Rochester: University of Rochester Press, 2010.

Nicholls, David, ed. *The Cambridge History of American Music*. Cambridge: Cambridge University Press, 1998.

Ostendorf, Ann. *Sounds American: National Identity and the Music Cultures of the Lower Mississippi River Valley, 1800–1860*. Athens: University of Georgia Press, 2011.

Paige, Paul. "Musical Organizations in Boston, 1830–1850." PhD diss., Boston University, 1967.

Pantaleoni, Hewitt. "A Reconsideration of Fillmore Reconsidered." *American Music* 3, no. 2 (Summer 1985): 217—28.

Pisani, Michael V. "Hiawatha to Wa-Wan: Musical Boston and the Uses of Native American Lore." *American Music* 19, no. 1 (Spring 2001): 39–50.

Platt, Heather. "Amalie Joachim's 1892 American Tour." *American Brahms Society Newsletter* 35, no. 1 (2017): 1–8.

———. "'For Any Ordinary Performer It Would Be Absurd, Ridiculous or Offensive': Performing Lieder Cycles on the American Stage." In Loges and Tunbridge, *German Song Onstage*, 111–31.

———. "Other Instrumentalists." In *Brahms in Context*, edited by Katy Hamilton and Natasha Loges, 215–26. Cambridge: Cambridge University Press, 2019.

Preston, Katherine K. *Opera for the People: English-Language Opera and Women Managers in Late 19th Century America*. New York: Oxford University Press, 2017.

———. "Opera Is Elite/Opera Is Nationalist: Cosmopolitan Views of Opera Reception in the United States, 1870–90." *Journal of the American Musicological Society* 66, no. 2 (2013): 535–39.

Purdy, Christopher. "Whither the Song Recital." CS Music (January 1, 2002), https:// www.csmusic.net/content/articles/whither-the-song-recital/.

Rademacher, Wiebke. "German Song and the Working Classes in Berlin, 1890–1914." In Loges and Tunbridge, *German Song Onstage*, 203–222.

Reich, Nancy. "Robert Schumann's Music in New York City, 1848–1898." In *European Music and Musicians in New York City, 1840–1900*, edited by John Graziano, 10–28. Rochester: University of Rochester Press, 2006.

Reynolds, Christopher. "Documenting the Zenith of Women Song Composers: A Database of Songs Published in the United States and the British Commonwealth, ca. 1890–1930." *Notes* 69, no. 4 (June 2013): 671–87.

———. "Growing the Database of Women Songwriters, 1890–1930." *AMS Musicology Now* (September 21, 2015): https://musicologynow.org/growing-the-database-of-women-songwriters-1890–1930/.

Roell, Craig H. *The Piano in America, 1890–1940*. Chapel Hill: University of North Carolina Press, 1989.

Rogers, Clara Kathleen Doria. *The Story of Two Lives: Home, Friends and Travels*. n.p.: Plimpton, 1932.

Ronyak, Jennifer. "Beethoven Within Grasp: The Nineteenth-Century Reception of 'Adelaide.'" *Music & Letters* 97, no. 2 (May 2016): 249–76.

———. *Intimacy, Performance, and the Lied in the Early Nineteenth Century*. Bloomington: Indiana University Press, 2018.

Saloman, Ora Frishberg. *Beethoven's Symphonies and J. S. Dwight: The Birth of American Music Criticism*. Boston: Northeastern University Press, 1995.

Samson, Jim. "Nations and Nationalism." In *The Cambridge History of Nineteenth Century Music*, 568–600. Cambridge: Cambridge University Press, 2001.

Saunders, Steven. "The Social Agenda of Stephen Foster's Plantation Melodies." *American Music* 30, no. 3 (Fall 2012): 275–89.

Savage, Heather de. "'Under the Gallic Spell': Boston's Embrace of Gabriel Fauré, 1892–1924." *Nineteenth Century Music Review* 19, no. 2 (2022) 255–72.

Schabas, Ezra. *Theodore Thomas: America's Conductor and Builder of Orchestras, 1835–1905*. Urbana: University of Illinois Press, 1989.

Schmidt, John C. "Osgood, George Laurie." *The Grove Dictionary of American Music*. 2nd ed. *Oxford Music Online, 2009*. www.oxfordmusiconline.com.

Scott, Derek B. "Music and Social Class." *Cambridge History of Nineteenth Century Music*, edited by David Nicholls, 544–67. Cambridge: Cambridge University Press, 2001.

———. *The Singing Bourgeois: Songs of the Victorian Drawing Room and Parlour*. Milton Keynes: Open University Press, 1989.

Scott, Michael. *The Record of Singing: To 1914*. New York: Scribner's, 1977.

Sears, Elizabeth Ann. "The Art Song in Boston, 1880–1914." PhD diss., Catholic University of America, 1993.

Shadle, Douglas W. *Antonín Dvořák's* New World Symphony. New York: Oxford University Press, 2021.

———. *Orchestrating the Nation: The Nineteenth-Century American Symphonic Enterprise*. Oxford: Oxford University Press, 2016.

Smith, Clifford P. "Early History of Christian Science in Germany." *Christian Science Journal* (1934). https://journal.christianscience.com/shared/view/1m6x5fr3egs.

Smith, Tim. "Songs of a Woman's Love and Loss, from a Stellar Messenger." *Baltimore Sun*, April 16, 2017, E5.

Snyder, Jean E. *Harry T. Burleigh: From the Spiritual to the Harlem Renaissance*. Urbana: University of Illinois Press, 2016.

Snyder, Suzanne. "The *Männerchor* Tradition in the United States: A Historical Analysis of Its Contribution to American Musical Culture." PhD diss., University of Iowa, 1991.

Solie, Ruth. "Whose Life? The Gendered Self in Schumann's *Frauenliebe* Songs." In *Music and Text: Critical Inquiries*, edited by Steven Paul Scher, 219–40. Cambridge: Cambridge University Press, 1992.

Spitzer, John. "Review of Lawrence Levine's *Highbrow/Lowbrow.*" *American Music* 8, no. 2 (1990): 233–36.

Stafford, Karen. "Binders' Volumes and the Culture of Music Collectorship in the United States, 1830–1870." PhD diss., Indiana University, 2020.

Stearns, David Patrick. "No Binoculars Needed." *Philadelphia Inquirer,* January 12, 2020, H4.

Stevenson, Robert. "Schubert in America: First Publications and Performances." *Inter-American Music Review* 1, no. 1 (1978): 5–10.

Stewart-MacDonald, Rohan H. "The Recital in England: Sir William Sterndale Bennett's 'Classical Chamber Concerts,' 1843–1856." *Ad Parnassum* 13, no. 25 (2015): 115–75.

Swenson, Rolf. "Pilgrims at the Golden Gate: Christian Scientists on the Pacific Coast, 1880–1915." *Pacific Historical Review* 72, no. 2 (2003): 229–63.

Tawa, Nicholas E. *The Coming of Age of American Art Music: New England's Classical Romanticists*. New York: Greenwood, 1991.

Theeman, Nancy Sarah. "The Life and Songs of Augusta Holmés." PhD diss., University of Maryland, 1983.

Thomas, Theodore. *Selected Orchestral Arrangements*, edited by Paul Luongo. Middleton: A-R Editions, 2017.

Tick, Judith. "Passed Away Is the Piano Girl: Changes in American Musical Life, 1870–1900." In *Women Making Music: The Western Art Tradition, 1150–1950*, edited by Jane Bowers and Judith Tick, 325–48. Urbana: University of Illinois Press, 1986.

Tischler, Barbara B. "One Hundred Percent Americanism and Music in Boston During World War I." *American Music* 4, no. 2 (1986): 164–76.

Tommasini, Anthony. "Devising an Experiment to Save the Song Recital." *New York Times,* January 18, 1997, sec. 1, 15.

Tunbridge, Laura. "Introduction" to Loges and Tunbridge, *German Song Onstage*, 1–9.

———. *Singing in the Age of Anxiety: Lieder Performances in New York and London Between the World Wars*. Chicago: University of Chicago Press, 2018.

———. "Singing Translations: The Politics of Listening Between the Wars." *Representations* 123, no. 1 (Summer 2013): 53–86.

———. *The Song Cycle*. Cambridge: Cambridge University Press, 2010.

Turner, Kristen M. "'A Joyous Star-Spangled-Bannerism': Emma Juch, Opera in English Translation, and the American Cultural Landscape in the Gilded Age." *Journal of the Society for American Music* 8, no. 2 (2014): 219–52.

———. "Opera in English: Class and Culture in America, 1878–1910." PhD diss., University of North Carolina, 2015.

Upton, William Treat. *Art-Song in America: A Study in the Development of American Music*. New York: Oliver Ditson, 1930.

Urrows, David. "Apollo in Athens: Otto Dresel and Boston, 1850–90." *American Music* 12, no. 4 (1994): 345–88.

———, ed. *Otto Dresel: Keyboard Music*. Middleton: A-R Editions, 2015.

Van Tassel, Eric. "'Something Utterly New': Listening to Schubert Lieder." *Early Music* 25, no. 4 (November 1997): 702–14.

Weber, Rolf, ed. *Land ohne Nachtigall: Deutsche Emigranten in Amerika*. Berlin: Der Morgen, 1981.

Weber, William. *The Great Transformation of Musical Taste*. Cambridge: Cambridge University Press, 2008.

———. "The History of Musical Canon." In *Rethinking Music*, edited by Nicholas Cook and Mark Everist, 336–55. Oxford: Oxford University Press, 1999.

———. *Music and the Middle Class: The Social Structure of Concert Life in London, Paris, and Vienna*. New York: Holmes & Meier, 1975.

Whitesitt, Linda. "'The Most Potent Force' in American Music: The Role of Women's Music Clubs in American Concert Life." *Musical Woman* 3 (1991): 663–81.

———. "The Role of Women Impresarios in American Concert Life, 1871–1933." *American Music* 7, no. 2 (1989): 159–80.

———. "Women as 'Keepers of Culture': Music Clubs, Community Concert Series and Symphony Orchestras." In *Cultivating Music in America: Women Patrons and Activists Since 1860*, edited by Ralph P. Locke and Cyrilla Barr, 65–86. Berkeley: University of California Press, 1997.

Wilson Kimber, Marian. *The Elocutionists: Women, Music, and the Spoken Word*. Urbana: University of Illinois Press, 2017.

———. "Listening to Loss in 'The Cry of Rachel.'" Women's Song Forum. https://www .womensongforum.org/2021/03/17/listening-to-loss-in-the-cry-of-rachel/.

Wirth, Julia. *Julius Stockhausen: Der Sänger des Deutschen Lieder*. Frankfurt am Main: Englert/Schlosser, 1927.

[Wolf, Hugo]. *The Music Criticism of Hugo Wolf*. Translated, edited, and annotated by Henry Pleasants. New York: Holmes & Meier, 1979.

Youens, Susan. "'Eine wahre Olla Patrida [*sic*]': Anna Milder-Hauptmann, Schubert, and Programming the Orient." In Loges and Tunbridge, *German Song Onstage*, 10–51.

———. *Heinrich Heine and the Lied*. Cambridge: Cambridge University Press, 2007.

Index

Abt, Franz Wilhelm, 5, 18, 96, 105, 233n79
African American songs, 10, 158, 160–64, 184, 186, 211, 260n110, 266n91, 272n64, 273n65
Aldrich, Richard, 150
Allen, B. D. (Benjamin Dwight), 54, 57, 71, 229n26
American songs. *See* African American songs; Creole songs; Native American songs; Tin Pan Alley songs; *and individual composers*
Apthorp, William, 40, 41, 200, 250n76
Arkansas, 176, 186

Bach, Johann Sebastian, 3, 58, 65, 78, 144, 158, 167, 181, 204, 233n76
Balakirev, Mily, 127, 205, 265n78
Beach, Amy, 92, 127, 190
Beethoven, Ludwig van, 5, 8, 31, 44, 49–51, 57, 74, 79, 174, 200, 203, 233n79, 270n17; "Adelaide" (op. 46), 18, 23, 28, 29, 38, 102, 155, 174, 204, 222nn23–24, 256n 50; *An die ferne Geliebte* (op. 98), 38, 50, 58, 62, 69, 85, 102, 105, 113, 150, 155, 172, 178, 180, 191, 225n69, 233n76, 256n50; "Kennst du das Land?" (op. 75, no. 1), 45, 52
Behrens, Conrad, 117
Bellini, Vincenzo, 125, 74, 222n20
Bergh, Arthur, 186, 264n66, 266n86
Bergmann, Carl, 29, 31
Bispham, David, 4, 7, 21, 84, 94, 122, 127, 128, 130, 132, 152, 164, 167–96, 204, 211,

214, 215, 256n70, 261n1, 261nn5–6, 263n31, 263n46, 264n48, 265n68, 265n77, 266n86
Bizet, Georges, 97, 204, 205
Blauvelt, Lillian, 86, 130
Bond, Carrie Jacobs, 188, 190, 203
Boston, 13, 23–24, 28–46, 52, 64, 67, 68, 73–82, 84–88, 91, 92, 98, 107–10, 113, 118–27, 137, 152, 156–58, 165, 174, 180, 181, 213–24, 222n25
Boston Conservatory, 40, 143, 144
Boston Symphony Orchestra, 73, 79, 82, 87, 97, 118, 127, 156, 206
Brahms, Johannes, 1, 12, 14, 31, 44, 55, 73, 80, 83, 87, 90, 91, 112, 121, 125, 132, 137, 143, 148, 181, 199, 269n4; "Auf dem Kirchhofe" (op. 105, no. 4), 113; "Es träumte mir" (op. 57, no. 3), 77; "Gestillte Sehnsucht" and "Geistliches Wiegenlied" (op. 91), 112; "Heimweh" (op. 63, nos. 7–9), 108, 150; *Liebeslieder* (opp. 52 and 65), 79; "Liebestreu" (op. 3, no. 1), 55; *Magelone Romances* (op. 33), 77, 113, 151–52, 158, 172–73, 180, 214; "Das Mädchen spricht" (op. 107, no. 3), 91; "Minnelied" (op. 71, no. 5), 90; "Ruhe, Süßliebchen" (op. 33, no. 9), 60; "Sonntag" (op. 47, no. 3), 60; "Spanish Serenade"/"Spanisches Lied" (op. 6, no. 1), 65; "Treue Liebe" (op. 33, no. 15), 172, 180; "Unüberwindlich" (op. 72, no. 5), 90; "Verrat" (op. 105, no. 5), 113; *Vier ernste Gesänge* (op. 121), 121, 127, 172, 173, 179, 180, 214; "Von ewiger Liebe" (op. 43, no.

Brahms, Johannes (*continued*)
1), 108, 180; "Wie bist du, meine Königin"
(op. 32, no. 9), 77; "Wie Melodien zieht
es mir" (op. 105, no. 1), 204; "Wiegenlied"
(op. 49, no. 4), 60, 155, 198; *Zigeunerlieder*
(op. 103), 241n91
Branscombe, Gena, 191
Brinkerhoff, Clara, 55–56
Brittan, Charles H., 40, 41, 64, 230n43
Brooklyn (NY), 59, 68, 70, 76, 78, 87, 118,
127–28, 130, 182, 187, 214, 232n56
Bruch, Max, 59, 97
Brückler, Hugo, 108, 111, 137, 201
Buck, Dudley, 173, 186, 233n79
Buffalo (NY), 42, 68, 78, 82, 97, 116, 187,
240n85
Burleigh, Harry, 164, 184, 186, 211, 266n82,
266n91
Burns, Robert, 70, 153
Burton, Frederick, 186, 266n80

Cady, Calvin, 161, 165, 259n99
California, 123, 128, 131, 155, 156
Calvé, Emma, 204, 205
Canada, 107, 108, 114, 118, 174, 176, 177,
244n48
Chadwick, George, 79, 109, 120, 126, 173
Chaminade, Cécile, 91, 125, 191, 205
Chicago, 41, 56–59, 63–65, 67, 80, 82, 89, 99,
102, 106, 107, 121, 122, 126, 128, 132, 137,
142, 151, 152, 160, 165, 173, 174, 180, 181, 192,
214; Amateur Musical Club, 87–88, 129,
143, 145, 146, 154, 188; Beethoven Society,
58, 59, 64, 79, 98, 116
Cincinnati, 11, 43, 50, 82, 97, 116, 211
Chopin, Frédéric, 33, 44, 54, 58, 74, 79, 200,
237n35
Clay, Frederic: "Gipsy John," 125, 129, 132;
"Sands o' Dee," 63
Cleveland, 91, 134, 145, 158, 173
Coleridge-Taylor, Samuel, 184–86, 205
Cook, Will Marion, 185
Cornelius, Peter, 112, 150, 152, 155, 200, 202
Creole songs, 158, 161, 163, 258n92
Crouch, Frederick Nicholls 52, 54
Culp, Julia 138, 183, 203, 215

Damrosch, Helene, 75, 236n16
Damrosch, Leopold, 3, 74, 75, 95–97, 105,
106, 112, 195
Damrosch, Walter, 8, 110, 145, 173, 174, 183,
187, 195
Davenport, Warren, 120

Davies, Fanny, 110, 112, 173
De Koven, Reginald, 173, 267n103
Delibes, Léo, 91, 125, 205
Densmore, Frances, 153, 164, 260n108
Denver, 132, 146, 156, 158, 170
Dillingham, Mary B., 144, 145, 165
Detroit, 128, 129, 135, 142
Ditson, Oliver, 9, 32, 35, 36, 38, 46, 63, 78,
109, 138, 150, 186, 198–201, 204, 205
Doria, Clara. *See* Rogers, Clara Kathleen
Dresel, Otto, 24, 28, 31–38, 40, 41, 71, 200
Dvořák, Antonín, 1, 91, 112, 130, 134, 162,
200, 240n78, 245n56, 259n101, 259n105
Dwight, John Sullivan, 3, 4, 11, 24, 28, 31–38,
40, 46, 52, 71, 73, 79, 115, 146, 166, 195, 201,
208
Dwight's Journal of Music, 5, 8, 15, 23, 29, 35,
37, 38, 41, 44, 45, 50–57, 64, 74

Eddy, Clarence, 65, 67, 233n79
Eddy, Mary Baker, 260n112
Eddy, Sarah (née Hershey), 56, 57, 65
Ehlert, Louis, 54–55
Eichberg, Julius, 30, 37, 40
Eisfeld, Theodore, 31, 33
Elgar, Edward, 181
Elson, Louis C., 16, 38, 40–41, 43, 110, 113,
121, 135, 153, 161, 163, 199, 200, 201
Esser, Heinrich, 49, 58, 59

Farrar, Geraldine, 138, 193, 204
Farwell, Arthur, 158, 164, 183, 186, 260n108,
266n80
Fauré, Gabriel, 91, 171, 205, 262n21, 265n72
Faure, Jean-Baptiste, 69, 235n99
Ferris, George T., 55, 71
Fielitz, Alexander von, 150, 152, 155, 156, 201
Fillmore, John Comfort, 161, 163
Fillunger, Marie, 112, 173
Finck, Henry, 104, 150, 170, 171, 197, 198, 200,
207, 269n6
Fletcher, Alice, 161, 163, 258n88
Florida, 177
folksong, 2, 6, 52–54, 59, 63, 68–70, 148,
150, 152–53, 171, 193, 199; American, 20,
160–62, 258n93; British Isles, 7, 24, 82,
152, 153, 156, 179, 205; German, 12, 35, 54,
148, 150
Foote, Arthur, 74, 86, 92, 109, 126, 129, 143,
173, 187
Foster, Stephen, 162, 259n102
Franz, Robert, 1, 3, 8, 23, 24, 31–42, 44, 46,
54, 55, 58, 59, 65, 67, 74, 76, 80, 91, 102,

132, 148, 199, 200; "Ave Maria" (op. 17, no. 1), 31, 35, 36; "Frühlingsgedränge" (op. 7, no. 5), 39; "Für Musik" (op. 10, no. 1), 39, 204; "Gewitternacht" (op. 8, no. 6), 39; "Mailied" (op. 33, no. 3), 43; "Mutter, O sing' mich zu Ruh'" (op. 10, no. 3), 36

Freer, Eleanor, 184, 188, 192

French songs, 2, 7, 16, 52, 59, 63, 68, 72, 82, 86, 87, 91–92, 103, 109, 117, 125, 136, 158, 171, 180, 182, 204–5, 214

Gade, Niels, 69

Gadski, Johanna, 78, 170, 174, 176, 177, 180–82, 194, 203, 239n62, 269n131

Gauthier, Éva, 205

Gems of German Song, 5, 38, 224nn59–60, 232n64

Gerhardt, Elena, 183, 203, 206, 215

Germania Musical Society, 29, 30, 33, 36, 219n31

German immigrants, 3, 11, 13, 17, 25, 29, 30, 95–97, 146, 221n7, 222n25, 223n33

Gilibert, Charles, 182, 204, 265n72

Gill, James, 58–59, 233n76

Gleason, Frederick Grant, 11, 65, 80, 89–90, 230n43, 233n77

Gluck, Alma, 193, 265n78

Gluck, Christoph Willibald, 51, 230n33

Goethe, Johann Wolfgang von, 12, 32

Gogorza, Emilio de, 177

Gordigiani, Luigi, 205

Goring Thomas, Arthur, 92, 109, 112

Gounod, Charles, 44, 56, 59, 63, 78, 103, 109, 113, 205, 227n97

Greene, Harry Plunket, 88, 116, 153

Greenfield, Elizabeth Taylor, 25

Grieg, Edvard, 1, 44, 68, 69, 91, 109, 171, 199, 201, 202, 269n4

Gutmann, Albert, 49, 50

Hahn, Reynaldo, 92, 182, 205

Hale, Philip 16, 121–23, 126, 133–35, 140, 176, 204

Hall, Marguerite, 86, 88, 151, 156, 165, 172, 180, 181, 262n28

Handel, George Frideric, 51, 65, 69, 74, 76, 84, 123, 137, 177, 194, 204, 230n33, 270n16

Hanslick, Eduard, 12, 80

Hartford (CT), 50, 120, 121, 156, 165, 247n16

Hayden, Charles R., 44, 74, 77, 236n10

Haydn, Joseph, 28, 31, 45, 74, 125, 230n33

Hayes, Roland, 93, 211

Heine, Heinrich, 12, 26, 46, 123

Heinrich, Julia, 20, 96, 112, 120, 122, 125, 128, 129, 132, 135, 136, 157, 198, 269n2

Heinrich, Max, 1, 70, 84, 85, 88, 95–141, 146, 155, 156, 167, 168, 192, 201, 202, 206, 212, 214, 215, 242n4, 244n48, 245n56, 247n16, 250n63, 250n76, 251n97, 261n1, 262n17

Heinrich, Mrs. (Annie), 20, 96, 113, 125, 135–36, 247n21

Heinrich, Wilhelm, 116, 152, 156–57, 158, 214, 222–23n25, 257n72, 264n55

Held, Anna (the second Mrs. Heinrich), 122–23, 248n28, 251n97, 251n101

Henderson, William James, 171, 172–73, 203, 204, 206–7, 210, 270n17

Henne, Antonia, 188

Henrotin, Ellen (Mrs. Charles), 158, 160, 161, 257n78, 257n84, 260n107

Henschel, George, 18, 63, 67, 70, 95, 97, 98, 102, 104, 105, 110, 113–15, 121, 126, 129, 131, 132, 135, 137, 146, 158, 165, 168, 170, 187, 201, 202, 210, 213, 215, 217n3, 240n78, 242n105, 242n4, 261n1

Henschel, Lillian (née Bailey), 74–75, 78, 79, 82, 84–87, 89, 91, 92, 125, 147, 210, 240n71

Henschels' recitals, The (George and Lillian), 72–94, 98, 99, 103, 104, 107, 111, 116, 130, 131, 135, 144, 145, 156–57, 173, 214, 215, 236n15, 237n29

Herder, Johann Gottfried, 54

Hershey, Sarah. *See* Eddy, Sarah

Hershey School of Musical Art, 57, 59, 60, 65, 67, 116, 233n76

Higginson, Henry Lee, 29, 73, 79

Hill, Mildred, 160, 162, 164, 258n95, 259nn96–99, 259n105

Hiltz, Grace, 56–57, 64, 65–68, 71, 93, 214, 233n73, 233n77, 233n79, 234n83

Homer, Sidney, 184, 265n69

Hopekirk, Helen, 153, 244n48

Horn, Charles Edward, 28–29

Horrocks, Amy, 125, 134, 137

Hull, Mrs. J., 56, 213

Huneker, James, 96, 114–15, 134, 136, 140, 261n1, 267n96

Huss, Henry Holden, 186, 267n96

Indianist movement, 164, 186, 266n80

Indiana, 67, 118, 128, 204

Iowa, 67, 145, 153, 158, 177, 265n68

Jensen, Adolf, 58–60, 91, 102, 104, 112, 125, 137, 199, 233n79, 269n4

Index   295

Jewett, Mrs. E. A. (Jennie M.), 56–57
Joachim, Amalie, 18, 60, 83, 85, 89, 111, 116, 144, 150–54, 165, 166, 219n37, 253n10, 254n19, 255n39
Joachim, Joseph, 73, 83, 110, 173, 185
Johannsen, Bertha, 31, 233n37
Jordan, Julius (Jules), 64, 67, 75, 79, 109, 214
Juch, Emma, 43, 97, 119, 130

Kansas, 171, 176
Kentucky, 158, 162, 163
Kirchner, Theodor, 44, 227n98
Kirpal, Margaretha, 108, 242n11
Knight, Joseph Philip, 28–29, 49, 213
Krehbiel, Henry, 4, 16, 153, 161–63, 179, 195, 245n57, 258n93, 266n80
Kreissmann, August, 13, 23–24, 30, 33, 36–41, 46, 51, 82, 110, 213, 224n60, 228n14
Kücken, Friedrich Wilhelm, 5, 18

Lacombe, Paul, 109
La Flesche, Francis, 161, 164, 258n90, 260n108
La Grange, Anna Caroline de, 67, 91
Lamperti, Francesco, 41, 59, 167
Lang, Benjamin J. (B. J.), 45, 74, 75, 78, 86, 118
Lang, Margaret Ruthven, 92, 109, 127, 190
Large, Josephine, 67, 165, 256n50
Lassen, Eduard, 108–9, 201, 233n79
Lawson, Corinne Moore, 172
Lehmann, Caroline, 30–31, 33
Lehmann, Lilli, 50, 89, 97, 121, 135, 140, 152, 170, 172, 214
Lehmann, Liza, 112, 158, 173, 179, 183, 188, 189
Leipzig Conservatory, 36, 37, 57, 58, 69, 73, 74
Leonhard, Hugo, 30, 37, 44
lieder: cycles, 26, 38, 45, 49, 69, 150–52, 155, 172–73, 179–81, 213, 214, 215 (*see also individual compositions*); in English translation, 2, 5, 6, 11, 16, 24–29, 35, 36, 38, 42, 46, 56, 58, 68, 77, 99, 103, 117, 123–25, 127, 130, 137, 138, 155, 171, 191, 204, 206, 209, 210, 218n14, 221n11, 224n59, 248n32, 252n107, 255n34, 267n108; *Innigkeit*, 12, 140; as understood by Americans, 6–7, 10–14, 26, 29, 38, 108, 132, 134, 166, 181, 201–3, 208, 210
Liederabende, 18, 20, 46, 48–50, 55, 59, 60, 76, 107, 214
Lind, Jenny, 25, 26, 54, 70, 72, 109

Liszt, Franz, 28, 33, 35, 36, 45, 49–52, 58, 59, 84, 91, 97, 108, 199, 210, 233n79, 270n17
Little, Lena, 111–13, 116–18, 127, 151
Loeffler, Charles Martin, 127, 249n44
Loewe, Carl, 1, 74, 85, 87, 91, 148, 177, 179; "Die Abgeschiedenen" (op. 9, Heft 2 no. 3), 225n73; "Abschied" (op. 3, no. 1), 225n73; "Edward" (op. 1, no. 1), 193; "Des Glockentürmers Töchterlein" ("The Bell Ringer's Daughter") (op. 112a), 69; "Hochzeitslied" (op. 20, no. 1), 38; "Der Totentanz" (op. 44, no. 3), 225n73; "Die Uhr" (op. 123, no. 3), 69; "Die Überfahrt" (op. 94, no. 1), 51; "Der Wirthin Töchterlein" (op. 1, no. 2), 38, 225n73
London, 59, 63, 69, 73, 82, 93, 111–14, 125, 167, 172, 173, 176, 183–85, 206, 209, 213, 214, 238n51, 240n71
Los Angeles, 123, 130, 131, 132, 155, 156, 191

MacDowell, Edward, 126, 171, 183, 184
MacKenzie, Alexander Campbell, 20, 102, 103, 113, 125–26, 132
Männerchöre 9, 13, 15, 23, 25, 37, 58, 75, 97, 107, 168, 220n61, 221n8
married couples performing lieder, 236n14. *See also* Henschels' recitals, The
Mason, Lowell, 30, 37, 230n35
Mason, William, 31, 33, 38, 39, 40, 213
Massenet, Jules, 78, 91, 92, 182
Mathews, W. S. B. (William Smythe Babcock), 3, 41, 42, 56–58, 60, 65, 71, 128, 136, 147, 191, 199, 201, 230n35, 231n52, 233n73
Mattullath, Alice, 138, 252n107
Maurel, Victor, 182, 204, 214, 264n56
McCormack, John, 93, 138, 205
Méhul, Ètienne, 230n33
melodramas, 122, 181. *See also individual composers*
Mendelssohn, Felix, 8, 26, 33, 35, 52, 58, 60, 65, 75, 79, 96, 143, 194, 199, 200, 230n33, 230n43, 244n48, 255n39; "An die Entfernte" (op. 71, no. 3), 45; "Auf Flügeln des Gesanges" ("On Wings of Song," op. 34, no. 2), 6, 25, 45, 91; "Frühlingslied" ("Spring Song," op. 8, no. 6), 45
Mendelssohn Quintette Club, 28, 30, 31, 37, 63, 75, 223n33
Merest, Mrs., 230n33
Mexico, 130
Meyerbeer, Giacomo, 59, 74, 182
Meyer-Helmund, Erik, 70
Meyn, Heinrich, 116, 151–52, 172, 214

296   Index

Michigan, 67, 129, 176. *See also* Detroit
Milwaukee, 97, 98, 99, 107, 214
Minneapolis, 144, 145, 151, 166, 253n15
Moore, Eva Perry (Mrs. Philip North), 160
Moore, Thomas, 63, 230n33
Mozart, Wolfgang Amadeus, 3, 28, 31, 56, 96, 168, 222n20, 230n33
Muldoon, Anita, 158, 160–63, 257n82, 259n100
Murphy, Jeanette Robinson, 164, 260n110

Nashville (TN), 88, 168
Native American songs, 158, 161, 163, 184, 186, 193, 259n105, 260n108, 260n111, 266n91
Nevin, Ethelbert, 7, 125, 187, 240n79, 248n37, 267n104
New York (NY), 11, 13, 15, 24, 25, 28, 29, 31, 33, 38–40, 44, 46, 51, 52, 55, 57, 72, 74–78, 82, 83, 86–88, 93, 97–99, 102–9, 112, 116, 117, 123, 127, 128, 143, 145, 147, 151, 167, 168, 184, 185, 172–74, 177, 179–82, 188, 192, 197, 202, 204–6, 209, 213–15, 223n38, 225n65, 228n13
Nordica, Lillian Norton, 110, 119, 152, 168, 170, 171, 176, 177, 215
normal music schools, 19, 48, 50, 56, 57, 60, 65, 152, 165, 198, 213, 227n1, 230n35, 230n44, 233n76, 256n50

Oakland (CA), 93, 131, 155
Ohio, 50, 67, 74, 134, 145, 177, 221n7
Osgood, George L., 24, 33, 36, 41–46, 54, 64, 65, 67, 109, 213, 233n78

Paderewski, Ignacy, 131, 172
Paine, John Knowles, 43, 54
Parker, Horatio, 109, 119, 120
Pasmore, Henry B., 57
Patti, Adelina, 82, 110, 237n35
Patti, Amelia, 24
Paur, Emil, 118, 127
Pennsylvania, 56, 67, 147, 181
Perabo, Ernst, 28, 30, 37, 38, 45, 225n73
Philadelphia, 15, 28, 31, 40, 57, 59, 75, 95–99, 102, 103, 108, 113, 114, 167, 171, 174, 214
piano, 4, 8, 30, 33, 54, 57–58, 65, 116, 143, 170, 198, 207, 264n48; accompanists, 15, 34–35, 44, 52, 54, 55, 69, 75, 76, 85, 99, 104, 111, 113, 127, 133, 144–45, 165, 174, 236n14, 249n51 (*see also under individual performers*); preludes/transitions, 85, 88, 239n70; role in lieder, 5, 32, 38, 39, 40, 51, 85, 103,

104, 108, 128, 135, 138, 202; transcriptions of lieder, 28, 36, 45, 225n73
Pischek, Johann Baptist, 48–49, 74, 213
Pollack, Ignaz, 57
Providence (RI), 64, 65, 67, 78, 129, 143, 150, 214, 245n56, 255n39
Purcell, Henry, 52, 205, 233n76

Raff, Joachim, 58, 233n79
recordings, 87, 89, 93, 122, 138, 179, 184, 190, 194, 198, 202, 205–7, 209, 239n56, 239n70, 240n78, 254n16, 265n72
Reger, Max, 180
Reichmann, Theodor, 111, 116, 246n2
Reimann, Heinrich, 150, 255n34, 255n37
Reinecke, Carl, 143, 201
Remmertz, Franz, 43, 84, 97, 107
Richter, Ernst Friedrich, 58
Richter, Hans 73, 110, 112, 114, 173
Rimsky–Korsakov, Nikolai, 127, 205
Ritter, Fanny Raymond, 48, 50–55, 57, 60, 70, 150, 213, 231n52, 236n15
Ritter, Frédéric Louis, 50–54, 64, 150, 228n14, 228n16, 229n17
Rochester (NY), 42, 88, 107
Rogers, Clara Kathleen (Clara Doria), 33, 43, 44, 74, 92, 127, 144, 154
Root, Frederick W., 160, 161, 257n85
Root, George F., 230n35
Rooy, Anton Van, 170
Rossini, Gioachino, 79, 109, 245n55
Rosenthal, Moriz, 86, 88, 131
Rubinstein, Anton, 46, 54, 55, 58–60, 74, 76, 89, 91, 102, 112, 200, 205, 227n98, 233n76, 233n79, 269n4
Rudersdorff, Mme. Erminia, 67, 74, 234n80
Russian songs, 171, 199, 204, 205

Salter, Mary Turner, 190, 268n113
San Diego, 123, 248n26
San Francisco, 57, 130–32, 155, 156, 174, 184, 231n46
Santley, Charles, 114, 125, 246n78
Saran, August, 35
Sbriglia, Giovanni, 67
Schubert, Franz, 1, 3, 5, 8, 18, 19, 23–26, 28–37, 39, 41–45, 55, 56, 59, 65, 68, 79, 82, 87, 90, 96, 99, 107, 115, 123, 132, 133, 138, 145, 148, 172, 177, 180, 192–94, 199, 202, 203, 214, 221n7, 221n11, 222n15, 227n91, 229n17, 230n43, 233n76, 233n79, 240n78, 269n4, 270n17; "Die Allmacht" (D. 852), 118; "Am Meer" (D. 957, no. 12), 271n45;

Index   297

Schubert, Franz (*continued*)
"An Schwager Kronos" (D. 369), 112; "An Sylvia" (D. 891), 193; "Aufenthalt" (D. 957, no. 5), 40; "Ave Maria" (D. 839), 28, 35, 52; "Die Post" (D. 911, no. 13), 128; "Der Leiermann" (D. 911, no. 24), 89; "Doppelgänger" (D. 957, no. 13), 43; "Frühlingsglaube" (D. 686), 128; "Erlkönig" (D. 328), 7, 28, 29, 42, 43, 50, 129, 130, 135, 155, 194, 198; "Die Forelle" (The Trout) (D. 550), 45; "Ganymed" (D. 544), 150; "Gretchen am Spinnrade" (D. 118), 74; "Gruppe aus dem Tartarus" (D. 583), 134; "Heidenröslein" (D. 257), 74; "Liebesbotschaft" (D. 957, no. 1), 97 ; "Lob der Tränen" (D. 711), 26; "Pax Vobiscum" (D. 551), 102; "Rastlose Liebe" (D. 138), 97; *Die schöne Müllerin* (D. 795), 49, 60, 64, 69, 80, 137, 150, 151, 155, 156, 179–81, 213, 239n70; *Schwanengesang* (D. 957), 64, 102; "Ständchen" ("Hark Hark! The Lark") (D. 889), 270n14; "Ständchen" ("Serenade") (D. 957), 6, 25, 28, 43, 52, 103, 218n20; "Trockne Blumen" (D. 795, no. 18), 31, 128; "Die junge Nonne" (D. 828), 103; "Die Waldesnacht" (aka "Im Walde") (D. 708), 32, 49; "Der Wanderer" (D. 489), 12, 25, 28, 43, 52, 103, 193, 223n38, 224n59; *Winterreise* (D. 911), 11–12, 13, 49, 64, 80, 102, 151, 180, 206, 209, 210, 213, 264n55; "Wohin?" (D. 795, no. 2), 85; "Das Zügenglöcklein" (D. 871), 224n59
Schumann, Clara, 37, 44, 73, 83, 110, 112, 153, 173, 188, 191, 267n108
Schumann, Robert, 1, 3–5, 7, 8, 18, 19, 23–26, 31, 33–42, 44, 49–56, 58, 59, 70, 74, 78–80, 83, 87, 90, 99, 102–4, 122, 128, 148, 177–81, 188, 192, 198, 199, 202–4, 227n91, 228n13, 229n17, 231n52, 233n76, 233n79, 240n78, 254n24, 255n39, 269n4, 269n7, 270n17; "An den Sonnenschein" (op. 36, no. 4), 25; "Dein Angesicht" (op. 127, no. 2), 104; "Die arme Peter" (op. 53, no. 3), 139, 140; "Die beiden Grenadiere" (op. 49, no. 1), 7, 76, 84, 97, 103, 107, 129, 132, 155, 193, 202, 204, 252n107, 271n45; *Dichterliebe* (op. 48), 26, 37, 38, 45, 58, 60, 65, 112, 137, 179, 180, 213, 225n66; "Du Ring an meinem Finger" (op. 42, no. 4), 26, 56, 96; *Frauenliebe und -leben* (op. 42), 26, 45–46, 65, 151, 180, 191, 213; "Frühlingsnacht" (op. 39, no. 12), 39, 96; "Hidalgo" (op. 30, no. 3), 134; "Ich grolle nicht" (op. 48, no. 7), 76, 96, 104; "Ich wandelte unter

den Bäumen" (op. 24, no. 3), 51; *Lieder-Album für die Jugend* (op. 79), 127, 154; "Die Lotosblume" (op. 25, no. 7), 51, 109, 242n105; "Mondnacht" (op. 39, no. 5), 39; "Der Nussbaum" (op. 25, no. 3), 45, 174; "Die Rose, die Lilie" (op. 48, no. 3), 26; "Sängers Trost" (op. 127, no. 1), 138; "Schöne Wiege meiner Leiden" (op. 24, no. 5), 51; "Verratene Liebe" (op. 40, no. 5), 204; "Waldesgespräch" (op. 39, no. 3), 39; "Wenn ich deine Augen seh'" (op. 48, no. 4), 26; "Widmung" (op. 25, no. 1), 36, 103, 202; "Zwei Venetianische Lieder" (op. 25, nos. 17 and 18), 102, 103, 123
Schumann-Heink, Ernestine, 10, 21, 150, 151, 168, 170, 171, 177, 182–84, 186, 189, 192, 194, 200, 204, 207, 214, 215, 239n62, 254n16, 266n82, 268n113, 270n15
Sembrich, Marcella, 125, 140, 170, 171, 174, 177, 180, 193, 215, 260n108
Shakespeare, William (English singing teacher), 167, 261n2
sheet music, 3, 5–9, 12, 13, 17–20, 24, 26, 36, 45, 63, 72, 92, 109, 125, 126, 128, 150, 170, 190, 197, 200, 227n101, 243n13
Sherwood, Mary (Mrs. W. H.), 143
Sherwood, William, 75, 78
Silcher, Friedrich, 5
Sontag, Henriette, 25
South Carolina, 177
Spies, Hermine, 111–13, 246n71
Stacey, Mrs. Clara D., 58
Staudigl, Josef, 49, 74, 110
Steinway, William, 17, 228n13
Sterling, Antoinette, 59, 232n56
Stevens, Nelda Hewitt, 164, 184, 260n111
Stigelli, Girogio (aka Georg Stiegel[e]), 25, 31, 49, 213
St. Louis, 160, 251n101, 254n24
Stockhausen, Julius, 12, 18, 30, 37, 38, 44, 45, 49, 50, 54, 57, 63, 65, 69, 73, 83, 112, 116, 121, 144, 152, 170, 213, 238n51, 239n70
Strauss, Richard, 91, 117, 122, 128, 137, 180, 181, 192, 199, 249n51, 252n105, 269n4
Sullivan, Arthur, 233n79

Taubert, Wilhelm, 25, 109, 154
Tchaikovsky, Pyotr, 137, 193, 199, 202, 205, 269n4
Thallon, Robert, 69, 70, 75
Texas, 68, 130, 176, 177, 181, 214
Thomas, Ambroise, 91
Thomas, Arthur Goring, 92, 109, 112

Thomas, Theodore, 3, 24, 25, 31, 33, 38–40, 43, 51, 70, 71, 75, 77, 79, 95, 114, 115, 146, 168, 195, 208, 213, 226n75, 226n89, 250n63, 271n45, 277n91; Thomas Orchestra, 28, 41, 42, 59, 97, 249n51, 260n107
Ticknor, Howard Malcolm, 85
Tin Pan Alley songs, 187, 207, 267n104

Van der Stucken, Frank, 109, 120, 245n57
Varley, Nelson, 44
vaudeville, 132, 184, 192, 211, 266n86
Verdi, Giuseppe, 168, 174
Viardot-Garcia, Pauline, 18, 49, 54, 67, 74, 79, 237n35
Vienna, 14, 20, 44, 48, 49, 59, 60, 80, 134, 201, 202, 213, 214
Vogl, Johann Michael, 133, 134

Wagner, Richard, 4, 108, 110, 114, 118, 145, 155, 168, 174, 200, 227n91, 230n43; *Tannhäuser*, 59, 91, 97, 105, 251n93; *Wesendonck Lieder* (WWV 91), 60, 172
Wallenreiter, Karl, 49, 50, 213
Wallnöfer, Adolf, 49
Walter, Gustav, 18, 20, 44, 49, 59, 60, 65, 76, 111, 213, 214, 227n98
Ware, Harriet, 187, 188, 190
Wassall, Grace, 181
Weber, Carl Maria von, 28, 85, 96
Weeden, (Maria) Howard, 184, 193, 266n84
Werrenrath, George, 48, 57–64, 68–70, 72, 75, 76, 78, 97–99, 214, 234n89, 234n97
Werrenrath, Reinald, 70, 232n57
Wetzler, Hermann Hans, 173, 184
White, Villa Whitney, 142–66, 180, 201, 214
Why, Greta and T. Foster, 236n14
Widor, Charles-Marie, 79
World War I, 7, 136, 194, 203–05

Wolf, Hugo, 14, 91, 116, 136, 180, 182, 192, 199, 202, 203, 214, 246n2, 265n68, 269n4, 271n31
Wolfsohn, Carl, 3, 19, 24, 31, 40, 57–60, 63–64, 71, 75, 79, 98, 116, 214, 223n34
women's clubs (not music), 158, 160, 162, 181
women's music clubs, 1, 4, 9, 15, 20, 78, 86–88, 92, 122, 142–47, 152–54, 164–66, 170, 171, 176, 183, 190, 191, 195, 197, 198, 201, 206–8, 240n85, 254n24, 256n70, 259n103, 260nn107–8, 262n23, 263n46; Amateur Musical Club, Chicago, 87–88, 129, 143, 145, 146, 188, 257n85; Fortnightly Club, Lincoln, Nebraska, 156; Fortnightly Club, St. Joseph, Missouri, 129; Fortnightly Music Club, Cleveland, 91, 145, 262n17; Ladies' Afternoon Musicale, Buffalo, 68; Ladies Musical Club, Burlington, Iowa, 153; Ladies Musical Club, Seattle, 260n108; Ladies Musical Club, Tacoma, Washington, 155; Matinee Musicale, Huntington, Indiana, 67; Mozart Club, Jamestown, New York, 145; Music Club, Lima, Ohio, 177; Musical Club, Portland, Oregon, 154, 155, 165; Philharmonic Society, Nashville, Tennessee, 88; Schubert Club, St. Paul, Minnesota, 88, 142–43, 145, 146, 153; Thursday Musical Club, Minneapolis, 164; Tuesday Afternoon Club, Akron, Ohio, 88; Tuesday Musical Club, Denver, 146, 156; Tuesday Musical, Detroit, 173; Tuesday Musicale, Rochester, New York, 88, 250n63; Wednesday Morning Musical Club, Nashville, Tennessee, 168–69
Wüllner, Ludwig, 133, 134, 180, 215, 252n108

Zelter, Carl Friedrich 18
Zur Mühlen, Raimund von, 133, 238n51

HEATHER PLATT is Sursa Distinguished Professor of Fine Arts and professor of music at Ball State University. She is the author of *Johannes Brahms: A Research and Information Guide,* second edition, and coeditor of *Expressive Interactions in Brahms: Essays in Analysis and Meaning.*

Music in American Life

Only a Miner: Studies in Recorded Coal-Mining Songs *Archie Green*
Great Day Coming: Folk Music and the American Left *R. Serge Denisoff*
John Philip Sousa: A Descriptive Catalog of His Works *Paul E. Bierley*
The Hell-Bound Train: A Cowboy Songbook *Glenn Ohrlin*
Oh, Didn't He Ramble: The Life Story of Lee Collins, as Told to Mary Collins
    Edited by Frank J. Gillis and John W. Miner
American Labor Songs of the Nineteenth Century *Philip S. Foner*
Stars of Country Music: Uncle Dave Macon to Johnny Rodriguez
    Edited by Bill C. Malone and Judith McCulloh
Git Along, Little Dogies: Songs and Songmakers of the American West
    John I. White
A Texas-Mexican *Cancionero*: Folksongs of the Lower Border *Américo Paredes*
San Antonio Rose: The Life and Music of Bob Wills *Charles R. Townsend*
Early Downhome Blues: A Musical and Cultural Analysis *Jeff Todd Titon*
An Ives Celebration: Papers and Panels of the Charles Ives Centennial
    Festival-Conference *Edited by H. Wiley Hitchcock and Vivian Perlis*
Sinful Tunes and Spirituals: Black Folk Music to the Civil War *Dena J. Epstein*
Joe Scott, the Woodsman-Songmaker *Edward D. Ives*
Jimmie Rodgers: The Life and Times of America's Blue Yodeler *Nolan Porterfield*
Early American Music Engraving and Printing: A History of Music Publishing in
    America from 1787 to 1825, with Commentary on Earlier and Later Practices
    Richard J. Wolfe
Sing a Sad Song: The Life of Hank Williams *Roger M. Williams*
Long Steel Rail: The Railroad in American Folksong *Norm Cohen*
Resources of American Music History: A Directory of Source Materials from
    Colonial Times to World War II *D. W. Krummel, Jean Geil, Doris J. Dyen,
    and Deane L. Root*
Tenement Songs: The Popular Music of the Jewish Immigrants *Mark Slobin*
Ozark Folksongs *Vance Randolph; edited and abridged by Norm Cohen*
Oscar Sonneck and American Music *Edited by William Lichtenwanger*
Bluegrass Breakdown: The Making of the Old Southern Sound *Robert Cantwell*
Bluegrass: A History *Neil V. Rosenberg*
Music at the White House: A History of the American Spirit *Elise K. Kirk*
Red River Blues: The Blues Tradition in the Southeast *Bruce Bastin*
Good Friends and Bad Enemies: Robert Winslow Gordon and the Study of
    American Folksong *Debora Kodish*
Fiddlin' Georgia Crazy: Fiddlin' John Carson, His Real World, and the World of
    His Songs *Gene Wiggins*
America's Music: From the Pilgrims to the Present (rev. 3d ed.) *Gilbert Chase*
Secular Music in Colonial Annapolis: The Tuesday Club, 1745–56 *John Barry Talley*
Bibliographical Handbook of American Music *D. W. Krummel*
Goin' to Kansas City *Nathan W. Pearson Jr.*

"Susanna," "Jeanie," and "The Old Folks at Home": The Songs of Stephen C. Foster
from His Time to Ours (2d ed.)   *William W. Austin*
Songprints: The Musical Experience of Five Shoshone Women   *Judith Vander*
"Happy in the Service of the Lord": Afro-American Gospel Quartets in Memphis
Kip Lornell
Paul Hindemith in the United States   *Luther Noss*
"My Song Is My Weapon": People's Songs, American Communism, and the Politics
of Culture, 1930–50   *Robbie Lieberman*
Chosen Voices: The Story of the American Cantorate   *Mark Slobin*
Theodore Thomas: America's Conductor and Builder of Orchestras, 1835–1905
Ezra Schabas
"The Whorehouse Bells Were Ringing" and Other Songs Cowboys Sing
Collected and Edited by Guy Logsdon
Crazeology: The Autobiography of a Chicago Jazzman   *Bud Freeman, as Told to
Robert Wolf*
Discoursing Sweet Music: Brass Bands and Community Life in Turn-of-the-Century
Pennsylvania   *Kenneth Kreitner*
Mormonism and Music: A History   *Michael Hicks*
Voices of the Jazz Age: Profiles of Eight Vintage Jazzmen   *Chip Deffaa*
Pickin' on Peachtree: A History of Country Music in Atlanta, Georgia
Wayne W. Daniel
Bitter Music: Collected Journals, Essays, Introductions, and Librettos   *Harry Partch;
edited by Thomas McGeary*
Ethnic Music on Records: A Discography of Ethnic Recordings Produced in the
United States, 1893 to 1942   *Richard K. Spottswood*
Downhome Blues Lyrics: An Anthology from the Post–World War II Era
Jeff Todd Titon
Ellington: The Early Years   *Mark Tucker*
Chicago Soul   *Robert Pruter*
That Half-Barbaric Twang: The Banjo in American Popular Culture   *Karen Linn*
Hot Man: The Life of Art Hodes   *Art Hodes and Chadwick Hansen*
The Erotic Muse: American Bawdy Songs (2d ed.)   *Ed Cray*
Barrio Rhythm: Mexican American Music in Los Angeles   *Steven Loza*
The Creation of Jazz: Music, Race, and Culture in Urban America   *Burton W. Peretti*
Charles Martin Loeffler: A Life Apart in Music   *Ellen Knight*
Club Date Musicians: Playing the New York Party Circuit   *Bruce A. MacLeod*
Opera on the Road: Traveling Opera Troupes in the United States, 1825–60
Katherine K. Preston
The Stonemans: An Appalachian Family and the Music That Shaped Their Lives
Ivan M. Tribe
Transforming Tradition: Folk Music Revivals Examined   *Edited by Neil V. Rosenberg*
The Crooked Stovepipe: Athapaskan Fiddle Music and Square Dancing in Northeast
Alaska and Northwest Canada   *Craig Mishler*

Traveling the High Way Home: Ralph Stanley and the World of Traditional
  Bluegrass Music   *John Wright*
Carl Ruggles: Composer, Painter, and Storyteller   *Marilyn Ziffrin*
Never without a Song: The Years and Songs of Jennie Devlin, 1865–1952
  Katharine D. Newman
The Hank Snow Story   *Hank Snow, with Jack Ownbey and Bob Burris*
Milton Brown and the Founding of Western Swing   *Cary Ginell, with special
  assistance from Roy Lee Brown*
Santiago de Murcia's "Códice Saldívar No. 4": A Treasury of Secular Guitar Music
  from Baroque Mexico   *Craig H. Russell*
The Sound of the Dove: Singing in Appalachian Primitive Baptist Churches
  Beverly Bush Patterson
Heartland Excursions: Ethnomusicological Reflections on Schools of Music
  Bruno Nettl
Doowop: The Chicago Scene   *Robert Pruter*
Blue Rhythms: Six Lives in Rhythm and Blues   *Chip Deffaa*
Shoshone Ghost Dance Religion: Poetry Songs and Great Basin Context
  Judith Vander
Go Cat Go! Rockabilly Music and Its Makers   *Craig Morrison*
'Twas Only an Irishman's Dream: The Image of Ireland and the Irish in American
  Popular Song Lyrics, 1800–1920   *William H. A. Williams*
Democracy at the Opera: Music, Theater, and Culture in New York City, 1815–60
  Karen Ahlquist
Fred Waring and the Pennsylvanians   *Virginia Waring*
Woody, Cisco, and Me: Seamen Three in the Merchant Marine   *Jim Longhi*
Behind the Burnt Cork Mask: Early Blackface Minstrelsy and Antebellum American
  Popular Culture   *William J. Mahar*
Going to Cincinnati: A History of the Blues in the Queen City   *Steven C. Tracy*
Pistol Packin' Mama: Aunt Molly Jackson and the Politics of Folksong
  Shelly Romalis
Sixties Rock: Garage, Psychedelic, and Other Satisfactions   *Michael Hicks*
The Late Great Johnny Ace and the Transition from R&B to Rock 'n' Roll
  James M. Salem
Tito Puente and the Making of Latin Music   *Steven Loza*
Juilliard: A History   *Andrea Olmstead*
Understanding Charles Seeger, Pioneer in American Musicology
  Edited by Bell Yung and Helen Rees
Mountains of Music: West Virginia Traditional Music from *Goldenseal*
  Edited by John Lilly
Alice Tully: An Intimate Portrait   *Albert Fuller*
A Blues Life   *Henry Townsend, as told to Bill Greensmith*
Long Steel Rail: The Railroad in American Folksong (2d ed.)   *Norm Cohen*
The Golden Age of Gospel   *Text by Horace Clarence Boyer; photography by
  Lloyd Yearwood*

Aaron Copland: The Life and Work of an Uncommon Man   *Howard Pollack*
Louis Moreau Gottschalk   *S. Frederick Starr*
Race, Rock, and Elvis   *Michael T. Bertrand*
Theremin: Ether Music and Espionage   *Albert Glinsky*
Poetry and Violence: The Ballad Tradition of Mexico's Costa Chica
   John H. McDowell
The Bill Monroe Reader   *Edited by Tom Ewing*
Music in Lubavitcher Life   *Ellen Koskoff*
Zarzuela: Spanish Operetta, American Stage   *Janet L. Sturman*
Bluegrass Odyssey: A Documentary in Pictures and Words, 1966–86
   Carl Fleischhauer and Neil V. Rosenberg
That Old-Time Rock & Roll: A Chronicle of an Era, 1954–63   *Richard Aquila*
Labor's Troubadour   *Joe Glazer*
American Opera   *Elise K. Kirk*
Don't Get above Your Raisin': Country Music and the Southern Working Class
   Bill C. Malone
John Alden Carpenter: A Chicago Composer   *Howard Pollack*
Heartbeat of the People: Music and Dance of the Northern Pow-wow   *Tara Browner*
My Lord, What a Morning: An Autobiography   *Marian Anderson*
Marian Anderson: A Singer's Journey   *Allan Keiler*
Charles Ives Remembered: An Oral History   *Vivian Perlis*
Henry Cowell, Bohemian   *Michael Hicks*
Rap Music and Street Consciousness   *Cheryl L. Keyes*
Louis Prima   *Garry Boulard*
Marian McPartland's Jazz World: All in Good Time   *Marian McPartland*
Robert Johnson: Lost and Found   *Barry Lee Pearson and Bill McCulloch*
Bound for America: Three British Composers   *Nicholas Temperley*
Lost Sounds: Blacks and the Birth of the Recording Industry, 1890–1919   *Tim Brooks*
Burn, Baby! BURN! The Autobiography of Magnificent Montague
   Magnificent Montague with Bob Baker
Way Up North in Dixie: A Black Family's Claim to the Confederate Anthem
   Howard L. Sacks and Judith Rose Sacks
The Bluegrass Reader   *Edited by Thomas Goldsmith*
Colin McPhee: Composer in Two Worlds   *Carol J. Oja*
Robert Johnson, Mythmaking, and Contemporary American Culture
   Patricia R. Schroeder
Composing a World: Lou Harrison, Musical Wayfarer   *Leta E. Miller and
   Fredric Lieberman*
Fritz Reiner, Maestro and Martinet   *Kenneth Morgan*
That Toddlin' Town: Chicago's White Dance Bands and Orchestras, 1900–1950
   Charles A. Sengstock Jr.
Dewey and Elvis: The Life and Times of a Rock 'n' Roll Deejay   *Louis Cantor*
Come Hither to Go Yonder: Playing Bluegrass with Bill Monroe   *Bob Black*
Chicago Blues: Portraits and Stories   *David Whiteis*

The Incredible Band of John Philip Sousa *Paul E. Bierley*
"Maximum Clarity" and Other Writings on Music *Ben Johnston,
    edited by Bob Gilmore*
Staging Tradition: John Lair and Sarah Gertrude Knott *Michael Ann Williams*
Homegrown Music: Discovering Bluegrass *Stephanie P. Ledgin*
Tales of a Theatrical Guru *Danny Newman*
The Music of Bill Monroe *Neil V. Rosenberg and Charles K. Wolfe*
Pressing On: The Roni Stoneman Story *Roni Stoneman, as told to Ellen Wright*
Together Let Us Sweetly Live *Jonathan C. David, with photographs by
    Richard Holloway*
Live Fast, Love Hard: The Faron Young Story *Diane Diekman*
Air Castle of the South: WSM Radio and the Making of Music City
    Craig P. Havighurst
Traveling Home: Sacred Harp Singing and American Pluralism *Kiri Miller*
Where Did Our Love Go? The Rise and Fall of the Motown Sound *Nelson George*
Lonesome Cowgirls and Honky-Tonk Angels: The Women of Barn Dance Radio
    Kristine M. McCusker
California Polyphony: Ethnic Voices, Musical Crossroads *Mina Yang*
The Never-Ending Revival: Rounder Records and the Folk Alliance
    Michael F. Scully
Sing It Pretty: A Memoir *Bess Lomax Hawes*
Working Girl Blues: The Life and Music of Hazel Dickens *Hazel Dickens and
    Bill C. Malone*
Charles Ives Reconsidered *Gayle Sherwood Magee*
The Hayloft Gang: The Story of the National Barn Dance *Edited by Chad Berry*
Country Music Humorists and Comedians *Loyal Jones*
Record Makers and Breakers: Voices of the Independent Rock 'n' Roll Pioneers
    John Broven
Music of the First Nations: Tradition and Innovation in Native North America
    Edited by Tara Browner
Cafe Society: The Wrong Place for the Right People *Barney Josephson,
    with Terry Trilling-Josephson*
George Gershwin: An Intimate Portrait *Walter Rimler*
Life Flows On in Endless Song: Folk Songs and American History *Robert V. Wells*
I Feel a Song Coming On: The Life of Jimmy McHugh *Alyn Shipton*
King of the Queen City: The Story of King Records *Jon Hartley Fox*
Long Lost Blues: Popular Blues in America, 1850–1920 *Peter C. Muir*
Hard Luck Blues: Roots Music Photographs from the Great Depression
    Rich Remsberg
Restless Giant: The Life and Times of Jean Aberbach and Hill and Range Songs
    Bar Biszick-Lockwood
Champagne Charlie and Pretty Jemima: Variety Theater in the Nineteenth Century
    Gillian M. Rodger
Sacred Steel: Inside an African American Steel Guitar Tradition *Robert L. Stone*

Gone to the Country: The New Lost City Ramblers and the Folk Music Revival
Ray Allen
The Makers of the Sacred Harp   *David Warren Steel with Richard H. Hulan*
Woody Guthrie, American Radical   *Will Kaufman*
George Szell: A Life of Music   *Michael Charry*
Bean Blossom: The Brown County Jamboree and Bill Monroe's Bluegrass Festivals
Thomas A. Adler
Crowe on the Banjo: The Music Life of J. D. Crowe   *Marty Godbey*
Twentieth Century Drifter: The Life of Marty Robbins   *Diane Diekman*
Henry Mancini: Reinventing Film Music   *John Caps*
The Beautiful Music All Around Us: Field Recordings and the American Experience
Stephen Wade
Then Sings My Soul: The Culture of Southern Gospel Music   *Douglas Harrison*
The Accordion in the Americas: Klezmer, Polka, Tango, Zydeco, and More!
Edited by Helena Simonett
Bluegrass Bluesman: A Memoir   *Josh Graves, edited by Fred Bartenstein*
One Woman in a Hundred: Edna Phillips and the Philadelphia Orchestra
Mary Sue Welsh
The Great Orchestrator: Arthur Judson and American Arts Management
James M. Doering
Charles Ives in the Mirror: American Histories of an Iconic Composer
David C. Paul
Southern Soul-Blues   *David Whiteis*
Sweet Air: Modernism, Regionalism, and American Popular Song
Edward P. Comentale
Pretty Good for a Girl: Women in Bluegrass   *Murphy Hicks Henry*
Sweet Dreams: The World of Patsy Cline   *Warren R. Hofstra*
William Sidney Mount and the Creolization of American Culture
Christopher J. Smith
Bird: The Life and Music of Charlie Parker   *Chuck Haddix*
Making the March King: John Philip Sousa's Washington Years, 1854–1893
Patrick Warfield
In It for the Long Run   *Jim Rooney*
Pioneers of the Blues Revival   *Steve Cushing*
Roots of the Revival: American and British Folk Music in the 1950s
Ronald D. Cohen and Rachel Clare Donaldson
Blues All Day Long: The Jimmy Rogers Story   *Wayne Everett Goins*
Yankee Twang: Country and Western Music in New England   *Clifford R. Murphy*
The Music of the Stanley Brothers   *Gary B. Reid*
Hawaiian Music in Motion: Mariners, Missionaries, and Minstrels
James Revell Carr
Sounds of the New Deal: The Federal Music Project in the West   *Peter Gough*
The Mormon Tabernacle Choir: A Biography   *Michael Hicks*

The Man That Got Away: The Life and Songs of Harold Arlen   *Walter Rimler*
A City Called Heaven: Chicago and the Birth of Gospel Music   *Robert M. Marovich*
Blues Unlimited: Essential Interviews from the Original Blues Magazine
  Edited by Bill Greensmith, Mike Rowe, and Mark Camarigg
Hoedowns, Reels, and Frolics: Roots and Branches of Southern Appalachian Dance
  Phil Jamison
Fannie Bloomfield-Zeisler: The Life and Times of a Piano Virtuoso
  Beth Abelson Macleod
Cybersonic Arts: Adventures in American New Music   *Gordon Mumma,*
  edited with commentary by Michelle Fillion
The Magic of Beverly Sills   *Nancy Guy*
Waiting for Buddy Guy   *Alan Harper*
Harry T. Burleigh: From the Spiritual to the Harlem Renaissance   *Jean E. Snyder*
Music in the Age of Anxiety: American Music in the Fifties   *James Wierzbicki*
Jazzing: New York City's Unseen Scene   *Thomas H. Greenland*
A Cole Porter Companion   *Edited by Don M. Randel, Matthew Shaftel,*
  and Susan Forscher Weiss
Foggy Mountain Troubadour: The Life and Music of Curly Seckler   *Penny Parsons*
Blue Rhythm Fantasy: Big Band Jazz Arranging in the Swing Era   *John Wriggle*
Bill Clifton: America's Bluegrass Ambassador to the World   *Bill C. Malone*
Chinatown Opera Theater in North America   *Nancy Yunhwa Rao*
The Elocutionists: Women, Music, and the Spoken Word   *Marian Wilson Kimber*
May Irwin: Singing, Shouting, and the Shadow of Minstrelsy   *Sharon Ammen*
Peggy Seeger: A Life of Music, Love, and Politics   *Jean R. Freedman*
Charles Ives's *Concord*: Essays after a Sonata   *Kyle Gann*
Don't Give Your Heart to a Rambler: My Life with Jimmy Martin, the King
  of Bluegrass   *Barbara Martin Stephens*
Libby Larsen: Composing an American Life   *Denise Von Glahn*
George Szell's Reign: Behind the Scenes with the Cleveland Orchestra
  Marcia Hansen Kraus
Just One of the Boys: Female-to-Male Cross-Dressing on the American
  Variety Stage   *Gillian M. Rodger*
Spirituals and the Birth of a Black Entertainment Industry   *Sandra Jean Graham*
Right to the Juke Joint: A Personal History of American Music   *Patrick B. Mullen*
Bluegrass Generation: A Memoir   *Neil V. Rosenberg*
Pioneers of the Blues Revival, Expanded Second Edition   *Steve Cushing*
Banjo Roots and Branches   *Edited by Robert Winans*
Bill Monroe: The Life and Music of the Blue Grass Man   *Tom Ewing*
Dixie Dewdrop: The Uncle Dave Macon Story   *Michael D. Doubler*
Los Romeros: Royal Family of the Spanish Guitar   *Walter Aaron Clark*
Transforming Women's Education: Liberal Arts and Music in Female Seminaries
  Jewel A. Smith
Rethinking American Music   *Edited by Tara Browner and Thomas L. Riis*

Leonard Bernstein and the Language of Jazz *Katherine Baber*
Dancing Revolution: Bodies, Space, and Sound in American Cultural History
Christopher J. Smith
Peggy Glanville-Hicks: Composer and Critic *Suzanne Robinson*
Mormons, Musical Theater, and Belonging in America *Jake Johnson*
Blues Legacy: Tradition and Innovation in Chicago *David Whiteis*
Blues Before Sunrise 2: Interviews from the Chicago Scene *Steve Cushing*
The Cashaway Psalmody: Transatlantic Religion and Music in Colonial Carolina
Stephen A. Marini
Earl Scruggs and Foggy Mountain Breakdown: The Making of an American Classic
Thomas Goldsmith
A Guru's Journey: Pandit Chitresh Das and Indian Classical Dance in Diaspora
Sarah Morelli
Unsettled Scores: Politics, Hollywood, and the Film Music of Aaron Copland and
Hanns Eisler *Sally Bick*
Hillbilly Maidens, Okies, and Cowgirls: Women's Country Music, 1930–1960
Stephanie Vander Wel
Always the Queen: The Denise LaSalle Story *Denise LaSalle with David Whiteis*
Artful Noise: Percussion Literature in the Twentieth Century *Thomas Siwe*
The Heart of a Woman: The Life and Music of Florence B. Price *Rae Linda Brown,*
edited by Guthrie P. Ramsey Jr.
When Sunday Comes: Gospel Music in the Soul and Hip-Hop Eras
Claudrena N. Harold
The Lady Swings: Memoirs of a Jazz Drummer *Dottie Dodgion and Wayne Enstice*
Industrial Strength Bluegrass: Southwestern Ohio's Musical Legacy
Edited by Fred Bartenstein and Curtis W. Ellison
Soul on Soul: The Life and Music of Mary Lou Williams *Tammy L. Kernodle*
Unbinding Gentility: Women Making Music in the Nineteenth-Century South
Candace Bailey
Punks in Peoria: Making a Scene in the American Heartland *Jonathan Wright*
and Dawson Barrett
Homer Rodeheaver and the Rise of the Gospel Music Industry *Kevin Mungons*
and Douglas Yeo
Americanaland: Where Country & Western Met Rock 'n' Roll *John Milward,*
with Portraits by Margie Greve
Listening to Bob Dylan *Larry Starr*
Lying in the Middle: Musical Theater and Belief at the Heart of America
Jake Johnson
The Sounds of Place: Music and the American Cultural Landscape
Denise Von Glahn
Peace Be Still: How James Cleveland and the Angelic Choir Created a Gospel Classic
Robert M. Marovich
Politics as Sound: The Washington, DC, Hardcore Scene, 1978–1983
Shayna L. Maskell

Tania León's Stride: A Polyrhythmic Life   *Alejandro L. Madrid*
Elliott Carter Speaks: Unpublished Lectures   *Edited by Laura Emmery*
Interviews with American Composers: Barney Childs in Conversation
   Edited by Virginia Anderson
Queer Country   *Shana Goldin-Perschbacher*
On the Bus with Bill Monroe: My Five-Year Ride with the Father of Blue Grass
   Mark Hembree
Mandolin Man: The Bluegrass Life of Roland White   *Bob Black*
Music and Mystique in Muscle Shoals   *Christopher M. Reali*
Buddy Emmons: Steel Guitar Icon   *Steve Fishell*
Music in Black American Life, 1600–1945: A University of Illinois Press Anthology
   Compiled by Laurie Matheson
Music in Black American Life, 1945–2020: A University of Illinois Press Anthology
   Compiled by Laurie Matheson
Ballad Hunting with Max Hunter: Stories of an Ozark Folksong Collector
   Sarah Jane Nelson
Play Like a Man: My Life in Poster Children   *Rose Marshack*
Samuel Barber: His Life and Legacy   *Howard Pollack*
Aaron Copland in Latin America: Music and Cultural Politics   *Carol A. Hess*
Stringbean: The Life and Murder of a Country Music Legend   *Taylor Hagood*
Danzón Days: Age, Race, and Romance in Mexico   *Hettie Malcomson*
Flaco's Legacy: The Globalization of Conjunto   *Erin E. Bauer*
Circle of Winners: How the Guggenheim Foundation Composition Awards Shaped
   American Music Culture   *Denise Von Glahn*
The Propaganda of Freedom: JFK, Shostakovich, Stravinsky, and the Cultural
   Cold War   *Joseph Horowitz*
The Possibility Machine: Music and Myth in Las Vegas   *Edited by Jake Johnson*
Union Divided: Black Musicians' Fight for Labor Equality   *Leta E. Miller*
Sound Pedagogy: Radical Care in Music   *Edited by Colleen Renihan, John Spilker,
   and Trudi Wright*
Lieder in America: On Stages and In Parlors   *Heather Platt*

The University of Illinois Press
is a founding member of the
Association of University Presses.

University of Illinois Press
1325 South Oak Street
Champaign, IL 61820-6903
www.press.uillinois.edu